Homes and Homecomings

Gender & History Special Issue Book Series

Gender & History, an international, interdisciplinary journal on the history of femininity, masculinity, and gender relations, publishes annual special issues which are now available in book form.

Bringing together path-breaking feminist scholarship with assessments of the field, each volume focuses on a specific subject, question or theme. These books are suitable for undergraduate and postgraduate courses in history, sociology, politics, cultural studies, and gender and women's studies.

Titles in the series include:

Homes and Homecomings: Gendered Histories of Domesticity and Return
Edited by K. H. Adler and Carrie Hamilton

Gender and Change: Agency, Chronology and Periodisation
Edited by Alexandra Shepard and Garthine Walker

Translating Feminisms in China
Edited by Dorothy Ko and Wang Zheng

Visual Genders, Visual Histories: A Special Issue of Gender & History
Edited by Patricia Hayes

Violence, Vulnerability and Embodiment: Gender and History
Edited by Shani D'Cruze and Anupama Rao

Dialogues of Dispersal: Gender, Sexuality and African Diasporas
Edited by Sandra Gunning, Tera Hunter and Michele Mitchell

Material Strategies: Dress and Gender in Historical Perspective
Edited by Barbara Burman and Carole Turbin

Gender, Citizenships and Subjectivities
Edited by Kathleen Canning and Sonya Rose

Gendering the Middle Ages: A Gender and History Special Issue
Edited by Pauline Stafford and Anneke B. Mulder-Bakker

Gender and History: Retrospect and Prospect
Edited by Leonore Davidoff, Keith McClelland and Eleni Varikas

Feminisms and Internationalism
Edited by Mrinalini Sinha, Donna Guy and Angela Woollacott

Gender and the Body in the Ancient Mediterranean
Edited by Maria Wyke

Gendered Colonialisms in African History
Edited by Nancy Rose Hunt, Tessie P. Liu and Jean Quataert

Homes and Homecomings

Gendered Histories of Domesticity and Return

EDITED BY

K. H. ADLER
AND
CARRIE HAMILTON

WILEY-BLACKWELL

A John Wiley & Sons, Ltd., Publication

CONTENTS

Boundaries

NOTES ON CONTRIBUTORS

K. H. Adler teaches history at the University of Nottingham. She is author of *Jews and Gender in Liberation France* and is working on a book about homecomings in post-war France. She is co-editor of *Gender & History*.

Quintin Colville is curator of naval history at the National Maritime Museum, London. He has held a Caird Senior Research Fellowship at the National Maritime Museum and a Junior Research Fellowship at Linacre College, Oxford, and was awarded the Royal Historical Society's Alexander Prize in 2002.

Vivian Bruce Conger is Associate Professor of History at Ithaca College, New York. She is the author of *The Widows' Might: Widowhood and Gender in Early British America* (2009). She is currently working on a book exploring gender in the early republic through the lives of Deborah Read Franklin and Sarah Franklin Bache.

Carrie Hamilton teaches History and Spanish at Roehampton University, London. She is the author of *Women and ETA: The Gender Politics of Radical Basque Nationalism* (2007) and numerous articles on cultural memory, oral history, gender and political violence and histories of activism. She is currently completing a monograph entitled *Sexual Revolutions: Passion and Politics in Socialist Cuba*.

Jane Hamlett is a lecturer in Modern British History at Royal Holloway University of London. She has published in *Women's History Review*, *Quaderni Storici*, *Cultural and Social History* and the *Journal of Consumer Culture*. Her book *Material Relations: Middle-Class Families and Domestic Interiors in England, 1850–1910*, is forthcoming from Manchester University Press.

Karen Harvey is Senior Lecturer in Cultural History at the University of Sheffield. She has ongoing research interests in gender, masculinity, the body, print culture (both visual and textual) and material culture during the British long eighteenth century. Her most recent book is the edited collection *History and Material Culture* (2009). Her next book will be *Domesticating Patriarchy: Male Authority in the Eighteenth-Century English Home* (to be published by Oxford University Press).

Bianca Murillo is Assistant Professor of History at Willamette University where she teaches courses on modern Africa. Her research interests include the history of global markets and trade, postcolonial state and society, and comparative consumer cultures. The chapter published here is based on research for a full-length book project, Market

Relations: Retailing, Distribution, and the Politics of Consumption in Ghana, 1930–1970s.

Lisa Pollard is Associate Professor in the History Department at the University of North Carolina, Wilmington. She is the author of *Nurturing the Nation: The Family Politics of Modernizing, Colonizing and Liberating Egypt (1805–1919)* (2005) and co-editor (with Lynne Haney) of *Families of a New World: Gender, Politics, and State Development in a Global Context* (2003). Her current projects include an examination of competing contemporary interpretations of the Sudanese Mahdiyya uprising (1881–85) and a history of the rise and spread of Egyptian social organisations under British colonial rule.

Carina E. Ray is Assistant Professor of History at Fordham University where she teaches African and Black Atlantic history. She is currently completing her book, *Policing Sexual Boundaries: The Politics of Race in Colonial Ghana*. She is co-editor of *Darfur and the Crisis of Governance in Sudan: A Critical Reader* (Cornell University Press, 2009) and *Navigating African Maritime History* (Memorial University of Newfoundland, 2010).

Susan E. Reid is Professor of Russian Visual Culture in the Department of Russian and Slavonic Studies, University of Sheffield. She has published widely on art, visual and material culture, and has edited numerous volumes, most recently, with David Crowley, *Pleasures in Socialism: Leisure and Luxury in the Bloc* (2010). The chapter published here draws on research for a book-length project, Khrushchev Modern: Making Home and Becoming a Consumer in the Soviet 1960s.

Nicole Rudolph is Assistant Professor in the Department of Languages and International Studies at Adelphi University, New York. She is working on a book called *At Home in Post-war France: The Design and Construction of Domestic Space, 1945–1975* and has previously published in *Modern and Contemporary France*.

Christina Twomey is a senior lecturer in the School of Historical Studies at Monash University, Australia. She is a cultural historian of war, and interested in issues of witnessing, captivity, the photography of atrocity, gender and memory. Her most recent book is *Australia's Forgotten Prisoners: Civilians Interned by the Japanese in World War II* (2007).

Gendering Histories of Homes and Homecomings

K. H. Adler

In the summer of 2009, a British government social attitudes survey which was designed to discover the happiest location in England, used an index of whether people felt that they belonged to the place where they lived.[1] The sense of belonging, the survey suggested, differed across the country by a margin of almost a third, with just 42 per cent of residents of the east London district of Tower Hamlets feeling as though they belonged there, against 71 per cent of the inhabitants of the rural county of Shropshire. Feeling as though one belonged, it would appear, was considered a real determinant of happiness in early twenty-first-century England, and something that could be geographically located. Indeed, the study was called the Place Survey and it seems to have been motivated by a concern to trace the feelings generated by certain locations though not, interestingly, to distinguish between inhabitants by other aspects such as their age, occupation, wealth or gender: 'belonging', we are meant to understand, is not only a generic sentiment uncoloured by social factors but one that is very much affected by geography and an individual's position in space.

The authors in this volume would no doubt refine and challenge these not uninteresting but somewhat crude findings. In their explorations of historical meanings of homes and homecomings, the chapters presented here investigate how the gendered interplay of a sense of belonging – or exclusion – have been made to work across time and space. Whether 'home' was a district – as the Place Survey claims – or a nation or community, or indeed just a dwelling, by looking at historical and gendered aspects of homes and homecomings we aim to upset historical assumptions about who belonged where in a dwelling, or what sort of impact the state and its agents might have on inhabitants. The kind of questions that this work asks are, why did the material objects that every home contains, and their arrangement, arouse such gendered fears? What type of surveillance was deemed necessary of the intimate relationships that the inhabitants of a home had with each other or those outside? If the nation represents itself as a home, what meanings might be attached to both? And what conditions are laid on those who move away or return? Assumptions made about the nature of the home, by those who designed it or sought to control it, are pared down to their ideological framework, much as the walls of Finnish artist Tea Mäkipää's full-scale rendition of the wonky but working skeleton of a typical northern European, suburban house are stripped away to reveal its inner workings.[2] Here, burning electric lamps are in perilous mid-air suspension and taps run water into sinks divested of all furniture and apparent human intervention. Mäkipää's refusal of the usual limits between public and private, by the simple expedient of removing all walls, ceilings and doors, exposes the extent to which those limits remain; the viewer 'sees' their presence and, by their very absence, knows all the more the work that they normally do. The very banality of the house's inner workings, in their western European context – the white ceramic lavatory, a stainless steel sink, a dull and unremarkable lampshade, as well as the wires and pipes via which these objects' functionality must derive – force reflection on the habits of those who live surrounded by such features, as well as on those who do not. But this particular incitement to reflection, while provocative, is still located in the present. It is the relation between the knowledge of the sense of home and its historical coming into being and developmental shifts at other times that the authors collected in this volume begin to explore.

A project to explore the historical sense of home recognises that 'home' is made up of more than actual or metaphorical sinks and pipes; as Mäkipää's skeletal house indicates, it is something full of constructed meanings.[3] But the nature of 'a' home as a single dwelling or community is in many instances defied. In her 1982–83 performance work, *Under Siege*, the artist Mona Hatoum elaborated the following interview dialogue:

> M: I like to walk through London with friends.
> *What do you talk about when you're walking?*
> M: We don't talk, we shout.
> *I'm sorry, I don't understand.*
> . . .
> M: I spend day after day on the phone, dialling and redialling.
> *Who are you calling?*
> M: I'm trying to locate my parents.
> *Why is it such a problem phoning home?*
> M: I'm not phoning home.
> *I'm sorry, I don't understand.*[4]

M is holding this conversation with her dim-witted interlocutor in the early 1980s, right around the time of the war in the Lebanon, where Hatoum spent much of her childhood with her family in exile from Israel. (More prosaically, this piece coincided with the release of the hit science fiction movie *E.T.* whose nostalgic command, 'phone home', rapidly entered Euro-American popular memory.)[5] The early 1980s was a period in which discussion of the refugee, the exile and the cultural dislocations that migration often entails was much less ubiquitous than it subsequently became. Nonetheless, a quarter of a century later, *Under Siege* retains an acuity to pinpoint the idea that 'family' and 'home' may each be located in entirely different places, that home might not be a place to which it is possible to return, and that these facts might condition ordinary behaviour so that it becomes extraordinary, even in a mundane activity – not possible in conditions of war – such as walking down the road with friends. The performance of *Under Siege*, described variously as lasting three or seven hours, was, in Gannit Ankori's words, 'gruelling', and it must have been for both artist and audience: the artist was contained in a transparent plastic box, struggling against a mixture of mud and clay, repeatedly trying to stand up and falling down, while speakers in the room where the box stood blasted out several three-hour tapes in Arabic, English and French, the languages of Hatoum's childhood and education.[6] Nevertheless, the interviewee's reply, 'we don't talk, we shout' amuses, not just in the bafflement of the questioner but in how the response sidesteps the original query and spotlights one of the most common aspects of misbehaviour unwittingly or consciously enacted by the migrant. The inappropriate loudness of migrants to western Europe, and what was perceived as their monstrous distortions of language, were often cause for concern from at least the late nineteenth century;[7] later on, for example, such was the fear of the potential disruption that outsiders might cause, that Jewish refugees arriving in Britain from Nazi-occupied Germany, Austria and Czechoslovakia before the Second World War were routinely handed a bilingual booklet of assimilatory guidance, admonishing them to avoid involvement with politics, and issuing the instruction, 'do not make yourself conspicuous by speaking loudly, nor by your manner or dress'.[8] Loudness is thus emblematic of the fact that home is both somewhere else and here; it is a series of multiplied homes; or a conglomeration; or a home nowhere. Home for many, for reasons of gender and sexual, as well as political, exile might be unreachable, unsafe or hostile. Home may well also be multiple, fragmented and transnational; not all of these conditions should be unconditionally interpreted as problematic.

If migrants' language has aroused disquiet, what are we to make of the language of home itself? What did home mean in the different contexts and periods that the authors in the volume address and in other contexts more broadly? How people understood their own 'being at home' is by no means self-evident, as a brief, and rather unscientific, linguistic excursion will make clear.[9] English is unusual in its ability to combine in one word the place where one lives and the sense of being in it: *home*. In English we are 'at home' when we are in our place of residence and when we are comfortable with our condition. That single word can express a multiplicity of relations and sensations. Not so other languages. 'So you're working on Heimat!' was the greeting my Germanist colleagues tended to repeat during the months leading up to publication of this volume whenever I mentioned *Homes and Homecomings* to them. The word 'Heim', as a literal translation of 'home', appears rarely in colloquial German, and its use (aside from complex sorts of residences, such as retirement homes) is confined to southern Germany and Austria. As a stem word it is far more common in the term *Heimat*, a concept that implies a certain Romantic, provincialised and gendered way of thinking about the home as an amalgam of the nation and its people, and their ideologically unequivocal attachment to the land. My colleagues' assumption indicates just how axiomatic it has become, when thinking about 'home' in the modern period in Germany, to refer to and problematise not the individual condition of homeliness but the nation. Of course, how a nation becomes a home, or stops being one, is one of the aspects of home that this volume seeks to tease out. But the German concept of *Heimat*, and its 'vacuously ideal' earth-bound, peasant inhabitants of a mythic nation, inaugurated in the Third Reich something very far from domesticity and homeliness, and the set of conceptual maps that *Heimat* implies have been revivified again and again in popular culture.[10]

While modern German draws on ideas of landscape and territory to define home and homeland, the classical languages suggest a vast array of different elements that can be expressed with a single word. In ancient Greek, οἶκος (oikos) could apply equally to the house, its inhabitants and their economic relations (i.e., the household), or to what we understand as the family. In other words, oikos contained suggestions about particular social relationships and their conduct. That root word now appears in our economic, as well as our ecological, considerations, and its meaning is discussed more fully by Karen Harvey in her chapter below. On the other hand, as far as forebears in medieval England, Wales and Scotland were concerned, the Latin word *domus* (home) delineated a structure, not what went on within its walls. It could be applied to any number of dwellings that housed anything from royalty to rabbits. It was built for activities far beyond living in the plain sense of eating, sleeping or receiving guests: domus might be a toll-house, a brothel, a prison or an office. It could house nuns, widows or scholars. In short, the house or home in medieval Britain had almost limitless functions, involving practically anything that went on in a building, that itself could be as enduring as a palace or as makeshift as a privy.[11] While this one Latin term could be applied to dozens of uses, in other modern languages, to say one is 'at home' requires the use of several other words, often using the metonym, 'house'. So one is *à la maison* in French, *en casa* in Spanish, *doma* in Russian, *ba bayit* in Hebrew, *alla casa* in Italian, *zu Hause* in German and *watan* in Arabic. Thus literally 'being in the house' – that is, being in a building – is a preferred way to express the idea of 'being at home' even in those languages such as German or Spanish where the word 'home' exists but is little used, or used in only a few regional settings (*das Heim* or *daheim*, and *el hogar* respectively). But the meaning of these terms is not necessarily similar, even if they appear to express the same thing. The Arabic 'watan' (lit. 'where you dwell'), has evolved since the nineteenth century to imply the dwelling within a nation, rather than a house, while the other term for 'being at home', *bil beit*, literally means 'where you spend the night'. 'Bil beit' further carries the implication of being with family members, not being alone. Furthermore, several other linguistic cultures do not confine the expression of being at home to a building; the concept of being with oneself, with another or with the family, can equally imply 'being at home-ness' in French (*chez soi*), German (*bei mir*), Hebrew (*etz li*) or Italian (*alla famiglia*). It should be clear, therefore, that of the few languages discussed here, English is extremely rare in having the term 'home'; it would be worth bearing this in mind when we come to analyse and translate the homes and homecomings of people in other linguistic groups, let alone in other historical periods.[12] Moreover, this is before we have even begun to embark on a discussion of the gendered and homely terminology of nation – *patria*, *Vaterland*, *Rodina*, and so on – which so often refer to the mother, the father, or even, as in the case of the French *la mère patrie*, both.[13]

It should be clear by now that 'home' is full of tangled meaning and that is certainly the case in Mona Hatoum's work, whose *Mobile Home II* features on the cover of this volume. The immense power of *Mobile Home II* derives in part from its transparency. The work consists of a space delimited by silvery metal barriers, 'within' which are several mundane objects on the floor. Above them trundle several pieces of cloth pegged to a moving clothesline. The viewer is invited visually to replace the metal bars with more solid walls, but the nature of the objects bounded by them – a cheap battered suitcase, some tatty teacloths, a flimsy laminated table, a rolled-up rug, some chairs arranged not to promote conviviality but in a way that indicates the absent sitters' separation from each other – only emphasise their, and the home's, provisionality. Hatoum's work has often featured planes made from metal bars; these ones are like the crash barriers used by western European police as a means of crowd control during demonstrations or visits by untouchable dignitaries. They are there to exclude. So we are confronted by a simultaneity of public and private: the apparently private walls of a dwelling, the home, are in this instance things normally seen on the street in the most public of contexts. Equally multi-layered is the mobility of *Mobile Home II*: not only do the children's drawings and teacloths pinned to the clothesline physically move, and the suitcases mark anticipated flight or recent arrival (or both), but again, the point of crash barriers is that they are moveable. Are we in fact looking at something discovered on a street? Or does the incessant circular movement of the washing line imply the sort of stasis combined with temporariness emphasised by one Palestinian interviewee in another art work, the video art project, *Roofs: 'Public-Private' Open Spaces in the Camp*? This project, by the feminist Palestinian architect, Sandi Hilal, explores via extended interviews the way that female residents of West Bank refugee camps experience their homes, in this instance, the spaces on the roofs. This particular interviewee explains in detail her love of running, and describes the geography of her neighbourhood, distinguished by a letterbox at the end of the road. Such are the gendered social constraints imposed by other residents of the refugee camp, however, in a place where there is little privacy, that she is forced to run round and round the flat roof of her building instead of down the road, with her husband measuring out the distance in recognisable terms.[14] 'Have I reached the post-box yet?' she reports herself asking, imagining that she is in fact running along the road outside her house, an activity forbidden to her because she is a woman. Thus, extraordinary amounts of movement, in this case running for the sheer pleasure of the sport, only serve to emphasise confinement and stasis, not passage or travel. To return to *Mobile Home II*, then, whether we see a mobility of flight, arrival or confined nervousness, Hatoum's whole installation evokes both sadness and confusion, far from any other of the culturally variable meanings its title may imply, be that pleasant family outing or impoverished marginality.

If contemporary art can remind one of the melancholy of home and of home's unreachability, much of the analytical work on these topics over the last two or three decades has emerged from a variety of disciplinary bases from which historians are often absent. For example, references to 'the growing, diverse and interdisciplinary study of home across the humanities and social sciences' by two geographers of gender and home, Alison Blunt and Ann Varley, point to anthropology, literature, material and visual cultures, sociology and feminist cultural studies – but not to history.[15] While much of the most exciting work on home has emerged from the discipline of geography, a great deal of it focused on the past as well as the present (and indeed the future), historians have tended to be absent from much of the recent theorising about home.

Feminist interest in the home, spurred in Britain and the USA by works such as Betty Friedan's classic, *The Feminine Mystique* or Ann Oakley's searing *Housewife*, explored what was effectively women's captivity in the home, and the housewife's sentence to a life of pointless cleaning.[16] While Friedan, as is well documented, concentrated on white, middle-class American women, sidelining the issues facing poor and black women after the Second World War – a critique that could not be levelled at Oakley – the association between the home and the normative place that women were required to occupy within it had been successfully made. Feminist historians took these ideas in several directions, most notably on the privacy of the dwelling against the public nature of the world beyond, and the gendered implications of such a divide. Their work aimed initially to establish that such a divide existed, though never to the extent that successive critics claimed,[17] and subsequently suggested interesting ways in which the separation of home and the world beyond helped in the development of a variety of social constructs.[18] These explorations were largely associated with the development of modernity in western Europe from the mid-eighteenth to the late nineteenth centuries, and made claims about how urban or urbanising women's increasing confinement to the home and areas associated with it – typically shops or philanthropy – laid the basis for social and socio-economic patterns that stretched into the twentieth century, in what Hilde Heynen calls 'a certain complicity between modernity and domesticity'.[19]

On one trajectory, this radical thinking about public and private coalesced imaginatively with new critical theoretical debates on space and mapping, with contributions by practitioners in the field of architecture and visual culture,[20] as well as, crucially, anthropologists and literary critics.[21] Questions of space and women's position in the home begin to cohere when the material cultures of home come under investigation. The scrutiny of domestic material objects is not simply a matter of bourgeois indulgence, but can contain the very bones of the heterosexual imperative that governed homemaking and people's lives for so long.[22] 'Stuff' was not merely a by-product of home, a class-bound and more or less irrelevant obsession with frippery and décor. As several of the authors in this volume indicate, and as Hatoum's *Mobile Home II* stresses, objects can often make a home in fundamental ways. Moreover, the retrieval of a lost home can be symbolised by efforts made to reacquire things, even when the actual spaces and the people they were supposed to contain, remained unavailable. Many of these efforts at retrieval are gendered.[23] Thus, for example, the articulations of 'at-homeness' made by Jewish claimants in their demands for the restitution of their stolen furniture in post-occupation Paris hide assertions of gender relations as well as relations to the state.[24] These relations to the state, and to the powers that control it, continue to provoke thinking around the public and private,[25] and the nation, for example, in the suggestion that particular methods of housework can become associated with national identity.[26] Discussions of public and private, combined with those of space, also led to new feminist – and consequently gendered and raced – ways to account for the nation, and its larger spatial, colonial ambitions.[27] With the idea of the home such a dynamic field, then, and with a reduction in the political desire for women to be released from the shackles of housework, it is not surprising that the gaze is now being turned towards homemaking as productive, and as a 'necessarily incomplete project'.[28] Clearly the home, in its domestic guise, generates pleasure as well as pain, but I am troubled that the work to restore the idea of pleasure to the analysis of the making of home and being in a home may wrest from it the politics that feminists worked so hard to extract.

The present volume to a large extent sidesteps the long-running deliberations on separate spheres. But the absence of historians in current debates about home is clear. As the editors of the journal *Home Cultures*, launched in 2004, clarify, part of their desire to publish such a journal was because,

> ...the Editors have each felt somewhat cut off from other disciplines, as disciplinary boundaries and traditions have isolated scholars who take the domestic sphere as their primary unit of analysis. Consequently, it has often been rather difficult to find out what others in various fields have discovered. Discussions seem to be confined within anthropology, architectural history, design history, literary criticism and geography, to name just a few areas where the domestic as a unit of analysis has proven to be particularly pertinent.[29]

That said, it is clear from their editorial, that the site of interest for *Home Cultures* is largely the problematisation of the dwelling and the domestic sphere it invokes. While questions about gender are put to the fore, and a historicisation of arguments is seen to be necessary, the home as something shifting or multiple does not appear to have been considered. On the other hand, gender might get short shrift even on some occasions when the complexity of home is taken into account. Nigel Rapport and Andrew Dawson's critical collection, *Migrants of Identity*, on the anthropologies of being at home and away, as it were, considers questions of home and movement, the politics of home, home and the expatriate, the immigrant, the dissident, the nation, the child, the house, urbanity and community. Yet in all these important approaches to home, none privileges an understanding of gender (and 'gender' is not even a term in the index), even though the making of a home has conventionally been seen to require the presence of a domestic arbiter, generally a female one.[30]

This volume sets out to reinvigorate many of these areas and to address some of the lacunae alluded to above. The sorts of homes and the way their inhabitants belonged in them that the authors collected here explore were all conditioned by multiple factors, but united by the significance of gender to those belongings or exclusions. What none of the authors in *Homes and Homecomings* considers, at least overtly, is the question of space. While this has preoccupied theorists for the last twenty years, its applicability to such a divergent set of understandings, and its inherent emptiness, also come in for some critique.[31] The apparently limitless readings available when one considers 'space' need to be set against the necessary materiality of historical study, even in its most theoretical guises, and it may be this that explains these chapters' disregard for the concept of space: it is place, and its social and economic control, as well as the relations that it provokes or that are permitted or forbidden to operate in it that, in part, motivate our interest here.

Whether investigating how people made themselves at home in eighteenth-century England or twentieth-century France, or the ways that domestic concerns played upon national demands in Egypt or the Soviet Union, we find that the gender of inhabitants, things, spaces and the domestic context overall, was significant in telling and sometimes surprising ways that *Homes and Homecomings* sets out to explore. The volume is divided into four parts which, if considered in terms of a dwelling itself, broadly move from the home's interior towards the outside, and survey several aspects of homeliness: Comfort, Utility, Inhabitants and Boundaries. In the first section, 'Comfort', the authors explore the elaborate, and elaborately gendered, means by which homes in the past were made homely. These efforts were significantly against the odds, in Susan Reid's case, involving resistance to Soviet state injunctions against the squishy and the baroque when it came to interior décor. Karen Harvey considers how masculinity was able to figure in eighteenth-century British ideas of home, while Quintin Colville explores the unlikely homemaker in the person of the British naval officer at war. Against 'comfort', planners and designers often set 'Utility', the subject of the next section. Here the nation comes more to the fore, when the duty to control the layout and function of a home became a battleground in post-war France, as Nicole Rudolph clarifies. Just what should go into a home and where, is set out in the 1960s Ghanaian case by Bianca Murillo, and the nineteenth-century British one by Jane Hamlett. The third section, 'Inhabitants', investigates who gets to live in a home and, more pertinently, make decisions over it. The instance of elite eighteenth-century north America is examined by Vivian Bruce

Conger, who finds that the house designed by Deborah Franklin for her and her absent husband Benjamin raises questions not just about the ability of wealthy women to make major architectural decisions, but how the household is defined when not all assumed members are present. Similar questions are tackled in completely contrasting ways by Carrie Hamilton, whose investigation of access to housing by poor Cubans since the Revolution, particularly lesbian and gay Cubans, reveals much about changing ideas of sexuality and the constraints that ideologies of home impose. It is the imposition of ideologies of home that are more deeply studied in the final section of this volume, 'Boundaries'. Here, the availability of homes, and the assumptions about who might belong in them, on both micro and macro levels, come under scrutiny. Carina Ray's chapter investigates what happened when people married across 'race', and wanted to live together in British-controlled west Africa. Lisa Pollard explores representations of marital strife as national anxiety in twentieth-century Egypt, while Christina Twomey investigates western women's return from Japanese internment after the Second World War. All three of these chapters suggest that anxieties about women being in the wrong place can provide ample evidence of how nations imagined themselves as home, as well as telling forgotten or long-buried stories about people whose homes the authorities frequently went to great lengths to make far from homely.

While most of the chapters collected here concentrate on single nations, they open up several new ways that historians can think about home. They take into account homes as sites to amass material objects, both hidden and displayed; they explore conflicts over the rights to construct and imagine a home; and they confront us with what happens when only some people are accorded rights to a home. In all of their explorations, gender is fundamental to elaborating our understanding of the historical meanings of homes and homecomings. But, given the amplitude of meanings of 'home' in the English language, this collection will necessarily range widely. Only one thing is definite: that, historically, there was something called 'home'. Precisely what the home is, though, is a little less certain.

Notes

I am very grateful to Carrie Hamilton and Sally Phillips for helping to make editing this volume such a pleasure.

1. The 2008 Place Survey. See http://www.communities.gov.uk/publications/corporate/statistics/placesurvey 2008; http://www.guardian.co.uk/news/datablog/2009/jun/24/communities-localgovernment (accessed 24 June 2009). Other indicators were whether respondents felt satisfied with their area as a place to live; thought that people of different backgrounds could get on well there; regarded anti-social behaviour as a problem; and thought their health was good. The survey did not analyse Wales or Scotland.
2. Tea Mäkipää's house at the exhibition Neue Heimat, Berlinische Galerie, Berlin, 2007. See http://www. berlinischegalerie.de/index.php?id=505&L=0 (accessed 1 June 2009).
3. For a relatively early excursion into the notion that home was a concept, see Witold Rybczynski, *Home: A Short History of an Idea* (1986; repr. London: Heinemann, 1988). For refinement and development of this idea, see Alison Blunt and Robyn Dowling, *Home* (London: Routledge, 2006).
4. Mona Hatoum, *Under Siege* (1983), in Michael Archer, Guy Brett and Catherine de Zegher, *Mona Hatoum*, (2nd edn. 1997; repr. Oxford: Phaidon, 1998), p. 122.
5. Steven Spielberg, *E.T.: The Extra-Terrestrial* (USA, 1982).
6. Gannit Ankori, '"Dis-Orientalisms": Displaced Bodies/Embodied Displacements in Contemporary Palestinian Art', in Sara Ahmed, Anne-Marie Fortier, Mimi Sheller and Claudia Castaneda (eds), *Uprootings/ Regroundings: Questions of Home and Migration* (Oxford: Berg, 2003), pp. 59–90, here p. 64. See also Edward W. Said, 'The Art of Displacement: Mona Hatoum's Logic of Irreconcilables', in *Mona Hatoum: The Entire World as a Foreign Land* (London: Tate Gallery, 2000), pp. 7–17.

7.   If not considerably earlier. See e.g., Roberto Fernandez Retamar, 'Caliban: Notes Toward a Discussion of Culture in Our America', tr. Lynn Garafola, David Arthur McMurray and Robert Marquez, *Massachusetts Review* 15 (1974), pp. 7–72; Sander L. Gilman, *The Jew's Body* (New York and London: Routledge, 1991).

8.   German Jewish Aid Committee, *While You Are in England: Helpful Information and Guidance for Every Refugee* (London: Jewish Board of Deputies, c.1938), p. 12.

9.   I make no claims to expertise in linguistics. The brief and highly provisional – not to say perfunctory – comments that follow are intended to be suggestive not conclusive. I am grateful to Ross Balzaretti, Julia Barrow, Lisa Pollard, Franziska Meyer, Sylvain Cypel, Carrie Hamilton, Hugh Goddard and Nick Baron for discussions about several languages.

10. Elizabeth Boa and Rachel Palfreyman, *Heimat: A German Dream. Regional Loyalties and National Identity in German Culture 1890–1990* (Oxford: Oxford University Press, 2000), quote on p. 5; see also Peter Blickle, *Heimat: A Critical Theory of the German Idea of Homeland* (London: Camden House, 2002). It should be noted that the land associated with Heimat is not confined to the place we understand as 'Germany', but at various times encompassed the German State's expanding and contracting colonies in Africa and Europe.

11. R. E. Latham and D. R. Howlett (eds), *Dictionary of Medieval Latin from British Sources* fasc. III (London: Oxford University Press, 1986), pp. 719–21.

12. On the lack of transferability between one language of home and another, see e.g., Volker Bückmann's discussion of the roots of the German term for a united or federal Europe, 'Haus Europa': http://www.linse.uni-due.de/linse/publikationen/Hass/Bueckmann_HausEuropa.pdf (accessed 24 July 2009).

13. Interestingly, Russia can be both *Rodina* (motherland) and *Otechestvo* (fatherland). A distinction is drawn between fighting for the nation's survival, where an oath is sworn to the motherland, and glorifying in its victory, where it becomes the fatherland. Note that the synonym of the British English term 'homely' is 'homey' in north American English; 'homely' in Britain carries none of the disdain that it does in America; on the contrary, it expresses comfort and what in German might be called *Gemütlichkeit.*

14. Part of Sandi Hilal, *Al-Qasas Project* (2008), at the exhibition, 'Palestine: La Création dans tous ses États', Institut du Monde Arabe, Paris, 2009. (My understanding is that this project was made in collaboration with Alessandro Petti and Eyal Weizman.)

15. Alison Blunt and Ann Varley, 'Geographies of Home', *Cultural Geographies* 11 (2004), pp. 3–6, here pp. 3, 5.

16. Betty Friedan, *The Feminine Mystique* (London: Victor Gollancz, 1963); Ann Oakley, *Housewife* (London: Allen Lane, 1974).

17. See e.g., the now canonised Leonore Davidoff and Catherine Hall, *Family Fortunes: Men and Women of the English Middle Class, 1780–1850* (London: Hutchinson, 1987).

18. There are plenty of works on separate spheres. I will just mention Amanda Vickery, 'Golden Age to Separate Spheres? A Review of the Categories and Chronology of English Women's History', *Historical Journal* 36 (1993), pp. 383–414; Marian Kaplan, *The Making of the Jewish Middle Class: Women, Family, and Identity in Imperial Germany* (New York: Oxford University Press, 1991).

19. Hilde Heynen, 'Modernity and Domesticity: Tensions and Contradictions', in Hilde Heynen and Gülsüm Baydar (eds), *Negotiating Domesticity: Spatial Productions of Gender in Modern Architecture* (London: Routledge, 2005), pp. 1–29, here p. 9.

20. See e.g., Shirley Ardener (ed.), *Women and Space: Ground Rules and Social Maps* (London: Croom Helm, 1981); Linda McDowell and Joanne P. Sharp (eds), *Space, Gender, Knowledge: Feminist Readings* (London: Arnold, 1997); Jane Rendell, Barbara Penner and Iain Borden (eds), *Gender Space Architecture: An Interdisciplinary Introduction* (London: Routledge, 2000); Leslie Kanes Weisman, *Discrimination by Design: A Feminist Critique of the Man-Made Environment* (Urbana and Chicago: University of Illinois Press, 1994); Mary Evans and Clare Ungerson (eds), *Sexual Divisions: Patterns and Processes* (London and New York: Tavistock Publications, 1983).

21. Mary Douglas, 'The Idea of a Home: A Kind of Space', *Social Research* 58 (1991), pp. 287–307; *New Formations* 17: special issue on 'The Question of "Home"' (1992); David Bell and Gill Valentine (eds), *Mapping Desire: Geographies of Sexualities* (London and New York: Routledge, 1995).

22. As Laura Mulvey suggested in 'Melodrama Inside and Outside the Home', in Laura Mulvey, *Visual Cultures and Other Pleasures* (Basingstoke: Macmillan, 1989), cited in Beatriz Colomina, 'The Split Wall: Domestic Voyeurism', in Beatriz Colomina (ed.), *Sexuality and Space* (New York: Princeton Architectural Press, 1992), pp. 72–128, here p. 82. Among Walter Benjamin's several modernist, Marxist aspersions that he cast on the softness and dark-coloured muddle he associated with nineteenth-century bourgeois women, see the section 'Blumeshof 12', in Walter Benjamin, *Berlin Childhood around 1900*, tr. Howard Eiland

(Cambridge: Belknap Press of Harvard University Press, 2006), pp. 86–92. Susan Reid develops this idea more fully in her chapter in this volume.

23. As I argued when discussing Jewish women's search for their stolen objects after their return to post-war Paris in K. H. Adler, *Jews and Gender in Liberation France* (Cambridge: Cambridge University Press, 2003), pp. 150–59.

24. Leora Auslander, 'Coming Home? Jews in Postwar Paris', *Journal of Contemporary History* 40 (2005), pp. 237–59, quote on p. 253.

25. For a recent investigation, see Amy Milne-Smith, 'Club Talk: Gossip, Masculinity and Oral Communities in Late Nineteenth-Century London', *Gender & History* 21 (2009), pp. 86–106.

26. Nancy Reagin, 'The Imagined Hausfrau: National Identity, Domesticity, and Colonialism in Imperial Germany', *Journal of Modern History* 73 (2001), pp. 54–86, here p. 58. Here the whole notion of home as homeland, and its imagined construction, needs to be mentioned, though I do not discuss it in detail. For important works which nonetheless ignore gender, see e.g., Salman Rushdie, 'Imaginary Homelands', in Salman Rushdie, *Imaginary Homelands: Essays and Criticism 1981–1991* (London: Granta, 1991), pp. 9–21; Benedict Anderson, *Imagined Communities: Reflections on the Origin and Spread of Nationalism* (London: Verso, 1983). For a useful reflection on home, gender and nation, see Wendy Webster, *Imagining Home: Gender, 'Race' and National Identity, 1945–64* (London: UCL Press, 1998).

27. See e.g., Catherine Hall and Sonya O. Rose (eds), *At Home with the Empire: Metropolitan Culture and the Imperial World* (Cambridge: Cambridge University Press, 2006).

28. Sarah Pink, *Home Truths: Gender, Domestic Objects and Everyday Life* (Oxford: Berg, 2004), p. 57.

29. Victor Buchli, Alison Clarke and Dell Upton, 'Editorial', *Home Cultures* 1 (2004), pp. 1–4, here p. 2.

30. Nigel Rapport and Andrew Dawson (eds), *Migrants of Identity: Perceptions of Home in a World of Movement* (Oxford: Berg, 1998).

31. Peter Wynn Kirby, '"Lost in Space": An Anthropological Approach to Movement', pp. 2–3; Tim Ingold, 'Against Space: Place, Movement, Knowledge', both in Peter Wynn Kirby (ed.), *Boundless Worlds: An Anthropological Approach to Movement* (Oxford: Berghahn, 2009), pp. 1–28 and 29–43.

1 Communist Comfort: Socialist Modernism and the Making of Cosy Homes in the Khrushchev Era

Susan E. Reid

The theme of this chapter – 'communist comfort' and the propagation, in Soviet mass housing of the 1950s–60s, of a socialist modernist aesthetics of domesticity – is rich with oxymoron.[1]

First, modernism was assigned, in the Cold War's binary model of the world, exclusively to the capitalist 'camp'. 'Socialist' and 'modernist' were positioned as incompatible. Although the conjunction of political and artistic radicalism in Soviet Russia of the 1920s is well known, the renascence there in mid-century of socialist modernism was unthinkable in Cold War terms and has only recently begun to be taken seriously.[2]

The second contradiction is that between modernity – along with its cultural manifestation, modernism – and domesticity. Modernity and dwelling have been assumed to be at odds. Pathologised by Walter Benjamin and others as a nineteenth-century petit-bourgeois addiction, domesticity and the need for comfort were to be shrugged off in favour of the freedom to roam. Homelessness, and not 'homeyness', was the valorised figure of modernity.[3] In revolutionary Russia of the 1920s, the modernist avant-garde designed portable, fold-away furniture more suited to the military camp; to supplant the soft, permanent bed of home was part of their effort to make the material culture of everyday life a launch pad to the radiant future.[4] Adopting unchallenged the established cultural identification between women and the bourgeois home, modernism's (and socialism's) antipathy for domesticity was also gendered, indeed misogynistic. Its wandering, exploring hero was imagined as male, while the despised aesthetics of dwelling from which he walked away – entailing ornament, concealment, confinement and the use of soft, yielding materials – particularly textiles – was construed not only as bourgeois but as feminine.[5] That the condition of modernity was to be restless, transient, constantly on the move became, however, a source of regret and nostalgic yearning for some after the destruction and dislocations of the Second World War. The philosopher Martin Heidegger, writing in 1954, lamented that in modern industrial society people had lost the capacity to dwell. It was particularly hard, he found, to be at home and at peace in modern housing, which is produced as a commodity or allocated by state bureaucracies, because we no longer reside in what we or our kin have built through generations but instead pass through the constructions of others.[6]

Third, the terms 'communist comfort' or 'socialist domesticity' are also, at first sight, as self-contradictory as 'fried snowballs'. 'Cosy' is unlikely to be the word that leaps to mind in association with Soviet state socialism, and least of all with the standard, prefabricated housing blocks that were erected at speed and in huge numbers in the late 1950s, which form the material context for this study. Indeed, home-life has hardly been the dominant angle from which to study the Soviet Union.[7] Socialism as a movement was traditionally associated with asceticism, sobriety and action; with production rather than consumption and rest; and with the collective, public sphere rather than the domestic and personal. Meanwhile, nineteenth-century socialist and feminist critiques, including those of Marx and Engels, identified the segregated bourgeois home as the origin of division of labour and alienation and a primary site of class and gender oppression. The bourgeois institutions of home and family, based on private property bonds, were supposed to be cleared away by the Bolshevik Revolution of 1917. John Maynard Keynes, speaking of left-leaning students in the 1930s, noted that, 'Cambridge undergraduates were never disillusioned when they took their inevitable trip to "Bolshiedom" and found it "dreadfully uncomfortable". That is what they are looking for'.[8]

If disdain for bourgeois domesticity was a stance sympathisers expected of the Soviet Union, neglect of human comfort was also one of the charges its detractors levelled against it. In the Cold War, Western accounts of the Soviet Union tended to focus on political repression and military hardware paraded in the public square. When Soviet Russian everyday life was addressed at all, it was in negative terms of lack and shortage, embodied in queues for basic necessities. Stereotypes of drab, austere comfort*less*ness reinforced the West's indictment and 'othering' of state socialism as the polar opposite of the Western, capitalist model of ever-increasing comfort, convenience and individual, home-based consumption.[9] The Soviet home, if it came within the sights of Western attention at all, stood – by contrast with Western prosperity – for the privation of Soviet people, their *lack* of privacy, convenience, choice, consumer goods and comforts. Alternatively, it figured as a flaw in the Soviet system's 'totalitarian' grasp, its Achilles heel, a site of resistance to public values, of demobilisation in face of the mobilisation regime's campaigns, and even a potential counter-revolutionary threat to the interventionist state's modernising project of building communism. Thus one Western observer surmised in 1955: 'if Russians got decent homes, TV sets and excellent food wouldn't they, being human, begin to develop a petit-bourgeois philosophy? Wouldn't they want to stay home before the fire instead of attending the political rally at the local palace of culture?'[10] Others asked, 'Can the Soviet system afford to allow a larger-scale retreat from the world of work and of collectivity to the world of cosy domesticity on the part of its women? . . . A type of socialism might appear that proved to be so pleasant that the distant vision of communism over the far horizon might cease to beckon'.[11]

You could have *either* communism *or* comfort, according to this model, *not* 'comfortable communism' or 'communist comfort'. Home and utopia – no-place – were incompatible. If comfortable homes were deemed by Cold War observers to exist at all in the Soviet Union then it was as spaces where the official utopia of the party-state was contradicted, as sites of potential resistance and as the germ of state socialism's potential undoing.

Associated with women's traditional roles as preservers of continuity with the past, with conventional female qualities and handed-down practices and know-how, the home's status as the recalcitrant last frontier of state modernisation was gendered. Thus Francine du Plessix Gray, a Russian émigrée resident in the United States, represents the Soviet Russian home as an antidote to official Soviet values:

> Moscow's other havens, of course, were and remain the homes of friends: Those padded, intimate interiors whose snug warmth is all the more comforting after the raw bleakness of the nation's public spaces; those tiny flats, steeped in the odor of dust and refried *kasha* in which every gram of precious space is filled, every scrap of matter – icons, crucifixes, ancient wooden dolls, unmatched teacups preserved since before the Revolution – is stored and gathered against the loss of memory.[12]

There, in Gray's view, authentic Russian qualities were preserved in spite of over sixty years of Soviet rule. Paramount among these is an apparently timeless and indomitable 'national tradition of *uyutnost'* [sic]: that dearest of Russian words, approximated by our "coziness" and better by the German *Gemütlichkeit*, denotes the Slavic talent for creating a tender environment even in dire poverty and with the most modest means'. *Uiutnost'* is 'associated with intimate scale, with small dark spaces, with women's domestic generosity, and with a nurturing love'.[13] It represents, in Gray's elegiac account, continuity between generations of women. The womb-like embrace of the Russian home is defined by explicit antithesis to an inhospitable, inhuman public sphere and to the chiliasm and collectivism of official ideology and culture. The opposition between the home and the Soviet state's official modernising project, which entailed rupture with the past, is represented in a series of negative/positive dyads that map onto the dichotomy public/private: bleak/snug; raw/cooked (or even re-cooked!); loss/gathering and storing; amnesia/memory. The striving, future-oriented public project of Soviet modernity, based on Enlightenment values of rationality, science and progress, is opposed by home as a warm, hospitable, unchanging and *essentially feminine* domain of authentic human relations materialised in 'scraps of matter' and unmatched teacups. The home appears as a hermetic cell, apparently untouched by historical contingency and the ruptures of the twentieth century. Padded by the accumulation of memories and memorabilia, dust and clutter, it is insulated from ideological intrusion, scientific and industrial progress, in short, from modernity and its specific Soviet mode (Figure 1).

One can almost hear Benjamin scream in his sleep. For the private realm Gray celebrates here is the stuff of any Marxist modernist's worst nightmares (dreams a Freudian might analyse in terms of fear of being absorbed back into the womb).[14] In such a space, even Faust might succumb to the temptation to abide and give up the quest for enlightenment. For many Soviet commentators, too, in the late 1950s and early 1960s, the period on which we focus here, the resilience of what they considered a regressive aesthetics of hyper-domesticity and bad taste among the Soviet people aroused fear of loss of political consciousness. But was the contradiction between domesticity and socialist modernity irreconcilable? Or could home be accommodated in the modernist, socialist utopia? If so, what should it look like? In what follows we will examine ways in which specialist agents in the Khrushchev era (1953–64) sought to overcome the contradiction between domesticity and socialist modernity and

Figure 1: Reconstruction of a Stalin-era domestic interior (Sillamae Ethnographic Museum, photo: Dmitrii Sidorov).

to delineate a modern socialist aesthetics of the domestic interior. As Gray indicated, the key Russian term in the image of homeliness is *uiut*, a word that encompasses both comfort and cosiness or snugness.[15] Intelligentsia experts redefined *uiut* in modernist terms. Did popular practice follow their prescription? Or did the material practices of *uiut* remain closer to a retrospective ideal of 'homeyness', as defined by anthropologist Grant McCracken, as the expression of a search for continuity, stability, and a sense of rootedness?[16] In the concluding section we will turn briefly to whether the aesthetics of modern housing and modernist advice were embraced, resisted, subverted or accommodated by primarily female homemakers in their homes.

An obsession with domesticity

In Boris Pasternak's 1957 novel, *Doctor Zhivago*, Lara (whose name references the Lares), watching a young girl construct a home for her doll in spite of the dislocations of the Revolution, comments on her instinct for domesticity and order: 'nothing can destroy the longing for home and for order'.[17] Unlike Pasternak's heroine, we should not take for granted, as some ahistorical, biological given, that the longing for home and order, for comfort and cosiness, are mandatory for dwelling, that these are essentially feminine instincts, or that domestic spaces need necessarily be projections of the occupant's self. Along with other apparently natural categories, such as childhood, the identification of home with comfort has to be historicised as the cultural product of particular historical and material circumstances. The emergence of the concept of comfort, like that of the 'private' to which it is closely aligned, was associated with industrialisation, the rise of the bourgeoisie, and the segregation of the home as a private sphere and women's domain, to which the exhausted male could return from the world of work and public life.[18] In the Soviet Union, the conditions for this historical phenomenon were supposed to be swept away: bourgeois capitalism, women's confinement in the segregated home, and the idea of home as a fortress of private property values.

Yet Soviet culture of the Khrushchev era, it is no exaggeration to say, became *obsessed* with homemaking and domesticity. This was a matter both of authoritative, specialist practice and intelligentsia discourse on one hand, and of popular culture and experience on the other. Soviet public discourse, whether intentionally or as an unintended effect, naturalised cosiness and comfort as essential attributes of home life, and as a legitimate concern of the modern Soviet person, especially women. The domestic interior was presented not only as a place to carry out everyday reproductive functions, but also as a site for self-projection and aesthetic production, where the *khoziaika* (housekeeper or, more literally, mistress of the house) displayed her taste and creativity. It involved making things for the home and exercising judgement in selecting, purchasing, adapting and arranging the products of mass serial production. What were the historical conditions for the preoccupation with home decorating?

The material premises for the production of domesticity began, at last, to be provided on a mass scale in the Khrushchev era. The shift of priorities towards addressing problems of mass living standards, housing and consumption had already begun before Stalin's death, at the Nineteenth Party Congress in October 1952, but the pace intensified from 1957 as the provision of housing and consumer goods became a pitch on which the post-Stalin regime staked its legitimacy at home and abroad. A party decree of 31 July 1957 launched a mass industrialised housing construction campaign: 'Beginning in 1958, in apartment houses under construction both in towns and in rural places, economical, well-appointed apartments are planned for occupancy by a single family'.[19] The results would transform the lives of millions over the next decade. Some 84.4 million people – over one third of the entire population of the USSR – moved into new accommodation between 1956 and 1965, while others improved their living conditions by moving into modernised or less cramped housing.[20] The construction of new regions of low-rise, standard, prefabricated apartment blocks fundamentally altered the urban – and even rural – environment, extending the margins of cities and accelerating the already rapid process of urbanisation. Above all, the new flats were designed for occupancy by single families, in place of the prevailing norm of collective living in either barracks or communal apartments (Figure 2).

A range of bureaucracies and specialist agents of the party-state were necessarily involved in shaping the interior, given the mass scale and industrial methods of construction and the accompanying shift towards serial production of consumer goods to furnish them. At the same time, the increased provision of single-family apartments could, it was feared, foster regressive, particularist mentalities and loss of political consciousness. It was necessary therefore to work actively to forestall this. Thus architects and designers, trade specialists, and health, hygiene and taste experts were concerned

Figure 2: 1960s standard apartment block, St Petersburg (photo: Ekaterina Gerasimova, 2004 for project Everyday Aesthetics in the Modern Soviet Flat).

not only with shaping the material structure of apartments, but with defining how people should furnish and dwell in them.

But, the obsession with homemaking and the terms of domesticity was also shared by the millions of ordinary citizens who moved into new or modernised living quarters, or who could realistically expect to do so in the near future. Moving in, they had to furnish and decorate their homes and accommodate their standard structures to their own lives, while at the same time accommodating themselves to the new, unfamiliar spaces. As public discourse acknowledged – and some specialists regretted – the making of the domestic interior was a work with multiple authors. Architects and planners – accredited experts interpreting the priorities and briefs of the party-state – might set the parameters and determine the material structures of the house, but their power was not total. In making housing into home, it was the occupant who had the last word, however limited her room for manoeuvre.[21]

The negotiations between these agencies, differently positioned in relation to the authority of the state and to the material fabric of the individual home, was convention-ally gendered as one between a masculine public sphere and its experts, on one hand, and female private interests and their amateur practices, on the other.[22] Women were construed as the primary consumers and homemakers and as such, their dominion and expertise within the domestic domain was acknowledged as a force to be reckoned with; women had to be brought on board the socialist modernising project if the new flats were not to become nests of regressive, petit-bourgeois mentalities.[23] A note of caution should be sounded, however: the gendering of the public/private, professional/amateur relationship did not necessarily correspond straightforwardly to an architect's biology. In the USSR, architecture was not so exclusively a male preserve as in the West at this time, although a gender hierarchy of specialisms did operate within it: female architects appear to have been more likely to get ahead in regard to the traditionally feminine sphere of the domestic interior than in large urban planning projects and prestigious public buildings, and the authorities who wrote on home decorating often had female names. But however they may have behaved in their personal lives, in their professional practice these female architects generally espoused the same dominant norms as their male colleagues (however patriarchal) rather than adopting eccentric or dissenting positions based on their gendered experience. A systematic examination of the gender relations within the architectural and newly emerging industrial design professions lies beyond our scope. Here, we will explore attempts both in authoritative discourse (historically and conventionally masculine), and to a lesser extent in every-day practice and experience (conventionally and in practice the domain of women) to transcend the antithesis of home comfort and communism.

Already in the 1920s, Russian avant-garde artists aspired to bring the Revolution 'home' by purging from people's everyday environments things which they regarded as the trappings of petit-bourgeois private life and materialisation of alien class values – ornate furniture, embroidered tablecloths and antimacassars, silk lampshades and use-less ornaments – and to replace them with rational, functionalist, industrial, modern and 'socialist' material culture.[24] However, beginning in the discourse of the 1930s and increasing in the postwar period of demobilisation and reconstruction, tablecloths, napkins and silk lampshades were reinstated as attributes of female virtue and markers of Soviet progress, signifying a modern, urban, cultured way of life (*kul'turnost'*). Vera Dunham has argued, on the basis of fictional representations, that the relegitimation of bourgeois cultural values and aspirations, as materialised in a retrospective aesthetics of homemaking and accumulation of possessions, constituted part of a 'big deal' with the new Stalinist 'middle class'.[25] There is little historio-ethnographic research on the popular material culture of the Stalin period by which to judge the relation be-tween representations and reality here. But Western visitors to the Soviet Union in the 1950s also frequently commented on the overstuffed 'Victorian' interiors they encoun-tered.[26] This may be put down, in part, to a tendency to seek out confirmation of the Cold-War stereotypes they brought with them (notably the contradiction between offi-cial claims for progress, based on heavy industry, and backwardness of living conditions and consumer goods). However, the resilience or resurgence of this aesthetic through the 1930s and 1940s at least as an ideal (if not as a reality),[27] is also suggested by the fact that, after Stalin's death in 1953, a laundry list of bad taste almost identical to that which the Constructivists had sought to purge in the 1920s became once again the object of a widespread campaign of anathema.

The Khrushchev era is best known for de-Stalinisation – that is, for efforts to reform the most coercive aspects of Stalinism and dismantle its institutionalisation of privilege. But it also saw a revitalisation of utopian elements of Marx's thought concerning such matters as the relation between people and things, and the self-actualisation of the individual; a restoration, in the fields of philosophy and the spatial arts, of Constructivist ideas of the 1920s about the nature of a socialist material environment, and about the relation between art, industry and everyday life; and a rapprochement with international modernism in architecture and design.[28] For cultural de-Stalinisers or modernisers, those pre-revolutionary teacups and ancient wooden dolls to which the émigrée Gray clung were the monsters brought forth by the Sleep of Reason; this home-life, a millstone around the neck of progress. What was needed was to fight for the liberation of man – and more particularly, given the conventional gendering of this discourse, *woman* – from the bondage of things, and to foster social forms of everyday life. Aesthetic reformers and utopian ideologues called to battle against what they disparaged as the 'cult of acquisitions' and 'the striving at any cost to build a nest'.[29] They cast the aesthetic they repudiated as 'petit-bourgeois' or 'philistine', a throwback to tastes and private property mentalities that were engendered by pre-revolutionary social and property relations. At the same time, this aesthetic was implicitly identified with Stalinism and, as such, an object of de-Stalinisation along with the other excesses and perversions of the Revolution.[30] Taste war was a form of 'class struggle' for hegemony by a sector of the intelligentsia against the bureaucratic middle class privileged in the Stalin era, whom the aesthetic reformers cast as uncultured parvenus.[31]

The great transmigration

The surge of attention to housing and homemaking in the late 1950s took place against the background of a chronic housing shortage, exacerbated by wartime destruction. The majority of Soviet people, in the post-war period, lived in barrack-type accommodation or in communal apartments, where an entire family or more would be cramped into a single room, sharing a kitchen and bathroom – if they existed – with many other families. One was lucky to have so much as a 'cot-place' in a hostel – one's 'private' space limited to the bed one slept in. Overcrowded, insanitary conditions and homelessness were recognised as the cause of major social and health problems.[32] Tuberculosis was rife. Recent research on post-war Soviet society presents a picture of peoples on the move, in flux, characterised by social dislocation.[33] Nomadic mobility might be embraced by modernism as a defining aspect of modernity, and it was romanticised in Soviet literature and film in the Khrushchev era (especially in regard to the Virgin Lands campaign).[34] But in life rather than fiction, after half a century of dislocation, rupture, flux and instability, to be homeless was associated with disorder, instability and marginality, and with elements of the population that eluded organisation. Lack of a legitimate, registered place of residence made one a misfit in Soviet society, a marginal type (*limitchik*) or person of no fixed abode; it disenfranchised and deprived one of civic personality.[35] The dialectics of home and homelessness, dislocation and dwelling, disenfranchisement and becoming a fully self-realised Soviet person, were at the centre of public discourse and mass individual experience in the Khrushchev era.

In the late 1950s and early 1960s, Soviet society was on the move once again, on such a scale that the satirical magazine *Krokodil* likened this mass relocation to the 'Great Transmigration of Peoples'.[36] The modern-day 'transmigration' was distinguished from earlier waves in Soviet history, however (resulting from collectivisation, from the enforced deportation of whole ethnic groups under Stalin, and from war), in that it was caused not by the *loss* of a home, but precisely the opposite; it was a mass homecoming. People were on the move because they had been allocated new homes thanks to the intensive mass housing campaign. The fundamental changes in people's everyday environment and way of living were arguably more momentous for more people than better-known political events such as Khrushchev's 'secret speech' to the Twentieth Party Congress in 1956, in which he denounced Stalin's excesses.[37] A new revolution took place in Soviet daily life in the late 1950s, as Svetlana Boym notes, 'consisting of resettlement out of communal apartments to outlying "micro-districts" where people were able to live in separate, albeit state-owned apartments – many for the first time in their lives'.[38] As a result, the newly founded industrial design journal *Tekhnicheskaia estetika* (*Technical Aesthetics*) declared, 'The creation of the interior of the contemporary urban apartment has become one of the most important state problems' (Figure 3).[39] If, in the comfort of one's new home, one opened a newspaper or turned on the television (a rapidly expanding leisure pursuit and medium in terms of airtime and number of sets in the early 1960s), one would get the impression that the entire Soviet population was on the move, running around worrying about colour schemes and the choice of wallpaper, furniture and lampshades.[40]

The new housing regions of the Khrushchev era were notorious for having sacrificed aesthetics to engineering, function and economy. One of Khrushchev's first decisive interventions, less than two years after Stalin's death in 1953, had been to denounce the extravagant, monumental style of Stalinist architecture and, seemingly prompted by modernisers in the architectural profession, to declare ornament a crime (or at least, a Stalinist excess).[41] This implied a rapprochement with modernist principles of design dictated by function, materials and mode of production. Architects and engineers looked back to indigenous Constructivism and across the Iron Curtain to recent international developments, in particular efforts to solve the housing shortage throughout post-war Europe through system building and factory prefabrication.

The imperatives of thoroughgoing industrialisation, speed and economy of construction, combined with still primitive technologies of prefabrication, required re-thinking the requirements of dwelling: eliminating architectural ornament, reducing the dimensions to a functional minimum, and minimising or eliminating auxiliary spaces such as corridors.[42] Standardisation was paramount: the use of a limited number of type plans, standard modules and unembellished elevations. As Russian design historian Iurii Gerchuk describes the new flats:

> 'Comfort' was also conceived in very frugal terms . . . In the standardized housing designs accepted and applied at the turn of the 1950s–60s, ceiling heights were reduced to 2.5 m. In the tiny, cramped flats the space for auxiliary rooms was cut to the bare minimum. The size of the kitchen was reduced from 7 to 4.5. sq m and it opened directly off the living room. The toilet was combined with the bathroom. Convenience was sacrificed not only to save space but to simplify the construction process.[43]

Functional and featureless, the new housing estates may not count today among the monuments of world architecture, worthy of preservation orders or heritage status. On the contrary, the new flats – known as *khrushchevki* (or worse, *khrushcheby*, a contraction of 'Khrushchev' and 'slum') – are widely regarded as a shameful aspect of the Soviet legacy, to be purged as quickly as growing prosperity allows.[44] Yet, notwithstanding the monotonous standardisation and minimum specifications of the new flats,

Figure 3: 'New furniture for new flats' (*Ogonek* 1959).

as well as numerous shortcomings in their design, materials, construction and finish, the improvement in millions of people's quality of life cannot be overestimated. As one elderly woman told me, they are 'monuments in our hearts'.[45] Most significantly, the flats were planned and designed for occupancy by single nuclear families, and were equipped with mains plumbing, inside toilets and kitchens. Many people in interviews conducted in 2004–07 still recall the joy of having their own bathroom or kitchen, however diminutive, for the first time, rather than sharing with up to fifty others.[46] After a lifetime under the gaze of nosy neighbours, it was bliss to have one's own four walls to shelter one from their view, even if poor soundproofing meant you could still hear everything going on next door.[47] Along with the spread of television and car ownership, the single-family apartments have been seen, with reason, as setting in train a process of 'privatisation' of Soviet life. It was the state that provided the premises for this process, which was one of a number of paradoxical unintended side effects of its policies.[48] While tenants had no legal rights of ownership or disposal, and one person's apartment shared the same standard plan as another's, it was nevertheless a place to settle at last and call one's own.

Mediating the move: giving public meaning to the separate apartments

Housing construction gave visual dramatisation to the party-state's commitment to raising living standards of the many, not just the few. The intensive housing campaign was kept in the public eye and mind through two linked themes that corresponded to the dichotomy of mobilisation and settling/dwelling: first, Happy Housewarming; and second, the process of making and maintaining a home in these government-issue spaces. Thereby the new housing was invested with public meaning as a gift that demonstrated the party-state's solicitousness for its people, and as a symptom of progress towards communism and of its superiority over capitalism.[49]

The theme of Happy Housewarming, *novosel'e* (lit. new settling), celebrated the dynamic, ritualised, transformative moment of moving in: turning the key in the new door for the first time, crossing the threshold, inviting friends and family inside to share one's happiness. 'Housewarming is becoming the most common festival genre', declared the state newspaper *Izvestiia*.[50] '"New home – new happiness", as the folk saying goes', began an article in the labour newspaper *Trud* in late 1959, entitled 'Happy Housewarming'. It focused on a newly built five-storey apartment block into which fifty-six families of workers and employees of a Moscow machine-building factory had just moved. 'Bright, cosy [*uiutnye*] rooms. A joyful, festive bustle. Human happiness takes up stable and permanent residence here'.[51] Housewarming was represented as a joyful rite of passage, associated with brightness, cosiness, stability and happiness, through which the new Soviet person would emerge, remade, in readiness for the new life under communism. It was a mass, common celebration, but unlike the major public festivals and parades in city streets and squares, this one was celebrated by individual families with their friends and kin in their own homes.[52]

The longer durée and mundane, everyday *process* of settling in, making home and dwelling in the new flats, was harder to dramatise and keep in the public eye than the ritual moment of changing places. How to maintain public consciousness about the relation between this blessing in the present day and the future perfection to come? How to keep people mobilised for the construction of communism once they had settled in?

The duration and daily round or *byt*, commonly designated 'private life', was articulated and reproduced again and again as the subject of public discourse through pervasive advice. Allegedly in response to readers' demand, the popular press, advice manuals and television offered instruction on how to arrange one's furniture in the unfamiliar spaces, how to select elements of décor and find an appropriate colour scheme, or how to maintain the new types of surface such as linoleum floor covering.[53] Housewarming and settling into one's new flat became the theme of much early television programming. Broadcasts with titles such as 'For Family and Home' or 'Help for the Housewarmer' represented this as the 'typical' experience of the present day, presuming their viewers were either already watching in a new flat or dreaming of receiving one soon. New norms of 'contemporary' (that is, modernist) 'good taste' and 'rational', function-based use of space were propagated through representations of model interiors in the form of ideal home exhibits and show homes, photographs and artists' impressions.[54] Advice also sought to introduce industrial, Taylorist standards of time-and-motion efficiency and mechanisation into the domestic workspace of the kitchen, thereby integrating the home (via the space most implicated, in the past, in its regressive role of enslaving and stultifying women) into the public modernising project.[55] *Izvestiia*'s 'home and family' page, a significant innovation introduced in July 1959, printed articles such as that cited above, entitled 'New Home – New Way of Life'. It argued that, as millions of Soviet citizens moved to new, well-appointed apartments, it was necessary to develop the new discipline of *domovodstvo*, domestic science, 'to teach how best to furnish [the new apartment] to make it more *uiutno* [cosy] to live in': 'Rational nutrition, knowledge of how to dress comfortably and beautifully, and how to furnish one's apartment: all this has to be taught'.[56]

Advice, addressed primarily to the female homemaker, was often a matter of informing her about consumer goods that were supposed to be available, if not now then in the near future, and how to choose, teaching her to make wise and tasteful purchases: that is, to be a skilled consumer. New consumer goods, including furniture and appliances for the home, which were promised in the 1959 economic plan, created new civic tasks and responsibilities for the housewife; they imposed the duty of rational consumption and correct choice. Advice also functioned as socialist realism, often implying a greater degree of choice than was available. According to a television programme on home furnishing: 'Many of us, when we receive a new apartment, want to change the colour of the walls or put up wallpaper, all the more since now in Moscow you can get any kind of wallpaper you want. But, comrades! – in buying wallpaper it is necessary to make the correct choice of colour, pattern and texture'.[57]

Many community activities in new neighbourhoods were also directed towards homemaking and making things for the home, in addition to communal campaigns to improve and maintain the external appearance of blocks of flats, monitor use of balconies, plant the yards and create children's playgrounds. The local housing administration might organise carpentry clubs for adults, exhibitions of houseplants and flower arranging, and cookery competitions, in addition to amateur art and photographic circles, musical ensembles and radio clubs.[58] Community activities included not only homecraft classes for women and girls, but also home-oriented activities for men such as woodwork. In one neighbourhood carpentry club, each member began with repairing furniture, making small things such as shelves, bedside cabinets and kitchen tables, and then moved on to making more complex items such as bookshelves, TV tables or sideboards. The members got so keen that they began to spend all their free time there.[59] Such clubs aimed to attract men, to keep them off the street, away from the bottle, and from antisocial behaviour or 'hooliganism', while engaging them in activities associated with the home and fostering a pride in making or mending things for their domestic space.[60] Thus, if homelessness deprived one of civic personality, becoming a homemaker (*novosel*) conversely made one a Soviet person and respectable member of the community, participating in the 'typical' experience of the present day.

Although activities associated with the home were a recognised way to integrate potentially antisocial men, advice on creating the domestic interior and keeping a rational, modern, tasteful home was still addressed predominantly, if not exclusively, to women, constructing them as the primary homemakers. Men might participate, but theirs was an auxiliary role. In 1955, a *Novyi mir* reader lamented that while she and her husband might discuss how to furnish their new marital home, in practice it fell to her alone.[61] There was also a conventional gender division of skills and materials. As the community activities confirmed, work that involved structures and hard materials such as wood or metal was appropriate to men, while the aesthetic decisions, attention to surfaces, decorative touches and soft furnishings belonged to women. Making *uiut* was women's responsibility, both in authoritative discourse and, recent interviews suggest, in everyday understandings. Men are absent altogether in many of the retrospective narratives of homemaking told by women.[62] As possibilities for private car ownership grew in the course of the 1960s, cars and the spaces associated with them and their time-consuming maintenance – yard, street and garage – increasingly became an alternative male homosocial space to which men retreated to escape the home and its obligations.[63] There were some exceptions, however, where homemaking became a shared family bonding experience. One woman who had moved into a newly completed house in 1960 with her parents when she was twelve years old recalled how the whole family was involved in the process of turning the new apartment into 'home'. 'We tried to make it nice and cosy in the apartment'. Although still young, she, too, had wanted their new home to be beautiful and actively participated in making the interior. So did her father. Forty years on, this woman still took great pride in the furniture her father had made for the family home. 'Dad did everything himself!' He had made a sideboard, beds and kitchen cabinets with his own hands. He also laid linoleum. She, meanwhile, brought home fabrics for curtains and soft furnishings to decorate the interior as soon as she was old enough to work in a shop.[64]

At the same time as publicists ascribed the key role in making and maintaining the home to women, they also regularly emphasised that this was only part of their identity. If, in the past, a good housekeeper was one who devoted all her time and energy to domestic affairs, the Soviet woman was not confined to her domestic role, but was also active in production and social life, which were vital to her self-realisation. The conclusion the experts drew from this was not, or rarely, that the gendered division of labour in the home should be restructured but, rather, that the housewife's domestic responsibilities now included the introduction of an industrial model of efficiency or scientific management into domestic space and domestic routines. She must learn to rationalise housework – to see to it, for example, that the kitchen was arranged rationally – so that it did not absorb all her energy and time.[65]

The sheer volume of press articles on taste, advice manuals offering 'help for the housewarmer', and television programmes about how to make home in the new standard apartment, as well as exhibitions of new furniture designs, together focused attention on interior decorating and home improvements and rendered these a normal and even normative concern and leisure pursuit for the modern Soviet person. Even zealous Marxists who were committed to reviving the spirit of the Revolution began to endorse cosiness as a legitimate aspiration along with the principle of one-family flats. For example, philosopher of material culture Karl Kantor – one of those active in reviving the suppressed legacy of the Constructivists, including the industrial modernist aesthetic they proposed as part of a reconfiguration of the relationship between people and things under socialism – distanced himself from the extreme asceticism of the 1920s. At that time, wrote Kantor:

> ...the struggle for the new way of life against the old bourgeois-philistine domesticity sometimes took on the form of a struggle against material comforts in everyday life, against the striving to have a separate apartment and make it comfortable. Attention to the external side of life was disparaged as little short of a betrayal of the Revolution.

However, Kantor corrected, 'the liberation from enslavement to things which the Revolution brought with it, could not mean liberation from things themselves; the striving to collective forms of life does not presuppose a rejection of individual forms of dwelling'.[66] 'The individual should not be lost sight of behind society, nor the family for the collective'. One-family flats were not, per se, counter-revolutionary, and concern with furnishing them was not to be confused with bourgeois fetishism or the consumerism identified with the capitalist West, he concluded. 'No-one today would dream of accusing a person of betraying revolutionary ideals by taking an interest in how to furnish an apartment in a new building comfortably and beautifully'.[67]

Accommodating industrial, standardised construction

The main task facing Soviet citizens moving into the new flats, public discourse acknowledged, was to overcome standardisation: how to create *uiut* in a mass-produced, concrete, prefabricated box. It was assumed that the new occupants would need and want to customise and interiorise their look-alike, industrially mass-produced living space to fit it to themselves. The official media encouraged the idea that the raw interiors of the prefabricated concrete blocks had somehow to be processed and worked over, to make them into cosy homes. While standardisation was acknowledged as a necessary condition of industrial production, it was represented more as a problem that needed to be mitigated, rather than as a virtue on account of its homogenising potential (with the exception that the elision of differences in living conditions between city and country was represented as a major benefit of extending such housing construction to rural areas). Responses to a 1968 survey of residents who had moved into new Moscow apartments in 1966 indicated that they saw standardisation as antithetical to *uiut*. Twenty-one out of eighty-five respondents named this as a defining characteristic of the interior, and 20 per cent said they did not want their apartment to look like their neighbours'.[68] Many thought lack of choice of consumer goods exacerbated the problem of standardisation of interiors. One wrote: 'Standard, lack of *uiut*: if one were to judge from the contemporary home it might seem that everyone has identical characters'. Conversely, *uiut* must presumably require a degree of individualisation.[69] It was *uiut* that made the difference between mere living space and a lived-in place, home.[70]

The problems and paradoxes of making 'private life' in both public and commodified housing – as a common problem of industrial modernity identified by Heidegger, for example, in his 1954 essay – have received much attention from anthropologists, design historians and others in different national contexts since at least the 1980s. They emphasise that residents do not passively submit to the given structures and the norms they materialise. As Marianne Gullestad, Daniel Miller and Nicky Gregson demonstrate, even if most people no longer reside in homesteads built with their own hands but in commodified or state-allocated housing, 'most do engage in sets of activities that are about seeking to constitute these dwelling structures as appropriate sites of habitation for them'; that is, they accommodate those spaces to their own lives, a process that includes both appropriation and compromise.[71] Studies of social housing in Britain, including Daniel Miller's important analysis of how residents of council housing overcame alienation, and Judy Attfield's work on how residents of rented public housing in Harlow New Town made themselves 'at home' in its modernist, open-plan structures, focus on the material practices of appropriation of space.[72] McCracken, in his 1989 study of North American owner-occupied homes, similarly found that individuals sought to mediate their relationship with the larger world, 'refusing some of its influences, and transforming still others' by creating 'homeyness'.[73] At issue is the possibility of exercising agency, control over boundaries and what Wolfgang Braunfels calls 'the freedom to participate in the design of one's own urban living environment'.[74]

The possibility of such agency and mutuality has often been denied by Western commentators in regard to the Soviet context. Writing of Soviet mass housing, historian Blair Ruble cites Braunfels with the gloss: 'The Western alienation from residence . . . was magnified in the Soviet Union, where all planning is done for strangers'.[75] Yet Soviet residents were expected to make a large input into transforming the concrete shell of their apartment into a liveable space. Experts writing in the popular and specialist design press in the Khrushchev era emphasised the labour of making the standard apartment into home, that is, the agency and responsibilities of the homemaker. People did not passively move in, or 'consume' the apartment as a ready-made, fully finished commodity, either in representations or in practice. If only because of shortcomings in the construction and finishing (rather than as a matter of state policy and design), this required personal investment of effort, and resourcefulness and skill on the part of the homemaker: people actively made the standard space into home through their purchases, taste decisions, and by making or adapting things. Many manufactured goods also presupposed the need for work on them by the user.[76] Advice literature assumed the necessary input of the tenant and included very practical directions on how to adapt or fit cupboards, equipment and labour-saving devices.[77] Some authors even acknowledged that choosing and arranging things for the new home was a semiotic process: an exercise in self-expression and differentiation. That one could and even *should* inscribe one's individuality upon the plan and walls of the new apartment and make the givens of the standard architecture personally meaningful and communicative of self-image and social position was an unexamined premise of much advice literature.[78]

Nevertheless, the degree of individualism envisaged was not only narrowly circumscribed by the physical structure of the building and by shortcomings of centrally planned production and distribution (shortages and lack of choice of consumer goods); it was also subject to widely promulgated norms and regimes of taste. Residents were not supposed to exercise their agency just anyhow, but in ways that accorded with the ideal identity of the Soviet Person and with modernist norms of good taste, rationality and hygiene – as these were defined by intelligentsia experts. Communism presupposed voluntary self-regulation, the internalisation of and submission to social norms, and accommodation of personal desires to the best interests of the collective. And this consciousness extended beyond 'communist morality' to matters of aesthetics.

Rationalisation and modernisation of *uiut*

Uiut remained the central term in discussions of domesticity in the context of Khrushchev-era remodernisation. There was much ambivalence, however, about the will to cosiness, and this was often expressed in misogynistic terms. Anxieties included, as Christine Varga-Harris summarises, 'trepidation over the rise of bourgeois desires, tastes and mores (gendered female); the emasculation of men within the household (metonymic of the emasculation of the working class as a whole, gendered male); and the disruption of social relations'.[79] Even as the search for *uiut* was legitimated and encouraged, the dream of a private realm such as Gray presented, seemingly insulated from the public sphere and from the forces of modernisation and sovietisation, was denigrated as 'philistine' and regressive by authorities on the interior. Thus Boris Brodskii, writing in the new design journal *Dekorativnoe iskusstvo SSSR* (*Decorative Art of the USSR*), condemned the idea of home 'as an island where one could build one's personal [*lichnuiu*] life "as I like"'. Repudiating this conception of privacy as a throwback to 'petit-bourgeois' values of the past, he, like other taste reformers, firmly identified it with a particular treatment of domestic space and residue of clutter: ornate furniture, embroidered tablecloths and antimacassars, and silk lampshades. These trappings of 'private life' not only failed to cement relations between people, Brodskii argued, but were fetishes that alienated them. 'The struggle with philistinism is the struggle for man's liberation from the bondage to things, which . . . appear to him more significant (and thence more beautiful) than they in fact are'.[80] A direct, seemingly causal link was assumed between things of a particular quantity, kind and style and a home-centred mentality, segregated from the public sphere. Such possessions chained people – especially women – to the home, and inhibited their engagement with public life. The assumption that padded and cluttered interiors stultified the individual was rationalised by reference to hygiene and women's enslavement to the unproductive labour of dusting, which (along with the 'kitchen slavery' Lenin had denounced as the source of women's stereotypical lack of political consciousness) prevented them from realising themselves as unalienated, all-round individuals.[81]

Brodskii and other publicists sought to distinguish the proper, socialist attitude towards the new apartments from the bourgeois 'home-is-my-castle' mentality in aesthetic terms. To prevent the new one-family apartments from becoming nests of particularist and regressive mentalities, their solution was to promote a modernist style known as the 'contemporary style'. The contemporary interior must be fitted to assist the process of opening up everyday life into the public sphere, to make the boundary between public and private transparent and shift the centre of gravity of everyday life out of the room or flat and into the public sphere. Thus, while *uiut* remained vital to homemaking in the 'new type of small-scale apartment for one family', and continued to be identified with 'the idea of an attentive female hand', the challenge was to produce it in ways that did not reproduce petit-bourgeois relations. *Uiut* must be redefined in austere, modern, hygienic terms explicitly opposed to those of the bourgeois and Stalinist past and appropriate to the present period of scientific technological revolution and imminent transition to communism.

What this modernised socialist *uiut* repudiated was clear already to the reader of the highbrow literary journal *Novyi mir*, cited above: it was *not* 'rubber plants with dusty leaves, nor a herd of marble elephants put out to pasture on one's dressing table "for good luck"'.[82] If in the past, *uiut* was identified with confinement and encumberment, entailing the use of all means 'to *reduce* living space, associated with cushions and drapes, dust and warmth', the (ideal) contemporary Soviet person, by contrast, strove for her home to be hygienic and spacious, to have more light and fresh air, to be furnished simply and conveniently with simple and beautiful objects of everyday life.[83] Modern beauty and comfort under socialism were the product of reason, dictated by function, convenience, hygiene, openness, stylistic homogeneity and good taste. Prime targets for the modernist broom were the accumulation of dust, clutter, useless ornaments and mementoes, that is, precisely those things which in Gray's and other accounts of the (traditional) Russian home were most closely identified with its female occupant and the status of the interior as an expression of femininity, identity and memory.

Among the most unforgivable taste gaffes were ersatz rugs hung on walls, on which swans, kittens, tigers, women's heads or portraits of important people were painted in oils.[84] These painted rugs, sold at stations and provincial markets, were a form of popular culture that had emerged in spite of the state, filling a vacuum left by the command economy. Producing them was a way in which collective farm peasants supplemented their income (Alexander Solzhenitsyn referred to them in his *One Day in the Life of Ivan Denisovich*, 1962).[85] Not only did such artisanal production occupy a shady area outside the state's economic planning and regulation, but it also undermined the intelligentsia's cultural hegemony. That it eluded quality control and aesthetic regulation by the professional artistic organisations was a matter of concern to taste experts in the late 1950s, as well as to the Komsomol (Party Youth League).[86] Moreover, to use rugs as wall hangings was a traditional practice of Russia's hinterland (while all negative practices tended to be branded indiscriminately as 'petit-bourgeois' their origins were often also rural and regional or ethnic), and attacks on this practice were part of a condescending *mission civilisatrice* by modernising urban professionals to reform and indeed Westernise popular practice. An architect instructed *Rabotnitsa*'s women readers in 1959: 'rugs hung on walls – that's bad! They are spread on the floor to muffle footsteps and keep feet warmer, or are hung behind a divan without a back so that one does not lean against the cold wall and also above the bed so as not to scratch the wall. Don't get carried away with rugs because they collect dust'.[87]

Other traditional uses of textiles were also inappropriate. A manual for teenage girls, *Podruga* (Girlfriend) showed 'before' and 'after' images of the same interior done in retrograde and good contemporary taste, where the key difference was the disappearance, along with little ornamental marble elephants, of the scalloped and embroidered cloths that covered every surface in the 'before' image (Figure 4). 'Many imagine that the more napkins, lampstands and sideboards, the cosier [the interior]', lamented a Novosibirsk taste manual, also for young people—but they were wrong! Along with beds covered in satin bedspreads and mountains of white, lace-covered cushions, intended proudly to proclaim the family's prosperity, they merely betrayed the householders' lack of discernment and failure to understand what beautifies and what spoils the appearance of the home (Figure 5).[88] Since all spaces and furniture in the modern Soviet flat had to serve multiple functions and the bedroom became the living room during the day, the bed had to double as a settee, not be set apart as a site of display of wealth.[89] Dust-catching and unhygienic, embroidered cloths were a

Figure 4: 'Good' and 'bad' taste in home furnishings, from M. Chereiskaia, 'Zametki o khoroshem vkuse' (*Podruga* [Girlfriend] (Moscow 1959), pp. 220–21).

throwback to petit-bourgeois models of domesticity and home-bound femininity. They were associated with the trousseau and the private property functions of the bourgeois and feudal family, with ostentatious display, with irrational, time-wasting practices of housekeeping and with an anachronistic conception of women's role, tied exclusively to the home. Embroidery testified to the confinement and oppression of women in the past, who were treated as chattels to be exchanged accompanied by a trousseau, rather

Figure 5: Kazan interior (photo: Sofia Chuikina, 2005, for project Everyday Aesthetics in the Modern Soviet Flat).

than as free, equal and entitled to develop their individuality, as they were supposed to be under socialism.[90]

Textiles had been used traditionally in Russian culture, including in the communal apartment from which many occupants of new flats had moved, to screen and conceal: nets hid intimate life from neighbours, valances around bedsteads concealed the things stored beneath them and curtains were widely used to hide messy shelves.[91] Victor Buchli insightfully analyses the ways in which, in the Stalin period, embroidered cloths were deployed to 'individualise' space and for the purpose of 'interiorisation' or 'privatisation' and 'withdrawal'.[92] The approved modernist aesthetics of transparency was conceived, by contrast, as opening up the 'private' interior onto the public space beyond, and maximising space and light. 'Don't clutter up the apartment with things. Let there be more space and light. Every item of furnishing you acquire must be

Figure 6: 'Contemporary' furniture (imported from Finland), mid-1960s, St Petersburg (photo: Ekaterina Gerasimova, 2004, for project Everyday Aesthetics in the Modern Soviet Flat).

essential for you ... Choosing furniture don't buy cumbersome things [... they] make it crowded and look very old-fashioned. The most important thing is stylistic unity. If you have only just started to equip your apartment then get contemporary, light, elegant and, at the same time, very simple furniture' (Figure 6).[93] Writing in *Rabotnitsa*, the magazine for women workers, architect Irina Voeikova, a frequent commentator in the popular press on how to furnish homes, instructed new homemakers to purchase

Figure 7: Model interior in the 'contemporary style' (from O. Baiar and R. Blashkevich, *Kvartira i ee ubranstvo*, Moscow, 1962).

furniture that left as much free space as possible. Thus, 'huge bedsteads on high legs disappear from our lives along with patterned valances,' for 'everyone knows that one doesn't hang valances nowadays'. They were to be replaced by 'convenient divans and chairs that easily transform into beds without taking up a lot of space'.[94] Others exhorted: 'Contemporary furniture must be convenient to use, compact, light and without carving or mouldings (scrolls, cornices), which are hard to wash and clean' (Figure 7). 'Contemporary lamps must be simple, light, hygienic, modest and elegant'.[95] Functional zoning was recommended, applying the modernist principle of spatial separation of functions in conditions where a single room had to serve multiple purposes. But this could be achieved without blocking off areas and daylight with solid partitions, by using differentiated colour schemes or light, open shelving units. Voeikova recommended a light frame with vertical cords above a narrow trough for plants. Trained to climb up the cords, the vegetation would form a light trellis, which corresponded with the fashionable aesthetics of transparency, lightness and irregular vertical lines.

Home as a site for display of cultural level and aesthetic discernment

One of the sins associated with embroidered cloths and lace pillows was that they served purely for display and were non-functional or even inhibited the proper use of an object or space. Was there any place at all for displays, mementoes, ornaments and other decorative elements in the socialist modern interior? In his 1954 call for industrialised construction, Khrushchev had condemned non-functional decoration in architecture as an expensive waste of resources, a luxury associated with Stalinist 'excess', which was unwarranted in modern socialist society. Signalling Soviet architecture's reorientation towards international modernism, with its minimalist aphorisms such as 'less is more' (widely attributed to modernist architect Ludwig Mies van der Rohe) and its identification of ornament with criminality, degeneracy and regression to a primitive evolutionary stage (Adolf Loos), the First Secretary's intervention (reinforced by subsequent decrees against 'excess'), rendered all forms of decorative art aesthetically and morally suspect.[96] Specialists extended the prohibition on 'superfluous' decorative elements to the domestic interior; these must be reduced to the minimum or eliminated, along with anything else that served purely the purpose of display or concealment. 'Some think that decorations create *uiut*. That's not quite right . . . To create genuine *uiut* in the apartment the main thing is convenience for people'.[97]

As in earlier modernist discourse in the West (and in the rants of nineteenth-century male taste reformers, for example in Great Britain), the decorative was identified, negatively, with the feminine, along with anything that was a matter of surface rather than substance. Women were represented as the chief perpetrators of clutter, hoarders of superfluous things and accumulators of knick-knacks.[98] But they were also their chief victims, taste experts cautioned, for useless decorative paraphernalia were among the chains that bound women into domestic slavery, since it fell to them to dust and polish them. As women saw the light of communist consciousness they were expected to recognise the tyranny of trash as an aspect of their oppression in the past, clinging to which was false consciousness. Ridding their lives of this dust-collecting ballast was in their own best interest. Combined with simplifications of the forms of furniture – stripping off the ornate mouldings from older items of furniture, for example – it would not only make their apartment look more contemporary, but would reduce the time they spent on cleaning, freeing them up for social and cultural activities.[99] As the 1955 *Novyi mir* reader had already grasped, ornaments popular in the recent past, such as miniature elephants, were out, as was the dysfunctional display of family status and wealth that characterised the bourgeois home.

Memory objects were particularly problematic, along with women's traditional role as custodians of memory. Public discourse represented moving into the new flat as a clean break with the past, its material and ideological residue, while taste experts' insistence on the unified contemporary style for all elements of the interior delegitimised alternative principles of unity based on biography, affect and personal ties. After repeated relocations and losses, in addition to the fear-induced excision of evidence associated with purged friends or family members, the material repositories of memory had often been reduced to the portable and concealable form of a small treasure box. But if any remaining material links with family history and repositories of personal memories had survived after decades of upheavals, destruction and loss, they were now to be cast away on the tide of progress, left behind in the move to the radiant future. This was often a physical necessity in practice: old pieces of furniture were too big to bring into the small flats. Their abandonment was also an imperative of modernity, however, according to advice that exhorted those moving to new apartments to do so unencumbered by the material trace of the past.[100]

There were mixed messages, however, concerning decorative touches in the apartment. These related to the centrality of aesthetics in the vision of the communist future. How to make the industrially prefabricated interior into a work of beauty and self-actualisation? The importance of aesthetic education in the formation of the fully rounded future citizen of communism was emphasised by philosophers and ideologues in the Khrushchev era, informed by a return to Marx (especially his earlier writings), and was written into the new Party Programme ('the Communist Manifesto of the present era') ratified in 1961. All Soviet people should have the opportunity to develop their aesthetic sensibilities and taste through access to art and aesthetic education. Moreover, they should themselves become producers of aesthetic value.[101]

The domestic interior was potentially a key site for daily encounter with art and for cultural activity. The household's cultural level (rather than its wealth, as in the past) was manifest, for example, through the presence of a piano or books.[102] Unique paintings might not be accessible for all, or even desirable in the modernist interior, according to some aesthetic specialists, because of their dust-collecting frames and spatial illusionism, which disrupted the flat plane of the wall. Judiciously chosen art prints were advocated, however, especially those in which decorative, formal qualities took precedence over naturalistic representation.[103] Voeikova recommended calm tints for walls on the grounds that these were easy on the eye, allowed one to use decorative fabrics for curtains and soft furnishing, and made a good background for prints, paintings, photographs and decorative elements. 'In such a room a brightly patterned rug or colourful decorative cushions on a divan will not look excessive, nor a vase in a saturated colour or picture on the wall'.[104] The choice, restrained deployment of such objects in the interior created contemporary beauty and revealed aesthetic discernment, and was quite distinct from mindless, eclectic, tasteless accumulation or vulgar display of luxury.

Moreover, creating the beautiful, tasteful interior was in itself a form of aesthetic production and not only of consumption.[105] For, as two television viewers (a married couple, both engineers) put it, writing in to the programme on homemaking mentioned above: 'everyone must become an artist in their home!'[106] A specialist in the new discipline of Technical Aesthetics indicated that, notwithstanding the value of rational-isation and standardisation, there was a place for purely expressive, aesthetic gestures. While advocating thoroughgoing standardisation of utilitarian routines and domestic fittings, because this would combat the regressive influence of the nuclear household and of any fetishistic tendencies that the increased availability of consumer goods might foster, she forestalled possible objections that fitted furniture would prevent the manifestation of individuality. For, the specialist asserted, the occupant's individuality would find full expression in the *aesthetics* of interior decoration.[107]

Handicraft

It will be clear by now that this did not mean open season: only certain kinds of
decorative objects, discerningly deployed in moderation, were acceptable. In regard
to curtains or wallpaper, for example, bold, abstracted patterns were deemed 'contemporary', but naturalistic designs that dissembled the flatness of the fabric or wall by
creating a spatial illusion were in bad taste. Not only was discrimination to be exercised according to the specific formal treatment; there were also hierarchies of virtue
pertaining to the materials and mode of production, where artefacts were made, and by
whom. The painted rugs discussed above were anathema not only for the romantic and
nostalgic images depicted on them and because they were 'dishonest' – a cheap ersatz
for woven rugs – but also because they were a form of unregulated artisanal production
for provincial bazaars, neither 'authentic' folk craft nor industrial manufactures.

Certain kinds of handmade objects, in limited numbers, were, however, acceptable
within the modern, industrially produced interior, notably traditional 'genuine' folk
craft and unique works of decorative art. Even in journals such as *Dekorativnoe
iskusstvo SSSR*, which staunchly promoted the stripped-down modernist 'contemporary
style', authors widely acknowledged that an increasingly standardised, industrially
mass-produced environment engendered an aesthetic need for the *faktura* (texture,
surface qualities that bear the trace of the process of making) of hand-made things.
They also discussed approvingly the discerning use of folk ornaments, craft and hand-
made *objets d'art* in the mass-produced modern interior. Illustrations of ideal modern
interiors regularly included carefully selected items of handcraft – a well-placed, hand-
thrown vase or a rough, hand-woven tapestry – amidst the stripped-down lines of the
new furniture.[108] The Estonian home decorating magazine *Kunst ja kodu* (*Art and the
Home*, also published in Russian as *Iskusstvo i domashnii byt*) celebrated handcraft as
part of the ideal modern interior (as it was in contemporary Scandinavian modernism,
an important model for Estonian design in this period).[109] Taste experts advocated
the restrained, discerning use in the contemporary apartment of traditional folk craft
identified with the specific traditions of various ethnic groups, regions and national
republics of the Soviet Union. 'The inexhaustible imagination and varied forms and
colours of folk craft provide unlimited choice of works of decorative-applied art to
beautify any room'. Voeikova recommended ceramics such as statuettes or dishes hung
on the wall, vases, painted figures from Viatka, Georgian black-fired pottery, carved
wooden figurines from Transcarpathia or Karelia, along with folk rugs, weavings,
Vologda lace, and other traditional textile arts from various national republics.[110] A
limited number of well-chosen and subtly deployed items of folk craft were desirable
in the industrial, standard urban apartment, then, for the splash of colour or contrasting
texture they added.

But what of amateur handicraft produced by women in the home? 'What is the
amateur of handicraft to do?' Voeikova put this question: 'Do embroidery and lace,
executed by the mistress of the house (*khoziaika*) herself have a place in the new
décor?' Could the definition of everyday aesthetic production embrace even embroidery, needlepoint and crochet? As we have seen, the legitimacy of deploying in the
interior cloths and embroidered napkins, which had played a significant role among
the repudiated forms of homemaking, had been under question in recent years. Needlework, along with other uses of textiles, was suspected of harbouring regressive relations,

as well as dust.[111] Yet Voeikova answered her own rhetorical question: 'not only do they go [in the interior], but these artefacts beautify the room'.[112] Her affirmation of amateur needlework's legitimacy in the modern interior should not automatically be explained by her gender. In part, this was a matter of finer distinctions to do with authenticity, allowing original or traditional designs appropriate to the medium and handmade (but not machine) lace. Needlepoint reproductions of popular, sentimental, naturalistic paintings based on crude patterns, sold in bazaars and in the hobby shop *Rukodelie* (handicraft), were still considered vulgar perversions.[113] It may also have been a compromise with the assumed tastes of Voeikova's readership, this being an article published in the magazine for women workers (a highbrow modernist aesthetic that excluded embroidery and crochet was still consistently pursued in the more specialist design magazine *Dekorativnoe iskusstvo SSSR*). Written in 1964, the article's willingness to admit amateur embroidery may also be an early indication of a growing critique, even among design professionals, of socialist modernism's asceticism and deracination. By the end of the 1960s, the tide had turned decisively. Intelligentsia discourse increasingly acknowledged the material and psychological losses entailed by industrial progress, by purging material links with past, and by the insistence on stylistic unity. It called instead for an 'ecology of culture' and sought to reconnect with suppressed personal and collective memories, as well as to embrace the heterogeneity of 'national' styles. In this changing climate of ideas, textiles, thread and tapestry began to be used as positive metaphors to reimagine the relationship between present identities and the past, revaluing the kind of connection between generations of women which needlework artefacts, patterns and skills materialised (Figure 8).[114]

Practice

Whatever misgivings the arbiters of taste held in the Khrushchev era, needlework and handicraft of various sorts remained popular leisure practices in Soviet urban homes throughout the 1950s to the 1980s. Not only were large quantities of needlework produced and deployed in the interior, but they were also carefully preserved through the years, even though storage space was at a premium in these small apartments.[115] Textiles, in various forms, deeply enmeshed in traditional notions of comfort, homecraft and female worth, remained essential material for creating home, a means to appropriate and individualise space and personalise standard goods. Rugs provided sound and heat insulation, while curtains were used to keep out draughts or to screen off areas of the shared main room (a niche where a child slept, for example) and demarcate functions. They also remained essential for creating privacy in the sense of concealment from external, uninvited eyes; although the separate apartments gave much greater privacy in this sense, a feature of their design was relatively large windows. In interviews and even in published accounts of moving in, the first thing a housewife has in mind when she says to her daughter 'we should start making it cosy' is to hang curtains or nets in order to enclose the interior.[116] The woman, cited above, who was proud of her father's cabinet-making recalled that making the apartment cosy had entailed the use of napkins, for example, to cover the television, and spreading a tablecloth when guests came.[117]

In this respect, the voluminous advice literature appears to have had little direct effect on many people's material practices of *uiut*, which were still determined by their

Figure 8: 'All of this is my mother's [work]. She did the housekeeping and crocheted.' Mother's needlework with a tapestry received as a gift *c*.1965 (photo: Ekaterina Gerasimova, 2004 for project Everyday Aesthetics in the Modern Soviet Flat).

habitus and remained closer to McCracken's 'homeyness' as the expression of a search for continuity, stability and a sense of rootedness, than to the modernist contemporary style.[118] When prototypes of furniture for mass production were presented to the population at an exhibition of model interiors in 1961, many who wrote in the visitors' comments books found the new style 'primitive', ugly, poorly finished and anonymous, lacking in 'national' characteristics. Many also found it priced well beyond their means, and moreover, it was still unavailable in the shops.[119] One respondent in the 1968 survey of new Moscow homes may have spoken for many when she denied that the minimal, 'contemporary', aesthetic that was so widely propagated could be either cosy or convenient to live in. On the contrary, for all that the modernisers condemned the way the old 'petit-bourgeois' (or Stalinist) interior subordinated function to non-functional display, the same criticism could, she pointed out, be levelled against the contemporary style they advocated. Its modernist minimalism and cool perfection rendered the interior like one in an exhibition or an illustration in a design magazine. *Uiut*, for this resident, depended on signs of being lived in.[120] Others identified it with the warmth of human relations or the presence of a nice cat.[121]

We can recognise this response to the socialist modernist 'contemporary style' as a version of the stock complaint about the unliveable-ness of the modernist interior familiar in the West. However, it would be wrong to represent this as a thoroughgoing or universal rejection of the new modernist style – and indeed of socialist modernity – regardless of social class, ethnicity or personal dispositions. Alongside the negative responses to the model interiors exhibited in 1961, there were many who welcomed the new light and simple furniture, and who would simply be glad to have an opportunity to buy any furniture whatever. The look of many of the apartments in the 1968 survey, according to its author Elena Torshilova, conformed to the official aesthetic of the contemporary style. And, asked 'How is *uiut* achieved?' 81 per cent of the informants rehearsed its widely promoted principles: 'through cleanliness' and 'a small number of things', 'convenience', 'unity of style' and 'harmony of the whole ensemble of the interior'.[122] That small survey made no claims to be representative, however. The informants, residents of an apartment block belonging to a Moscow research institute, included an unrepresentatively large number of people with higher education and doctorates. It is probable that take-up was highest among this, the same social stratum as the specialists who promoted the cosmopolitan modernist contemporary style, who were also more able to afford the new furniture. A much larger sample than Torshilova's or than the interview and visual data I have been able to gather from some seventy households would be necessary to draw meaningful generalisations concerning class, ethnic and urban–rural (first or second generation urban dwellers, etc.) distinctions. The available evidence would suggest, however, that the effort to propagate the contemporary style met with neither universal acceptance nor with total rejection, but had a varied and mixed response. While take-up was limited by factors from taste and habitus to price and shortage, and adoption of the approved style in popular practices of homemaking and ideals of beauty and *uiut* was patchy and selective, many interiors were hybrids of new and old: not an outright rejection of the modern, but its accommodation and absorption/integration into an established conception of *uiut*.

Conclusion

This chapter has explored attempts in authoritative discourse to transcend the antithesis of home comfort and communism, cosiness and socialist modernity, and to redefine cosiness in ways that could be reconciled with the Enlightenment values of progress, science and reason through a modernist aesthetics. To a large extent this discourse was addressed to women, aiming to reform their notions of taste and delegitimate traditional practices of homemaking. The hegemony of the state, as materialised in the invasive effects of modern housing, is often seen as an assault on women's domain and dominance within the domestic sphere. Yet, while architects and planners set the parameters of the new housing, and specialists sought to shape the ways in which women made home in the new flats, they were dependent on individual householders to materialise the norms of the contemporary aesthetic. Home and women's practices in it tested the jurisdiction of the state. The continued production of decorated cloths and the use of textiles by women and girls in many homes are just two of the ways in which advice on good taste and rational living was ignored in everyday practice.

How are we to interpret this? Is this a case of what anthropologists in other contexts have described as resistance by female occupants who persist in traditional practices and uses of space even when these have been designated 'irrational', or otherwise denigrated or countered by 'creative and sometimes subversive alternatives'?[123]

For Henri Lefebvre, home is inherently an oppositional, 'private' space that 'asserts itself . . . always in a conflictual way, against the public one'.[124] Moreover, as we saw, the 'private' space of home in the Soviet scheme of things was regarded by outside observers as communism's 'other', a flaw in the Soviet system's supposedly 'totalitarian' grasp or consummate grid of surveillance, where the state project of socialist modernity was contradicted. We should not resort to this model uncritically, however, it being one of the binaries that sustained and legitimated the Cold War and blinkered Western understanding of Soviet experience. The Soviet discourse we have analysed was aimed precisely at overcoming this antithesis and accommodating home comfort within socialist modernity. Did that spell the beginning of the end of communism as cold-war observers predicted? Was the preoccupation with nest-making a symptom of degeneration of the Soviet project, marking a retreat from building communism, into private values, personal consumption and home-is-my-castle mindsets? Or was it, rather, a way to sustain the Soviet regime and lend new legitimacy to the project of building communism?

So large a question cannot be resolved here. To construe the practices of home-making as resistance to the hegemony of the state or the cultural elitism of intelligentsia specialists, however, invests them with too much conscious, programmatic intention. They are more accurately described by the model of ad hoc coping tactics and making do, as people's everyday ways of negotiating and coming to terms with the material constraints and possibilities of their lives, as suggested by Michel de Certeau.[125] As Attfield found in British social housing in the same period of the mid-twentieth century, residents made themselves 'at home' in a variety of ways that mitigated the homogeneous unity of modern design: 'Yet it cannot be said that tenants rejected modernity as such, even when they clung to family heirlooms and traditional furnishing conventions. On the contrary, it was the adaptability with which tenants took over their domestic space, stubbornly arranging it in contravention to the designers' intentions, that shows how they appropriated modernity to their own designs'.[126] Soviet homemakers got what they could afford or get hold of and incorporated it as best they could into their conception of beauty and *uiut*. In the course of the 1960s, as prosperity and consumer goods production grew, many people gradually acquired the new modular furniture to replace the older bulky items that wouldn't fit or looked out of place in the new flats – and learned to live with and even to love it. Incorporating the new into eclectic, hybrid combinations along with older pieces in more ornate styles, with hand-made things and with memory objects, they assimilated it into their domestic space and routines, accommodating modernity and socialism in ways that allowed them and their families to live comfortably within these givens. Thus home was where the contradiction between the forward thrust of modernity and chiliasm of communism, on one hand, and dwelling, on the other, was accommodated: a heterotopia rather than a counter-utopia.

Notes

1. This chapter is drawn from a larger project, Everyday Aesthetics in the Modern Soviet Flat, generously supported by the Leverhulme Trust.
2. Conference, 'Different Modernisms, Different Avant-Gardes' (KUMU, Tallinn, 2007); Susan E. Reid and David Crowley (eds), *Style and Socialism: Modernity and Material Culture in Post-War Eastern Europe* (Oxford: Berg, 2000); Paul Betts and Katherine Pence (eds), *Socialist Modern: East German Everyday Culture and Politics* (Ann Arbor: University of Michigan Press, 2007); Susan E. Reid, 'Toward a New (Socialist) Realism: The Re-Engagement with Western Modernism in the Khrushchev Thaw', in Susan E. Reid and Rosalind P. Blakesley (eds), *Russian Art and the West: A Century of Dialogue in Painting,*

Architecture, and the Decorative Arts (DeKalb: Northern Illinois University Press, 2006), pp. 217–39; Susan E. Reid, 'Khrushchev Modern: Agency and Modernization in the Soviet Home', *Cahiers du Monde russe* 47 (2006), pp. 227–68.

3. Christopher Reed (ed.), *Not at Home: The Suppression of Domesticity in Modern Art and Architecture* (London: Thames & Hudson, 1996); Hilde Heynen, 'Modernity and Domesticity: Tensions and Contradictions' and Karina van Herck, '"Only Where Comfort Ends Does Humanity Begin": On the "Coldness" of Avant-Garde Architecture in the Weimar Period', both in Hilde Heynen and Gülsüm Baydar (eds), *Negotiating Domesticity: Spatial Productions of Gender in Modern Architecture* (London and New York: Routledge, 2005), pp. 1–29, 123–44 respectively. For 'homeyness', see Grant McCracken, '"Homeyness": A Cultural Account of One Constellation on Consumer Goods and Meaning', in Elizabeth C. Hirschman (ed.), *Interpretive Consumer Research* (Provo, UT: Association for Consumer Research, 1989), pp. 168–83.

4. Olga Matich, 'Remaking the Bed: Utopia in Daily Life', in John Bowlt and Olga Matich (eds), *Laboratories of Dreams: The Russian Avant-Garde and Cultural Experience* (Stanford, CA: Stanford University Press, 1996), pp. 59–78; Svetlana Boym, *Common Places: Mythologies of Everyday Life in Russia* (Cambridge, MA: Harvard University Press, 1994), esp. pp. 73–88; Walter Benjamin, *Moscow Diary* (Cambridge: Harvard University Press, 1986), p. 48; Walter Benjamin, 'Moscow', in Walter Benjamin, *Reflections: Essays, Aphorisms, Autobiographical Writings* (New York: Schocken, 1978), pp. 97–130; Heynen, 'Modernity and Domesticity', p. 17; Karen Kettering, '"Ever More Cosy and Comfortable": Stalinism and the Soviet Domestic Interior, 1928–1938', *Journal of Design History* 10 (1997), pp. 119–35; Christina Kiaer, *Imagine No Possessions: The Socialist Objects of Russian Constructivism* (New Haven: Yale University Press, 2005).

5. See Tag Gronberg, 'Decoration: Modernism's "Other"', *Art History* 15 (1993), pp. 547–52; Roszika Parker and Griselda Pollock, *Old Mistresses: Women, Art and Ideology* (2nd edn, London: Pandora, 1987); Bridget Elliott and Janice Helland (eds), *Women Artists and the Decorative Arts 1880–1935: The Gender of Ornament* (Aldershot: Ashgate, 2002); Penny Sparke, *As Long as It's Pink: The Sexual Politics of Taste* (London: Pandora, 1995); Judy Attfield, *Bringing Modernity Home: Writings on Popular Design and Material Culture* (Manchester: Manchester University Press, 2007); Janet Wolff, 'Feminism and Modernism' and 'The Invisible Flaneuse: Women and the Literature of Modernity', both in Janet Wolff, *Feminine Sentences: Essays On Women and Culture* (Cambridge: Polity Press, 1990), pp. 51–66 and 34–50 respectively; Jane Rendell, Barbara Penner and Iain Borden (eds), *Gender Space Architecture: An Interdisciplinary Introduction* (London: Routledge, 2000).

6. Martin Heidegger, 'Building, Dwelling, Thinking' [1954], in D. Farrell Krell (ed.), *Basic Writings: Martin Heidegger* (London: Routledge, 1978), pp. 347–63, here p. 348; Nicky Gregson, *Living with Things: Ridding, Accommodation, Dwelling* (Wantage: Sean Kingston, 2007), pp. 21–3.

7. Exceptions include Victor Buchli's groundbreaking *An Archaeology of Socialism* (Oxford: Berg, 1999), Ekaterina Gerasimova, 'Sovetskaia kommunal'naia kvartira kak sotsial'nyi institut: istoriko-sotsiologicheskii analiz' (unpublished doctoral thesis, European University, St Petersburg, 2000); Steven Harris, 'Moving to the Separate Apartment: Building, Distributing, Furnishing, and Living in Urban Housing in Soviet Russia, 1950s–1960s' (unpublished doctoral thesis, University of Chicago, 2003); Christine Varga-Harris, 'Constructing the Soviet Hearth: Home, Citizenship and Socialism in Russia, 1956–1964' (unpublished doctoral thesis, University of Illinois at Urbana-Champaign, 2005).

8. Cited in Robert Skidelsky, *John Maynard Keynes* (London: Papermac, 1992), p. 519; cited by Victoria de Grazia, *Irresistible Empire: America's Advance through 20th-Century Europe* (Cambridge: Belknap Press, Harvard University, 2005), p. 113.

9. Compare Richard Nixon's position in dispute with Nikita Khrushchev: BBC News: On This Day, 24 July 1959, <http://news.bbc.co.uk/onthisday/hi/dates/stories/july/24/newsid_2779000/2779551.stm> (accessed 7 September 2009).

10. Marguerite Higgins, *Red Plush and Black Bread* (Garden City, NY: Doubleday, 1955), p. 125. Cited in David and Vera Mace, *The Soviet Family* (London: Hutchinson, 1963), p. 187.

11. Mace, *Soviet Family*, pp. 187–8; Bruce and Beatrice Gould, 'We Saw How Russians Live', *Ladies Home Journal*, February 1957, pp. 58–61, 176, 179, here p. 176.

12. Francine du Plessix Gray, *Soviet Women Walking the Tightrope* (New York: Doubleday, 1989), p. 2.

13. Gray, *Soviet Women Walking the Tightrope*, pp. 2–3.

14. Walter Benjamin, *The Arcades Project* (Cambridge: Harvard University Press, 1999), p. 220; Heynen, 'Modernity and Domesticity', esp. p. 17.

15. Gray, *Soviet Women*, p. 2; Herck, 'Only Where Comfort Ends', p. 141 *n.* 3; Buchli, *Archaeology*, pp. 56–62; Marianne Gullestad, *The Art of Social Relations* (Oslo and Oxford: Scandinavian University Press, 1992), pp. 79–80.

16. McCracken, 'Homeyness'; Susan J. Matt, 'Why the Old-Fashioned Is in Fashion in American Homes', in Regina Lee Blaszczyk, *Producing Fashion: Commerce, Culture, and Consumers* (Philadelphia: University of Pennsylvania Press, 2007), pp. 273–92, esp. pp. 283–4.

17. Boris Pasternak, *Doktor Zhivago* (Milan: Feltrinelli Editore, 1957), pp. 443–4 [*Doctor Zhivago*, tr. Max Hayward and Manya Harari (London: Collins Harvill, 1958), p. 360)]; Mace, *Soviet Family*, pp. 186–7.

18. John Crowley, *The Invention of Comfort: Sensibilities and Design in Early Modern Britain and Early America* (Baltimore and London: Johns Hopkins University Press, 2000); Philippe Ariès, *Centuries of Childhood* (Harmondsworth: Penguin, 1973); Philippe Ariès and Georges Duby (eds), *History of Private Life*, 5 vols. Vol. 5: *Riddles of Identity in Modern Times*, ed. Antoine Prost and Gerard Vincent, tr. Arthur Goldhammer (Cambridge: Belknap Press, Harvard University, 1991). Literature on the public/private dichotomy and on the gendered segregation of spheres is extensive: see Dorothy Helly and Susan Reverby (eds), *Gendered Domains: Rethinking Public and Private in Women's History* (Ithaca: Cornell University Press, 1992); Jeff Weintraub and Krishan Kumar (eds), *Public and Private in Thought and Practice* (Chicago: University of Chicago Press, 1996); Lewis Siegelbaum (ed.), *Borders of Socialism: Private Spheres of Soviet Russia* (New York and Basingstoke: Palgrave, 2006).

19. Decree of CPSU Central Committee and USSR Council of Ministers, 'O razvitii zhilishchnogo stroitel'stva v SSSR', 31 July 1957, *Pravda*, 2 August 1957; reprinted in *Sobranie postanovlenii pravitel'stva* (Moscow: Gosiurizdat, 1960), article 102, pp. 332–48; Nikita S. Khrushchev, *O kontrol'nykh tsifrakh razvitiia narodnogo khoziaistva SSSR na 1959–1965 gody* (Moscow: Gospolitizdat, 1959).

20. Gregory D. Andrusz, *Housing and Urban Development in the USSR* (London: Macmillan, 1984), p. 157, table 7.5; Harris, 'Moving to the Separate Apartment'; K. Zhukov, 'Tekhnicheskaia estetika i oborudovanie kvartir', *Tekhnicheskaia estetika* 2 (1964), p. 1.

21. B. Merzhanov and K. Sorokin, *Eto nuzhno novoselam* (Moscow: Ekonomika 1966), p. 4; Russian State Archive of Literature and Art (RGALI), f. 2329, op. 4, ed. khr. 1388, ll. 51–2 (transcript of discussion of exhibition 'Iskusstvo- v byt!', 6 June 1961); Boris Ionovich Brodskii, *Khudozhnik i gorod* (Moscow: Iskusstvo, 1965), pp. 65–9; Boris Ionovich Brodskii, 'Novyi byt i kamufliazh meshchanstva', *Dekorativnoe iskusstvo SSSR (DI)* 8 (1963), pp. 23–8, here p. 25; Ol'ga Baiar, 'Dekorativnoe ubranstvo kvartiry', *DI*, Jubilee edition (Moscow, 1957), pp. 17–20; Irina Voeikova, 'Vasha kvartira', *Rabotnitsa* 9 (1962), p. 30; Lynne Attwood, 'Housing in the Khrushchev Era', in Melanie Ilič, Susan Reid and Lynne Attwood (eds), *Women in the Khrushchev Era* (Basingstoke: Palgrave Macmillan, 2004), pp. 189, 200–01, nn. 72–3. Compare Daniel Miller (ed.), *Home Possessions: Material Culture behind Closed Doors* (Oxford: Berg, 2001), pp. 9–11.

22. These negotiations are examined more fully in the wider project from which this chapter is drawn.

23. For detail, see Susan E. Reid, 'Women in the Home', in Ilič, Reid and Attwood (eds), *Women in the Khrushchev Era*, pp. 149–76; Susan E. Reid, 'Cold War in the Kitchen: Gender and Consumption in the Khrushchev Thaw', *Slavic Review* 61 (2002), pp. 211–52.

24. Christina Kiaer and Eric Naiman (eds), *Everyday Life in Early Soviet Russia: Taking the Revolution Inside* (Bloomington: Indiana University Press, 2006).

25. Vera S. Dunham, *In Stalin's Time: Middleclass Values in Soviet Fiction* (Cambridge: Cambridge University Press, 1976); Sheila Fitzpatrick, 'Becoming Cultured: Socialist Realism and the Representation of Privilege and Taste', in Sheila Fitzpatrick, *The Cultural Front: Power and Culture in Revolutionary Russia* (Ithaca: Cornell University Press, 1992), pp. 216–37; Kettering, 'Ever More Cosy and Comfortable', pp. 119–35.

26. See e.g., Mace, *Soviet Family*, pp. 187–8; Gould, 'We Saw How Russians Live', p. 176; Santha Rama Rau, *My Russian Journey* (New York: Harper & Brothers, 1959), p. 5.

27. Paucity of consumer goods, overcrowding and the loss of homes and possessions in the course of serial dislocations which structure life stories of this period as narrated in interviews conducted under my project 'Everyday Aesthetics in the Modern Soviet Flat'. Over seventy interviews were conducted between 2004 and 2007 in St Petersburg, Kazan, Samara, Kaluga, Kovdor, Apatity and Tartu, with people who moved into new apartments in the early 1960s.

28. Jukka Renkama, *Ideology and Challenges of Political Liberalisation in the USSR, 1957–1961: Otto Kuusinen's 'Reform Platform', the State Concept, and the Path to the 3rd CPSU Programme* (Helsinki: Suomalaisen Kirjallisuuden Seura, Bibliotheca Historica 99, 2006); Jerome M. Gilison, *The Soviet Image of Utopia* (Baltimore: Johns Hopkins University Press, 1975).

29. Brodskii, 'Novyi byt', p. 24.

30. For further discussion, see Susan E. Reid, 'Destalinization and Taste, 1953–1963', *Journal of Design History* 10 (1997), pp. 177–201, esp. pp. 190–92.

31. Boym, *Common Places*, pp. 39–40.

32. N. I. Andreeva, 'Gigienicheskaia otsenka novogo zhilishchnogo stroitel'stva v Moskve (period 1947–1951 gg.)', *Gigiena i sanitaria* 6 (1956), pp. 23–4; Timothy Sosnovy, 'The Soviet Housing Situation Today', *Soviet Studies* 11 (1959), pp. 1–21; Timothy Sosnovy, *The Housing Problem in the Soviet Union* (New York: Research Program on the USSR, 1954), pp. 114–15.

33. Donald Filtzer, 'Standard of Living Versus Quality of Life: Struggling With the Urban Environment in Russia During the Early Years of Post-War Reconstruction' and Rebecca Manley, '"Where Should We Resettle the Comrades Next?" The Adjudication of Housing Claims and the Construction of the Post-War Order', both in Juliane Fürst (ed.), *Late Stalinist Russia: Society between Reconstruction and Reinvention* (London and New York: Routledge, 2006), pp. 81–102 and 233–46 respectively; Elena Zubkova, *Russia after the War: Hopes, Illusions, and Disappointments, 1945–1957*, tr. Hugh Ragsdale (Armonk, NY: M. E. Sharpe, 1998); Brian LaPierre, 'Private Matters or Public Crimes: The Emergence of Domestic Hooliganism in the Soviet Union, 1939–1966', in Siegelbaum, *Borders of Socialism*, pp. 191–210. Tuberculosis was frequently cited in cases considered for rehousing in new apartment blocks. Tsentral'nyi arkhiv goroda Moskvy [Moscow City Centre Archive] (TsAGM), f. 62, op. 15, d. 267; TsAGM, f. 62, op. 15, d. 266.

34. Boym, *Common Places*, pp. 73–88; Katerina Clark, *The Soviet Novel: History as Ritual* (2nd edn, Chicago and London; University of Chicago Press, 1985), pp. 227–33; Miki Pohl, 'Women and Girls in the Virgin Lands', in Ilič, Reid and Attwood, *Women in the Khrushchev Era*, pp. 52–74.

35. For the identification between housing registration and civic identity or enfranchisement, see Nadezhda Mandel'sham, *Kniga vtoraia* (Moscow: Moskovskii rabochii, 1990), p. 13, cited in Boym, *Common Places*, p. 93; Tsentral'nyi arkhiv literatury i iskusstva St Petersburg (TsGALI SPb), f. 341, op. 1, d. 357, l. 32; Manley, 'Where Should We Resettle the Comrades Next?', p. 233; Vladimir Papernyi, 'Men, Women and Living Space' and Stephen Kotkin, 'Shelter and Subjectivity in the Stalin Period', both in William Brumfield and Blair Ruble (eds), *Russian Housing in the Modern Age* (Cambridge: Cambridge University Press, 1993), pp. 149–70 and 171–210 respectively. The term *BOMZh*, is an acronym for *bez opredelennogo mesta zhitel'stva* ('of no fixed abode'), Irena H. Corten, *Vocabulary of Soviet Society and Culture: a Selected Guide to Russian Words, Idioms and Expressions of the post-Stalin Era, 1953–1991* (Durham: Duke University Press, 1992), p. 31. This spatial organisation of the population was not new. See Stephen Kotkin, *Magnetic Mountain: Stalinism as a Civilization* (Berkeley: University of California Press, 1995).

36. I. Semenov, 'Velikoe pereselenie narodov', *Krokodil* 22, 10 August 1964, pp. 8–9.

37. See also Steven Harris, '"I Know all the Secrets of my Neighbors": The Quest for Privacy in the Era of the Separate Apartment', in Siegelbaum (ed.), *Borders of Socialism*, pp. 171–90, here p. 171.

38. Boym, *Common Places*, p. 125. The role of such public agencies in the ownership of housing increased in the 1950s, giving the 'state' a virtual monopoly over urban housing construction, although cooperatives represented an alternative. Sosnovy, 'The Soviet Housing Situation Today', p. 9.

39. Zhukov, 'Tekhnicheskaia estetika', p. 1; Victor Buchli, 'Khrushchev, Modernism, and the Fight against Petit-Bourgeois Consciousness in the Soviet Home', *Journal of Design History* 10 (1997), pp. 161–76.

40. See e.g., V. Rybitskii, 'Dlia doma, dlia sem'i. V pomoshch' novoselam', 5 January 1963, script in State Archive of the Russian Federation (GARF), f. 6903 (Gosteleradio), op. 2, d. 449; Kristin Roth-Ey, 'Finding a Home for Television in the USSR, 1950–1970', *Slavic Review* 66 (2007), pp. 278–306.

41. Nikita S. Khrushchev, *O shirokom vnedrenii industrial'nykh metodov, uluchshenii kachestva i snizhenii stoimosti stroitel'stva* (Moscow: Gospolitizdat, 1955); Blair Ruble, 'From *Khrushcheby* to *Korobki*', in Brumfield and Ruble, *Russian Housing*, pp. 232–70.

42. A decree of 23 April 1959 extended the moratorium on superfluous embellishment to public interiors: 'Ob ustranenii izlishestv v otdelke, oborudovanii i vo vnutrennem ubranstve obshchestvennykh zdanii', *Sobranie postanovlenii pravitel'stva SSSR* (Moscow: Gosiurizdat, 1959), pp. 166–71; see also Harris, 'Moving to the Separate Apartment', ch. 8, pp. 467–546.

43. Iurii Gerchuk, 'The Aesthetics of Everyday Life in the Khrushchev Thaw in the USSR (1954–64)', in Susan E. Reid and David Crowley (eds), *Style and Socialism*, pp. 81–100, here p. 88.

44. Vadim Movchaniuk, 'Reshaetsia sud'ba "khrushchevok": v interesakh grazhdan', and Mikhail Shvarts, '"Krushchevki" eshche postoiat', *Etazhi* 2, 1 March 1998.

45. Concierge, Union of Architects, St Petersburg, April 2005.

46. Interviews for 'Everyday Aesthetics'; Aleksei Adzhubei, *Te desiat' let* (Moscow: Sovetskaia Rossiia, 1989), p. 118.

47. Harris, 'I Know all the Secrets', pp. 171–90.

48. Vladimir Shlapentokh, *Public and Private Life of the Soviet People: Changing Values in Post-Stalin Russia* (Oxford: Oxford University Press, 1989); Lewis Siegelbaum, 'Cars, Cars, and More Cars: The Faustian

Bargain of the Brezhnev Era' and Susan E. Reid, 'The Meaning of Home: "The Only Bit of the World You Can Have to Yourself"', both in Siegelbaum, *Borders of Socialism*, pp. 83–103 and 145–70 respectively; Deborah A. Field, *Private Life and Communist Morality in Khrushchev's Russia* (New York: Peter Lang, 2007).

49. See special issue on the gift, *Journal of the Royal Anthropological Institute (N.S.)* 12 (2006); Jeffrey Brooks, *Thank You Comrade Stalin! Soviet Public Culture from Revolution to Cold War* (Princeton: Princeton University Press, 1999).

50. M. Nikol'skii, 'Novyi dom – novyi byt', *Izvestiia*, 19 December 1959.

51. 'Schastlivoe novosel'e', *Trud*, 7 November 1959.

52. I discuss representations of *novosel'e* more fully in Susan E. Reid, 'Happy Housewarming! Moving into Khrushchev-Era Apartments', in Marina Balina and Evgeny Dobrenko (eds), *Petriphied Utopia: Happiness Soviet Style* (London: Anthem Press, 2009), pp. 133–60.

53. See e.g., *Izvestiia*'s 'For Home and Family' page and the illustrated magazine *Ogonek*'s rubric, 'Women – This Is For You'; Merzhanov and Sorokin, 'Eto nuzhno novoselam' (published in a series 'For Home and Family'); Deborah A. Field, 'Communist Morality and Meanings of Private Life in Post-Stalinist Russia, 1953–1964' (unpublished doctoral thesis, University of Michigan, 1996), p. 41; Catriona Kelly, *Refining Russia: Advice Literature, Polite Culture, and Gender from Catherine to Yeltsin* (Oxford: Oxford University Press, 2001).

54. See e.g., the 1958 novel by Daniil Granin, *Posle svad'by* (Leningrad: Sovetskii pisatel', 1959; Moscow: Khudozhestvennaia literatura, 1964); Ol'ga Baiar and Rimma Blashkevich, *Kvartira i ee ubranstvo* (Moscow: Stroiizdat, 1962); regular features in magazines such as *Ogonek* (e.g. 11 (8 March 1959) back cover), *Dekorativnoe iskusstvo SSSR, Kunst ja kodu, Sem'ia i shkola*. Among exhibitions of model interiors, the most significant was 'Iskusstvo – v byt' (Art into Life), Moscow, 1961.

55. For argumentation, see Susan E. Reid, 'The Khrushchev Kitchen: Domesticating the Scientific–Technological Revolution', *Journal of Contemporary History* 40 (2005), pp. 289–316.

56. Nikol'skii, 'Novyi dom'. See also A. Lapin, 'Malen'kie zaboty bol'shogo novosel'ia', *Izvestiia*, 14 November 1959.

57. Rybitskii, 'Dlia doma, dlia sem'i. V pomoshch' novoselam'.

58. Moscow Central Archive of Social and Political Movements (TsAOPIM), f. 4, op. 139, d. 35: ll. 12–16.

59. TsAOPIM, f. 4, op. 139, d. 35, ll. 8–12.

60. TsAOPIM, f. 4, op. 139, d. 35. On efforts to engage men with domesticity, see M. Edel', 'Divan', *Krokodil* 12, 30 April 1958, p. 12.

61. 'Tribuna chitatelia: O vospitanii vkusa', *Novyi mir* 2 (1955), pp. 247–54, here p. 247.

62. Interviews for 'Everyday Aesthetics'.

63. Siegelbaum, 'Cars, Cars, and More Cars', p. 97.

64. Interview with L. G., St Petersburg 2004, 'Everyday Aesthetics'.

65. I. Abramenko and L. Tormozova (eds), *Besedy o domashnem khoziaistva* (Moscow: Molodaia gvardiia, 1959), p. 4. See also Reid, 'Khrushchev Kitchen', pp. 289–316.

66. Karl M. Kantor, 'Chelovek i zhilishche', *Iskusstvo i byt* 1 (1963), pp. 26–48; S. Strumilin, 'Rabochii byt i kommunizm', *Novyi mir* 7 (1960), pp. 203–20, here p. 213; A. Baranov, 'Sotsiologicheskie problemy zhilishcha', in A. G. Kharchev, S. M. Verizhnikov and V. L. Ruzhzhe (eds), *Sotsial'nye probelmy zhilishcha* (Leningrad: LenZNIIEP, 1967), p. 17.

67. Kantor, 'Chelovek i zhilishche', pp. 29–30.

68. Elena Torshilova, 'Byt i nekotorye sotsial'no-psikhologicheskie kharakteristiki sovremennogo zhilogo inter'era', in A. G. Kharchev and Z. A. Iankova (eds), *Sotsial'nye issledovaniia* 7: *Metodologicheskie problemy issledovaniia byta* (Moscow: Nauka, 1971), pp. 137–44, esp. pp. 141–3.

69. Torshilova, 'Byt', pp. 141–3.

70. M. Chereiskaia, 'Zametki o khoroshem vkuse', in R. Saltanova and N. Kolchinskaia (eds), *Podruga* (Moscow: Molodaia gvardiia, 1959), pp. 220–34, here p. 220.

71. Gregson, *Living with Things*, p. 23; Gullestad, *Art of Social Relations*; Daniel Miller, 'Accommodating', in Colin Painter (ed.), *Contemporary Art and the Home* (Oxford: Berg, 2002): pp. 115–30.

72. Daniel Miller, 'Appropriating the State on the Council Estate', *Man* 23 (1988), pp. 353–72; Judy Attfield, 'Bringing Modernity Home: Open Plan in the British Domestic Interior', in Irene Cieraad (ed.), *At Home: An Anthropology of Domestic Space* (Syracuse, NY: Syracuse University Press, 1999), pp. 73–82.

73. Ronald Paul Hill, 'Homeless Women, Special Possessions, and the Meaning of "Home": An Ethnographic Case Study', *Journal of Consumer Research* 18 (1991), pp. 298–310, here p. 300, with reference to McCracken, 'Homeyness', p. 179.

74. Wolfgang Braunfels, *Urban Design in Western Europe: Regime and Architecture, 900–1900*, tr. Kenneth J. Northcott (Chicago: University of Chicago Press, 1988), p. 38; compare Hill, 'Homeless Women', pp. 298–310.

75. Braunfels, *Urban Design in Western Europe*, p. 38; Nathan Glazer, 'The Prince, the People, and the Architects', *American Scholar* 59 (1990), pp. 507–18; Ruble, 'From *Khrushcheby*', pp. 243–4.

76. On the input of labour from the consumer, which Soviet consumer goods presupposed in the 'post-commodity' phase before the item could be used or assimilated, see Ekaterina Gerasimova and Sof'ia Chuikina, 'Obshchestvo remonta', *Neprikosnovennyi zapas (NZ)* 34 (2004), <http://magazines.russ.ru/nz/2004/34/ger85.html>, (accessed 1 November 2004). See also Galina Orlova, 'Apologiia strannoi veshchi: Malen'kie khitrosti' sovetskogo cheloveka', *NZ* 34 (2004) <http://magazines.russ.ru/nz/2004/34/orll10.html>.

77. See e.g., Baiar and Blashkevich, *Kvartira i ee ubranstvo*, p. 15; 'Svoimi rukami', *DI* 3 (1961), pp. 48–9; and regular features in *Kunst ja kodu*. Compare Aleksandr Vysokovskii, 'Will Domesticity Return?', in Brumfield and Ruble, *Russian Housing*, p. 284; RGALI, f. 2329, op. 4, ed. khr. 1391, l. 29, l. 47 (visitors' book for exhibition 'Iskusstvo – v byt', 1961).

78. Iu. Sharov and G. Poliachek, *Vkus nado vospityvat' (besedy dlia molodezhi)* (Novosibirsk: Novosibirskoe knizhnoe izdatel'stvo, 1960), pp. 66–79. See also Chereiskaia, 'Zametki o khoroshem vkuse', p. 220; Buchli, *An Archaeology*.

79. Christine Varga-Harris, 'Homemaking: Keeping Appearances and Petticoat Rule', presented at conference 'The Thaw', University of California at Berkeley, May 2005.

80. Brodskii, 'Novyi byt', p. 24.

81. I. Sidorov, 'Tsvety v komnate', *Ogonek* 24 (June 1960), inside back cover; Vladimir I. Lenin, 'Velikii pochin. (O geroizme rabochikh v tylu)', *Polnoe sobranie sochinenii*, vol. 39 (5th edn, Moscow, 1970), p. 24.

82. 'Tribuna chitatelia', p. 247.

83. Chereiskaia, 'Zametki o khoroshem vkuse', p. 220; Torshilova, 'Byt', p. 140; Editorial, *Iskusstvo i domashnii byt (Kunst ja kodu)* 2 (1962), pp. 1–2; I. Voeikova, 'Uiut – v prostote', *Rabotnitsa* 10 (1964), pp. 30–31; A. Gol'dshtein, 'Chto takoe uiut?', *Rabotnitsa* 1 (1959), p. 30; E. Krasnova, 'Khoroshii vkus v ubranstve zhil'ia'', *Sem'ia i shkola* 1 (1960), pp. 44–5.

84. Sharov and Poliachek, *Vkus nado vospityvat'*, p. 73.

85. Alexander Solzhenitsyn, *One Day in the Life of Ivan Denisovich*, tr. Ralph Parker (Harmondsworth: Penguin, 1963), p. 192.

86. 'O merakh bor'by s antikhudozhestvennymi, khalturnymi izdeliiami', March 1959 to TsK VLKSM otdel Komsomol'skikh organov propagandy i agitatsii Russian State Archive of Social and Political History (RGASPI), f. M–1, op. 32, d. 972, ll. 58–63; Andrew Jenks, 'The Art Market and the Construction of Soviet Russian Culture', in Siegelbaum, *Borders of Socialism*, pp. 47–64.

87. A. Gol'dshtein, 'Chto takoe uiut', p. 30.

88. Sharov and Poliachek, *Vkus nado vospityvat'*, p. 73.

89. On beds as outdated 'prejudice', see A. Briuno, 'Vasha kvartira', *Sem'ia i shkola* 10 (1960), p. 46; Voeikova, 'Vasha kvartira', p. 30; Buchli, 'Khrushchev, Modernism', pp. 161–76.

90. On the gendered meanings of textiles and on modernism's delegitimation of women's aesthetic practices, see Sparke, *As Long As It's Pink*; Attfield, *Bringing Modernity Home*; Judy Attfield, *Wild Things: The Material Culture of Everyday Life* (Oxford: Berg, 2000), pp. 129–36; Heynen, 'Modernity and Domesticity'.

91. Interview with L. G., St Petersburg, female.

92. Buchli, *Archaeology*, p. 128.

93. Voeikova, 'Uiut – v prostote', p. 30; Ol'ga Baiar, 'Sdelaem kvartiru udobnoi i uiutnoi', *Sovetskaia zhenshchina* 7 (1956), pp. 47–8; Baiar and Blashkevich, *Kvartira*.

94. Voeikova, 'Uiut – v prostote', p. 30; Voeikova, 'Vasha kvartira', p. 30.

95. Gol'dshtein, 'Chto takoe uiut', p. 30.

96. The Austrian architect-journalist Adolf Loos's influential essay 'Ornament and Crime' written in 1908, tied the elimination of ornament to progress in a Darwinian argument. See Adolf Loos, *Ornament und Verbrechen (Ornament and Crime)* tr. and repr. in Ludwig Münz and Gustav Künstler (eds), *Adolf Loos: Pioneer of Modern Architecture* (New York: Praeger, 1966), pp. 226–31; Le Corbusier denounced ornament in his *The Decorative Art of Today*, tr. James Dunnett (Cambridge: MIT Press, 1987); and *Towards a New Architecture*, tr. Frederick Etchells (New York: Praeger, 1960).

97. Gol'dshtein, 'Chto takoe uiut', p. 30.

98. One speaker in discussion considered entresol storage 'a superfluous seedbed of rubbish, which housewives always have and which must simply be liquidated'. TsGALI SPb, f. 341, op. 1, d. 386, l. 16.

99. Abramenko and Tormozova (eds), *Besedy o domashnem khoziaistva*, p. 4; E. Nikol'skaia, 'Ob uiute v obstanovke kvartiry', in Abramenko and Tormozova (eds), *Besedy o domashnem khoziaistva*, pp. 7–56; Chereiskaia, 'Zametki o khoroshem vkuse', pp. 220–34; E. Nikol'skaia, 'Uiut i obstanovka v dome', *Sem'ia i shkola* 11 (1958), pp. 46–7; E. Nikol'skaia, 'Blagoustroistvo zhilishcha', *Sem'ia i shkola* 1 (1958), pp. 42–4. See also Buchli, 'Khrushchev, Modernism', pp. 161–76; Reid, 'Destalinization and Taste', pp. 177–202; Gerchuk, 'Aesthetics of Everyday Life', pp. 81–99.

100. The contemporary interior as a site of memory and women's use of objects and embroidery to materialise memories are central issues of my interviews for 'Everyday Aesthetics' and, as represented in painting, of Susan E. Reid, 'The Art of Memory: Retrospectivism in Soviet Painting of the Brezhnev Era', in Matthew Cullerne Bown and Brandon Taylor (eds), *Art of the Soviets* (Manchester: Manchester University Press, 1993), pp. 161–87; and of Susan E. Reid, 'Representing Past and Presence: The Brezhnev Era Paintings of Tat'iana Nazarenko', unpublished paper, Association of Art Historians Annual Conference, University of Nottingham, 2004.

101. 'Programme of the CPSU', in Grey Hodnett (ed.), *Resolutions and Decisions of the Communist Party of the Soviet Union*, vol. 4: *The Khrushchev Years, 1953–1964* (Toronto: University of Toronto Press, 1974), pp. 167–264, esp. pp. 255–6.

102. Books were an essential attribute of the cultured home, for the absence of which no amount of luxury could compensate. GARF f. 6903, op. 26, d. 449, item no. 459, script of programme for Moscow Television: 'Dlia doma, dlia sem'i: vasha lichnaia biblioteka', 2 February 1963. However, a piano in a home where no-one played was a useless ornament. Sharov and Poliachek, *Vkus nado vospityvat'*, pp. 70–72.

103. Voeikova, 'Vasha kvartira', p. 30; Krasnova, 'Khoroshii vkus', p. 45; Interview with I. A., St Petersburg, *b*.1927, engineer, female; Iu. Filatov, 'Veshchi, sovremennost', zhivopis'', *Zvezda* 2 (1961), pp. 176–9, esp. p. 177.

104. Voeikova, 'Uiut – v prostote', pp. 30–31.

105. Briuno, 'Vasha kvartira', p. 4; 'Khudozhnik prishel na kvartiru', *Sluzhba byta* 6 (1963), p. 26; G. Liubimova (All-Union Institute of Technical Aesthetics, VNIITE), 'Ratsional'noe oborudovanie kvartir', *DI* 6 (1964), pp. 15–18.

106. 'Dlia doma, dlia sem'i. V pomoshch' novoselam', 5 January 1963, GARF, f. 6903, op. 2, d. 449.

107. Liubimova, 'Ratsional'noe oborudovanie kvartir', p. 16.

108. See the Estonian journal *Kunst ja kodu*; A. Goncharov, 'Vkhodi v nash dom, narodnoe iskusstvo', *Ogonek* 42 (16 October 1960), p. 24; Krasnova, 'Khoroshii vkus', p. 45.

109. Mart Kalm, 'Sauna Party at the Summer Cottage: Soviet Estonians Play at Being Western', in Pekka Korvenmaa and Esa Laaksonen (eds), *Universal versus Individual: The Architecture of the 1960's* (Helsinki: Alvar Aalto Academy, 2002), pp. 52–65.

110. Voeikova, 'Uiut – v prostote', p. 31; Goncharov, 'Vkhodi', p. 24.

111. See Buchli, *Archaeology*, p. 128.

112. Voeikova, 'Uiut – v prostote', p. 31.

113. I. Suvorova, 'Na urovne plokhogo rynka', *DI* 6 (1962), p. 46.

114. For detail, see Reid, 'Art of Memory', pp. 161–87.

115. Everyday Aesthetics interviews, 2004–07, St Petersburg, Tartu, Samara, Kaluga, Kazan.

116. Interview with I. A., St Petersburg, *b*.1927, engineer, female; Edel', *Divan*, p. 12.

117. For the affective meanings of textiles, their close identification with the human body, see Attfield, *Wild Things*, pp. 129–36; Heynen, 'Modernity and Domesticity', pp. 1–29.

118. McCracken, 'Homeyness', pp. 168–83.

119. RGALI, f. 2329, op. 4, ed. khr. 1391; TsAGM f. 21, op 1, d. 125, d. 126, d. 127 (visitors' book for exhibition 'Iskusstvo- v byt!', 1961); Torshilova, 'Byt'.

120. Torshilova, 'Byt', p. 140.

121. Ekaterina Gerasimova, interview for project 'Intelligentsia and Philistinism in Russian History and Culture', funded by Finnish Academy of Sciences, 2000–02, accessed with kind permission of Timo Vihavainen. See also Timo Vihavainen, *Vnutrennii vrag: bor'ba s meshchanstvom kak moral'naia missiia russkoi intelligentsii* (St Petersburg: Kolo, 2004).

122. Torshilova, 'Byt', pp. 138–9.

123. Donna Birdwell-Pheasant and Denise Lawrence-Zúñiga, 'Introduction' to Birdwell-Pheasant and Lawrence-Zúñiga (eds), *HouseLife: Space, Place and Family in Europe* (Oxford; Berg, 1999), pp. 23–8.

124. Henri Lefebvre, *The Production of Space* (Oxford: Blackwell, 1991), pp. 361–2.

125. Michel de Certeau, *The Practice of Everyday Life* (Berkeley: University of California Press, 1984).

126. Attfield, 'Bringing Modernity Home', p. 81.

2 Corporate Domesticity and Idealised Masculinity: Royal Naval Officers and their Shipboard Homes, 1918–39

Quintin Colville

In recent years, the relationship between masculinity and domesticity in nineteenth- and twentieth-century Britain has received increasing historical scrutiny. In a 2002 review article, for instance, Martin Francis took issue with the notion of a late nineteenth-century 'flight from domesticity', and equally with narratives of the unproblematic 're-domestication' of the male in interwar Britain.[1] In their place, he identified a continuum of ambivalence in which, whether in fantasy or reality, men sought 'to reconcile and integrate the contradictory impulses of domestic responsibility and escapism'.[2] This reassessment has, in turn, been complicated by Amy Milne-Smith's recent exploration of the Victorian and Edwardian gentlemen's club. While if anything reinforcing the contention of the 'flight from domesticity' thesis that her middle- and upper-class subjects were disaffected with, and keen to disassociate themselves from, the family home, Milne-Smith points out that their desired alternative surroundings were far from an exterior world of escapist adventure. Instead, their allegiances were unevenly divided between two rival incarnations of domesticity: the first feminised, familial and apparently demanding; the second corporate, homosocial and apparently harmonious. In the process, Milne-Smith argues convincingly that the concept of domesticity can be meaningfully disentangled from the context of family life, and that men's 'deep emotional attachment' to their club reflected its nature as 'a substitute for and a complement to the home'.[3]

The aim of this chapter is to consider further this idea of surrogate, corporate male domesticity through the example of Royal Naval officers and the quarters they occupied on board ship during the 1920s and 1930s. The accommodation allocated to the navy's non-officer personnel – collectively termed 'ratings' – will not be examined here. It is a subject that raises immediate parallels with Milne-Smith's research. To begin with, the social spaces allocated to officers afloat took the gentlemen's clubroom as their guide and inspiration throughout this period. Descriptions of these interiors as 'well-arranged clubrooms',[4] 'equipped club-fashion',[5] with a 'club-like atmosphere',[6] and resembling 'a section of a London club',[7] abound in memoirs and Admiralty papers. Both sets of environments shared an essential communality, to which expressions of privatised and exclusive ownership were subordinated. In addition, the insistence of clubland that its doors should remain closed to female applicants was mirrored by the navy's anathema to women serving at sea, and neither context can be said to have prioritised the cultivation of family life.[8] However, this distancing from the feminised and familial, and the limited scope for individualised possession, did not constitute a rejection of domesticity *tout court*: officers, like clubmen, viewed their quarters as alternative homes, profoundly relating to their appearance and to the relationships and lifestyles nurtured within them.

At the same time, of course, navalised domesticity was also highly idiosyncratic. Extended cruises offered little escape from its familiar features, while distance and time intensified and complicated its separateness from rival definitions of home. Although understood as separate from work, officers' living spaces were nonetheless fused not only to the site of their daily professional activities, but to their professional status. For instance, a ship's complement of officers might range from midshipmen under training to a full admiral, and the accommodation and access to the ship's domestic facilities enjoyed by each varied in accordance with a sliding scale of age and rank. Shipboard domesticity was, therefore, complex and multivalent and what follows will analyse some of the agendas that informed the design, the use and the imagining of these spaces. In so doing, the chapter will draw into this institutional arena conclusions reached by Alison J. Clarke about the family home: that it 'objectifies the [idealised] vision the occupants have of themselves ... it becomes an entity and process to live up to'.[9] From this perspective, particular attention will be paid to the role of the shipboard home in broadcasting the qualities from which an idealised persona of the naval officer was fashioned, while also stressing its simultaneous ability to support a range of contradictory corporate and individual behaviours.

However, the interpenetrating categories of class and masculinity from which this persona was constructed can only be addressed in this setting if we first reconsider an important embargo within the history of masculinity itself. Reacting against early work in the field, John Tosh and later Martin Francis have cautioned that concentrating on 'exclusively male contexts' fails to advance the essential task of illuminating the gendered and relational nature of all masculinities.[10] The naval home explored here was certainly exclusively male, and its design and use primarily reflected male ma-noeuvring for power and status either within the officer corps or with reference to a spectrum of male out-groups. Nonetheless, the dynamic engineered by these spaces between rival 'male' and 'female' domesticities made them relational from the outset. Even at sea, elements of a gendered and gendering dialogue also persisted, with every careful eradication of female association competing with projections and memorial-isations of real or imagined femininity. On closer inspection, too, once in port this male ghetto became the location for a range of mixed-sex entertaining. The cloistered home was reassigned to corporate display, to hospitable social performance and, not least, to courtship. Naval officers' alternative, homosocial domesticity, therefore, con-tained in itself the ambivalence, contradiction and conflict perceived by Francis in more straightforwardly relational negotiations between family home and masculine escapism.

Before exploring this case study of corporate homemaking, it is necessary briefly to sketch the social configuration of the navy's officer corps. By the late nineteenth century, and in the context of increasing professionalisation and the introduction of competitive entrance exams, the upper-class monopoly of naval officer status had been considerably eroded. In its place, the institution came to be dominated by men from a social fraction often referred to as the upper middle class or the public school middle class – the sons of lawyers, clergy, civil servants, politicians, doctors, bankers and stockbrokers.[11] This was, of course, as much a transition of norms as of personnel, and upper-middle-class officers refashioned the institution around their own interests and cultural agendas. Still strongly in evidence by the Second World War, these involved defining themselves against individualism, ostentation and leisured excess (upper-class, plutocratic or bohemian); against middle-class commercialism, 'money-grubbing' and 'materialism'; against the working class in general and the navy's rank and file in particular; and against their interwoven understandings of femininity, effeminacy and homosexuality. The idealised identity that officers strategically brought into focus through opposition to these varied 'others' was a version of the upper-middle-class reconfiguration of the gentleman as plotted by Harold Perkin.[12] This persona was by no means monolithic or unchanging, and received especially searching re-evaluations in the years following each world war.[13] However, throughout the 1920s and 1930s it continued to prioritise qualities of self-control and self-discipline, conformity, corporatism, respect for seniority, duty, service, selflessness and leadership ability. The cultural authority of this masculine identity during the interwar period was such that the navy's significant minorities from upper-class or non-professional middle-class backgrounds had, broadly, conformed to them.[14]

Whether in Admiralty houses, shore bases or warships, the construction of naval domesticities was central to this class-related project. Until the late 1880s, for instance, officers had used their private means, in the words of an Admiralty memorandum, 'to furnish their cabins according to their own ideas'.[15] From the 1890s onwards, however, the Admiralty reserved this power substantially to itself through a minutely orchestrated and bureaucratised programme of corporate consumption spanning the full range of officers' material culture from soup tureens to lampshades. Presented as a drive 'to promote uniformity … by restricting supply to articles of established patterns', the homogenising nature of this vast enterprise was also far from arbitrary.[16] In fact, the materiality it disseminated was a stylistically unified borrowing from various upper-middle-class sources, and was revealingly sensitive to shifts in upper-middle-class fashion. At the turn of the century, for example, officers' accommodation afloat comprised the full range of Victorian domestic paraphernalia: elaborately carved and upholstered furniture, patterned carpets and wallpapers, tassels and pot plants, clusters of ornaments and curios. By the First World War, though, these spaces were assuming the stripped aesthetic, white-painted walls, plain carpets, chintz soft furnishings, and neo-Georgian furniture, mantelpieces and dado rails which, with some alteration, epitomised upper-middle-class style throughout the interwar period.[17] As a result, when officers moved from ship to ship they would have experienced a standardised consistency in the design of their surroundings, albeit modified to the scale of a 40,000-ton battleship or a 2,000-ton destroyer.

A more detailed impression of the resulting domestic material culture can be gained from the officers' quarters on board one of the few surviving warships from the era: HMS *Belfast*, a cruiser launched in 1938 and ultimately preserved for the nation as a museum. The contract documents sent between 1936 and 1939 to the ship's builders, Harland & Wolff, contain the Admiralty's exhaustive specifications for how

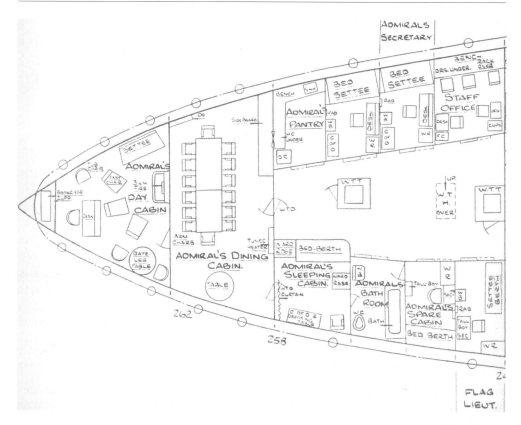

Figure 1: Schematic from 1959 showing the admiral's quarters located at the stern of HMS *Belfast* (image courtesy of the Admiralty Collection at the National Maritime Museum, Greenwich, London).

these spaces should be fitted and furnished and, together with photographs and the ship's interiors themselves, it is possible to recreate them in some detail. Out of a total crew of 750, *Belfast* carried approximately forty-five officers whose living areas occupied large areas of two decks. On the lower deck, and towards the stern of the ship, were a series of white-enamelled lobbies.[18] Doors in the first lobby gave access to the admiral's quarters: a large day cabin, a large dining cabin with a table capable of seating fourteen people, a sleeping cabin, a spare cabin, a bathroom and cabins for three of the admiral's staff (see Figures 1 and 2).[19] The second lobby gave access to the captain's day cabin, sleeping cabin and bathroom. Further forward were two more lobbies with doors leading off to a large number of more compact cabins allocated to officers of decreasing seniority.[20] On the deck above their cabins, and also at the ship's stern, were the officers' communal areas, known as the wardroom (see Figure 3). They occupied an enclosed and self-sufficient block of the ship's superstructure and, like the cabins, were entirely separate from the living spaces of the bulk of the crew.[21] On the right, looking towards the bow, were the wardroom anteroom and the wardroom dining room with its adjoining pantry into which food descended by lift from the officer's galley.[22] Across a passageway from the wardroom complex were two smaller spaces. The first was set aside for the warrant officers – former ratings who had been promoted to officer status but who remained barred from membership of the wardroom until the

Figure 2: Admiral Sir John Tovey dealing with correspondence in the day cabin of his flagship during the Second World War (photograph courtesy of the Imperial War Museum, London. Negative number A.10327).

later 1950s. The second, known as the gunroom, was occupied by the ship's eighteen- and nineteen-year-old midshipmen, recently graduated from cadet college.[23]

What is especially striking about the organisation of these quarters is the degree to which *Belfast*'s officer accommodation mediated or disguised the ship's structural realities. For instance, the honeycomb of partition walls that articulated both the cabin and wardroom areas served no structural function at all. This stood in sharp contrast to the messes occupied by ratings, the shapes of which generally conformed to the ship's watertight subdivisions, and were thus boundaried by the unlined steel plates of the hull and bulkheads.[24] In the cabin, the ship's ubiquitous steel watertight doors were supplemented by a neo-Georgian, panelled wooden design and, where officers' cabins were delineated on one or more sides by the ship's hull, the plating was lined and the rivet heads concealed with flat metal discs.[25] Porthole openings were cut in the hull plating to suit each cabin, and 'ornamental mouldings' were fitted to the beams of the admiral's and captain's apartments.[26] In the wardroom and wardroom anteroom, the sheet metal outer walls were thickly clad on the inside and then wallpapered.[27] On their ceilings, the otherwise inescapable ventilation ducts, pipes and wiring vanished behind white-painted panels and, rather than portholes, these spaces were given small, neo-Georgian, wood-framed sash windows.[28]

As this begins to reveal, rather than their accommodation being determined by the ship, the ship had been moulded around officers' upper-middle-class domestic

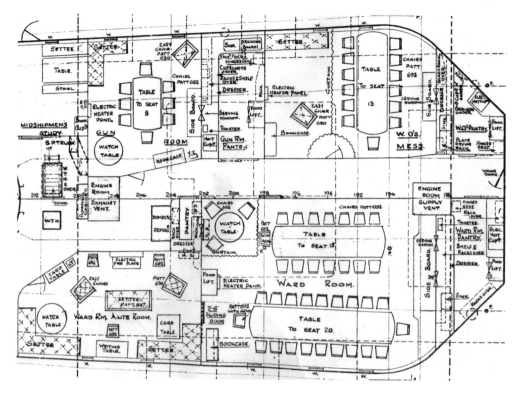

Figure 3: Schematic from 1939 showing part of the upper deck of HMS *Belfast*. The lower half of the image shows the wardroom and wardroom anteroom with, above them, the gunroom and warrant officers' mess (image courtesy of the Admiralty Collection at the National Maritime Museum, Greenwich, London).

familiarities. The domestic projections that this comprised were, however, varied and closely associated with hierarchies of age and rank. For instance, *Belfast*'s communal gunroom for midshipmen was a facsimile of another engine of upper-middle-class identity: the public school common room. Officers immediately above them (sub-lieutenants, lieutenants and lieutenant-commanders) were provided with small, single-room cabins fitted with the following: a bed/settee with drawers, a wash basin and toiletry cabinet, a secretaire, bookshelves, a wardrobe and a chair. In dimensions and furniture (and in the necessity of sharing separate bathroom facilities with other officers), these spaces were redolent of a number of parallel upper-middle-class institutional domesticities designed for bachelor males, among them the study/bedroom of the undergraduate student. The more spacious, multi-room admiral's and captain's apartments were equipped, in addition, with bedsteads, dressing tables, chests of drawers, card tables, settees, easy chairs and roll-top desks, as well as possessing *en suite* bathrooms.[29] Their design strongly suggested a more privatised, almost familial upper-middle-class domesticity; indeed, even on the building drawings, their furniture was grouped in a homely fashion around tables and fireplaces (see Figure 1).[30] Officers of lieutenant's rank and above also had access to the communal spaces of the wardroom, whose relationship to the gentlemen's club (and, indeed, to the golf or yachting club) has already been noted. *Belfast*'s schematics make this kinship explicit with the

Figure 4: Officers gathered in the wardroom anteroom of the battleship HMS *King George V*. Pictured here in 1941, many of the wardroom's furnishings and trophies had been removed for the duration of hostilities (photograph courtesy of the Imperial War Museum, London. Negative number A.1778).

wardroom anteroom's appropriate assemblage of card tables, button-back settees, easy chairs, letter racks and servants' bells, and its focal electric fireplace, club fender, and fitted bar complete with a hatch through to the stewards' pantry (see Figures 3 and 4). Equally in keeping were the wardroom dining room's long mahogany dining tables and leather-upholstered wooden dining chairs.[31]

HMS *Belfast*'s officer accommodation was, therefore, characterised by a plurality of jostling, age-related domesticities. Each, however, was bound conceptually and stylistically to a wider upper-middle-class context. From the chintz porthole curtains to the rectilinear, slab-sided easy chairs, every element thereby proclaimed its, albeit standardised, membership of a coherent socio-cultural world. And what made this programme of corporate control so significant was the fact that these designed environments had come to represent, both within and beyond the navy, the idealised upper-middle-class masculine qualities already listed. In a similar fashion, naval officers' uniform was configured around the template of the gentlemen's suit, with its connotations of restraint, self-discipline and authority.[32] The enforced conformity of officers' living spaces to this stylistic treatment was thus a clear statement of upper-middle-class hegemony within the institution. But it was also one that placed considerable demands on its inhabitants. The warship interior did not simply broadcast a range of approved qualities, it notionally or actually suppressed contradictory or disruptive characteristics. The experience of living within the ship was, therefore, one in which domesticity had a strenuously pedagogical function for all officers, urging them towards a flawless, corporate ideal. Moreover, the sublimation of male individuality that this system appeared to demand was intensified beyond civilian upper-middle-class usage by the navy's creed that claims of duty and service were absolute. In the opinion of Admiral Sir Richard Onslow, for example, naval officers 'put service before self: service to their Queen, their country and their fellow men, without thought for gain or glory or indeed of any reward save the knowledge of a job well done'.[33]

The nature of the warship interior as a gymnasium of authorised corporate masculinity was also consciously exploited to mould officers, and particularly the lowly midshipmen. Close physical proximity and a complete absence of privacy were the key features of their shared gunroom, with the seclusion of a cabin denied in favour of serried rows of hammocks. In the words of Captain Augustus Agar, 'There is nothing better than cramped and confined quarters to wear off the edges ... [among] youngsters';[34] and, as another naval officer, Kenneth Oram, put it, '[the gunroom] played an essential part in moulding "young gentlemen" into an acceptable professional pattern'.[35] Ritualised subordination to the norms and hierarchies of the gunroom was entrenched through a barrage of frequently humiliating initiation practices conducted to eradicate weakness, aloofness, pride or effeminacy. Newcomers were hurled from one end to the other of the gunroom table or dispatched, blindfolded and on all fours, on an 'Angostura hunt' following a scent trail of pungent droplets over an obstacle course around their mess and its adjoining spaces.[36] Failure to complete these exercises, or to submit to the endless mess rules and regulations, invariably resulted in canings. The alternative agendas that might have propelled the activities of this naval home – emotional isolation, sadism or sexual desire – were hidden beneath their stated service function. When Charles Morgan made them embarrassingly public in his 1919 autobiographical novel, *The Gunroom*, naval officers' outraged rebuttals swiftly identified Morgan's own selfish shortcomings and questionable masculinity as the root cause of his critique. As a midshipman, they declared, he had been an introvert and a 'budding Oscar Wilde', always keen to 'get away in a corner and read his favourite author'.[37] As such, his inability to participate in the gunroom's transformation of self into service explained the jaundiced and distorted nature of his subsequent recollections.

Departure from the gunroom accompanied promotion to the rank of lieutenant, and the 'short journey ... to the wardroom door' that came next had the significance of a ritualised passage from boyhood to adulthood.[38] The officer's new environment, however, had much in common with the homogenising, character-forming function of its predecessor, tacitly communicating the never-ending nature of this journey to masculine completeness. The continuing premium placed on communality is clear from the considerable space allocated on board ship to the wardroom complex, in contrast to the relatively cramped cabin accommodation for all but the highest-ranking officers. As one observer put it in 1913, '[cabins] are pathetically tiny, those little centres of privacy in a British warship. Outside of them, the life is entirely public'.[39] Within each wardroom, prominently hung portraits of the king and queen radically simplified the naval calling into an expression of loyal corporate service. More noticeably still, wardrooms were richly populated with references to the normative male upper-middle-class obsessions of physical fitness, team sports, field sports and adventure, with their prioritisation of activity over contemplation, experience over bookishness. A collection of silver trophies, won in inter-ship and inter-squadron sports and regattas, usually adorned the sideboard. Copies of yachting and golfing periodicals, as well as *Blackwood's Magazine, Country Life, The Country Sportsman, The Countryman, Field Sports, The Shooting Times* and *The Field* were piled on occasional tables. Even the novels by C. S. Forrester, H. Rider Haggard and John Buchan that often filled the limited wardroom shelving asserted that the moments of concentrated interiority required to read them were, in fact, engagements with the unimpeachable man of action.

A variety of accounts also make it clear that specific linkages were drawn between the uniform, plain and restrained decoration of officers' quarters and the dutifulness, self-denial and self-discipline of their inhabitants. Lieutenant-Commander John Irving's 1945 guide to naval customs commented repeatedly on the 'amazing Spartan simplicity' of captains' shipboard living spaces, marvelling at the dedicated rejection of self-indulgence they revealed.[40] Describing officers' quarters during the late 1920s, the erstwhile Royal Marine officer and writer, Sir George Aston, emphasised that they contained 'no trace of luxury'.[41] In similar vein, the naval officer-turned-naval author, 'Bartimeus', endlessly reiterated the nature of the officer corps as a 'brotherhood of self-immolation and hardship',[42] or a 'brotherhood of discipline and control, of austerity'.[43] Some officers took this creed to extremes. Sam Lombard-Hobson, for instance, remembered that, 'to toughen himself up for the job in hand', his commanding officer 'discarded his mattress and elected to sleep on the bare iron springs of his bunk'.[44]

These depictions of willing sacrifice and spurned extravagance substantiated the notion that service itself was an officer's sole motivation and sufficient recompense. The self-discipline demanded by this lifestyle was also dramatised through the warship's physical removal from normal society. According to John Irving, officers 'gladly forsake the fleshpots of the civilian life with its comforts, its safeties and its glittering prizes ... With their eyes wide open they choose a life of exile, hardship, and maybe, danger'.[45] Their ability to live contentedly and self-sufficiently under these conditions was commonly remarked. A discussion on the benefits of shore-based domesticity prompted one officer to describe these as 'pleasures which the naval officer is quite content to indulge in when they are accessible, but for which he does not pine, and whose total disappearance for months on end is no cause for distress'.[46] 'Most of the men have little use for the shore', wrote Sir George Aston, 'excepting for ... healthy and strenuous games and sports'.[47] Officers' supposed renunciation of the dividends of civilian life was also presented as evidence that they were equally removed from the everyday drives of personal ambition and financial acquisitiveness. Instead, the capacity for such unworthy motivations was projected outwards and away from the naval home to a variety of different masculine groupings ashore. 'The navy', insisted Commander Eric Bush, 'is not a money-making profession'.[48] The working classes, however, '[thought] only in pounds, shillings and pence; their principles ... engulfed in avariciousness'.[49] John Irving revealingly concluded his description of one senior officer's accommodation: 'none of the rose-wood-panelled boardroom of industry here'.[50] Even 'success in the city' could not compare to a naval career in which, 'one is not making money or amassing wealth. One is learning to be an officer and a gentleman'.[51]

Unsurprisingly, however, the impersonal and unreachable standards encoded in naval domesticity also generated a host of tensions and concealed, more or less

Figure 5: Officers reading and relaxing in the wardroom of HMS *King George V*, 1941 (photograph courtesy of the Imperial War Museum, London. Negative number A.2997).

successfully, a range of discordant attitudes and activities, both corporate and indi-vidual. To begin with, the immediate surroundings within which officers voyaged into dutiful 'exile' not only mirrored civilian norms but borrowed many of their most com-fortable domestic amenities. Indeed, the level of personal service enjoyed by officers afloat – from wine stewards, wardroom stewards and personal naval servants – far exceeded that in any interwar, civilian middle-class home.[52] One rating, William Lang, could barely control his resentment that, at the height of the First World War, his captain had 'required the services of six able-bodied men to attend to his creature comforts . . . at a time when men over forty years of age, fathers of families . . . were being called up to man the trenches in France'.[53] Nor, in peacetime, could ratings fail to notice the officers' motorcars, polo ponies, sailing dinghies, fishing rods, golf clubs and shotguns conveniently carried on board from port to port; or the frequency with which warships anchored in spots around the world known for their excellent riding, shooting, fishing, golf and yachting; or, for that matter, the coinciding of cruises with social seasons at Cowes on the Isle of Wight or on the French Riviera.

This tight alignment of the officer and his naval home to a class-specific identity also defined the nature and limits of the service officers felt duty-bound to provide. The wardroom, for example, replicated the gentlemen's club with its emphasis on casual conversation, communal relaxation and light reading (see Figure 5). In so doing, it entrenched an upper-middle-class rejection of introspection, individualism and intellectual endeavour. Attempts to appropriate the space for solitary, studious application – even for purposes of professional betterment – were thus met with deep disapproval, and such activities were relegated to the cabin. However, officers who continually sought the seclusion of their cabins for private study soon found themselves branded unhealthy and 'mouldy' for not participating in wardroom conviviality, and were dismissively labelled 'brain workers', 'brains men' or 'paperwork fiends'.[54] In this way, the wardroom's domestic usages supported the broad upper-middle-class preference for the clubbable and conservative median over the antisocial, uncorporate and unmanly associations of intellectual distinction and expertise.[55] As one officer commented, 'for leadership ... intellect is of secondary importance and may be quite inferior', and in the words of another, 'Heaven forbid that we get a navy officered by exceptional or above average men only. The average man is the backbone of any profession'.[56]

In this connection, the years following the First World War witnessed growing alarm among officers at the threat to this identity posed by the increasingly technical, specialised and scientific nature of their work.[57] Every step towards this economy of classroom-taught knowledge undermined the vision of gentlemanly, upper-middle-class masculinity which the officer corps sought to epitomise, captured in a nostrum still rehearsed in the 1930s: 'It is your character, not the character of your job, that counts'.[58] Within wardrooms, and between the pages of their independent professional journal, the *Naval Review*, officers dilated on the 'deadening shackles of scientific and material slavery' and 'the deadening study of intricate machinery'.[59] Solemn, but anxious, warnings were delivered concerning 'the insidious and well-known danger that continuous work with machinery and material militates against the development of certain faculties which are essential for command' and stressing the greater importance 'for a leader of men to develop a military character than to be a skilled mechanic'.[60] As this begins to demonstrate, officers also saw this as a social challenge. The roots of this aggressive 'materialism' in engineering and technology, with their proximity to trade, industry and manual work, suggested an assault on class hierarchy, and on the socio-cultural homogeneity of the mess. 'If these methods were correct', wrote one officer, 'an engine fitter would make the best managing director of a railway'.[61]

In this regard, the stylistic conformity of the navy's officer accommodation to a set of neo-Georgian, pre-industrial, anti-urban and gentlemanly principles asserted that these remained the governing values not just of the ship, but of the institution. For the small minority of engineer officers in each wardroom, and for officers of any branch with an excessive enthusiasm for technical detail, the message was plain: conformity to the dominant code was required. The wardroom's sporting trophies, for instance, associated naval efficiency and achievement (and also chances for promotion) not with a mastery of specialised equipment, but with physical prowess and gamesmanship. The nature of the wardroom as a space separate from work reinforced these expectations still further. Even in the 1930s, the injunction against 'talking shop'[62] could be fiercely upheld, and one officer sourly recalled the infractions of a gunnery lieutenant in his mess: 'meal after meal we were forced to listen to the rival merits of electric and percussion firing and to details of the results of some gunnery test or other'.[63] Officers' constructions of domesticity were, therefore, central to their conceptual domestication of the navy as a whole. As one tellingly commented, 'A housekeeper does not require to be a plumber'.[64]

Through their control of the institution, therefore, upper-middle-class officers were able not merely to occupy their quarters on board ship, but to corporately own them. In fact, once insulated from accusations of individualised acquisitiveness, officers reformulated and rehabilitated some of the usages of the upper class they had largely displaced. As one recruiting pamphlet declared to its often suburban and semi-detached readers, '[When] the officer goes from wardroom to wardroom he always feels at home; it is as if his quarters had been moved to another wing of the family mansion'.[65] Comparisons of the warship itself to the stately home were also common, particularly in the context of the navy's self-promotional open days, when hordes of unwelcome visitors were shown on board.[66] 'I remember them [members of the public] gazing down through the skylight at the officers eating their lunch',[67] noted one disconcerted admiral while another testily recalled that the public 'left us with our decks dirty; littered with cigarette ends, empty ice-cream cartons and the grisly and gummy remains of shrimps and other edibles . . . crammed into odd holes and corners'.[68] A similar, class-inflected frustration with uncouth trespassers was visible when dockyard repairs interrupted the smooth functioning of the corporate home. As John Ellis observed, 'The ship is no longer ours and strangers, with no feeling for the beauty and dignity of our vessel, swarm aboard, invading every compartment . . . Spots of oil begin to appear on the once snowy woodwork and greasy hands leave a trail . . . on hatch combings and doors'.[69]

These corporate disjunctures from messages of disinterested service were also joined by more individualised infractions. The navy, for example, made much of the officer corps' scrupulous meritocracy. As Rear-Admiral Harold Hickling put it in 1946, 'the status of officers in the Royal Navy depends on merit, nothing else . . . We do not bolster up any section of the officers . . . by privilege or by patronage'.[70] Of course, this overlooked the fact that the initial costs of training and uniform placed officer status beyond the means of all working-class and most lower-middle-class incomes. Nonetheless, among those able to afford the career, this level playing field for talent was corroborated by the warship's hierarchical domesticities. Within these environments, material perquisites had been substantially decoupled from the differentiating potentialities of birth and wealth, and were hitched instead to the standardised criteria of age and rank – a lieutenant had a lieutenant's cabin, a captain had a captain's. Before they even served afloat, officers were habituated to this system by their cadet training at Dartmouth Naval College. The dormitories, with their regimented rows of identical bedsteads and clothes chests, and the prohibition from adorning the stark, white walls with photographs or personal memorabilia of any kind, militated against individual ostentation. In fact, within this domestic context, attempts at personalised display were classified as vainglorious and antisocial.[71]

However, while conformity to this code was both obligatory and formative, it concealed a number of ways in which upper-middle-class connections, or the continuing influence of a title, could quietly sidestep its egalitarian implications.[72] Numerous accounts echo the recollection of one officer that, 'even such low forms of life as midshipmen could get their appointments wangled – if they had the right family contacts . . . so to come under the eye of a father's, or uncle's, friend', who would duly smooth their path to rapid promotion.[73] The coveted position of flag-lieutenant to an admiral fell with notorious frequency to socially adept scions of titled families. Officers with a private income could also arrange for the exterior of their naval home to be beautified by purchasing emery paper, 'Globe' polish, enamel paint and gold leaf in advance of an all-important admiral's inspection.[74] There were even a few officers whose royal connections and wealth overpowered the iron grip of rank-related domestic materiality, resulting in islands of conspicuous individualism that were clearly neither meritocratic nor upper-middle-class in spirit. In 1940, for instance, Lieutenant John Ellis recalled visiting the 'fabulous', custom-built living quarters on board HMS *Kelly* occupied by Lord Mountbatten, then a naval captain: 'Everyone in the navy had heard about Lord Louis' cabin', he began, before describing its attractive shades of pale green, the signed portraits of royalty and 'world famous personages', the 'magnificent radio-gram' and the 'celebrated showpiece, a luxuriously tiled bathroom fitted with a deep sunken bath'.[75] For the officer corps' less fortunate upper-middle-class majority, the rumblings of jealousy and resentment occasioned by these varied levels of privilege ran through their shipboard accommodation as surely as its messages of devoted corporate service.[76]

Other domestic rumblings clustered around generational fault lines. The 1920s, for instance, saw a number of young officers voice their frustration that socio-cultural resistance to technical expertise had allowed many senior ratings to outstrip their officers in professional knowledge.[77] This, in turn, was part of a broader critique of the navy's educational shortcomings and its emphasis on sport. Tentative plans were made for the rehabilitation of intellect, initiative and originality, and for their right to claim 'a fair share of the pedestal at present occupied almost exclusively by muscle and manual dexterity'.[78] Particularly in the context of the deep naval cutbacks of the 1920s, these and other elements of disaffection coalesced around the space most profoundly implicated in shaping the communal officer persona: the wardroom mess. Some young officers continued to describe its homosocial communality in affirming and sustaining terms, as a 'crowd of jolly good fellows', or 'the very finest comrades in the world'.[79] But an alternative picture was also presented of this home as a place of stultification and atrophy, of poorly educated officers 'with no mental occupation' snoozing through their off-duty afternoons in wardroom easy chairs, or turning 'for comfort to the gin bottle'.[80] This 'thoroughly unnatural life ... not very high up the scale of social evolution' was compared with civilian employment where 'prospects are immeasurably greater', and its communal celibacy was contrasted with marital domesticity. For many who left, or considered leaving, the service at this time, the naval home had become 'an inhuman monster, crushing the brains and binding the bodies of its servants'.[81]

Much of the power of this institutional vice to constrict individual identity came, of course, from the gendered construction of masculinity that had been drawn into the warship, and which the warship was used to propagandise. Above all, and as Michael Roper and Peter Lewis have noted, the contours of upper-middle-class masculinity were consistently drawn in opposition to understandings of femininity.[82] Among naval officers, the key qualities of self-control, self-discipline, leadership ability and service were routinely represented as inherently male, while characteristics such as vanity, frivolity, sentimentality, weakness, suggestibility and irrationality were externalised and projected onto women.[83] At the level of fantasy, therefore, the exclusion of women from shipboard life was also an eradication of 'female' character traits inconsistent with the officer ideal. Clearly, however, officers 'purgings of the "feminine" parts of them-selves' were as fragile as their possession of the idealised qualities they prized.[84] Sam Lombard-Hobson remembered, for instance, that after each shore leave, his captain felt the need to drive the ship especially hard, 'to get the canker out of the system, planted there by over-caring mothers and too-demanding wives'.[85] As a result, this neat conceptualisation of two naturally distinct and opposite sexes co-existed with a wary watchfulness for corrupting feminine encroachment. Given the broad cultural associ- ation of femininity with domesticity, it is consequently unsurprising that a gendered struggle between artificial ideal and troublesome reality was fought out in the context of officers' accommodation on board ship.

This process of prising apart male and female identity was considered most urgent among junior officers, who might still bear the imprint of maternal cosseting. With its extrovert communality and suppression of compassionate love, the male domesticity of the gunroom (as with its public school equivalent) was intended to distance midshipmen from feminised contexts that would weaken resolve and impede progress to manhood.[86] Within this space, feminised stereotypes of domestic perfection were overturned through a rhetoric of scruffy dilapidation. Its messages – captured in the well-worn armchairs, the initials carved in the gunroom table and the dart holes liberally scattered beyond the circumference of the dart board – were of masculine vigour, hard use and freedom from female rules. The suggestive and objectified images torn from *La Vie Parisienne* and stuck to the lockers only served to accentuate female remoteness and difference. For adult officers, the modelling of the wardroom on the gentlemen's club also signalled that their corporate domesticity was one of purified masculinity. Even the association of interior space with femininity was countered by the environment's relentless focus on exterior activity. The custom of concluding a wardroom dinner with 'an impromptu speech upon some aspect of female life or habit – or costume' was an additional opportunity to underline the foreignness and irrelevance of all such issues to their surroundings.[87] Within the wardroom, and throughout the naval home, the corporate control of material culture that underpinned the officer ideal also freed officers from a feminising engagement with interior decoration and taste-making. And a still more radical conformity to this pared-down masculinity was achieved in officers' descriptions of the warship to family and friends. The naval home, with its softness, warmth and comforts tended to recede, and the cold, hard exterior and warlike utilitarianism of the ship came to the fore. As one officer portrayed it to his wife, his ship was just an 'iron box with the lid down'.[88]

And yet, a wide range of sources suggest that the naval home also functioned as a setting for acquiring and mastering the skills of upper-middle-class, mixed-sex sociability. As the warship moved from port to port in Britain and around the empire, its officers established or strengthened their connections with an influential upper-middle- class diaspora. At each destination, the reassuring appearance of the wardroom, the drawing-room vocabulary of the senior officers' quarters, and elaborate transforma- tions of the upper deck, allowed these spaces to host lunch and tea parties, dinners, full-blown dances and the wardroom's significantly titled 'At Homes'. Under these circumstances, the warship also became a stage for courtship and the contracting of socially advantageous marriages, with its corporate grandeur and punctilious staff bol- stering the credentials of even the most impecunious officer. John Ellis's description of the preparations for a shipboard dance in 1938 is worth quoting at length:

> The quarterdeck and adjoining waists were transformed into a fairyland with little coloured lanterns strung between the stanchions, masses of greenery and bright flowers decoratively arranged and

bathed in soft indirect lighting . . . The crowing achievement was the '*Brasserie de Londres*' in which an illuminated waterfall gurgled and splashed from a fountainhead of fernery into a miniature rock garden. This was one of several secluded bars and sitting out places which were strategically placed . . . to enable full advantage to be taken of the . . . starry night.[89]

A recruitment pamphlet from 1935 elaborated on the prospects for young officers, insisting that, 'the most junior lieutenants have cabins in which they will not hesitate to "organise a tea fight", graced by three or four damsels'.[90] While still a midshipman, Ellis reserved a small dining room in HMS *London*, then docked in Malta, for 'a private *tête à tête* with . . . [a] local beauty called Harriet Caruana'.[91] And far from restricting access to these protected masculine environments, a proprietorial desire to impress meant that female guests were given tours of ships that often long outlasted their enthusiasm.

These bachelor social activities, and their associated idealised qualities of smooth urbanity and masterful gallantry, may only have accentuated the conceptual distance between masculinity and femininity. Certainly a predatory and objectifying gaze was directed at many female visitors, and Brian Smalley recalled one officer who 'made sure that he was in the wardroom when the girls came on board to cast his eye over the "talent"'.[92] However, sustained attempts to dispute the gendered boundaries of naval manliness, and to internalise feminised qualities of sentiment, attachment and dependency can be detected in the privatised domesticity of married officers' cabins (see Figures 6 and 7). While the fixtures and furnishings of these spaces remained of service pattern, a greater degree of personal decoration was permitted, and officers used their partly contrived and partly genuine bafflement at aesthetic decision-making – particularly on the subject of soft furnishings – as a pretext to co-opt female assistance.[93] Officers and their wives would duly select patterns of chintz from Admiralty samples, and the latter would be 'allowed' to make the cabin into 'a home from home with warm, bright covers and curtains'.[94] The cabin thereby became a symbolically companionate space, and a means of mediating the dislocations of naval life. On a visit to her husband's ship, Joy Packer 'prowled into his sleeping cabin', noting with some relief that 'on the bunk was the silver jackal karross I had given Bertie in South Africa', and that photographs of herself and their son stood on the chest of drawers.[95] During a long separation from his wife in 1937, Admiral Sir Angus Graham made his quarters 'as homelike as I could' with a series of purchases, including a Rockingham dessert service, a Turkish silver dish, dwarf willows from Iceland and a reproduction Ching dynasty vase. All were described and pondered in letters to his wife, and many were subsequently moved to corresponding locations in his family home.[96]

Such officers, however, stepped from their superficially companionate cabins into the lobby and wardroom beyond, whose loud messages of masculine self-sufficiency reasserted the oppositional nature of feminised and masculine worlds. Married officers could never reconcile this dialectic, and its implications became clear in a bitter tussle between marital and institutional domesticities that, for many, made it impossible to live contentedly in either. The first threatened a contamination and deterioration of masculinity. As one officer complained to his wife while dressing for dinner ashore, 'when I laid out my coat on that chair I found it covered in powder . . . what I need is a nice plain man's cabin and a good capable marine servant'.[97] The second involved

Figure 6: A portrait of Lieutenant-Commander R. B. Stannard in his cabin on board HMS *Vimy*, 1943 (photograph courtesy of the Imperial War Museum, London. Negative number A.15018).

renouncing, for long periods, the emotional satisfactions and securities of marriage and fatherhood. In fact, whether in their cabins or in the studies of their family homes, officers prominently displayed tokens of their divided domestic loyalties. Framed portraits of wife and children often stood next to framed photographs of warships, some with beaming crews crammed onto the decks and upperworks. Admiral Lord

Figure 7: Rear Admiral P. J. Mack photographed in his cabin on board ship, 1943 (photograph courtesy of the Imperial War Museum, London. Negative number A.14298).

Chatfield ruminated on the 'difficult and correct balance between zeal for the service and affectionate duty to wife and family'.[98] But for many officers' wives, the nature of the navy as a protected space where dreams of masculinity coalesced and evolved from boyhood to retirement made this contest between homes rather one-sided. Celia Johnson's character in the film, *In Which We Serve* (the wife of Noel Coward's Captain Kinross) spoke with an authentic voice:

> Wherever she [the naval wife] goes, there is always in her life a permanent and undefeated rival: her husband's ship. Whether it be a battleship or a sloop . . . it holds first place in his heart, it comes before wife, home, children, everything. Some of us try to fight this and get badly mauled in the process; others, like myself, resign themselves to the inevitable.[99]

The naval home consequently made a number of claims on behalf of its upper-middle-class occupants – a prescriptive and idealising ambition common to many domestic contexts. By carefully identifying and appropriating a range of governing qualities, it helped to define the norms and propagandise the self-image of a ruling class, while simultaneously stigmatising the characteristics of other social collectivities. At the same time, these surroundings were equally integral to the configuration of a ruling masculinity, resolved through a purging of feminised and unorthodox masculine traits. In fact, the inhabitants of the wardroom also frequently considered themselves the finest specimens of a ruling race: 'samples of the best kind of Englishman'; and the warship's far-flung diplomatic duties made it a global reception room whose timbre would suitably improve or intimidate the foreign guest.[100] Moreover, while commonly presenting the components of this corporate officer persona as innate and unacquirable, the naval home also offered an age-related process of personal development and discipline to stabilise them piece by piece. And yet, of course, instability was the constant companion of this institutionalised fusion of identity and domesticity. The intensity with which each approved quality was pursued guaranteed that its obverse flourished within the shipboard environment. The central rhetoric of service, selflessness and self-denial was, for instance, invariably and creatively intertwined with corporate and individual self-interest. Above all, though, the masculine priorities that sought to distance this home from female presence and feminised characteristics ensured that officers (and their domesticity) lurched between gendered extremes, trapped by their own ambitions for masculine status within a setting that corporately rejected synthesis and reconciliation. Even the alternative emotional sustenance that the naval home offered – the brotherly feeling of the wardroom, or the frequently stressed paternal responsibilities to the crew – were undermined by the messages of impermanence and human interchangeability in naval life. In John Ellis's words again,

> . . . for months one is part of a ship, one becomes firm friends with a group of people, one gets to know them intimately and confidences are exchanged . . . and then an appointment is received to another ship. Within a few weeks . . . their faces become vague and shadowy . . . The saddest thing is to return to your old ship after two or three months. You find that the wardroom which you knew so well is strangely unfamiliar; some other officer has taken your place in this intimate circle and you are a stranger, just a guest.[101]

Notes

1. Martin Francis, 'The Domestication of the Male? Recent Research on Nineteenth- and Twentieth-Century British Masculinity', *Historical Journal* 45 (2002), pp. 637–52.
2. Francis, 'The Domestication of the Male?', p. 643.
3. Amy Milne-Smith, 'A Flight to Domesticity? Making a Home in the Gentlemen's Clubs of London, 1880–1914', *Journal of British Studies* 45 (2006), pp. 796–818, here p. 799. See also Amy Milne-Smith, 'Club Talk: Gossip, Masculinity and Oral Communities in Late Nineteenth-Century London', *Gender & History* 21 (2009), pp. 86–106.
4. C[harles]. E. W. Bean, *Flagships Three* (London: Alston Rivers, 1913), p. 82.
5. Lieutenant-Commander John Irving, *Naval Life and Customs* (Altrincham: Sherratt & Hughes, 1945), p. 56.

6. Britannia Royal Naval College archive (BRNC), John Ellis, unpublished manuscript, p. 155.
7. Eric Bush, *How to Become a Naval Officer* (London: Gieves, 1935), p. 6.
8. The Women's Royal Naval Service, established during the First World War, was demobilised altogether between 1919 and 1938.
9. Alison J. Clarke, 'The Aesthetics of Social Aspiration', in Daniel Miller (ed.), *Home Possessions: Material Culture behind Closed Doors* (Oxford: Berg, 2001), pp. 23–46, here p. 42.
10. John Tosh, *Manliness and Masculinities in Nineteenth-Century Britain: Essays on Gender, Family and Empire* (Harlow: Pearson Longman, 2005), p. 2. See also Francis, 'The Domestication of the Male?', p. 652.
11. See e.g., Ross McKibbin, *Classes and Cultures: England 1918–1951* (Oxford: Oxford University Press, 1998), p. 35; Noreen Branson and Margot Heinemann, *Britain in the 1930s* (London: Weidenfeld & Nicolson, 1971), p. 152; David Cannadine, *The Decline and Fall of the British Aristocracy* (London: Papermac, 1996), p. 274.
12. Harold Perkin, *The Rise of Professional Society: England since 1880* (London: Routledge, 1990), pp. 121, 368.
13. See e.g., 'Training and Instruction of Junior Officers', *Naval Review* 9 (1921), pp. 584–95.
14. See Quintin Colville, 'The Role of the Interior in Constructing Notions of Class and Status: A Case Study of Britannia Royal Naval College Dartmouth', in Susie McKellar and Penny Sparke (eds), *Interior Design and Identity* (Manchester: Manchester University Press, 2004), pp. 114–32.
15. National Archives (NA), ADM 116/315, memorandum, 21 November 1887.
16. NA, ADM 116/315, 'Regulations as to Supply of Furniture, Plate and Linen', circular 29, 8 December 1876.
17. See Deborah Cohen, *Household Gods: The British and their Possessions* (New Haven: Yale University Press, 2006), pp. 194–5.
18. National Maritime Museum (NMM), Ships Plans Collection, NPA 6748, 'HMS *Belfast* Lower Deck Plan', 8 November 1939.
19. HMS *Belfast* was fitted as a flagship, which meant that accommodation had to be provided for an admiral in addition to the quarters occupied by the ship's captain.
20. NMM, Ships Plans Collection, NPA 6748.
21. NMM, Ships Plans Collection, NPA 6745, 'HMS *Belfast* Upper Deck Plan', 8 November 1939.
22. NMM, Ships Plans Collection, NPA 6745.
23. NMM, Ships Plans Collection, NPA 6745.
24. NMM, Ships Plans Collection, NPA 6748.
25. NMM, Ships Plans Collection, 211 (612), 'Contract for HMS Belfast; Specifications for Building a Cruiser of the 1936 Programme'.
26. NMM, Ships Plans Collection, 211 (612).
27. NMM, Ships Plans Collection, 211 (612).
28. NMM, Ships Plans Collection, 211 (612).
29. NMM, Ships Plans Collection, NPA 6748.
30. NMM, Ships Plans Collection, NPA 6748.
31. NMM, Ships Plans Collection, NPA 6745.
32. Quintin Colville, 'Jack Tar and the Gentleman Officer: The Role of Uniform in Shaping the Class- and Gender-Related Identities of British Naval Personnel, 1930–1939', *Transactions of the Royal Historical Society* 13 (2003), pp. 105–29.
33. BRNC, speech by Sir Richard Onslow at Britannia Royal Naval College, 11 April 1960, p. 5
34. Augustus Agar, *Footprints in the Sea* (London: Evans, 1959), p. 23.
35. Kenneth Oram, *The Rogue's Yarn* (London: Leo Cooper, 1993), p. 21.
36. Charles Morgan, *The Gunroom* (London: A. & C. Black, 1919), p. 167.
37. 'The Gunroom', *Naval Review* 9 (1921), p. 165.
38. Irving, *Naval Life*, p. 56.
39. Bean, *Flagships Three*, p. 92.
40. Irving, *Naval Life*, p. 45.
41. Sir George Aston, *The Navy of To-Day* (London: Methuen, 1927), p. 41.
42. Bartimeus, *Naval Occasions; and Some Traits of the Sailor-Man* (London: Penguin, 1936), p. 62.
43. Bartimeus, *The Navy Eternal* (London: Hodder & Stoughton, 1918), p. 43.
44. Sam Lombard-Hobson, *A Sailor's War* (London: Orbis, 1983), p. 42.
45. Irving, *Naval Life*, p. 9.
46. 'The Age of Entry of Naval Cadets', *Naval Review* 8 (1920), pp. 535–38, here p. 538.

47. Aston, *The Navy of To-Day*, p. 15.
48. Bush, *How to Become a Naval Officer*, p. 4.
49. 'The Spirit of Democracy and the Navy', *Naval Review* 9 (1921), pp. 342–55, here p. 347.
50. Irving, *Naval Life*, p. 45.
51. 'Advice to a Young Officer', *Naval Review* 15 (1927), p. 426.
52. See e.g., the account of one naval steward: J. N. James, *A Piece of Gin* (London: Excalibur, 1993).
53. William Lang, 'Lower Deck and Wardroom', *Naval Review* 8 (1920), pp. 147–51, here p. 147.
54. 'The Slough of Dispond', *Naval Review* 9 (1921), pp. 340–41; 'Games', *Naval Review* 8 (1920), pp. 204–10, here p. 206.
55. See McKibbin, *Classes and Cultures*, pp. 96–7.
56. 'Early Entry *v.* Late Entry', *Naval Review* 13 (1925), pp. 59–62, here p. 61.
57. See e.g., 'The Training of Officers', *Naval Review* 9 (1921), pp. 364–88, here p. 380.
58. Bush, *Naval Officer*, p. 12.
59. 'The Atrophy of the Lieutenant', *Naval Review* 2 (1914), pp. 25–30, here p. 25.
60. 'Thoughts on the Service', *Naval Review* 9 (1921), pp. 48–54, here p. 54.
61. 'Atrophy of the Lieutenant', p. 25.
62. 'The Junior Lieutenant', *Naval Review* 8 (1920), pp. 355–9, here p. 358.
63. George Hartford, *Commander R.N.* (London: Arrowsmith, 1927), p. 180.
64. 'Naval Education', *Naval Review* 1 (1913), pp. 279–80.
65. Bush, *How to Become a Naval Officer*, p. 7.
66. John Hayes, *Face the Music: A Sailor's Story* (Edinburgh: Pentland, 1991), p. 86.
67. Admiral of the Fleet Lord Chatfield, *The Navy and Defence* (London: Heinemann, 1942), pp. 3–4.
68. Michael Simpson, *A Life of Admiral of the Fleet Andrew Cunningham* (London: Frank Cass, 2004), p. 116.
69. BRNC, Ellis, p. 117.
70. NA, ADM 116/5496, evidence of Rear-Admiral Harold Hickling to the Noble Committee, 1 October 1946.
71. See Colville, 'The Role of the Interior'.
72. See James Dalglish, *Life Story of a Fish* (London: Adelphi Press, 1992), p. 24.
73. Alastair Mars, *Court Martial* (London: Frederick Muller, 1954), pp. 58–9.
74. Chatfield, *The Navy and Defence*, pp. 28–9.
75. BRNC, Ellis, p. 213. Mountbatten was uncle to Philip, later Queen Elizabeth's husband.
76. See Mars, *Court Martial*, pp. 58–9.
77. 'Training and Instruction of Junior Officers', p. 584.
78. 'The Higher Naval Education of Executive Officers in Relation to Staff Work', *Naval Review* 7 (1919), pp. 276–81, here p. 276.
79. 'Thoughts on Leaving the Service', *Naval Review* 8 (1920), pp. 502–7, here p. 505; Letter from the Duke of Montrose, quoted in 'Naval Education', *Naval Review* 15 (1927), pp. 146–54, here p. 146.
80. 'Thoughts on Leaving the Service', pp. 502, 504.
81. 'Thoughts on Leaving the Service', pp. 506–7.
82. Michael Roper, *Masculinity and the British Organisation Man since 1945* (Oxford: Oxford University Press, 1994); Peter Lewis, 'Mummy, Matron and the Maids: Female Presence and Absence in Male Institutions, 1934–1963', in Michael Roper and John Tosh (eds), *Manful Assertions: Masculinities in Britain since 1800* (London: Routledge, 1991), pp. 168–89, esp. pp. 168–9.
83. See Colville, 'Jack Tar', pp. 114–18.
84. Roper, *Masculinity*, p. 112.
85. Lombard-Hobson, *A Sailor's War*, p. 56.
86. See Lewis, 'Mummy, Matron and the Maids', pp. 168–9.
87. Irving, *Naval Life*, p. 59.
88. Joy Packer, *Grey Mistress* (London: Eyre & Spottiswoode, 1949), p. 43.
89. BRNC, Ellis, p. 137.
90. Bush, *How to Become a Naval Officer*, p. 6.
91. BRNC, Ellis, p. 120.
92. Brian Smalley, *Aft through the Hawsepipe* (Stanhope: Memoir Club, 2004), p. 128.
93. See Dalglish, *Life Story of a Fish*, p. 234.
94. BRNC, Ellis, p. 214.
95. Packer, *Grey Mistress*, pp. 44–5.

96. Admiral Sir Angus Cunninghame Graham, *Random Naval Recollections, 1905–1951* (Cardross: self-published, 1979), pp. 84, 239.
97. Joy Packer, *Pack and Follow* (London: Eyre & Spottiswoode, 1945), p. 334.
98. Chatfield, *The Navy and Defence*, p. 99.
99. David Lean and Noel Coward (dirs), *In Which We Serve* (Britain, 1942). See also Packer, *Grey Mistress*, p. 42.
100. 'Meditations', *Naval Review* 13 (1925), pp. 45–9, here p. 47.
101. BRNC, Ellis, p. 75.

3 Men Making Home: Masculinity and Domesticity in Eighteenth-Century Britain

Karen Harvey

In 1807, the great visual caricaturist Thomas Rowlandson designed a pair of images, ruminating on men and their relationship to 'home' (Figure 1). In the first, 'At Home and Abroad' (1807), a man at home with his unavoidably large and unmistakably ugly wife drinks himself into a stupor. The room is messy, uncomfortable and saggy. The bed curtains are wide open: perhaps to fit the woman's bottom through, perhaps to signify the age and openness of her body. She, with some effort it seems, is engaged in domestic tasks, stretching to the fire to boil water and warm bed-clothes. There is certainly no warmth or relief between husband and wife: the man seems to have fallen asleep in his chair reading; the book that falls from his left hand is entitled *Memoirs of an Amorous Fat Rumped old Tabby*. Sure enough, the mantelpiece displays not fine china or shiny silver, but restoration drops. The man is physically at home, but not really there; he is at home, but away; at home, but abroad.

In the second image, 'Abroad and At Home', the same man is in a very different place (Figure 2). He is away from home, but is 'at home'. Here, the man reclines, legs naughtily astride, holding a typically plump Rowlandson beauty who looks adoringly into the man's eyes. The sofa is firm and comfortable, large enough for two lovers, enveloped by the lush red curtains that have yet to be opened. The mantelpiece shows appropriate objects, and the fire is not blowing smoke, but giving out heat: it is a resting place for a poker, glowing red hot at one end and pointing at the woman's feet.

Significantly, the protagonist in Rowlandson's narrative is the man; these images are 'about' his relationship with 'home'. In this chapter, I want to consider the cultural terrain in the century or so before the production of these images, exploring some of the issues about masculinity and home that inform Rowlandson's illustrations. I seek to extend our currently poorly developed view of men's gendered engagement with home, as part of a developing history of masculinity.[1] One aim is to write men back into a history from which they have been written out. At the same time, I contend that training the light on masculinity broadens our understanding of the experience and meaning of home in a period when these changed significantly. Attention to how men made homes and homes made men, I propose, necessarily transforms our idea of 'home' and 'domesticity'.

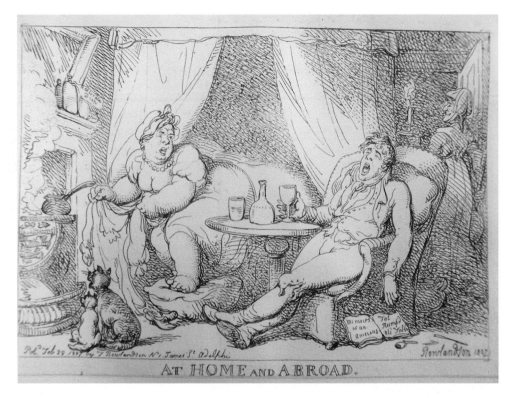

AT HOME AND ABROAD.

Figure 1: Thomas Rowlandson, 'At Home and Abroad' (1807). Courtesy of Special Collections, Western Bank Library, University of Sheffield.

Missing men

As gendered individuals, and certainly compared to women, men are notable for their absence in accounts of the eighteenth-century domestic interior. Part of the explanation is historiographical. To some extent, the older genealogy of women's history explains why the attention to women and the home has been more fulsome than to men. More substantially, though, men's absence has been shaped by the categories, models and narratives developed and deployed in historical work.

First, in much published work on the eighteenth century, narratives about changes in the tenor of domestic relationships, and theories of political obligation more broadly, shape a decline in men's engagement with home. There is general agreement that before the mid-seventeenth century, the house and its social relationships were critical to men's wider social status and indeed their masculinity. Following the Reformation, Lena Orlin writes, political patriarchalism elevated the individual household as 'the primary unit of social control', and the householder's authority was utilised for 'macrocosmic benefit'.[2] Susan Amussen shows how the role of the household as a key instrument of social order continued in the seventeenth century, declining after the Restoration because a more secure social elite were able to use more subtle forms of discipline.[3] It was here, Amussen argued, that the roots of the private eighteenth-century family and the separate spheres family of the nineteenth century were to be found. A similar trajectory has been drawn for Anglo-America. Mary Beth Norton characterises the

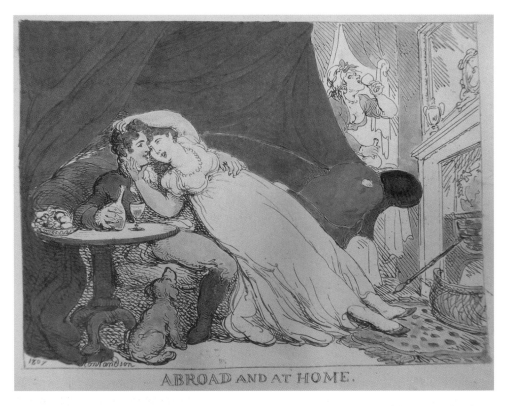

Figure 2: Thomas Rowlandson, 'Abroad and At Home' (1807). Courtesy of Special Collections, Western Bank Library, University of Sheffield.

shift as one from paternal power to maternal care between the mid-seventeenth and mid-eighteenth centuries, and Carole Shammas's *A History of Household Government* (2002) argues more recently that while the household head's jurisdiction continued for much longer than in western Europe, by 1880 the paterfamilias was offstage and remote, and 'separate spheres domesticity' had arrived.[4] The most detailed study of how such changes might have played out in people's lives in England is Anthony Fletcher's *Gender, Sex and Subordination* (1995). Fletcher presents a sixteenth- and seventeenth-century world of subordination and discipline, but over time patriarchy was revised and reinvigorated, and a new form of patriarchy emerged: a secular ideology based less on law and religion than on education, through which men and women internalised the values that ensured their fulfilment of appropriate roles.[5] Fletcher's depth of research gives texture to what Elizabeth Kowaleski-Wallace has termed a 'new-style patriarchy'.[6]

Such analyses of cultural representations and social experiences of the household echo, to varying degrees, work on political theory. The classic is Gordon J. Schochet's *The Authoritarian Family and Political Attitudes in 17th-Century England* (1975). Beginning with Sir Robert Filmer's *Patriarcha* (1680), in which magistrates gained their authority from and were due the same obedience as fathers, both divinely ordained, and ending with John Locke's *Two Treatises of Government*, which sought to distinguish between political and patriarchal authority and to craft a new basis for allegiance to a magistrate, Schochet tracks what he refers to as 'the disappearance of the family from Anglo-American political thought over two hundred years ago'.[7] It is this lifting of the political burden from the household in canonical political treatises that many subsequent histories reconstruct in practice; the absence of men in the eighteenth-century home mirrors this absence of the household from eighteenth-century theories of political obligation.

The second body of work that has obscured men's engagements with the eighteenth-century home chronicles the birth of domesticity. Created in the constructions of new domestic architecture, embedded in modern concepts of the self through new forms of narrative, or performed through sociability using new items of material culture, for many it was during the eighteenth century that modern domesticity was invented, before coalescing into the more intense nineteenth-century domestic culture.[8]

In some influential studies, this domesticity displays an increasingly close relationship with women and/or femininity. This has become an important strand of studies of the eighteenth-century middle class, including those by Leonore Davidoff and Catherine Hall, and by John Smail, in which an ideology of feminine domesticity is seen as central to the construction of middle-class identity.[9] Important work on nineteenth-century Britain, in contrast, argues that domesticity became a vital political discourse only after the late 1820s and 1830s.[10] Domesticity *is* politically relevant, here – these are studies of class culture and identity, after all – but domesticity itself is characterised as one half of a separation, part of a broader discourse of 'separate spheres', and predicated on new ideals of both womanhood and manhood.

Thus, the home in studies of the British long eighteenth century has a rather feminine feel. And this raises at least one significant question: what happened to the domestic patriarch, and to men's engagements with home more generally, during the eighteenth century?[11] The figure of the household patriarch is well-developed in works on early modern masculinity,[12] while for the nineteenth century John Tosh makes the emphatic statement that 'the Victorian ideal of domesticity was in all respects the creation of men as much as women'.[13] Viewed in this light, the eighteenth-century home appears to be peculiarly women's business. And there is much at stake here: domesticity might be critiqued as constraining, but in redemptive histories of domesticity, women accrue status through their responsibility for the fitting up and running of the home. As Amanda Vickery begins the chapter on 'Prudent Economy' in her book *The Gentleman's Daughter*, 'The writers of advice literature groomed genteel women for the exercise of power'.[14] This constitutes a significant shift from the home being critical for men's authority in the seventeenth century: the eighteenth-century home becomes a source of authority for women, not men.

Historical narratives can be seductive and satisfying; yet while they are useful, even necessary, they can also over-simplify. There is no easy characterisation of the home and of men's and women's relationships to it. In her important book, *The Middling Sort: Commerce, Gender, and the Family in England, 1680–1780* (1996), Margaret Hunt demonstrates that the home was of considerable importance to middling-sort men and vice versa, elaborating the 'common culture' shared by middling men and women in the home.[15] Instead of gendered divisions between spheres of home and work, Hunt's study elevated 'the market' as that which '*transcended* the so-called "public sphere" and went to the heart of family life'.[16] Joanne Bailey's *Unquiet Lives: Marriage and Marriage Breakdown in England, 1660–1800* (2003) offers an invaluable analysis of the tensions between domesticity and masculinity. Normal marital life depended on co-dependency between men and women, Bailey insists, and conflict in marriage often arose when tensions between 'the ideal of manhood and realities of marital material life could not be accommodated'.[17] The necessary expertise and authority held by women in the household undercut the normative ideal of 'the male provisioner' and 'male autonomy in the household'.[18] Men's patriarchal authority could be contested, ignored, or challenged, then, yet Bailey's study suggests how the ideal of manly provisioning shaped married lives and sparked ongoing tensions.

In this light, we can see the historical significance of Shawn Lisa Maurer's literary finding that 'the bourgeois family man emerged as the prototype of desirable mas-culinity' in early eighteenth-century periodicals.[19] Maurer believes that this 'ideology' problematises critics' distinctions between 'public and private, male and female'.[20] Bailey's study suggests that it problematised contemporaries' distinctions too. Yet it seems that men could concern themselves with home in ways that did not produce obvious tensions, battles or breakdown. Hannah Barker finds in her recent study of the diaries of four Manchester men that they were preoccupied by 'the concerns of family life and the "private" sphere'.[21] These rather unremarkable northern men had somewhat ordinary and everyday engagements with home. Barker's article exposes the oddity of a historiography that has occluded such ordinariness, and provides an invaluable piece as we reassemble the jigsaw.

In this chapter, I wish to develop the body of work that reconstructs men's domestic activities against a lightly drawn 'ideal of manhood'. But I wish to do this by employing a thorough-going cultural–historical approach that can generate in fuller form the meaningful historical concepts with which contemporaries understood the complicated nature of men's relationship with home. Narratives proposing an absence of domestic authority and a feminine domesticity can work against an historically sensitive account of men and the eighteenth-century home. Here I seek to develop a convincing framework through which we can study men's engagements with the home, one to join the ranks of 'domesticity', 'separate spheres' and 'political patriarchalism' as something for historians to think with. But is also important that such a framework enables us to envisage texts not as prescriptive normative ideals or prototypes, but as flexible discourses that were adopted as meaningful ways of seeing, thinking and living and that operated materially in practice.

In this venture, I take one significant lead from Michael McKeon's important book *The Secret History of Domesticity: Public, Private, and the Division of Knowledge* (2005).[22] Gender is not a central organising concept in this book; the primary concern is with separation, and the differing ways in which the concepts of 'public' and 'private' are applied to knowledge and experience over time. By the late seventeenth century, the long process of separation is under way and an ever-increasing series of divisions between public and private ensues: of the family and state, home and public, women and men. During the eighteenth century, all manner of things come to be explicitly separated through the shifting categories of 'public' and 'private'. Significantly, though, while in this modern world things are explicitly separated into 'public' and 'private', they are ultimately conflated. It is within domesticity, argues McKeon, that the conflation of 'public' and 'private' takes place.

In an historiographical context where 'home' is the 'private', feminine and largely female element of a world shaped by 'separate spheres', McKeon's case for separation but also *conflation* is an original and provocative thesis. This chapter shares with McKeon's project a desire to move past arguments for the separation of public and private and also to expose the political and ethical issues that continued to be embedded within domesticity, but it does so through a particular focus on masculinity. Thinking about men and the home – or about the home through men – will hopefully yield new insights about both. In words that owe a conscious debt to feminist and women's historians, my intention is not simply to put men back into the historical record of home, but to consider the revision of that historical record.

Meanings of home

In suggesting that attention to masculinity changes our understanding of home, I want to explore first what 'home' meant in this period. What is the 'it' with which men engaged, and how did this change over time? Several historians have attended to contemporary meanings of the descriptors used to portray the domestic unit. These cultural–linguistic studies revise earlier demographic and social history approaches, producing conceptual frameworks nurtured ground up from the historical sources, rather than modelled by the historian. David Sabean's groundbreaking study *Property, Production, and Family* (1990) included a sustained analysis of terms associated with '*haus*' ('house') in the south German village of Neckarhausen between 1700 and 1870.[23] Occurring in various forms in other words, *haus* was the term most commonly used until the nineteenth century to refer to the family. The term had wide application, alluding to many issues relating to economy, management and power, while also accommodating the flux of connections within, without and through the house. There are many echoes of Sabean's study in the work of Naomi Tadmor on England. Tadmor proposes the concept of 'household-family' as that which accords most closely with contemporaries' descriptions and understandings of their own experience; household-families were delimited not by blood and marriage, but by 'the boundaries of authority and of household management'.[24]

These studies demonstrate that the definition of our unit of study impacts upon our vision of gender and the home. The findings of both Sabean and Tadmor are highly suggestive for a study of men and the home. Sabean showed that *haus* was invariably tied to management, and that in a range of discourses the person responsible for this at a general level was a man.[25] In Tadmor's study, a 'household-family' comprised 'persons living under the same roof and under the authority of a householder'.[26] Cultural–historical approaches have opened up rich, complex and labile contemporary definitions of house, household and household-family; definitions that often have men woven into their very fabric.

We lack a comparable in-depth study of the term or concept of 'home' in everyday use, though in this chapter there is space and warrant for a brief analysis. We could look to various types of source to outline these points; printed dictionaries are admittedly limited sources, but as they are necessarily concerned with distilling precise, concise and clear meanings, they offer a useful starting point. The main finding here is that 'home' was increasingly distinguishable from related terms such as 'house', 'household' and 'family'. Contemporary meanings of home, particularly in the later eighteenth century, suggest something other than a collection of social relationships (family), an economic unit (household), a physical construction (house or domestic interior), or a co-resident unit bounded by household management (household-family). Instead, 'home' encompassed all these meanings and more, connoting emotional states and serving imaginative or representational functions. In any analysis, we must keep in mind both the instability of these meanings and the possibility that users of terms could activate different meanings at different times; the term referred to many different levels of experience, but over time became a noun of state.

English printed dictionaries show that while 'family' and 'house' appear through-out the seventeenth century, 'home' appears as a later inclusion in the eighteenth cen-tury.[27] In Edward Phillips's *The New World of Words* (6th edn, 1706), 'home' is defined simply as 'House or Place of Abode'. Notably, the description continues: 'Homely, ugly, disagreeable, course, mean': 'home' had ambivalent connotations, here.[28] John Kersey's *A New English Dictionary* (1731) similarly defined home as, 'a House or Place of Abode', and it was this definition that endured in dictionaries throughout the first half of the eighteenth century.[29] Similarly brief definitions were given in early entries for the term 'domestic'. The 1658 edition of *The New World of Words* gave 'tame, belonging to a family, or houshold'.[30] The 1724 edition of the *Universal Etymo-logical English Dictionary* expanded upon this, defining 'domesticity' as 'the being a Servant' and 'domestick' as 'belonging to a Household, or one's Country in Opposition to *Foreign*'.[31] Home and domestic may have later become interchangeable, yet they were not partnered at this stage.

As the century progressed, and as the printed dictionary genre itself transformed, dictionary definitions gave fuller meanings to these two terms, and also began to con-nect them. Samuel Johnson's unique volumes were, of course, particularly fulsome. 'Domestical. Domestick' meant 'Belonging to the house; not relating to things pub-lick', 'Private; done at home; not open', 'Inhabiting the house; not wild', and 'Not foreign; intestine'. According to Johnson, 'To domesticate' was 'To make domestick; to withdraw from the publick'. The definitions of 'home' in Johnson's work were similarly rich. Home was '*His* own house; the private dwelling' – illustrated by a quotation from Dryden in which 'Home is the sacred refuge of our life, / Secur'd from all approaches but a wife – and '*His* own country'. The possessives here chime with Sabean's and Tadmor's emphasis on male management or authority. Third, 'home' was 'The place of constant residence', and fourth, united to a substantive, 'home' signified 'domestick, or of the same country'.[32] Change occurred in other dictionaries too, if a little later. The 25th edition of Bailey's *Universal Etymological English Dic-tionary* (1783) expanded earlier definitions of 'domesticate' into, 'to make domestic, to withdraw from the public'.[33] Ambivalence has all but gone, now, and 'home' is a capacious entity: separate, comforting and familiar, a place of belonging but also of possession.

Dictionaries are suggestive, but they do not give a full sense of the contemporary meaning or resonance of words. They also often fail to capture the speed of change. It is clear from the sources used by Johnson, but also from many other types of document, that home had already come to mean more than 'house' some time before 1755. Modern editions of the *Oxford English Dictionary* also suggest a shift in the early decades of the eighteenth century. The first definition of domestic, 'The quality or state of being domestic, domestic character; home or family life; devotion to home; homeliness', is supported with citations from 1721 and 1726, both of which refer to 'domesticity'. The earliest use of 'domesticate' given by the modern *OED* is 1639, with the second dating from 1773. Following definitions of home as a simple noun (commonly as a dwelling-place), the *OED* lists the third as a noun of state: 'The place of one's dwelling or nurturing, with the conditions, circumstances, and feelings which naturally and properly attach to it, and are associated with it'. Though there are no uses from the eighteenth century, the earliest is from *c.*1460, with increasing frequency from 1813.[34] In pursuing our question 'what did home mean and how did this change?', dictionaries show an increasing range of meanings, and point to the nineteenth century as a period of particularly frequent use.

If, as I noted earlier, eighteenth-century Britain was the birthplace of domesticity, then for many it was certainly in nineteenth-century Britain that this culture of home became fully realised. John Tosh identifies a specifically nineteenth-century concept of domesticity, combining 'privacy and comfort, separation from the workplace, and the merging of domestic space and family members into a single commanding concept (in English, 'home')'. Tosh adds that domesticity worked symbolically, acquiring 'psychological and emotional dimensions'.[35] Davidoff and Hall have demonstrated that in the final two decades of the eighteenth century a number of writers began to draw on the rich emotional pull of this kind of home.[36] In these (often rural) scenes, the 'fireside enjoyments [and] home-born happiness' are constituted by the family circle, rather than by a wife or mother.[37] Significantly, it is a male narrator who eulogises the experience of the space from within. This was mirrored in much late eighteenth-century writing. An emerging middle-class domesticity of such emotional and psychological depth did not exclude men; they were a (literally) central part of its constitution.

As several scholars of eighteenth-century domestic novels demonstrate, though, home had accommodated such psychological and representational depths some decades earlier.[38] I have already offered some examples from dictionaries, though there is ample opportunity to undertake a more extensive analysis of uses of 'home' in sources such as novels and diaries, that (as Tadmor reminds us) show words in 'active' use.[39] Many examples could be marshalled to demonstrate how home meant much more than an abode; it could be congruent with contentment and relaxation, juxtaposed against the outside, and fulfilling many of the functions mentioned by Tosh.[40] The simple point, here, is that late eighteenth-century notions of home were not entirely new. While meanings of 'home' were unstable throughout the eighteenth century, and it is difficult to offer a very precise chronology, it is possible to tell a story of a gradual shift towards deeper and also broader definitions of 'home'.

Yet before tracing the origins of nineteenth-century understandings of home back-wards, we can render this general picture more precisely by establishing a clearer chronology of eighteenth-century developments and of what kind of 'domesticity' we can find and when. While the foregoing brief analysis might suggest a gradual pro-gression in changes in meaning, when combined with other sources we can identify one distinct stage in the development of eighteenth-century 'domesticity' followed by a period of rapid intensification. The first stage involves material changes relating to comfort and sociability. Focusing on domestic possessions over the period 1550–1774, Carole Shammas identifies an important shift in the 1720s, as female work patterns became oriented towards home consumption and sociability, opposed to the sociability outside the home engaged in by men. Using tea objects as 'tools of domesticity', women gleaned autonomy through a new kind of home. 'Domesticity', Shammas claims, was 'largely a female cause'.[41]

This period is also regarded as a turning point in the domestic environment by Lorna Weatherill, who found that the new consumer goods were found in a range of inventories by *c*.1725.[42] Unlike Shammas, though, Weatherill is not convinced that women were the catalysts. Studying possessions between 1660 and 1740, Weatherill found no evidence of a female subculture of material culture values. Notably, men and women apparently consumed utensils for hot drinks in equal measure.[43] For the later period 1751 to 1781, evidence has been uncovered for gendered patterns of consumption amongst the gentry, with men's intermittent, impulsive, expensive and dynastic consumption contrasting with women's pattern of regular, visible, mundane and repetitive purchasing.[44] Margot Finn's study of middling-sort men shows that we have underestimated male consumption. She insists that men were keenly acquisitive and had great personal investment in small things.[45] 'Consumption', of course, refers equally well to the act of purchase, decision-making prior to purchase, the provision of resources to enable the purchase, or the responsibility for the care of the object, and it is difficult to determine who may have been involved more actively in each aspect. Even work on detailed accounting records is inconclusive with regard to general patterns of decision-making between married couples.[46] So, while we might expect – and there is indeed evidence for – differences in some of the things that men and women selected and bought, it is not entirely clear that women consumed (in any sense of the word) more of the material things from which home was made. Indeed, taking the work on consumption on its own terms, with a focus on purchase, possession and use, there is ample evidence that men were fully engaged in this new material world of home.[47]

Whether or not men and women played an equally significant role in these material changes in the home, it is precisely at this time that Michael McKeon sees crucial changes in literature. Once the small had explicated the large, the familiar conveyed the unfamiliar; thus the small and familiar issues of the domestic represented the big, arcane issues pertaining to public. In the decades after 1714–15, literary works display 'the gradual shift of normative weight from the public referent to the private reference – more precisely, the gradual absorption of the public realm's traditional priority and privilege by the realm of private experience'.[48] Subsequently, the domestic shifted from 'a means to an end, from an instrumental signifier to a self-sufficient signified'.[49] Within the domestic novel, domesticity comes to represent the public by itself. This becomes clearest following experiments in the early novel, crystallising (in McKeon's narrative) in Jane Austen's *Pride and Prejudice* (1813). McKeon ends his study with an account of how, in the character of Mr Darcy, Austen displays 'the politics that inhere within the domestic realm of the family in politically resonant conflicts'; McKeon uses this as exemplary of the separation but also conflation of public and private in the domestic novel.[50]

Teasing out this chronology in the development of domesticity – the culture that surrounds 'home' – registering as a material shift in inventories from the early eighteenth century, and in a range of imaginative literature culminating in the (political) 'domestic novel' in the later eighteenth century, shows that 'home' was an entity created at a number of different levels. It reinforces evidence for the unstable, varying and intertwined meanings of the concept discussed above. And the engagement of men in making the eighteenth-century home can be more fully exposed if we recognise the different dimensions to domesticity. Whether constituted by authority, things, emotional or representational richness, men were implicated in, even necessary to, its constitution.

At home or abroad?

Having examined what home meant and some of the things from which it was made, I now want to focus on the substantive content of texts that discuss men's and women's roles in the home. For this, I draw on a survey of a large body of literature commonly described as 'prescriptive', and which gives us a much better sense of the labour involved in making 'home'. It is not difficult to find a straightforward gendering of home and outside in the rich and fulsome print culture of late seventeenth- and eighteenth-century England. Gervase Markham's works – which were republished several times throughout this period and are exemplary of a sub-genre of print on the home – are typical in this regard.[51] Markham placed 'the perfect Husbandman, who is the Father and Master of the Family', most assuredly 'for the most part abroad or removed from the house', while his 'English House-wife, who is the Mother and Mistress of the family ... hath her most general imployments within the house'.[52] Richard Bradley, a later prolific writer of books on household and family, echoed Markham's distinctions. Bradley's book on housewifery of 1732 made a clear statement of gendered domains: 'The Art of Oeconomy is divided, as Xenophon tell us, between the Men and the Women; the Men have the most dangerous and laborious Share of it in the Fields, and without doors, and the Women have the Care and Management of every Business within doors'.[53]

Such statements – of women's responsibility for housewifery and men's for husbandry – are undoubtedly prominent in many printed books on household and family. Separation is central to the discussions of home in these works. But these sources are not mono-vocal texts that simply disassociate men and the home. In the case of books like those by Markham and Bradley, these are works authored by men, and in which those authors often included lengthy autobiographical prefaces that openly address the male author's engagements with the domestic. Bradley, for example, apologised for publishing a book which 'falls within the Ladies' Jurisdiction, excusing himself on the grounds that he was seeking 'rather to assist, than to direct'.[54] Modest excuses notwithstanding, the second part of Bradley's *The Country Housewife and Lady's Director* is dedicated to a man: 'Sir Hans Sloane, Bart. President of the Royal Society'.[55] And no longer is the tone one of advising knowledgeable women: the first letter in the book is from a man telling Bradley how he has firmly directed his wife in the matter of salting meat, and then advising Bradley on how it should be done.[56] Here are men with intimate knowledge of (and strong opinions about) the minutiae of domestic life, at least in the kitchen. Despite some of the rhetoric, men were indoors, writing domestic manuals in an authoritative tone, serving as dedicatees, directing women in kitchen practices and reporting the results to male writers.

On the other side of the household venture was husbandry. Books on husbandry were written by men and directed at male readers. The preface of Gervase Markham's *Cheap and Good Husbandry* (14th edn, 1683) was directed 'To the courteous reader' seeking to 'preserve and keep *his* Horse from all suddain extremities'.[57] And in practice, of course, skill in working the ground took men away from the house (Figure 3). One plate accompanying Richard Bradley's *A Complete Body of Husbandry* (1727)

Figure 3: Richard Bradley's *A Complete Body of Husbandry* (1727). © The British Library Board (R.B.23.a.12058)

shows the husbandman watering his horse in open land in the foreground, with the house behind and surrounded by land enclosed by a fence.[58] Such books certainly described some overlap between the roles of men and women; sections on malting and beekeeping, for example, talked about the shared responsibilities of husband and wife. But while separation was not complete, the emphasis was on interdependence rather than the equivalency of tasks.

To interpret printed works on husbandry as merely practical guides to working the land and as 'sources' of information about who was thought to do what misses some of the functions of these texts, though. These were not simply practical manuals. Alongside discussion of men's work, for example, treatises on husbandry include many allusions to men's leisure. Robert Brown's *The Compleat Farmer; or, the Whole Art of Husbandry* (1759) is illustrated with a title-page that smacks of eighteenth-century fantasies of the pastoral, and contains advertisements for books on letter writing, sport, jests and wooing.[59] Reading about husbandry could be a form of recreation. Moreover, husbandry in these works becomes a site of fantasy. As indicated by the full title of Gervase Markham's *Country Contentments; or the Husbandman's Recreations. Containing The Wholesome Experience, in which any ought to Recreate himself, after the Toyl of more Serious Business*, such rural activity operated imaginatively as a refuge.[60]

In this way, these books were domestic objects. John Flavell's *Husbandry Spiritualized* (1669) described his reader – a male husbandman – inside the house during the evening.[61] In line with this image of the male reader in the home (rather than the field), many books on husbandry lack contents pages and/or indexes that would allow a reader to navigate the work for practical purposes. Instead, they are sometimes long, dense discussions about the idea of husbandry. The frontispiece to *Husbandry Moralized; or, Pleasant Sunday Reading for a Farmer's Kitchen* (1795?) seems to display its reader and his wife in a room, presumably the kitchen of the sub-title. In this way, frontispiece and title page work together to proclaim the book a domestic object to be consumed in the home.[62] Such books are not geared to the practice of husbandry. Just as 'home' served representational functions, so husbandry was used to think with. In both the examples noted above, husbandry held spiritual meanings: Flavell's *Husbandry Spiritualized* begins, 'In the laborious Husbandman you see, / What all true Christians are, or ought to be'.[63] The religious aspects of home continued to be prominent themes in writing about the home and husbandry well before the evangelical revival so crucial to some later formulations of domestic ideology.[64] Josiah Woodward's *The Necessary Duty of Family Prayer* (first published in 1717 and running to at least thirteen editions before 1800) was expressive of this persistence, targeted at the 'good Housholder' and 'the little Assembly of his Family'.[65] Yet whether as a spiritual aid or not, the content of these books cautions against seeing them as evidence for a masculine part of a gendered inside/outside dichotomy. Moreover, while invariably directed to male readers, they were surely used by both men and women: the 'husbandman' to which one copy of Flavell's book belonged, and who inscribed their name on its pages, was 'Phebe Chiselden'.[66]

Printed guides to housewifery and husbandry establish a gendered interior and exterior and deploy an undeniable rhetoric of separation, but this is disrupted by their content and 'objectness'. Moreover, there was another sub-genre that projected the family as a shared enterprise. Family advice books, particularly from the mid-eighteenth century, were geared to both men and women, to 'private Families',[67] or to 'Master, Mistresses, and Servants'.[68] And in many of these family advice books and general books on household economy, while certain sections were directed at men specifically (notably hunting), most were simply directed to the general (genderless) reader. If anything, this became more pronounced as the long eighteenth century wore on. The terms used in printed texts to refer to the key players in this shared endeavour reflect a contemporary understanding of the overlapping and shared responsibilities in the household. 'House-keeper', for example, applied to both men and women: Dudley North, the author of *Observations and Advices Oeconomical* (1669), proudly reassured his readers, 'I have been a House-keeper a great part of my dayes'.[69] Markham refers to 'the general profit which accreweth and ariseth to the *Husband House wife*, and the whole Family' through malting,[70] and in a later discussion of oats explains, 'no *Husband Housewife*, or *House keeper*, whatsoever hath so true and worthy a friend, as his Oats are'.[71] The terms 'housewife' and 'housekeeper' were not reserved solely for women.

The image projected by family advice books reinforces the 'common culture' of home shared by middling-sort men and women and noted by Hunt. It also provides some support for Bailey's finding that 'co-dependency breaks down the crude assignment of differently gendered ideas and expectations to these activities'.[72] Yet as Bailey is aware, co-dependency does not mean men and women did the same things; indeed, there are distinct gendered differences observable in the application of terms such as 'housewife' and 'housekeeper'. When used positively by, or relating to, men, 'housekeeping' referred to the process of setting up, or the period of being in, a house that belonged to them. Thomas Naish had been married and living with his wife for some years, when he described how, in 1701, he 'parted from my father and mother and went my selfe to house keeping'.[73] Daniel Renaud and his wife Christine shared their house with Daniel's uncle, until the latter married in 1730 and, as Daniel notes, 'We began To keep House'.[74] Neither Naish nor Renaud owned their houses, though they were both married. But starting to 'keep house' was not necessarily undertaken by married men. The Lancaster tradesman William Stout made frequent reference to keeping house, though he remained unmarried throughout his life. Each new stage in Stout's housekeeping usually coincided with a physical move but always involved the arrival of a new female presence in the home: he first reports how he 'began to keep house' with his sister in 1691, how, in 1734, he 'resolved to keepe house' with his two nieces, and how, from *c*.1739–1742 he was joined by the servant Mary Bayley with whom he, 'kept house . . . with good content'.[75]

In these men's lives, housekeeping was more to do with ownership or authority than with the detail of domestic chores. It is here, in unpicking the gendered application of words in print and manuscript, that we can detect the different relationships with home imagined for men and women. While both were expected to have a close and involved engagement with home – both were housekeepers – the nature of that engagement was different. For contemporaries, 'housekeeping' undertaken by men was understood as management – 'oeconomy' – taking place at a global level. In the final section of this chapter, I will examine more closely how oeconomy was understood, how it maps onto changing meanings of home and domesticity, and some of the implications of this for the historical study of the home.

The extensive sense of oeconomy

It was through a model of oeconomy that contemporaries framed and articulated men's engagement with the many components of 'home' noted so far: management and authority, material objects, emotional and representational functions and a continuing political and national relevance. Given the chronology of domesticity outlined above, it is significant that the 1720s were an important decade in printed works on oeconomy. In 1725, Richard Bradley revised and translated Noel Chomel's *Dictionaire Oeconomique: or, The Family Dictionary*.[76] This monumental work brought together all the topics one might find scattered in a host of other family books. As in the original, Bradley's two-volume work is organised alphabetically. There are entries on bread, brewing and brick-making, on gout, grafting and gravy, and on lemonade, lettice and 'loosness'. Bradley's preface, however, imposes a spatial, rather than alphabetical, order on the work's main body: 'Having now instructed us in the Manner of improving Estates without Doors', Bradley writes of Chomel, 'he then brings us home, and prescribes the best and cheapest Way of providing and managing all manner of Meats and Sauces in the Kitchen'.[77] In framing Chomel's dictionary with outside/inside distinctions, Bradley brought this work into line with the many English printed works on the topic (several of which he himself was writing). And yet such spatial distinctions, as discussed above, were disrupted. The definition of oeconomy in the main text of the dictionary straddled inside and outside: 'OECONOMY, a certain Order in the Management of a Family and domestick Affairs: Hence the Word Oeconomist, for a good Manager. But Oeconomy may be taken in a more extensive Sense, for a just, prudent, and regular Conduct in all the Parts of Life, and relative Capacities'.[78] This definition takes us to the heart of oeconomy as a general system of management and order; but it also shows how the 'extensive sense' was predicated on relations between – not separation of – 'all the Parts of Life'.

Such connections were also foregrounded in Bradley's 1727 translation of Xenophon's classic work on oeconomy. Xenophon's work had already served as a model for many more 'popular' household books in this period.[79] Bradley's translation continued this tradition but, whereas Chomel's dictionary was a practical guide, Xenophon's text was a work of philosophy and the most thoroughgoing discussion of the topic published in English in the first half of the century. Yet there were important overlaps between the works. In the translation of Xenophon, Bradley gave the definition of oeconomy as, 'the just and regular Distribution of a Man's Goods, or the wise Management of his Possessions, or of his Household'.[80] The major theme was order: the practice of oeconomy was 'the Ordering of a House'.[81] This involved the husband paying close attention to the items bought for the home and the nature of interior decoration: the house should not, Bradley explains, be filled with 'unnecessary Decorations', but be 'built with due Consideration, and for the Conveniency of the Inhabitants'.[82] Men were participants in the mundane and everyday in the popular books, and they were also global managers or instructors. The 'extensive sense' of this participation remained pronounced in Xenophon, too. Oeconomy rendered the home a training ground for skills that were at the heart of all manly behaviour. Oeconomy earned men 'Honour and Reputation' and taught them self-governance, an important virtue of any man seeking masculine status.[83] A man who can manage his household, argued Xenophon, can command kingdoms.

The classical theory of oeconomy envisaged the *oikos* – the household community – being governed with two aims in mind: 'securing and increasing the wealth of the household and the proper use of the wealth thereby created'.[84] The involvement of men in the many levels of this venture in early modern texts is not surprising. Yet in classical theory, the household is ordered by a hierarchy separate from and different to that operating in the market and the polity.[85] It is noteworthy that early modern oeconomy armed men with a political role. Dudley North's *Observations and Advices Oeconomical* (1669) high-end treatise is a good example. Here, oeconomy in the family is critical for the state: 'the government of private Families may be considerable even with Princes', North writes in the Preface, 'because . . . they who are known to have well governed their private fortunes, are the rather judged fit for Publick Offices'.[86] He continued: 'Writers very considerable fetch their chief argument for Monarchy (as being the most natural and ancient Government) from its Conformity with the Paternal'.[87] Late seventeenth-century writers melded theories of oeconomy with political patriarchalism.

Typical of oeconomy's usage in the many early eighteenth-century household manuals that later emerged was the discussion by Daniel Defoe in *The Family Instructor* (1715). Defoe's book delineated the appropriate and mutual duties of all family members. The first part concerned 'paternal Duty, such as Instruction, Reproof, Authority and Discipline in a Father'; the second part described 'the Duty of Heads of Families as Masters of Servants, and how Servants ought to submit to Instruction and Family Regulation'; while the final part attended to 'the Duty of Husbands and Wives to exhort and perswade, intreat, instruct, and *by all gentle Means* if possible, prevail and engage one another to a religious holy Life'.[88] Such relatively secular household manuals about order were a new genre for the burgeoning audience of print. And here, political patriarchalism is less pronounced; this is partly due to genre (this is a household manual not a philosophical work). But it is also because writers are speaking not to landowners with stewards and a fleet of other servants, but to smaller householders who nevertheless might occupy (or seek to acquire) positions of moral or social status in the local community.

Yet the political significance of order in the household remains in works throughout the period. Of particular note is the popular *The Oeconomy of Human Life*, first published in 1751, with 142 editions between 1750 and 1800, and a further ninety-five from 1801.[89] This text – the substantive sections of which remained the same through the many editions – repackaged patriarchalism and oeconomic order for a new audience. Oeconomy is here a system of morality built upon and exercised through ordered domestic relationships. The first part laid out guides for the conduct of men in a series of roles – husband, father, son, brother – and then in position to others outside the home: wise and ignorant, rich and poor, masters and servants, magistrates and subjects. Benevolence is a key theme, but strict obedience is also necessary. Describing the relationship between master and servant, there is little trace of reciprocity, but rather a taxonomy of the powers and responsibilities of the king: he who is 'clothed in purple' creates laws for his 'subjects', is merciful and punishes justly; 'His people therefore look up to him as a father', the author explains, 'with reverence and love'.[90]

The Oeconomy of Human Life was a general guide to living, not a manual on the everyday ordering of the household economy. While the use of the terms 'housekeeper' and 'housekeeping' discussed above demonstrates men's application of notions of oeconomy to the home, men also employed oeconomy in its extensive sense. In court depositions, some uses pertained to household management or relations, but others reveal oeconomy's moral elements. For example, at his trial for deception in 1747, some of the questioning naturally focused on Hugh Pelling's character. The witness John Thomson gave a good account, explaining that he 'found him to be a Man of great Probity and Honour . . . a Man of good Oeconomy'.[91] In this case, which alleged the falsification of papers to defraud, Pelling's financial probity was clearly central, and he was acquitted. Here, 'oeconomy' connoted the value of rules of right living. Oeconomy also facilitated independence – from some other men and women, but also from the passions and emotions – and thus enabled a man to be truly just, fair and honest. This affected the home but could also be applied outside, sometimes in the most public of arenas. Writing on the value of literary reviews in 1760, the clergyman and novelist Lawrence Sterne commented that in the context of 'the inconstancy of what is called the Public', 'a well judged œconomy . . . provided against the temptations of a mean and servile dependency'.[92] Men used oeconomy to indicate the provisioning and governance of the home, but also the uniting of economy and morality, along with the public relevance of this.

Importantly, though, such extensive meanings and applications of oeconomy remained tethered to a concern for men's involvement in the nitty-gritty of household. To his *Rural Oeconomy* (1770), Arthur Young appended a translation of a German text called *The Rural Socrates*, describing it as an example, 'not only of oeconomy, industry, sobriety, and every domestick virtue, but also of most spirited husbandry'.[93]

Alongside Young's practical advice for husbandry, the translation compares the need for the regulation of a man's 'domestick affairs by the rules of a wise and prudent oeconomy', to that of 'the wisest systems of legislature, and the best political institutions' that also require 'a general scheme of oeconomy, sensibly executed'.[94] Throughout the century, this 'vernacular tradition' – interested in the practical involvement of men in the mundane and everyday domestic within a vision of virtuous and useful masculinity – ran alongside works such as Bradley's translation and *The Oeconomy of Human Life*. This tradition incorporated many different levels of activity within an overarching model of moral and economic domestic management. The Newcastle periodical the *Oeconomist* (published monthly in Newcastle upon Tyne at the very end of the eighteenth century, between January 1798 and December 1799) is a rare and late example.[95] Essays and miscellania discussed the topics of the cottage, food, farming, poverty and diet, while a banner in the frontispiece read 'Truth Liberty Virtue'. Throughout, morality and economy closely connect. Thus articles on the rights of men and their conduct in society, soup kitchens in Newcastle and English history sit side by side. Oeconomy was no longer a classical model of ordering the household's resources to safeguard and increase wealth and exercise one's skills as a manager; in the later examples, oeconomy is a model of order and management designed to ensure prudence and a public-spirited virtue.

There were, therefore, contours to and changes in the discourse of oeconomy. But from Dudley North's *Observations and advices oeconomical* (1669), to Arthur Young's *Rural Oeconomy* (1770), and through the many editions of *The Oeconomy of Human Life* and issues of *The Oeconomist*, oeconomy was reiterated and developed as a viable model of household living built around male domestic management. The late date of some of these works is very important. Shammas has suggested that the term 'oeconomy' was used by liberal theorists to discuss production, speculating that it was adapted from the household to give 'private activities primacy in the generation of wealth and downplaying the importance of government policies'.[96] McKeon has similarly argued that the management of household economy became the model for management of the larger economy through 'political economy'. This left 'the household divested of its economic function [which] became the model for the "domestic sphere"'.[97] 'Oeconomic' would thus be an earlier version of 'economic', and furthermore the development of 'political economy' – with its focus on the market rather than household – would indicate the declining importance of the household to the polity. The significance of such a shift for the home is evident in Davidoff and Hall's comment that the home became 'the basis for a proper moral order in the amoral world of the market, [because] the new world of political economy necessitated a separate sphere of domestic economy'.[98] Here we have the linguistic and philosophical separation necessary for gendered separate spheres, perhaps.

In some instances, 'oeconomic' was certainly replaced by 'economic', but in others the meaning remained the same. William Cobbett's *Cottage Economy* (1822) explained, 'ECONOMY means, management, and nothing more; and it is generally applied to the affairs of a house and family'.[99] Works on political economy from this period described the etymology of the term. Jean-Baptiste Say explained that economy meant 'the law which regulates the household', and that 'political' referred to the extension of that law to society or the nation. Order in the household was an important illustration of the need for order in the political economy: 'A household, conducted without order, is preyed upon by all the world'.[100] These discussions indicate the persistence of a late seventeenth-century version of oeconomy in which the economic (and indeed political) function of households was not wholly absorbed by political economy. They show that oeconomy remained distinct from economy and political economy well into the eighteenth century and beyond, bringing together the home and the world, primarily through men's activities.

Conclusion

By the end of the eighteenth century, 'home' was understood to mean more than one's dwelling; it was a multi-faceted state of being, encompassing the emotional, physical, moral and spatial. New meanings jostled with old, though, and 'home' continued to encompass the political. This range of meanings was essential to the discourse of oeconomy. Male oeconomy insisted not only on homes as houses to keep and as households to manage, but also on homes as tools of management in a much broader context. As a meaningful discourse of masculinity, oeconomy emphasised a man's managerial engagement with home. It made 'housekeeping' central to manly status. It also made men central to the home. Oeconomy shows the ways in which men made homes and homes made men.

With its emphasis on provisioning and the physical environment, oeconomy focuses historians' attention on men's engagements with the important and changing material aspects of domesticity. But oeconomy further reorients our vision of home by foregrounding the continuing significance of men's domestic authority. Men's domestic management connected the most mundane domestic activity with governance within and without the house. Home remained a place with political resonance in ways that destabilise the supposed 'privacy' of domesticity. If 'public' and 'private' were conflated during the eighteenth century, then oeconomy was surely one instrument of this conflation. Oeconomy did change in this period but if explicit analogies between the household and polity faded, this was replaced by an emphasis on the skills and virtues of the benevolent citizen, and subsequently by attention to frugality and honest virtue in a national community. In the later texts, the actions of men in the home have become an implicit comment on ethical and political topics. Only then – when home had come to mean so much – could Rowlandson draw on such rich meanings for his visual narrative. Exploring the intersections of masculinity with this multi-faceted home shows why a satire on fidelity, hypocrisy, female power and male desire among the British elite was told through a story about a man and his homes.

Notes

1. For a recent summation of work in this area, and suggestions for future research, see Karen Harvey and Alexandra Shepard, 'What Have Historians Done with Masculinity? Reflections on Five Centuries of British History, circa 1500–1950', *Journal of British Studies* 44 (2005), pp. 274–80. I develop the ideas presented in this chapter in *Domesticating Patriarchy: Male Authority in the Eighteenth-Century English Home* (Oxford: Oxford University Press, in preparation).
2. Lena Cowen Orlin, *Private Matters and Public Culture in Post-Reformation England* (Ithaca and London: Cornell University Press, 1994), p. 3.
3. Susan Dwyer Amussen, *An Ordered Society: Gender and Class in Early Modern England* (New York: Columbia University Press, 1988), pp. 31–2, 101–3, 186.

4. Mary Beth Norton, *Founding Mothers and Fathers* (New York: A. A. Knopf, 1996), esp. pp. 404–5; Carole Shammas, *A History of Household Government* (London and Charlottesville: University of Virginia Press, 2002), p. 144.

5. Anthony Fletcher, *Gender, Sex and Subordination in England, 1500–1800* (New Haven and London: Yale University Press, 1995).

6. Elizabeth Kowaleski-Wallace, *Their Fathers' Daughters: Hannah More, Maria Edgeworth and Patriarchal Complicity* (New York and Oxford: Oxford University Press, 1991), p. 17.

7. Gordon J. Schochet, *The Authoritarian Family and Political Attitudes in 17th-Century England* (1975; repr. New Brunswick: Transaction Books, 1988), p. xxv. See also Gordon J. Schochet, 'The Significant Sounds of Silence: The Absence of Women from the Political Thought of Sir Robert Filmer and Locke (or "Why can't a woman be more like a man?")', in Hilda L. Smith (ed.), *Women Writers and the Early Modern British Political Tradition* (Cambridge: Cambridge University Press, 1998), pp. 220–42.

8. Key works on changes in domestic architecture include: Frank E. Brown, 'Continuity and Change in the Urban House: Developments in Domestic Space Organisation in Seventeenth-Century London', *Comparative Studies in Society and History* 28 (1986), pp. 558–90; Mark Girouard, *Life in the English Country House: A Social and Architectural History* (1978; repr. Harmondsworth: Penguin, 1980); Matthew Johnson, 'Redefining the Domestic', in Matthew Johnson, *An Archaeology of Capitalism* (Oxford: Blackwell, 1996), pp. 55–78. On the self, see e.g., Michael Mascuch, *Origins of the Individualist Self: Autobiography and Self-Identity in England, 1591–1791* (Cambridge: Polity Press, 1997); Patricia Meyer Spacks, *Privacy: Concealing the Eighteenth-Century Self* (Chicago and London: University of Chicago Press, 2003); Dror Wahrman, *The Making of the Modern Self: Identity and Culture in Eighteenth-Century England* (London and New Haven: Yale University Press, 2004).

9. Leonore Davidoff and Catherine Hall, *Family Fortunes: Men and Women of the English Middle Class, 1780–1850* (1987; repr. London: Routledge, 1992); John Smail, *The Origins of Middle Class Culture: Halifax, Yorkshire, 1660–1780* (Ithaca, NY: Cornell University Press, 1995).

10. Anna Clark, *Struggle for the Breeches: Gender and the Making of the British Working Class* (Berkeley, Los Angeles and London: University of California Press, 1995); Dror Wahrman, *Imagining the Middle Class: The Political Representation of Class in Britain, c.1780–1840* (Cambridge: Cambridge University Press, 1995), pp. 377–408.

11. For a fuller discussion of this, see Karen Harvey, 'The History of Masculinity, circa 1650–1800', in Karen Harvey and Alexandra Shepard (eds), 'Special Feature on Masculinities', *Journal of British Studies* 44 (2005), pp. 298–300.

12. See e.g., Elizabeth Foyster, *Manhood in Early Modern England: Honour, Sex and Marriage* (Harlow: Addison, Wesley, Longman, 1999).

13. John Tosh, *A Man's Place: Masculinity and the Middle-Class Home in Victorian England* (New Haven and London: Yale University Press, 1999), p. 50. See also Deborah Cohen, *Household Gods: The British and their Possessions* (New Haven and London: Yale University Press, 2006), pp. 81–121.

14. Amanda Vickery, *The Gentleman's Daughter: Women's Lives in Georgian England* (New Haven and London: Yale University Press, 1998), p. 127. The degree of actual power women gleaned through this domestic role is a topic of some debate. See e.g., Kathryn Shevelow, *Women and Print Culture: The Construction of Femininity in the Early Periodical* (London: Routledge, 1989); Nancy Armstrong, *Desire and Domestic Fiction: A Political History of the Novel* (Oxford and New York: Oxford University Press, 1987).

15. Margaret Hunt, *The Middling Sort: Commerce, Gender, and the Family in England, 1680–1780* (Berkeley: University of California Press, 1996), p. 170.

16. Hunt, *Middling Sort*, p. 9.

17. Joanne Bailey, *Unquiet Lives: Marriage and Marriage Breakdown in England, 1660–1800* (Cambridge: Cambridge University Press, 2003), p. 199.

18. Bailey, *Unquiet Lives*, p. 199.

19. Shawn Lisa Maurer, *Proposing Men: Dialectics of Gender and Class in the Eighteenth-Century English Periodical* (Stanford, CA: Stanford University Press, 1999), p. 3.

20. Maurer, *Proposing Men*, pp. 3, 231.

21. Hannah Barker, 'Soul, Purse and Family: Middling and Lower-Class Masculinity in Eighteenth-Century Manchester', *Social History* 33 (2008), pp. 12–35, here p. 18.

22. Michael McKeon, *The Secret History of Domesticity: Public, Private, and the Division of Knowledge* (Baltimore and London: Johns Hopkins University Press, 2005).

23. David Sabean, *Property, Production, and Family in Neckarhausen, 1700–1870* (Cambridge: Cambridge University Press, 1990), pp. 88–123.

24. Naomi Tadmor, 'The Concept of the Household-Family in Eighteenth-Century England', *Past & Present* 151 (1996), pp. 111–40, here p. 120. See also Naomi Tadmor, *Family and Friends in Eighteenth-Century England: Household, Kinship and Patronage* (Cambridge: Cambridge University Press, 2001), pp. 18–43.

25. Sabean, *Property, Production, and Family*, pp. 107–13.

26. Tadmor, 'Concept of the Household-Family', p. 118.

27. These findings are based on a sample of twenty dictionaries published between 1658 and 1800.

28. Edward Phillips, *The New World of Words: or, Universal English Dictionary* (6th edn, London: J. Philips, 1706).

29. John Kersey, *A New English Dictionary* (3rd edn, London: Robert Knaplock, 1731).

30. E.[dward] P.[hillips], *The New World of English Words: Or, a General Dictionary* (London: E. Tyler, 1658).

31. These definitions remained consistent over at least two editions: N[athan] Bailey, *An Universal Etymological English Dictionary* (2nd edn, London: E. Bell et al., 1724). N[athan] Bailey, *An Universal Etymological English Dictionary* (10th edn, London: R. Ware et al., 1742).

32. These definitions remained consistent over at least two editions. Samuel Johnson, *A Dictionary of the English Language*, 2 vols (2nd edn, London: W. Strahan, 1755–56), vol. 1. Samuel Johnson, *A Dictionary of the English Language* (4th edn, London: W. Strahan et al., 1773). Italics my emphasis.

33. N[athan] Bailey, *An Universal Etymological English Dictionary* (25th edn, Edinburgh: Neill and Company, 1783).

34. *Oxford English Dictionary* (2nd edn, Oxford: Oxford University Press, 1989).

35. Tosh, *Man's Place*, pp. 4, 30.

36. Davidoff and Hall, *Family Fortunes*, pp. 149–92.

37. William Cowper, *The Task* (London: J. Johnson, 1785), p. 144.

38. Christopher Flint, *Family Fictions: Narrative and Domestic Relations in Britain, 1688–1798* (Stanford, CA: Stanford University Press, 1998); Ruth Perry, *Novel Relations: The Transformation of Kinship in English Literature and Culture, 1748–1818* (Cambridge: Cambridge University Press, 2004).

39. Tadmor, 'Concept of the Household-Family', p. 113.

40. See e.g., Letter 8, 'On the Method of employing Time', 'Mrs. T—ss's Advice to her Daughter', *Lady's Magazine* (1775), p. 720.

41. Carole Shammas, 'The Domestic Environment in Early Modern England and America', *Journal of Social History* 14 (1980), pp. 3–24, here pp. 5, 16.

42. Lorna Weatherill, *Consumer Behaviour and Material Culture in Britain, 1660–1760* (London: Routledge, 1988).

43. Lorna Weatherill, 'A Possession of One's Own: Women and Consumer Behaviour in England, 1660–1740', *Journal of British Studies* 25 (1986), pp. 131–56.

44. Amanda Vickery, 'Women and the World of Goods: A Lancashire Consumer and her Possessions, 1751–81', in John Brewer and Roy Porter (eds), *Consumption and the World of Goods: Consumption and Society in the Seventeenth and Eighteenth Centuries* (London: Routledge, 1993), pp. 274–301.

45. Margot Finn, 'Men's Things: Masculine Possession in the Consumer Revolution', *Social History* 25 (2000), pp. 133–54.

46. Amanda Vickery, 'His and Hers: Gender, Consumption and Household Accounting in Eighteenth-Century England', *Past & Present* Supplement 1 (2006), pp. 12–38.

47. See also Karen Harvey, 'Barbarity in a Teacup? Punch, Domesticity and Gender in the Eighteenth Century', *Journal of Design History* 21 (2008), pp. 205–21; Harvey, *Domesticating Patriarchy*, ch. 4.

48. McKeon, *Secret History of Domesticity*, p. 621.

49. McKeon, *Secret History of Domesticity*, p. 327.

50. McKeon, *Secret History of Domesticity*, p. 716.

51. Markham's book on husbandry, first published in 1614, was published as late as 1707. Markham's book on housewifery, first published in 'A Way to get Wealth' in 1623, was published as late as 1695.

52. Gervase Markham, *The English House-Wife, containing The inward and outward Vertues which ought to be in a Compleat Woman* (9th edn, London: Hannah Sawbridge, 1683), pp. 1–2.

53. Richard Bradley, *The Country Housewife and Lady's Director, in the Management of a House, and the Delights and Profits of a Farm* (6th edn, London: D. Browne, 1736), pp. vii–viii.

54. Bradley, *Country Housewife*, p. viii.

55. Bradley, *Country Housewife*, p. iii.

56. Bradley, *Country Housewife*, pp. 2–3.

57. Gervase Markham, *Cheap and Good Husbandry* (14th edn, London: Hannah Sawbridge, 1683), p. iv [unnumbered]. Italics my emphasis.

58. Richard Bradley, *A Complete Body of Husbandry, Collected from the Practice and Experience of the most considerable Farmers in Britain* (London: James Woodman, 1727), Plate IV (between pp. 114–15).

59. Robert Brown, *The Compleat Farmer; or, the Whole Art of Husbandry* (London: J. Coote, 1759).

60. G[ervase] Markham, *Country Contentments; or the Husbandman's Recreations. Containing The Wholesome Experience, in which any ought to Recreate himself, after the Toyl of more Serious Business* (11th edn, London: I. B., 1683).

61. John Flavell, *Husbandry Spiritualized* (London: Robert Boulter, 1669), fol. 15.

62. [Anon.], *Husbandry Moralized; or, Pleasant Sunday Reading for a Farmer's Kitchen* (Dublin: William Watson, n. d. 1795?).

63. Flavell, *Husbandry Spiritualized*, p. 17

64. Davidoff and Hall, *Family Fortunes*.

65. Josiah Woodward, *The Necessary Duty of Family Prayer* (6th edn, London: J. Downing, 1722), pp. 7, 8.

66. Flavell, *Husbandry Spiritualized*, fol. 11. This is in the British Library copy, shelfmark 4404.l.17.

67. *The Complete Family-Piece: and, Country Gentleman, and Farmer's Best Guide* (2nd edn, London: A Bettesworth and C. Hitch, 1737), p. x.

68. *The Universal Family-Book: or, a Necessary and Profitable Companion for All Degrees of People of Either Sex* (London: D. Midwinter and T. Leigh, 1703), p. ii.

69. Dudley North, *Observations and Advices Oeconomical* (London: T. R., 1669), fol. 10.

70. Markham, *English House-Wife*, p. 152.

71. Markham, *English House-Wife*, p. 176.

72. Bailey, *Unquiet Lives*, p. 203.

73. *The Diary of Thomas Naish*, ed. Doreen Slatter (Devizes: Wiltshire Archeological and Natural History Society, 1964), vol. 20, p. 46.

74. Notebook of Daniel Renaud, *c.*November 1769, William Andrews Clark Memorial Library, MS R395Z1 N911 [*c.*1769] Bound, fol. 37.

75. J. D. Marshall (ed.), *The Autobiography of William Stout of Lancaster, 1665–1752*, 3rd series, vol. 14 (Manchester: Chetham Society, 1967), pp. 103, 215, 232.

76. Noel Chomel, *Dictionaire Oeconomique: or, The Family Dictionary*, revised by Richard Bradley (London: D. Midwinter, 1725).

77. Bradley, 'Preface', in Chomel, *Dictionaire Oeconomique*, p. v.

78. Chomel, *Dictionaire Oeconomique* (page unnumbered).

79. See Craig Muldrew, *The Economy of Obligation: The Culture of Credit and Social Relations in Early Modern England* (Basingstoke: Macmillan, 1998), p. 159.

80. *The Science of Good Husbandry: or, the Oeconomics of Xenophon*, tr. Richard Bradley (London: Tho. Corbet, 1727), p. i. Xenophon was first published in English in 1532.

81. *Science of Good Husbandry*, p. 37.

82. *Science of Good Husbandry*, p. 61.

83. *Science of Good Husbandry*, pp. 1–2.

84. William James Booth, *Households: On the Moral Architecture of the Economy* (Ithaca and London: Cornell University Press, 1993), p. 39.

85. Booth, *Households*, pp. 39–40.

86. North, *Observations and Advices Oeconomical*, p. 8.

87. North, *Observations and Advices Oeconomical*, pp. 32–3.

88. Daniel Defoe, *The Family Instructor* (2nd edn, London: Eman. Matthews, 1715), pp. 296–7.

89. *The Oeconomy of Human Life. Translated from an Indian Manuscript. Written by an Ancient Bramin* (London: Robert Dodsley, 1751). See Donald D. Eddy, 'Dodsley's "Oeconomy of Human Life", 1750–1751', *Modern Philology* 85 (1988), pp. 460–79.

90. *Oeconomy of Human Life*, pp. 71, 73, 74.

91. *Old Bailey Proceedings Online*, <http://www.oldbaileyonline.org/> (accessed August 2007), 16 January 1747, trial of Hugh Pelling (t17470116–27).

92. *Letters of the Late Rev. Mr. Laurence Sterne*, 3 vols (London: T. Becket, 1775), vol. 1, pp. 103–4.

93. Arthur Young, *Rural Oeconomy: or, Essays on the Practical Parts of Husbandry* (London: T. Becket, 1770), pp. 375–6.

94. Young, *Rural Oeconomy*, p. 360.

95. *The Oeconomist, or Englishman's Magazine* (Newcastle upon Tyne: M. Angus).

96. Carole Shammas, 'Anglo-American Household Government in Comparative Perspective', *William and Mary Quarterly* 52 (1995), pp. 104–44, here p. 105 *n.* 6.

97.   McKeon, *Secret History of Domesticity*, pp. 179–80.
98.   Davidoff and Hall, *Family Fortunes*, p. 74.
99.   William Cobbett, *Cottage Economy* (London: C. Clement, 1822), p. 1.
100. See Jean-Baptiste Say, *A Treatise on Political Economy* (Philadelphia: Lippincott, 1803; tr. from 4th edition by C. R. Prinsep, ed. Clement C. Biddle, 1855). The same translation was published in London in 1821.

4 'Who Should Be the Author of a Dwelling?' Architects versus Housewives in 1950s France

Nicole Rudolph

In 1950s France, publicly-funded high-rise housing complexes known as *grands en-sembles* were widely viewed as the best solution to the housing crisis that had plagued France since the end of the Second World War. Inside the complexes, housing professionals boasted that inhabitants would find a modern resolution of the 'problem of family life'. Drawing on Taylorist time and motion studies, functionalist design theory and state of the art standardised construction processes, modernist architects had created an apartment known as the *cellule* (or cell, the building block of the *grand ensemble*), whose efficient, rationalised floor plan offered a reconfiguration of domestic space as a streamlined site that actively minimised labour and maximised comfort in the form of central heating and indoor plumbing.

This form of habitat *was* new: commentators noted that it was really the first time families from different social backgrounds enjoyed the same amenities. Inside this 'one-size-fits-all' modern home, families, depending on their class origins, had to acclimatise either to the absence of a parlour and separate dining room or, instead, to having an apartment with differentiated rooms instead of simply a common room surrounded by a satellite bedroom or two. The technocratic state, having wagered on the mass construction of *grands ensembles* to create the 240,000 housing units a year demanded by the General Planning Commission's Second Plan in 1954, embarked upon the construction of these 'ideal homes' with a feeling of experimentation, hoping that the provision of amenities would compensate for small and unfamiliar spaces. Gérard Blachère, an engineer who became head of the powerful Scientific and Technical Centre for Building (CSTB), described the process of providing modern housing as 'putting families in different kinds of apartments and seeing how they would react'.[1]

In 1959 and 1960, the results of this experiment began to appear, with two events questioning the modernist orthodoxy about the functionalist cell as ideal home. First, faced with anecdotal and journalistic complaints about the *grand ensemble*, the French housing ministry put the modern home back under the microscope with its 'Referendum Apartment', an apartment designed according to the wishes and practices described by women in interviews and surveys and shown at the 1959 Salon des Arts Ménagers (or SAM, the equivalent of Britain's Ideal Home Show).

The second event was the publication of the two-volume *Famille et habitation*, a scholarly work by a team of researchers led by urban sociologist Paul-Henry Chombart de Lauwe. The first volume appeared in 1959; surveying the social scientific literature about homes over time and across cultures, it offered an interdisciplinary view of housing. The second volume, published the following year, focused on three apartment complexes belonging to the first generation of *grands ensembles* and provided the most in-depth study of residents in public housing to date.

Modernist architects had heralded the *cellule* as, in Le Corbusier's famous formulation, a 'machine for living'; the *cellule* was based on scientific management and efficiency instead of status-oriented designs derived from a bourgeois desire for display. It is striking, then, that architects vociferously rejected the critiques and practical suggestions of these homes' 'users', especially those of women. Architects' insistence on the superiority of their own design criteria with regard to interiors denied women's expertise as homemakers of the house. Why, in an era of technocracy that celebrated the 'expert', would housing professionals demean the housewife's know-how and attempt to modify – instead of adapt to – her domestic practices?

In answering that question, this chapter attempts to highlight the complex relationship between gender, domestic space and the nation. First, I briefly describe the role of domestic space in French reconstruction during the immediate post-war period: the newly created housing ministry looked to modernist architects to lead reconstruction and 'build a new France'. Shaped by both professional and socio-political concerns, modernists believed their streamlined interiors, as well as the comfort and *art de vivre* they would purportedly produce, to be key to building a classless society and restoring French *grandeur*. The stakes were such that women lost any opportunity to contribute to the formulation of the modern home.

As the chapter goes on to demonstrate, however, Frenchwomen ignored – to the best of their ability – architectural dictates when it came to homemaking and, in the changed political climate of Fifth Republic France after 1958, their preferences convinced the housing ministry to redefine its norms and standards for *grand ensemble* apartments. Though architects vaunted their designs as state of the art solutions, the failure of women to feel at home in the spaces designed by modernists undermined that expertise. The gendered understanding of the home as a feminine sphere meant that women's preferences and practices ultimately triumphed.

Building homes, rebuilding a nation

Before proceeding to a closer examination of the dynamic between architects and housewives at the end of the 1950s, it is useful to review the larger historical context in which the *cellule* was developed. As they did in other nations, modern homes resonated with the French in the post-war period; modern homes were symbols of progress and comfort, both of which spoke to the French after the trauma of war. Even the creation of the Fourth Republic in 1944 signalled an intentional rupture with the past. Policymakers and citizens were eager to put the past behind them and to build a new nation, one worthy of wartime sacrifices. To avoid the perceived pitfalls of the past – Third Republic corruption and stagnation, class conflict and unplanned urbanisation, and the moral failures and collaboration of the Vichy Regime – France embraced the technocratic welfare state: a political and social order designed by experts, who would direct the planned economy, administer the national health system and social security, and modernise France so that it could reassume its position on the world stage.

To a large extent, these policymakers were successful: their project of national modernisation led to such economic growth and prosperity in France that the period spanning 1945 to 1975 has come to be known as the *trente glorieuses*, Thirty Glorious Years. Though this prosperity did not affect everyone equally, in general wages rose, production soared and consumption took off. The protection of the welfare state, the expansion of education and the development of mass culture all contributed to a process of social democratisation. Another factor in both the economic boom and democratisation was state-led housing construction.

Housing was of critical political, economic and social importance during the Thirty Glorious Years. The extent of the wartime destruction – one out of every twenty buildings was destroyed and one out of every five was damaged – was such that reconstruction came to the fore as a national priority. Nor did the national attention to housing wane in the years following the first decade of reconstruction; demographic factors, including the baby boom, arrival of French citizens from Algeria, immigration and rural exodus, contributed to an enduring housing crisis. By 1975, the end of the Thirty Glorious Years, over eight million new housing units had been built. Lodging this many people meant literally incorporating them into a collective project to build modern France.

When historians of post-war France address housing, they rarely cross the threshold. Instead, interiors are folded into larger narratives of reconstruction or urbanisation, homes considered solely as units of a more or less successful mass plan. Architectural historians have written wonderful studies of the exceptional contributions of the great figures of architecture, evaluating homes for their technical, structural or formal innovations.[2] Yet the everyday interiors, those that can still be found within the public housing towers and bars that stud the French landscape, are the ones in which modernisation was brought home, as it were, and few existing studies give us a real sense of either what the spaces looked like when they were built or how, exactly, they were supposed to modernise their inhabitants.

Indeed, because the production of space is never neutral but reflects instead normative beliefs about social life, examining proposals and counterproposals for the home tells us much about what was understood to be at stake in a modernising France. Housing professionals planned the home as a response to potential threats to the family posed by middle-class women in paid employment and by working-class men who spent more time at cafés or racetracks than with their families. Intended to house a breadwinning father, a stay-at-home mother and three or four children, the functionalist interior would, ideally, promote the integrity of the nuclear family by offering a setting in which a family could thrive within a planned urban environment. The rationally organised modern home would lessen women's homemaking burdens, making the domestic sphere a place where she would want to spend her days. This would, in turn – and particularly in combination with the technological comfort offered by central heating and indoor plumbing – contribute even further to making the home a happy place to which her husband would want to hurry and relax while playing with his children. It would alleviate the burden of the middle-class woman who could no longer find household help, and soothe the class antagonism of the factory worker whose home now shared the same plumbing and central heating system as that of the bank manager. Instead of being a nation of 'haves' and 'have-nots', modern France would be populated by urban individuals who shared equal access to safe and warm living environments, environments that would permit every French person to develop his or her potential to the fullest.[3] In this sense, state actors conceived of domestic space as a national social space, one in which relationships of class and gender could be organised for the nation's benefit.

The architectural profession and French reconstruction

For assistance in rebuilding the nation, the housing ministry turned to modernist architects. Since France needed to rebuild from the ground up, why not build something new and avoid repeating past mistakes? In 1945, Raoul Dautry, the first minister of the newly created Ministry of Reconstruction and Urbanism,[4] wrote of the 'common and ardent desire to make a new France',[5] and his successor, Eugène Claudius-Petit, who held the post from 1948 to 1952, rhetorically asked, 'Surely we are not going to, as we did in 1918, rebuild the same little houses along the same little streets? We are not going to sacrifice to the spirit of the old décor the possibilities of man's liberation that a new décor can bring us?'[6]

The need to ease the housing shortage as rapidly and inexpensively as possible imposed standardisation at the expense of traditional building methods, and this gave proponents of the Modern Movement an advantage. If, before the war, modernists had been fighting for legitimacy in architectural and governmental circles, after the war it was their very research into and experiments with prefabrication and mass production during the 1930s that gave modernist architects a certain amount of authority and momentum.

At the same time, the prospect of standardisation called into question the parameters and goals of the architect's work. Mass production not only threatened the free exercise of the architect's 'liberal' profession, but also had the potential to dehumanise those who dwelt within by ignoring their individuality. Claudius-Petit, a former cabinet maker and ardent modernist, argued the case for standardisation on aesthetic grounds, claiming that Paris's Place Vendôme, in its uniformity, was far more beautiful than the 'chaos' of neighbourhoods where all the houses looked different.[7] Modernist architect and editor of *L'Architecture d'aujourd'hui*, Alexandre Persitz, took a more pragmatic tack, dismissing the objections of those opposed to mass production as inappropriate, indeed unethical, given the enormity of reconstruction tasks:

> Whatever the reasons they invoke, these in fact can be summed up by the fear of seeing the profession limited ... We believe that the role of the architect is undergoing profound transformation ... The architect who sees himself as doing battle with the problem of rehousing thousands of families, can he, humanely, materially, create for one neighbourhood or district dozens of individual models, and is this even necessary? For such work on this scale, a certain standardisation imposes itself whether one likes it or not.[8]

The standardisation of domestic architecture would indeed become the order of the day and, from the modernists' point of view, uniform, normalised housing units, imposed by economy, had aesthetic, social and even moral qualities to recommend them.

Persitz's observation that the architectural profession was changing was astute. In December 1940, the Hautecœur law created the Order of Architects. Although membership in the Order did not guarantee that architects alone would receive contracts to design monuments, buildings or other edifices, only those in the Order could claim the title of architect. To be eligible, one had to have graduated from a select number of (mostly Parisian) architecture schools. By 1944, the number of official architects had dropped from approximately 12,000 to 6,400.[9]

Furthermore, competition from urbanists and engineers also constricted the boundaries of the architect's field of expertise. In 1946, the state established a professional hierarchy with its Architect's Charter, which placed town planners above architects. In charge of each urban reconstruction project was a chief urbanist. By subsuming the chief architect to the chief urbanist, the ministry affirmed the primacy of town planners in reconstruction efforts. Engineers, too, found their way into the central and local administrations of the housing ministry. Unlike architects, engineers could work autonomously, beyond the supervision of the senior urbanist. Moreover, as historian Danièle Voldman indicates, the industrialisation of construction pointed clearly to the need for technical advisers, assuring a role for engineers in reconstruction.[10]

Despite potential threats to the profession posed by standardisation, government regulations and the 'jurisdictional claims' of engineers and town planners, modernist architects remained optimistic about their capacity to provide a substantive contribution to French reconstruction.[11] Indeed, the housing shortage offered domestic space as a privileged sphere of activity and an opportunity to fulfil the architect's social mission by improving the average French family's standard of living. Roger Gilbert, head of the National Front of Architects, wrote, 'We can be the principal artisans of France's recovery. Our role is not limited, in fact, to translating current needs and tailoring our projects to the manner in which the French used to live and live today. *We could and we should anticipate and orient social evolution*'.[12] For Gilbert, the modernists' goal of creating functionalist, needs-based housing would hasten the democratisation of French society by eliminating status or wealth as the basis for design. Making human needs the starting point of art, architecture would valorise nature instead of the bourgeois concern for status.

Not coincidentally, this modern 'art of living' meant a specialised area of expertise for architects within the contested field of housing construction. In a 1950 issue of *Techniques et Architecture*, the modernist architect André Hermant opined:

> We know that an exact response can be given now to each demand, to each call to live better in a dwelling and in surroundings worthy of the human mind and favourable to its development. But this call can not be heard if it is not formulated, and most people, crippled by the tasks of everyday life, caught up in the cogs of routine and prejudices, do not even suspect that part of their difficulties and fatigue comes from clutter, from disorganisation, from the ugliness of a dwelling that they think normal . . . but that they flee as soon as they can. In every milieu, the majority is completely unaware of this art of living that is one of the conditions for *joie de vivre* . . . Materials and science are at our disposal. All we need now are beings capable of accomplishing the most beautiful of tasks: to fashion surroundings that are in accordance with their time and for the true happiness of all.[13]

Hermant thus claimed for architects the responsibility of shaping the aesthetics of everyday life and for teaching an appreciation of that aesthetic to the French public. In so doing, Hermant echoed his fellow modernist Jean Prouvé, who had announced five years earlier, 'We must show them [the French] the home of the future and give them the idea of what it can be. We must educate them'.[14] Queried about the architect's role, Marcel Lods agreed: 'He must teach people how to live, because they don't know how'.[15] In other words, housewives were reactionaries; to make the modern home, male experts were needed.

Architects began, then, to redefine their field of competence by emphasising their aesthetic jurisdiction, reinventing themselves as creators of domestic space and teachers of a modern art of living. Having debated and delineated the modern home since the 1920s, they believed themselves to be the experts who would give the French renaissance its shape and content, building homes whose very walls would create an urban, democratised and civilised populace. It is not surprising that architects became quite invested in the success of the rationalist, functionalist modern home.

The *grand ensemble* 'cell'

What did that home look like? The 1950s HLM cell had its roots in the interwar period.[16] Much of the received knowledge about rationalised domestic space in France came from the pre-war time and motion studies of housework conducted by German, Swedish and American advocates of scientific management for the home.[17] The chief goal of rationalist home design was to improve household efficiency by reducing the expenditure of time, labour and material resources. In this regard, French modernists had been deeply impressed by Ernst May's *existenzminimum* apartments in Germany, and especially by their kitchens, designed by the Austrian architect Grete Schütte-Lihotsky. Inspired by Taylorism, Lihotsky conducted time and motion studies, consulted housewives about their daily activities and measured standard utensils in order to come up with a more efficient kitchen. This kitchen (which became known as the Frankfurt kitchen because of its realisation in that city) was a workspace only: the dining area lay just outside the kitchen, and it was there that the families would take their meals. What was most striking to contemporaries was the capacity of the Frankfurt kitchen to reduce labour and exhaustion by decreasing the number of movements a housewife had to perform during meal preparation. Furthermore, the Frankfurt kitchen raised the standard of living for its inhabitants by coming fully equipped. It was standard practice for renters to supply most of their own kitchen equipment, from cupboards to stoves. Incorporating these into the kitchen design, a possibility made feasible by the low costs of mass production, raised all the inhabitants' standard of living equally and quickly.

Rationalism's partner in good design was functionalism, which posited usage as the basis of a blueprint. The plans of HLM units rested upon a theory of common human needs: no longer would homes be planned around extraneous considerations of status or neoclassical aesthetics; instead, they would be built, literally, to the proportions of human bodies and in accordance with the activities that these bodies needed to accomplish in domestic space. Writing in a 1951 issue of *L'Architecture française*, architect Louis-Georges Noviant affirmed that class was no longer factored into home design due to the principle of universal functions: 'This plan, aside from a few details, will be identical, no matter the size or social status of the family to be housed, since its principal elements and their necessary relations will be defined with the goal of satisfying the essential needs of the inhabitant, needs (material, physical, psychological) which are the same for everyone'.[18] Beyond common human necessities, other requirements might be differentiated by gender and age; architects posited that men needed a restful environment after a long day at work, women required equipment that would minimise their household labour and children needed a space in which to play and do schoolwork.

While the late 1940s saw much discussion of proposals for domestic architecture, by the 1950s, a consensus had emerged about the key elements of modern housing. The *cellules* of the 1950s HLMs shared a number of features: plans eliminated hallways (a waste of space), and the apartments all had Frankfurt-style kitchens, which became known in France as 'laboratory' or 'lab' kitchens on the basis of their 'scientific' design. The largest space was always the living room–dining room area, a new kind of living space referred to by a neologism: the *séjour*. This living room–dining room area represented a real innovation, replacing the separate dining rooms and parlours of pre-war middle-class housing. The functions of corporeal care and meal preparation were clustered together so bathrooms and kitchens were juxtaposed. To preserve individual privacy, none of the bedrooms communicated with each other. (Occasionally, to maximise space, a third bedroom was placed off the *séjour* or the sofa was considered to double as a bed for parents or an older child living at home.)

By 1953, in order to speed construction, the *cellule*'s form had been condensed into a finite number of possibilities by the *Plans-types*, a limited series of model blueprints designed by nearly thirty different architects and approved by the housing ministry. Builders using these plans received bonuses from the state, encouraging proliferation of the models. Even builders not using the model plans were constrained by new regulations to be applied to any construction receiving state aid. These regulations specified things like the minimum temperature in a bedroom, maximum ceiling height and the number of sinks per room; meeting these requirements obliged certain layouts and prohibited others.

With consensus emerging about the ideal form of the modern apartment and facilitated by state regulations and incentives for mass construction, HLM construction boomed during the 1950s. In 1951, Strasbourg's Cité Rotterdam had been France's first *grand ensemble*, with a dizzying 800 units; by 1959, Nancy's Haut-du-Lièvre complex dwarfed it, with a long strip housing 3,500 families. Did these mass-produced modern homes solve 'the problem of family life'?

The Referendum Apartment

Upon becoming head of the housing ministry in 1958, Pierre Sudreau began to offer an answer to this question. Sudreau, born in 1919, was from a bourgeois family, although the death of his father contributed to a difficult childhood. He was a great friend of the pilot and writer Antoine de Saint-Exupéry and, after studies in law and political science, Sudreau joined the French Resistance as part of the Brutus Network. He was captured and sent to Buchenwald. At Liberation, Sudreau joined the Interior Ministry, then became prefect of the Loir-et-Cher, invented the sound-and-light shows for châteaux and, in 1955, took the position of commissioner of construction and town planning for the Paris region. His success there led President Charles de Gaulle to appoint him as the new Fifth Republic's housing minister.[19] As commissioner, Sudreau had instituted a committee to study life in the *grands ensembles*, and now, as minister, he wished to appoint a consultant to evaluate the *cellules* themselves.[20] Sudreau decided that women needed a voice in the evaluation and planning of domestic space and, in search of an experienced consultant, he turned to Jeanne Picard. Picard had a long career representing working-class families as a member of the Young Christian Women Workers (Jeunesse Ouvrière Chrétienne Féminine), the Working Family Movement (Mouvement Populaire des Familles), the National Union of Family Associations (Union Nationale des Associations Familiales) and the Economic and Social Council. By 1958, Picard had already spent three decades working with and for working-class women and their households.

Her first task was to survey families in new HLMs about their homes, and she visited approximately 300 households. When asked specifically about their interiors, occupants complained about the absence of entryways, the lack of a door between the kitchen and the *séjour*, the absence of privacy for bedrooms integrated into the living room–dining-room area, picture windows that were too large (further limiting privacy and requiring costly window treatments) and rooms whose walls, broken up by windows, radiators, doors and closets, left few or poor choices for furniture placement. They also objected to mediocre soundproofing, cheap fixtures, and wall and floor coverings that were difficult to clean.[21]

Apprised of these criticisms, Sudreau invited Picard to assemble a team to form policy recommendations to improve resident satisfaction. Picard joined with three home economics organisations and consulted with nearly thirty different women's groups; their collective membership, Picard boasted, represented three million Frenchwomen. Picard worked with the housing ministry's house architect, Marcel Roux, to give form to the women's recommendations, and the ministry showed a life-size model of *their* modern home at the 1959 SAM home exhibition. In order to maximise the extent to which the remodelled 'cell' could be representative of the average French person's dwelling preferences, the housing ministry surveyed exhibition visitors on their reactions to the space. Moreover, the plan, photos and description of the apartment were widely published, and readers (particularly those from the provinces who rarely visited the home exhibition in person) were encouraged to send in their comments as well, making the apartment a 'referendum' on the present and future of modern housing.

When the Referendum Apartment appeared, the most obvious difference between its plan and that of existing HLMs was size: Picard's team had increased the overall, habitable surface area of the apartment by approximately twelve square metres, well exceeding the housing ministry's existing maximum norm of seventy square metres for a typical HLM three-bedroom apartment. In and of itself, this change represented a critique of ministerial policy, a critique rendered explicit by Picard's call for an official change in norms.

The Referendum Apartment still bore marks of modernism. Marcel Gascoin, the premier French modernist interior decorator, had furnished it, and tour guides noted that it did not suffer from 'useless' or 'outmoded' furnishings. They reminded visitors that the *séjour* had 'definitively dethroned' the conventional dining room.[22] But if the *séjour* followed modernist orthodoxy, the kitchen represented heresy. Picard's apartment featured a large, eat-in kitchen. At twelve square metres, the Referendum Apartment kitchen reflected the reality that families routinely dined there and that the kitchen fulfilled another function besides that of 'laboratory'.

Other changes included bedrooms that were separate from the *séjour* and designed to accommodate the size and placement of standard furnishings. The master bedroom connected to one of the children's rooms, so that parents could check on small children

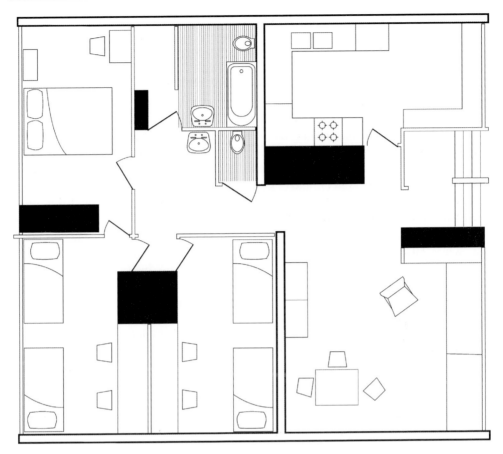

Figure 1: The Referendum Apartment, 1959 (Author's rendering, based on the original by Marcel Roux).

at night. A long hallway and entryway restored independent circulation. A second sink facilitated morning and bedtime preparation for the family of six for whom this three-bedroom apartment had been designed (Figure 1). Some of the changes seemed minor but reflected major improvements for daily living in the eyes of those surveyed. For instance, a small bathtub replaced the shower stall ubiquitous in HLMs, which mothers found difficult to use when bathing small children. In response to residents eager to use new (and old) appliances, twice as many electrical outlets appeared in each room than called for in the ministry's existing regulations.

The public took the referendum literally, and thousands offered their evaluation of the space. SAM visitors filled out surveys, and letters poured in to Picard at the housing ministry. Letter-writers noted that they had heard Picard on the radio or had seen the apartment in popular magazines. They suggested adaptations for rural homes or proposed adding a play space for young children. Others signalled approbation by simply wondering how they could acquire the plans for such a home.[23]

One group, though, voted no – unanimously – on the referendum. One might think that the architectural community, whose classical, Beaux-Arts education had not stressed popular housing, would be eager to have 'real-world' feedback on their designs. And, indeed, they concurred with residents that more space was not simply desirable, but imperative. Architects felt that the state's norms for surface area forced them to advocate solutions that were, aesthetically speaking, compromises (such as the third sleeping area either in or adjacent to the *séjour*).

Consensus ended there, however. The design community's reactions to the Referendum Apartment were particularly violent. One trade publication observed, 'The respect that we owe these women, all belonging to very reputable family associations, should not prevent us from writing that we have rarely seen, within the walls of the Salon des Arts Ménagers, a more banal and backward presentation'.[24] Françoise Choay, the noted architecture critic, supported this assessment in *France-Observateur*, as did an article in *Combat*. Architects and designers, while concurring that the housing ministry should increase the norms for surface area, rejected Picard's model. *Techniques et architecture* devoted an entire issue to a reconsideration of the *cellule* in the spring of 1959 and featured a spread on the Referendum Apartment. The magazine noted that, while HLM tenants had every right to complain about a lack of space, poor soundproofing and faulty materials, these deficiencies were due to the administration, not to architecture; moreover, the problems occupants reported with ventilation, the editors claimed, demonstrated that residents simply did not know how to use their new spaces.[25]

Some reacted even more virulently. Ionel Schein, architect of a futuristic, shell-shaped Plastic House that had caused a sensation at the 1956 SAM, drafted a five-page letter to Jeanne Picard. He rejected the very premise of the Referendum Apartment and railed against its traditional hallway and eat-in kitchen:

> We aspire to an intense domestic life, opened up, rid of the artificial barriers and limits engendered by the lifestyle of old societies! We condemn the fake chaste education engendered by a deceptive lifestyle: slipcovers and house slippers, parlour, corridors, decorative facades and shutters ... The public cannot do this work and neither can three million women, even though they are users [of the spaces]. You don't go to the doctor to have him sign a prescription that you've written yourself ... it's the same for a dwelling! ... As soon as one enters [the Referendum Apartment], one is surrounded, in a hostile manner, by long walls and closed doors. There are not only unwanted visitors in a dwelling! How will a child evolve in such an environment? Have the three million mothers thought of *that*? But they haven't even thought of themselves! The problems of the kitchen, the dining area and the living room have been thoroughly analysed for over forty years by those who have been fascinated from the beginning by the question of the organisation of the home with respect to new modes of living.[26]

Even Marcel Roux, the architect who had drawn up the Referendum Apartment blueprint, distanced himself from the project: 'The plan presented here puts feminine aspirations into concrete form, but it should not be considered an ideal apartment, neither from an architectural point of view, nor from my own'.[27]

The 'problem' of the kitchen, as Schein called it, was a particularly thorny one, into which issues of space, efficiency, status, ventilation and propriety were packed. Most women living in HLMs wanted to serve family meals in the kitchen. Not only did they have to travel less distance to prepare the table, but keeping food out of the living room area allowed this space to remain tidy for longer, especially for families with small children. In this sense, their decision to dine in the kitchen was entirely compatible with one of the fundamental goals of modern housing: to reduce household labour.

Yet this preference for eat-in kitchens conflicted with the modernist design principle of separation of functions. Having identified the kitchen as a laboratory for meal preparation, architects found it difficult to countenance its dual use as a dining area. Architect Georges-Henri Pingusson justified the spatial tyranny of the lab kitchen:

> One ought not have a lot of people in there. [The laboratory kitchen] is the exact opposite of the peasant kitchen, the hearth around which the family gathers, where you have the radio, and the laundry drying … This is a way of being together, but in a place where you shouldn't be. I consider the trend of combining the kitchen and living/dining area to be a fleeting one. It's both an American-bourgeois and a French-peasant trend, one that I judge to be a backward step for the art of dwelling and a social decline.[28]

Furthermore, architects were sceptical of the motivations behind women's efforts to keep the living room clean. They attributed this preference not to the reduction of labour but to an inappropriate attempt to imitate the always-ready-to-receive bourgeois parlour. However, despite the rhetoric of abandoning the false and pretentious modes of living that distinguished the bourgeois apartment, architects still believed that family life required a separate, specialised site for meal-taking. The 'need' for the dining ritual trumped the 'need' for efficiency in this case and resulted in the design 'solution' of the dining corner in the living room. It did not seem to occur to architects that their own opposition to dining in the kitchen bore the stamp of class preference.

As members of an educated elite, particularly an elite explicitly engaged in building – literally – a new France, architects assumed that they knew best what functions the modern home needed to fulfil for any family. This is why Schein opened his letter to Jeanne Picard by asking, 'Who should be the author of a dwelling?' After all, as he had pointed out, patients did not go to the doctor and tell him what medicine to prescribe; similarly, residents shouldn't diagnose their own design problems. It was an attack on an architect's professional competence to ask him simply to build what people thought that they wanted.

The following year, in a more constructive vein, the Syndicat des Architectes de la Seine (SAS), an architectural collective led by Jean Balladur, another former Resistance member and a follower of Le Corbusier, exhibited a rebuttal apartment called the 'Experiment in Adaptive Housing', at the SAM. The authors of the project attempted to accommodate inhabitant preferences in a more modernist form, one that they believed would represent progress and not simply reconstruct traditional interiors in a smaller space.

The SAS identified a static floor plan as the real source of resident dissatisfaction; these architects proposed that user frustration was inevitable if domestic space could not evolve with the arrival of more children or with the different needs children had as they grew. They therefore proposed a central service core, around which a number of moving partitions articulated rooms (Figure 2).

By moving the partitions, residents could change room size and also attribute room usage as they wished. Believing this option to be an elegant and satisfactory response to the needs of inhabitants, the SAS appealed to Minister Sudreau for state sponsorship of the Experiment at the 1960 SAM, but Sudreau replied that the ministry had already accorded its patronage for the 1960 exhibit to Jeanne Picard's follow-up project, the Family House, a detached home version of the Referendum Apartment.[29]

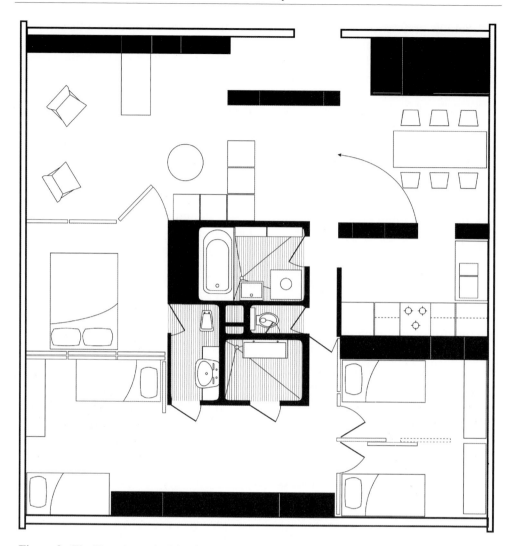

Figure 2: The Experiment in Adaptive Housing, 1960 (Author's rendering, based on the original by the Syndicat des Architectes de la Seine).

SAS exhibited on their own at the 1960 SAM, however, and the Experiment received a laudatory response from the prominent proponents of modern architecture who had rejected the Referendum Apartment. In *L'Architecture française*, a feature on the Experiment claimed that the high quality of the model demonstrated the superior expertise of architects when it came to housing design. *France Observateur* praised the SAS's effort, and one L. Veillon-Duverneuil penned two glowing reviews in *Combat* and in the *Revue de l'ameublement et des industries du bois*. In the *Combat* piece, Veillon-Duverneuil belittled the participatory aspect of Picard's model:

> Last year, a charming learned assembly of matrons, all housewives, right-thinking and well-intentioned, in response to the ridiculous vague impulses of one amongst them, presented a 'referendum' apartment, which seemed at the same time – we can say it now – both a practical joke and a do-it-yourself home! ... Architects, who, when these ladies permit them, also deal with questions of housing, reacted individually and collectively within their professional organisations. They reacted

discreetly, as well-bred men. Courteous and gallant, they were careful not to upset this witty bevy of delightful little faces (delightful, but sure of themselves!). They gathered together, modestly, and thought – men too have such ideas! – that perhaps they, too, by joining forces, who knows? could present the apartment of their dreams.[30]

Veillon-Duverneuil and Schein both affirmed the architects' expertise and undermined women's contributions and wishes by referring to them in sarcastic, condescending and sexist terms. Yet their attempts to marginalise women's contributions ultimately failed when the urban sociologists, led by Paul-Henry Chombart de Lauwe, published *Famille et habitation* and dealt another blow to architects' authority and competence.

Famille et habitation: whose functionalism? Whose expertise?

The son of an army colonel, Paul-Henry Chombart de Lauwe was born in 1913 into a 'half-aristocratic, half-bourgeois' family.[31] At twenty, he began working with Robert Garric's Catholic organisation, Equipes sociales, which brought together young people from the upper and working classes in study groups; Chombart de Lauwe worked with them for six years. When he was twenty-one, he spent a year studying painting and sculpture but soon decided to study ethnology with Marcel Mauss in Paris.

After first fulfilling his obligatory military service during the 1930s, at which time he befriended the urbanist Robert Auzelle, Chombart de Lauwe joined the French leadership school at Uriage in 1940 and then the Resistance; he also flew for the Royal Air Force. It wasn't until Liberation that Chombart de Lauwe was able to begin building his academic career in earnest. He founded the Social Ethnology Group at the Musée de l'Homme to study aspects of working-class life, and he invited Auzelle to join. In 1952, Chombart de Lauwe published *Paris et l'agglomération parisienne*.[32] Combining ecology, history, demography, sociology and ethnography, his project centred on the anthropology of Parisian neighbourhoods, with particular attention paid to the needs of working-class communities. Chombart de Lauwe had received funding for his study from housing minister Eugène Claudius-Petit, to whom he had been introduced by Auzelle.

For the administration, an organisation devoted to sophisticated analysis of working-class populations was a welcome associate, offering expertise to technocratic offices lacking the resources to acquire such knowledge on their own. After obtaining sponsorship from Claudius-Petit at the housing ministry, in 1955 Chombart de Lauwe garnered a commission from the Scientific and Technical Centre for Building to study three new HLMs in the Paris area. In the autumn of that year, his newly formed group for applied research, the Centre for the Study of Social Groups, conducted interviews at apartment complexes in the working-class Paris suburbs of Aubervilliers, Villeneuve Saint-Georges and Argenteuil to determine the sources of resident satisfaction and dissatisfaction. The results of this study appeared in the *Cahiers du CSTB* in 1957 and were well known at the housing ministry: Jeanne Picard even drew upon them for her Referendum Apartment.[33]

Chombart de Lauwe built upon this body of work when he published the first volume of *Famille et habitation* in 1959. In that volume, he also sketched a brief history of functionalism in architecture and, in an effort to identify contemporary trends, contained interviews with a dozen leading modernist architects and designers of the day, including Michel Bataille, André Wogenscky (Le Corbusier's partner),

Bernard Zehrfuss, André Hermant, Charlotte Perriand, Georges-Henri Pingusson and Marcel Lods. Acknowledging the vanguard position of Le Corbusier in the architectural field, a separate section addressed his work and opinions.

Chombart de Lauwe's team asked architects questions that went straight to the heart of the debates that had filled the pages of the professional press since before the war. The interviewers asked architects to take a position on collective versus individual housing, the eat-in kitchen, the place of aesthetics in architecture, and the relative importance of the *cellule* in a housing complex's mass plan. Zooming in on the subject of their inquiry, the interviewers also posed specific questions about family dwellings. What did the architects see as the particular needs of families, and how did they integrate these into their designs? What should be a family's role in the elaboration of an apartment plan?

With regard to this last question, virtually all the architects were sceptical about the contributions families could make regarding the equipment and layout of their homes. Echoing Ionel Schein's analogy to physicians, André Wogenscky argued for the architect's absolute expertise: 'Their [families'] attitude vis-à-vis the doctor is different: when they consult him, they explain what they are feeling, but they don't dictate the medicine that they should take. It's the opposite with architects. *Women, in particular, are astonishing, they describe exactly what they want. Naturally, the architect should take people's desires into account, to the extent that their opinions seem justified to him*'.[34] Women's input, in particular, weighed little in architects' minds. This position derived from the commonly held belief that women, as homemakers whose expertise and preferences derived from inherited knowledge and local norms, were responsible for perpetuating the very dwelling practices that the modernists aimed to eliminate. Bataille spoke for his colleagues when he asserted, 'Families think they have opinions, but they really only have habits'. André Hermant conceded that families could have some freedom as to the equipment and organisation of their apartments, but only under the architect's guidance or tutelage. Pingusson summed up their general position, asking rhetorically, 'Should we be democratic and follow the desires of families, who have confused ideas based on what they have always seen, or should we advise them, orient them in an imperative fashion toward the norms of the new way of living?'[35]

Having opted for the latter, architects were willing to wait residents out. Resident dissatisfaction made little impact on these architects' beliefs about good design. Rather than accept that 'the customer is always right', the architects surmised that users had not yet learned their lesson. Rural or working-class dwelling practices that deviated from the new art of living simply had not been exposed long enough to the spaces designed to eliminate them. In other words, resistance to residents' input stemmed not only from the perception that their professional competence was being threatened. It also originated in the belief that there was a teleology of dwelling, and that architects, through good design, could – and should – educate users in the art of living for the greater good of socio-cultural progress and of the nation.

The first volume of *Famille et habitation* concluded with a vivid critique of this pedagogy of dwelling. Chombart de Lauwe accepted the modernists' claim that modern architecture distanced itself from its Beaux-Arts antecedent because human needs – not abstract aesthetic principles or concerns about social status – governed design. Yet the questions of Chombart de Lauwe's team exposed architects' tendencies to identify those needs in an individualised, unscientific and arbitrary manner. Hence, in

Chombart de Lauwe's opinion, modern architecture was unable to satisfy what was, in fact, a complex plurality of requirements. He argued (somewhat self-servingly) that only methodical observation by social scientists could accurately designate, categorise and rank the needs of *all* classes of families.[36]

Such methodical observation was the subject of the second volume of *Famille et habitation*, which brought the voices of 135 households onto the page. Workers, salaried employees and managers, teachers and civil servants contributed their evaluations of life in Le Corbusier's Cité Radieuse in Nantes-Rezé, in Jacques Carlu's Cité de la Benauge in Bordeaux and in Robert Auzelle's Cité de la Plaine, in the Paris suburb of Clamart. In this second volume, Chombart de Lauwe emphasised the historical novelty of mixed classes inhabiting one apartment complex and stressed the specificity of needs and aspirations, which varied not only by class, but also by age, gender, family size and religion. He observed that needs were socially constructed; hence it followed that the reception of new HLM homes, designed for a single set of requirements, would vary as well.[37]

Chombart de Lauwe's team set out to identify, categorise and measure changes in individuals' and groups' behaviour, satisfaction and expectations as a result of living in the HLMs. Over 80 per cent of families expressed satisfaction with their new homes, but 93 per cent of them had modified their apartments in some fashion: painting, carpeting the floors, moving electrical outlets or putting blinds over the large picture windows.[38]

Other findings exposed the difficulty of life in the housing complexes when apartments suffered from overcrowding, when complexes lacked certain collective facilities, such as child care centres, or when they were far from shops and serviced infrequently by mass transport.[39] In general, apartments fared better in residential evaluations than did the *grands ensembles* as a whole. Still, Chombart de Lauwe's team recommended that policymakers allow at least fourteen square metres per person in an apartment; otherwise, they warned, dissatisfaction would inevitably result. They also asserted a 'critical threshold' of eight to ten square metres per person, below which serious psychological disturbances threatened family unity.[40]

Additional improvements that inhabitants suggested for their domestic spaces, summarised in the conclusion to Chombart de Lauwe's second volume, sound familiar: 'Renters do not like having a bedroom right off the living room. On the other hand, they often would like a hallway that facilitates the isolation of the other rooms. Finally, a larger kitchen permitting family dining is desired, particularly by working-class and lower-middle-class households'.[41] Thus, the residents of these new complexes also approved – indirectly – the Referendum Apartment.

State planners adapt

Having sponsored the Referendum Apartment and recruited Chombart de Lauwe for one of his *grand ensemble* working groups, it is not surprising that Minister Sudreau was receptive to reports of inhabitant preferences.[42] The housing ministry implemented a number of changes that responded to residents' concerns. Most significantly, in accordance with the unanimous critique of small spaces, Sudreau revised the size requirements for state-funded housing. In April 1960, the ministry increased the maximum surface area norms for HLMs. On the other hand, the fact that it took until

1963 to raise the *minimum* surface norms for the HLMs tempered the achievements of the administration with regard to satisfying public demand.

In addition to augmenting the surface area of the apartments, Sudreau proceeded to improve their quality. A new set of regulations, issued by Sudreau in June 1960, eliminated differences in the quality of equipment, fixtures and materials employed in the different categories of HLMs.[43] These regulations spoke directly to criticisms highlighted by Picard and Chombart de Lauwe by stipulating that kitchens could no longer open directly into the *séjour* (except for studio and one-bedroom apartments) and implicitly endorsed the eat-in kitchen by specifying a minimum combined surface area for the kitchen and living room-dining room area of twenty-one square metres. (The *séjour* retained its status as the most important room in the home, however, since regulations specified that it had to measure at least twelve square metres.)

Other improvements included an increase in the amount of storage space in HLMs and an increase in the minimum temperature of a centrally heated apartment from twelve degrees Celsius in the bedrooms and sixteen degrees in the *séjour* to a consistent eighteen degrees throughout the entire apartment. Ideas about what constituted a minimum level of comfort were evolving as France entered the second half of the Thirty Glorious Years.

In addition to these rather modest responses to the residential critiques unearthed by Picard and Chombart de Lauwe, the ministry assisted attempts to prolong the life of Picard's Referendum Apartment. First, with the benefit of state funds, a private HLM company built over 400 'referendum apartments' in Thiais, in the southern suburbs of Paris.[44] Second, reincarnations of the Referendum Apartment appeared at both the 1960 and 1961 SAMs. As mentioned above, Picard showed the Family House, essentially the Referendum Apartment in detached house form, at the 1960 SAM. The National Building Federation, which had co-sponsored the Family House, received approval from the housing ministry to use a modified version of the plan as a *plan-type*. In 1961, *Arts ménagers* magazine exhibited the 'Prefabricated Apartment', another design based on the Referendum Apartment.[45] It was built by SERPEC, a conglomerate of the largest construction companies. Like the National Building Federation, SERPEC received *plan-type* certification.[46] Now the ministry's model plans included not only those designed by modernist architects but those incorporating residential preferences.

Finally, another official initiative to incorporate French inhabitants' expectations took place in the belly of the technocratic beast: the Scientific and Technical Centre for Building. In a 1961 issue of the centre's journal, Jacques Dreyfus and Jean Tribel published an article entitled, 'The Cellule-Lodging: Analysis of its Problems; Search for New Solutions'.[47] Tribel was an architect, and Dreyfus was an engineer in charge of the centre's research office on functionalism. Together, they set out to determine the design implications of Chombart de Lauwe's results, agreeing with him that family structures – and not an idealised art of living – should be at the centre of a needs-based functionalism. Dreyfus and Tribel commented wryly, 'The picture of the large family gathered together in the *séjour*, the father reading and the mother performing some household task (sewing, for example), while an older child does their homework and the young ones play on the floor with blocks is somewhat idyllic'.[48] Families did not spend all their waking time at home in the living room–dining room area, so they needed more space elsewhere in the home to accommodate the different requirements of fathers, mothers, adolescents and small children. Dreyfus and Tribel proposed that parents had to maintain prestige in their children's eyes in order to enforce parental authority; they thus needed a separate and large master bedroom apart from the *séjour*. Adolescents wanted to entertain friends away from smaller children, who themselves had to have room to play, so Dreyfus and Tribel recommended small but autonomous rooms for the former and play spaces outside shared bedrooms for the latter. Dreyfus and Tribel argued that a family's needs changed over time, and they laid out six different 'examples of non-traditional solutions', each accompanied by a chart listing the advantages and disadvantages. Their model plans juggled new arrangements incorporating children's play areas, more privacy for parents and adolescents, eat-in kitchens and hallways of different dimensions.

It was hoped that these new arrangements might improve inhabitant contentment in the *grands ensembles* for, although Fifth Republic policymakers sought to incorporate inhabitant input into decision-making, they were not willing to give up on the huge complexes, which still seemed the best way to meet the continued demand for housing. A record-setting number of 275,000 new units was built in 1959, and more homes were built in the two years between 1958 and 1960 than during the four years previously.[49] If modifying elements of the apartment would ensure greater satisfaction with collective housing, state planners – unlike modernist architects – were willing to compromise on interiors and give residents some voice in the design process.

Conclusion

In the immediate post-war context, state actors had targeted domestic space as a site for rebuilding the nation: new home design would help to reorganise relationships of class and gender destabilised by the war. The modernist architects to whom state planners turned for expertise agreed with those policymakers that housing would be a key site for their national modernising project. In order to prove that France had entered a modern era of democratised comfort and leisure, homes could not bear any marks of rural, traditional or 'backward' habits and, in the name of socio-political progress, architects evacuated women's preferences and practices – their inherited and acquired expertise – from home design.

In other words, the modern home became a synecdoche for a modern nation. One of the lessons that can be taken from this study is that when domestic space signifies the nation, as it can during or after times of major conflict, it is public men who make decisions about the homes assumed to be part of the 'private' or 'feminine' sphere. Architects, supported by Fourth Republic housing ministers who shared their top-down approach to design, understood their contributions to the nation as a 'civilising mission'. In paternalist fashion, they hoped to mould inhabitants, acculturating the lower and middle classes to an urban and efficient (read: upper-middle-class) lifestyle via pedagogical spaces designed to reduce users' labour and maximise their comfort and self-actualisation.

Once architects' designs had left the drawing board and evolved into concrete blocks and towers housing real families, however, these modern interiors became sites of conflict. The 'cell's' floor plans turned out not to be as prescriptive as architects had hoped. Female HLM dwellers did not challenge the gendered assumption that they were responsible for a home's upkeep and management, nor that it should be a place of rest for their spouses, but they did argue, via intermediaries like Jeanne Picard and Paul-Henry Chombart de Lauwe, that these 'ideal' interiors often impaired their ability to use, maintain and enjoy their homes. Their understanding of rational and efficient dwelling practices simply did not coincide with architects' and, ultimately, it was the gendered understanding of the interior as 'women's space' that undermined the architects' agenda. A home that failed to please women was not an ideal home. The compromise signified by the proliferation of the Referendum Apartment as a *plan-type* indicates that for technocratic state planners, women's expertise trumped modernist architects' prescriptions. By 1960, in a changed political and economic climate, pragmatic housing professionals were willing to let homemakers become modern in their own ways, at least within the four walls of their 'cells'.

Notes

I would like to thank Karen Adler, Carrie Hamilton, Sally Phillips and the participants in the Homes and Homecomings conference held at the University of Nottingham 26–28 March 2008, as well as the two anonymous reviewers for *Gender & History*, for their helpful comments on the original article.

1. Minutes of the meeting of the working group on 'L'Etude de l'amélioration des dispositions des logements', 18 February 1958. Article 4, 770775, Archives nationales, Centre des archives contemporaines, Fontainebleau (AN, CAC). All translations are the author's own.
2. The literature on post-war housing includes Danièle Voldman's canonical text, *La Reconstruction des villes françaises de 1940 à 1954: Histoire d'une politique* (Paris: L'Harmattan, 1997); Hélène Sanyas, 'La Politique architecturale et urbaine de la reconstruction. France: 1945–1955' (unpublished doctoral thesis, University of Paris VIII, 1982); Anatole Kopp, Frédérique Boucher and Danièle Pauly, *L'Architecture de la reconstruction en France, 1945–1953* (Paris: Editions du Moniteur, 1982); Bruno Vayssière, *Reconstruction, deconstruction: Le hard French ou l'architecture française des trente glorieuses* (Paris: Picard, 1988). Most of these works emphasise the housing ministry's incapacity to implement a real policy of new construction while coping with the imperatives, struggles and constraints that accompanied reconstruction in the strict sense of the word. Jean-Paul Flamand's work on public housing, *Loger le peuple: Essai sur l'Histoire du logement social* (Paris: La Découverte, 1989), considers housing as an aspect of urbanisation. Joseph Abram's *L'Architecture moderne en France*, vol. 2: *Du chaos à la croissance 1940–1966* (Paris: Picard, 1999) is an example of a valuable work that focuses primarily on the history of architecture and urban planning with only perfunctory attention to interiors. Christian Moley's *L'Architecture du logement: Culture et logiques d'une norme héritée* (Paris: Anthropos, 1998) looks at interiors with an emphasis on technical questions of construction, but also includes some sociological and anthropological discussion of these.
3. On the state's conceptualisation of modern homes after Liberation, see Nicole Rudolph, 'Domestic Politics: The Cité Expérimentale at Noisy-le-Sec in Greater Paris', *Modern and Contemporary France* 12 (2004), pp. 483–95.
4. The name of the ministry changed several times during the Fourth and Fifth Republics. I refer to it here as the 'housing ministry', although its functions also encompassed urban planning.
5. Raoul Dautry in Voldman, *La Reconstruction des villes françaises*, p. 124.
6. Pierre Claudius [Eugène Petit], 'Renaissance', *L'Architecture d'aujourd'hui* 1 (1945), pp. 5–6. Pierre Claudius was Eugène Petit's Resistance alias; after the war he became officially known as Eugène Claudius-Petit.
7. Claudius, 'Renaissance', p. 6.
8. Alexandre Persitz, 'A Propos de la Première Exposition de la Reconstruction', *L'Architecture d'aujourd'hui* 4 (1946), p. 64.
9. Voldman, *Reconstruction*, p. 248.
10. Voldman, *Reconstruction*, pp. 247, 258–63.
11. The term is from Andrew Abbott, *The System of Professions* (Chicago and London: University of Chicago Press, 1988).
12. Roger Gilbert, 'L'Architecte devant la Reconstruction', *L'Architecture d'aujourd'hui* 1 (1945), p. 25. My emphasis.
13. André Hermant, 'Réflexions', *Techniques et Architecture* 9–10 (1950), p. 95.
14. Cited in Kopp, Boucher and Pauly, *L'Architecture de la reconstruction*, p. 88.
15. Cited in Paul-Henry Chombart de Lauwe, *Famille et habitation*, vol. 1: *Sciences humaines et conceptions de l'habitation* (Paris: CNRS, 1959), p. 192.

16. HLM stands for *Habitations à Loyer Modéré* and refers to state-subsidised public housing.

17. This research was disseminated in France primarily by Paulette Bernège, a home economist. Bernège was involved with architects and home planners from the 1930s to the 1950s. See also Jackie Clarke, 'L'Organisation ménagère comme pédagogie: Paulette Bernège et la formation d'une nouvelle classe moyenne dans les années 1930 et 1940', *Travail, genre et sociétés* 1 (2005), pp. 139–57.

18. Louis-Georges Noviant, 'Le Logis d'aujourd'hui: Eléments et conditions de son plan', *L'Architecture française* 111–112 (1951), p. 11.

19. Pierre Sudreau, *Au-delà de toutes les frontières* (Paris: Odile Jacob, 1991), pp. 31, 44, 95, 97, 107.

20. Annie Fourcaut, 'Les Premiers grands ensembles en région parisienne: Ne pas refaire la banlieue?', *French Historical Studies* 27 (2004), pp. 195–218, here p. 214.

21. See 'Nos desiderata en matière de logements', AN, CAC, 850023/120; 'L'Enquête de Mme Picard', *Techniques et Architecture* 19/2 (1959), p. 114.

22. Script for 'Visite guidée', AN, CAC, 850023/120.

23. The survey responses are no longer traceable in the Housing Ministry archives.

24. L. Veillon-Duverneuil, 'Le Syndicat des Architectes de la Seine réagit contre l'appartement de "ces dames" présenté en 1959', *Revue de l'ameublement et des industries du bois* 2 (1960), p. 35.

25. 'L'Enquête de Mme Picard', p. 114.

26. Ionel Schein, letter to Jeanne Picard, 16 February 1958. AN, CAC, 850023/120.

27. 'Points de vue des architectes', *Techniques et architecture* 19:2 (1959), p. 114.

28. Cited in Chombart de Lauwe, *Famille et habitation*, vol. 1, p. 178.

29. Pierre Sudreau, letter to Jean Balladur, 2 February 1960. AN, CAC, 790660/11.

30. L. Veillon-Duverneuil, 'Les Cloisons de l'appartement de demain seront mobiles', *Combat*, 22 February 1960, p. 8. See also his 'Le Syndicat des Architectes de la Seine réagit', p. 35; Françoise Choay, 'Un appartement sur mesures', *France Observateur*, 25 February 1960, pp. 15–16; Françoise Choay, 'Essai d'habitation évolutive', *L'Architecture française* 211–212 (1960), p. 112.

31. The biographical information about Chombart de Lauwe in this section is taken from André Grelon, 'In Mémoriam. Paul-Henry Chombart de Lauwe, 1913–1998', *L'Année sociologique* 49 (1999), pp. 7–18; Paul-Henry Chombart de Lauwe, *Un anthropologue dans le siècle: Entretiens avec Thierry Pacquot* (Paris: Descartes & Cie., 1996), pp. 157, 181–2.

32. Paul-Henry Chombart de Lauwe, *Paris et l'agglomération parisienne* (Paris: Presses Universitaires de France, 1952).

33. W. Brian Newsome, 'The "Apartment Referendum" of 1959: Toward Participatory Architectural and Urban Planning in Postwar France', *French Historical Studies* 28 (2005), pp. 329–58, here p. 342.

34. Chombart de Lauwe, *Famille et habitation*, vol. 1, p. 191. My emphasis.

35. The three citations in this paragraph come from Chombart de Lauwe, *Famille et habitation*, vol. 1, pp. 188, 190.

36. Chombart de Lauwe, *Famille et habitation*, vol. 1, p. 212.

37. Chombart de Lauwe, *Famille et habitation*, vol. 2: *Un essai d'observation expérimentale* (Paris: CNRS, 1960), pp. 11, 13–14.

38. Chombart de Lauwe, *Famille et habitation*, vol. 2, pp. 66–7.

39. Because collective facilities like schools, post offices and shops fell outside the housing ministry's aegis, new housing complexes often opened their doors to residents well before construction had begun on the other projected elements of a mass plan.

40. Chombart de Lauwe, *Famille et habitation*, vol. 1, p. 108.

41. Chombart de Lauwe, *Famille et habitation*, vol. 2, p. 267.

42. Chombart de Lauwe participated in the working group for 'improving apartment layouts'. See minutes of their meetings in AN, CAC, 770775/4.

43. See 'Cahier des Prescriptions Techniques et Fonctionnelles Minima Unifiées', *Journal Officiel de la Republique Française*, 3 July 1960, pp. 6039–49.

44. 'Thiais: Groupe d'HLM', *Techniques et Architecture* 24 (1963), p. 116; Anne-Marie Pajot, 'Mode d'emploi pour un HLM 4 pièces', *Arts ménagers* 171 (1964), pp. 210–14.

45. Anne-Marie Pajot, 'L'Appartement préfabriqué', *Arts ménagers* 136 (1961), pp. 226–32.

46. Newsome, 'The "Apartment Referendum" of 1959', p. 354.

47. Jacques Dreyfus and Jean Tribel, 'La Cellule-logement: Analyse des problèmes; recherche de solutions nouvelles', *Cahiers du CSTB* 48, cahier 382 (1961), pp. 3–56.

48. Dreyfus and Tribel, 'La Cellule-logement', p. 23.

49. Marcel Roncayolo (ed.), *La Ville d'aujourd'hui*, vol. 5: *Histoire de la France urbaine*, ed. Georges Duby (Paris: Seuil, 1985), p. 646.

5 Ideal Homes and the Gender Politics of Consumerism in Postcolonial Ghana, 1960–70

Bianca Murillo

> A little over two decades ago an ordinary bed in the room was a dream which could come true for a few Ghanaians. Then, unlike today, talk of refrigerators, gas or electric cookers or of bedroom and sitting room suites seemed sheer day dreams. They were 'luxuries' far beyond the reach of all but a few privileged people, the 'Beentos',[1] lawyers and doctors. But the times have changed and with them the means and the modes of living of the people of Ghana. These changes have brought new tastes, new cravings and new longings, among them the desire for new look homes that are comfortable and cosy – the ideal home.
>
> A Correspondent for the Ideal Home Exhibition, 1967[2]

In November 1967, more than 50,000 people gathered to attend the Ideal Home Exhibition in Ghana's capital city, Accra.[3] This week-long event held at the Accra Community Centre sought not only to promote 'the improvement of Ghanaian homes', but also to encourage the use of locally manufactured goods and assist in the growth of Ghanaian industry.[4] Exhibitors, including state and private business and large multinationals, such as Lever Brothers and S. C. Johnson, used the venue to advertise and sell new products and educate Ghanaian consumers on 'modern' modes of living. Super Furniture Works and the Ashanti Furniture Company constructed model showrooms and Accra cosmetic firm Atico offered free samples and beauty treatments. In addition, guests could purchase their favourite beverages and snacks and view demonstrations for products like household cleaners, aluminum cookware and plastics.

Reporters described most attendees as 'young women and men from top forms of secondary schools and teacher training colleges' and the *Daily Graphic*, a popular newspaper among urban readers, published lengthy articles and detailed photographs of the event throughout the week.[5] The exhibition's theme – 'Ideas that Directly Contribute to Civilisation and Improvement to Ghanaian Homes' – celebrated the ideal home in connection with specific family forms and gendered behaviours. Through advertisements and displays, exhibitors presented a 'domestic ideal' based on the notion of a stereotypical middle-class housewife/breadwinner model, stressing above all a woman's importance as wife, housekeeper and caregiver and a man's authority as head of household.

This chapter uses the 1967 Ideal Home Exhibition as a lens for exploring the gender politics of consumerism in postcolonial Ghana. Planning for the exhibition took place against the backdrop of major political and economic changes in the country. In February 1966 a military and police coup overthrew Ghana's first prime minister and president Kwame Nkrumah. The National Liberation Council (NLC), which would be the first of many military regimes to rule the country, embraced a free-market economy, encouraged private business, and welcomed foreign investment and economic aid programmes.[6] While a local publishing firm, Anowuo Educational Publications (AEP), organised the exhibition, the NLC government supported the show by offering publicity and acting as a major exhibitor.

AEP's owner, Samuel Asare Konadu, an Accra businessman and popular novelist, also had direct links with the new administration.[7] After the coup, the NLC awarded Konadu exclusive contracts to produce textbooks and other instructional materials for the growing number of Ghanaian school children. In 1966 he established AEP, and by 1967 his publishing house grossed around half a million dollars in sales, making him one of the wealthiest men in Ghana.[8] Konadu's motivations for organising the show were varied. While he undoubtedly used the venue to promote and sell his novels, he may have also done so to maintain the favour of NLC officials and secure further government publishing contracts.

Whatever the motivation behind Konadu's involvement, the NLC supported his efforts both financially and ideologically. In order to jump-start Ghana's private sector, attract foreign investors and garner popularity among elite and middle-class consumers, the NLC threw their support behind the show. In addition, the NLC was keen to attract the support of local Ghanaian businessmen and other aspiring entrepreneurs, as their interests had been neglected under Nkrumah's socialist agenda.[9] Similar to the Ideal Home Exhibition's advertisements and displays, the military-controlled media situated the 'Ghanaian home' as a space that represented national stability and the goods inside as testimony to the country's rising level of development.[10]

As other scholars have noted, the number of men and women living as conjugal partners or in any kind of 'middle-class' domestic household during the 1960s was very small.[11] Because the 'domestic ideal' epitomised by the exhibition and its advertising did not reflect the majority of men's and women's experiences in 1960s Ghana, this chapter is less concerned with problematising this ideal, and more with understanding why it was rearticulated, especially in the postcolonial period, thorough state rhetoric, public exhibitions and the press. The Ideal Home Exhibition was part of a larger post-Nkrumah self-fashioning project that emphasised the home and rigid gender roles as a means to enforce social order. After the coup, the NLC accused Nkrumah's regime of dismantling older systems of authority, such as that of chiefs, elders and parents, and of corrupting the morals of youth, especially young women.[12] The show presented a disciplined form of domesticity as vital for the country's economic and political reconstruction.

For the most part, the colonial period has been the main focus of gender historiography for Ghana, and Africa in general.[13] These studies have emphasised how colonial institutions, wage labour, urbanisation and an expanding cash economy have shaped gender relations and ideas about marriage, family and domestic life. In addition, gender history is dominated by studies on rural and non-elite women.[14] This chapter shifts the focus onto the second half of the twentieth century and builds on work from scholars like Amina Mama and Claire Robertson on the gendered nature of postcolonial statecraft. It also contributes to comparative gender histories and engages in larger questions about how gender ideologies and the home are mobilised by the state during periods of economic uncertainty and national reconstruction.[15]

Background: independence and economic decline

Ten years prior to the Ideal Home Exhibition, Ghana, then known as the Gold Coast, became the first West African country to gain political independence from Britain. The 1950s was a period of steady economic growth, and numerous Ghanaians witnessed higher incomes and increased purchasing power. For many, independence symbolised a chance to improve their material lives and provided hope for a more equitable distribution of the country's wealth. President Kwame Nkrumah envisioned a new Ghana 'where hunger, unemployment, poverty, and illiteracy no longer exist[ed] . . . [and] where every person [could] use his talents to the full and contribute to the general well being of [the] nation'.[16] At the time of independence, Ghana's economic prosperity was at its peak and Nkrumah's promises for a better future seemed within reach.

Nkrumah's Convention People's Party (CPP) government adopted an African socialist philosophy, promoting a one-party system, state control of the economy and a reduction of private and foreign business interests. His regime undertook large-scale development projects, such as the Akosombo Dam and Tema Harbour, and implemented policies supporting import substitution, government marketing boards and state-owned factories.[17] By the mid-1960s a drastic drop in the world market price of cocoa, the state's main source of revenue, and excessive government spending slowed economic growth. As potential remedies, Nkrumah introduced import licence regulations and a series of commodity price controls.[18] Intended to halt inflation and decrease import dependence, Nkrumah's policies instead created periodic shortages and bred corruption at all levels of distribution.

Restrictive import policies and continued economic decline dealt a severe blow to rising consumer expectations of the 1950s. During a 1965 government investigation on trade malpractices, consumers reported difficulties in obtaining essential commodities like sugar, milk, flour and rice.[19] Investigators held that 'the immediate causes of the shortages were first and foremost the non-issuing of import licenses in a rational manner', which they claimed had been exacerbated by the practice of hoarding by firms and traders and the inability, logistically, of the state-run Ghana National Trading Corporation (GNTC) to distribute large quantities of goods.[20] In addition, by late 1964 shortages in materials required in both manufacturing and export industries had reached serious proportions.[21] Combined with increasing levels of unemployment, lack of housing and growing disparities of wealth, many Ghanaians grew disillusioned with the outcomes of independence.[22] While not the only reasons, unfulfilled economic and consumer demands substantially weakened support of the CPP government and in 1966 a military and police coup, staged by members of the National Liberation Council (NLC), overthrew President Nkrumah and ousted CPP officials.[23]

In the first week of rule, the NLC cut all ties with Communist powers, expelling Soviet and Chinese technical personnel and some of their diplomatic staff. Not only did the new military government position free-market capitalism as the key to Ghana's economic recovery; it also saw it as a means to gain Western support and financial aid.

Although the state and local press celebrated the Ideal Home Exhibition as a major turning point from government-controlled to private-owned business, many companies at the show were jointly owned by the military state.[24] For instance, the NLC government still jointly controlled firms such as the State Brick and Tile, State Footwear and State Farms Corporations that had previously been part of Nkrumah's group of state-run enterprises.[25] As other scholars have shown, post-Nkrumah governments still thought in terms of a close partnership between the state and private capital, despite rhetoric used to win Western sympathy and financing.[26] Furthermore, these alliances reflected a continued connection between government and business bureaucracies, a relationship that, feminist scholars argue, concentrated postcolonial political and economic power in the hands of a male elite.[27]

Exhibition politics and motivations

Home exhibitions emerged in the twentieth century as marketing tools and as venues for domestic education. In places like Britain and the United States, home shows emphasised rational consumption, introduced new labour-saving devices and defined ideas about modern living, articulating what sponsors believed were women's fantasies of domestic liberation. The original Ideal Home Exhibition appeared in Britain in 1908. Sponsored by London's *Daily Mail* as a venue for advertisers, the first exhibitions also reflected major transformations in British society. While advertisers focused on alleviating stresses connected to the rapid growth of Britain's suburbs by promoting household goods as solutions for the emerging 'servant problem' among middle- and upper-class women, they later expanded efforts to include lower-middle- and working-class consumers.[28] Exhibitions situated the possession of household goods as opportunities for social mobility and the construction of a collective British identity. Increased wealth, decreasing costs of consumer goods and easier accessibility to these goods fuelled the exhibition's ongoing success.

While public festivals and gatherings were not new to Ghanaians, the content of such gatherings did change over the course of the twentieth century. Local chiefs, royal families and prominent community members had long used festivals and annual gatherings as spaces to gain support and legitimise political authority.[29] During colonial rule, British administrators attempted to expand the scope of these gatherings by promoting colony-wide events, such as Empire Day. In addition, regional officials, supported by Christian missions and voluntary organisations, sponsored special events such as baby pageants in places like Kumasi and funded travelling demonstrations on cooking, infant welfare and needlepoint to more rural areas.[30] In the post-war period, large multinational firms expanded on colonial models. For example, Lever Brothers used fashion shows, cinema and demonstration vans, and public contests and give-aways to promote and sell products.[31] Unlike past events, commercial marketers and advertisers targeted Africans as consumers. The 1967 Ideal Home Exhibition drew from these past influences – political, commercial and religious. It served both educational and profit-driven interests, and, like the exhibitions and festivals before it, was a manifestation of the politics of the day.

Although publicly presented as such, the 1967 Ideal Home Exhibition was not the first of its kind. In 1956, the Federation of Gold Coast Women (FGCW), a mainly urban elite organisation established in 1953, in conjunction with the Departments of

Housing and Social Welfare and Community Development, organised the first exhibition.[32] Modelled on the British version, the FGCW used the show to encourage their fellow countrywomen to raise their standards of living and as a tool to educate all 'classes' on the benefits of 'modern living'.[33] The FGCW's Ideal Home Exhibition was part of a broader trend undertaken by elite Ghanaian women, who, as early as the 1930s, had set up their own domestic education programmes to teach young girls the 'art of housekeeping' and other vocational skills.[34] For example, Nancy Tsiboe, the wife of a wealthy local newspaper proprietor, founded the Happy Home Institute in Kumasi, and urban organisations and clubs, like the Ideal Homemakers Club in Accra, focused on teaching home management and cookery.[35] Through press coverage, the FGCW declared, 'Let those who see the exhibition go to their towns and villages and do likewise'.[36]

While the 1967 exhibition was similar to its 1956 predecessor in its display of household goods and emphasis on modern living, it was fuelled by a very different set of expectations and ideologies. Male sponsors criticised past exhibitions organised by women's groups as too 'individualistic', failing to advise consumers on how properly to use and display home goods. In addition, they claimed the 1967 exhibition marked a major turning point in Ghana's history.[37] Not only did the event feature consumer goods in abundance within the reach of 'all' Ghanaians; it connected ideas of material prosperity with the transition from government to private business. By proclaiming democratic, free-capital interests, the exhibition reflected similar developments happening on a global scale. The connection between consumer 'free choice', and political freedom and democracy, was made frequently during the Cold War.[38] Probably the best known example of this is the 1959 'kitchen debate' at the American National Exhibition in Moscow, where Vice President Richard Nixon argued with General Secretary Nikita Khrushchev that a consumer-based economy gave American housewives freedom from domestic drudgery and opportunities for leisure, individuality and a higher standard of living.[39]

The NLC clearly publicised these ideals at the Ideal Home Exhibition, which was an extension of Ghana's First International Trade Fair held earlier the same year.[40] Although Nkrumah's administration had originally planned the fair and constructed the permanent Trade Fair site in Accra, the NLC took over planning after the 1966 coup.[41] The NLC re-spun the fair's goals to focus on strengthening Ghana's private sector. In a published message to participants, Lieutenant-General Joseph A. Ankrah, Chairman of the NLC stated, 'Our economy is looking forward to a chance of survival from the bleak past and for continual growth . . . come, businessmen of the world. Let us work together for our mutual benefit and in the true spirit of free enterprise'.[42] The NLC celebrated the trade fair, like the Ideal Home Exhibition, as ushering a new era of private business and used the fair not only to attract foreign investors, but also to assure international audiences that Ghana was on the road to economic stability.

The fair attracted more than 950,000 visitors, two and half times the population of Accra. Observers noted that visitors were largely from Ghana and other neighbouring African countries.[43] In addition, an estimated 2,000 firms participated, displaying all types of items ranging from heavy agricultural equipment to everyday household goods. Exhibitors included participating governments and commercial organisations showing goods made both in and outside Ghana.[44] Although participants' motivations varied, decisions in many cases were motivated by the Ghanaian government's undertaking to give twenty-two old cedis (about £10) worth of import licences for every square foot of space rented.[45]

Following in the footsteps of President Nkrumah, who vehemently used mass media coverage to promote his political agenda, the NLC used the international and Ghanaian press to publicise their economic policies and gain local and international support.[46] Photographs and details of the trade fair, its state-of-the-art facilities and crowds of visitors, including groups of Ghanaian school children, appeared in the pages of both mainstream and business-oriented presses.[47] In addition, newspapers showed several images of NLC members welcoming local chiefs and foreign dignitaries.[48] Under Nkrumah, the authority and power of chieftaincy was positioned as an obstacle in constructing a modern nation-state. Nationalist leaders viewed chiefs as 'antique', 'feudalistic' and 'unprogressive'.[49] Through NLC images, the military state illustrated intentions to restore relations between local chiefs and the state. In a confidential letter to the Secretary of State for Commonwealth Affairs describing the fair's outcomes, Harold Smedley, the British High Commissioner, concluded:

> Internally it was a great morale booster for the people of Ghana; and for the NLC . . . demonstrating as it did, the stability and popularity of the new regime. It provided evidence both of the significant progress the Government had already made in combating the economic difficulties caused by bad administration in the past, and the potential for economic growth in Ghana.[50]

In addition to motivations and ideologies, links between the First International Trade Fair and the Ideal Home Exhibition can be made in terms of the products displayed. The NLC constructed a smaller version of an ideal home show with model kitchen and bathrooms and many of the participating companies at the trade fair also exhibited their goods at the larger Ideal Home Exhibition nine months later.[51] Thus, the November 1967 exhibition should be understood as an extension of the International Trade Fair. Both used consumer goods to publicise, locally and internationally, Ghana's transition to a capitalist economy and both reflect NLC efforts to construct a new image of Ghana.[52] One major difference was that the propaganda represented the trade fair as an almost all-male event. While women did visit and also acted as 'female pavilion guides', women were largely excluded from the narrative.[53] In contrast, while also controlled by male elites, the Ideal Home Exhibition incorporated and attempted to appeal to female audiences. Although targetting mostly elite and middle-class consumers, sponsors and companies, thorough promotion of different household items, propagated specific gender roles for Ghanaian men and women and promoted the home as a key to national stability.

The Ghanaian home and national stability

Ideas about family and domesticity were at the centre of press advertisements and displays at the 1967 Ideal Home Exhibition. The exhibition directed consumer practices towards household consumption. It promoted not only housewife/breadwinner gender roles, stressing a woman's importance as wife, housekeeper and caregiver, and a man's authority as head of household, but also rational consumerism within the confines of an ideal home.[54] The state-controlled press positioned the 'Ghanaian home' as a space that represented national stability and an abundance of household goods as symbols of the country's promising economic future.

Unlike the trade fair, the exhibition featured products exclusively for the home, ranging from provisions to furniture. While some displays were constructed by large established multinational firms, like Lever Brothers and S. C. Johnson, others were sponsored by privately owned Ghanaian and foreign businesses. The Ideal Home Exhibition operated on multiple levels. Participating companies used the venue to promote and sell goods and publicise their business. The NLC supported the show publicly to demonstrate their commitment towards building the country's private sector and towards fulfilling Ghanaian consumer demands. In addition, through the press, the state reflected images of Western-style homes and housewife/breadwinner models back to Western audiences in hopes of securing aid and convincing donors to invest.[55]

Some of these motivations are reflected in exhibition advertising and publicity. For instance, the Tema-based Ghana Pioneer Aluminum Factory advertised that its brand of cooking utensils, pots and frying pans formed an 'important section of a home' where the 'hungry husband' could be satisfied after a 'day's hard work'.[56] Not only did this statement imply specific gender roles that cast men as breadwinners; it also positioned women as homemakers entrusted with the responsibility of transforming the home into a refuge from the cares of the outside world. Through its advertisements, the Ghana Pioneer Aluminum Factory suggested that its cookware allowed wives to prepare better tasting food, allowing them to satisfy their husbands and maintain an ideal home.

A Ghanaian-owned cosmetic firm, Atico, claimed that its line of soaps, powders, pomades and perfumes gave 'girls ... what it takes to create an ideal home'.[57] Atico advertisements portrayed an attractive African woman posing in her bedroom amid various Atico products, connecting ideas about consumption to beauty and domestic happiness. It also promoted its beauty products as suitable for the Ghanaian climate, as well as for African hair and skin. By highlighting problems such as the melting of make-up in hot weather, or the lack of matching skin-tone options on the market, Atico hoped to appeal to local women's needs.[58] Owner S. O. Atiemo claimed that his products enhanced the beauty of African women and were priced to meet their budgets.

The Ghana Pioneer Plastic Company also linked its line of products with ideals of housewifery, emphasising a woman's role as a knowledgeable and effective household manager. Pioneer Plastic advertisements situated its products, ranging from 'High Vinyl Floor Tiles' to plastic wig stands, as necessary for the 'average' housewife to create a happy home.[59] The company promoted its line of storage containers as essential for the housewife who knew the importance of household budgeting and understood the value of money. The ideal home was one that was run economically, and in turn a thrifty household contributed to improving the country's economy.

The exhibition also positioned consumerism as an act of patriotism and as an important feature of the post-Nkrumah economy. An exhibition reporter wrote that consumption of locally manufactured goods and support of local business was, 'a patriotic act'.[60] In the hope of gaining support for their free-market policies, the government propagated an image of the democratisation of goods. The show publicised products that had previously been considered 'luxuries far beyond the reach of all but a few privileged people' as affordable and available to all.[61] While some companies like Ghana Pioneer Plastic did attempt to incorporate more consumers by packaging smaller individualised items and keeping prices moderate, larger items displayed, such as gas stoves and air conditioners, were most likely still out of reach for the majority of Ghanaian consumers.[62]

Similar to the attempted sale of larger domestic items, the show's promotion of breadwinner/housewife ideals was largely disconnected from the majority of Ghanaian men's and women's experiences.[63] In his 1960s study of households in Adabraka, a socially and ethnically diverse residential area of Accra, Roger Sanjek argues that the majority of consumption decisions took place outside the household. Women tended to spend money on clothes and wigs to attend community and church functions, and men on going out to places like bars, football matches and nightclubs. Husbands and wives had individual incomes, separate sets of friends and made separate decisions about consumption activities.[64] In addition, as others have shown, conjugal partnership was not the norm or was only temporary in a couple's early years of a marriage, and many married couples lived apart.[65]

Moreover, the single-family homes and spacious kitchens and living rooms portrayed at the exhibitions did not reflect the realities of housing in urban Ghana. Consisting mainly of multi-household buildings, urban houses contained from four to forty rooms that were mostly rented out to numerous tenants. While wealthier residents did occupy multiple-room apartments and own larger domestic items like televisions and refrigerators, and some among the lower-middle and working classes had electric irons, fans and phonographs, 'most live[d] in a single room about twelve feet square, with only a bed, storage containers, chair, table, cooking utensils, and perhaps a radio as furnishings'.[66] Even when the state constructed new single-family developments in places like Tema, tenants converted extra rooms into places of business such as provision stores, drinking bars, and chop bars (a place to buy prepared meals). Since most domestic cooking was done outside on balconies or verandahs, tenants used indoor kitchens as places to sleep or for commercial activities rather than everyday cooking.[67]

While elite and some middle-class women did prefer monogamous, conjugal partnerships, they did so not because they fully supported Western imported notions of housewife/breadwinner gender roles, although some did, but because they considered these unions as a source of security.[68] A legally registered or church marriage provided wives with some legal protection and leverage in asserting both conjugal and inheritance rights.[69] In addition, since the colonial period monogamous marriages and Christian marriage ceremonies had been strong markers of elitism. Advertisers may have capitalised on this correlation to appeal to elite and emerging middle-class consumers and used images of the monogamous happy home to sell products.

Visitors to the Ideal Home Exhibition and readers/viewers of the published photographs, advertisements and features articles no doubt took different messages away from the show. The majority of those who did purchase products and drew inspiration from the show were probably already established elite and middle-class wives and daughters, and perhaps also their husbands. For many urban Ghanaians in the 1960s, the 'home' was not the centre of social or personal life. According to historian Dennis Austin, the NLC desired a return to 'a reformed past', or what I would refer to as an 'imagined past'.[70] The NLC presented versions of the ideal Ghanaian home to forward their political and economic agendas and address social changes. Echoed in social commentaries, like the article 'Social Reform and Economic Planning: They Must

Begin and End with the Kitchen', the state supported the idea that order and discipline began in the home.[71]

Disciplined domesticity

The ideal home was a space characterised by a neat division of labour and the enactment of gender roles that assumed the subordination of wives under the authority of their husbands. While these rigid ideals were not new, they do reflect anxieties about changes, or perceived changes, in social systems and political and economic opportunities for women and youth in post-Nkrumah Ghana.[72] According to Colonel A. A. Afrifa, Chairman of the NLC, Nkrumah's socialist programmes had undermined 'the authority of parents, teachers and elders' and dismantled the Ghanaian family system by seducing the 'youth to look upon the state as a better substitute for the parent'.[73] In addition, members of the CPP engaged in lavish consumption habits and seduced young girls with money and luxuries. While these allegations were often exaggerated, editorials and articles in the press reveal that these issues did circulate widely.

During the anti-colonial struggle, women had actively supported and organised the nationalist effort. In this period a limited number of educated women also began moving into jobs traditionally considered the preserve of males, as journalists, police officers, typists, clerks and employees in trading firms.[74] After independence, Nkrumah made special provisions for the election of women to the National Assembly, and removed discriminatory practices in education and employment. During his term, female education rates rose, more women entered universities and several took on new opportunities and entered professions previously closed to them. Although Nkrumah's efforts made visible changes in women's presence in politics and wage employment, opportunities remained limited and benefited mostly upper- and middle-class women and CPP party members.[75] The rigidly defined breadwinner/wife model promoted at the Ideal Home Exhibition spoke to some of these changes.

Social commentaries echoed these concerns over gender, while stressing the importance of increased discipline and the re-education of youth as possible solutions. An article entitled 'Maintaining Authority in the Home' argued that, while parents should never use excessive force or the 'iron hand', they should uphold the virtues of obedience in the home and instill this value in their children. According to the anonymous author, parents must urge children to respect and understand authority; anything less was a sign of parental weakness.[76] Additionally, in a lecture at Nkonya Secondary School, Economics Lecturer and NLC supporter Dr Jones Ofori-Atta urged students and all youth to unite to save Ghana 'from drowning in a moral cesspool'. He argued that the stability of Ghana required a new deal based on moral rearmament.[77] Taking up 'arms', a military-derived term in support of the military government, was the only way to stamp out what Ofori-Atta believed was a type of social chaos created by the past regime.

Some writers also called directly for government intervention in promoting discipline. For example, the president of the Eastern Region of Chiefs, Nene Annorkwei II argued that 'the indecent behaviour of students in the schools and colleges ... was brought on by ... the old regime'.[78] He encouraged the NLC and organisations, like the Christian Council of Ghana, to enforce moral education programmes in schools and universities. Similarly, women's organisation leader Emma Jiagge argued that now, more than ever, Ghana needed 'an organisation which would help restore traditional discipline'.[79] In particular, she blamed the degeneration of Ghanaian womanhood on Nkrumah's regime and called for the participation of more women's groups to 'curb the evils' growing over the past decade.

In addition to corrupting the morals of youth and women, the CPP was also criticised for its consumption habits, which the NLC saw as evidence of moral laxity and corruption. Although Nkrumah attempted to impose property limitations and dismissed various officials for abusing their positions to gain personal wealth, he could not contain them all.[80] After the coup, detailed reports appeared on the lavish consumption habits of CPP officials, such as Kwaku Boateng (Minister of the Interior) and Atta Mensah (Secretary to the Ministry of Communications and Works).[81] The most infamous was CPP Propaganda Secretary and Minister of the Interior Krobo Edusei, who owned a large number of houses and '(allegedly) a gold bed'.[82] In a confidential report to the Secretary of State for Commonwealth Relations and the British Prime Minister, the High Commissioner in Ghana wrote that local newspapers attacked Mr Krobo Edusei, in particular, 'for his wife's jewellery, his champagne parties and his joy riding', and there were 'veiled references to the *droit de seigneur* he and his friends are said to exercise over Ghana Airways hostesses'.[83] The implication of these allegations is that Edusei and his fellow CPP colleagues had unlimited access to the sexual services of the young and famously attractive Ghana Airways attendants.

CPP officials, as historian Emmanuel Akyeampong has argued, initiated a new elite culture characterised by the accumulation of houses, cars, young girlfriends and the consumption of expensive imported items.[84] However, while political elites were the initial targets of criticism about excessive consumerism, their relatives and especially their wives, young mistresses and girlfriends, also shouldered the blame. Takyiwaa Manuh argues that it was during the Nkrumah period that the 'sugar daddy syndrome' emerged.[85] Young women were lavished with gifts, found jobs and had apartments rented for them by older CPP men. During the latter part of Nkrumah's term, when items like sugar and milk became more expensive and often in short supply, reports highlighting the extravagant consumption habits of CPP members, as well as the young women benefiting from their patronage, intensified anxieties about the declining morals of women, in addition to the dangers of consumerism.[86]

The pitfalls of conspicuous consumption were captured in a 1966 article published in the *Ghanaian Times* by popular female journalist, Mabel Dove:

> Kwame Nkrumah, his gang, and his followers, taught people that the best type of citizen in the community was the man who lives in luxurious surroundings, owned long expensive cars, whose palaces or flats were so furnished that the visitor feared to walk on the soft carpet or sit on the comfortable chair.[87]

It is ironic that almost two years after the coup the NLC supported the Ideal Home Exhibition aimed at promoting and selling these same types of goods. What differed between the two forms of consumption was that consumerism under the NLC was based on free-market ideologies that assumed access to all Ghanaians. Consumerism was also posited as a patriotic act that supported Ghana's private sector and contributed to the country's increased economic development. Moreover, comfortable living, married couples, and the desire for consumer goods to maintain an ideal home, furthered an image of national stability that was deemed legitimate.

Through advertisements and the press, the ideal Ghanaian housewife, under her husband's authority, was glorified and represented as the essence of a respectable modern woman. In opposition to earlier portrayals of modern women as single, self-indulgent and incompetent, the married 1960s ideal housewife could be glamorous and fashionable as well as a good mother, housekeeper and cook.[88] Her consumption habits were not self-centered, like CPP members or those young girls that relied on them as 'sugar daddies', but contributed to creating a modern stable family and assisted in Ghana's national development.

Conclusion

Economic and political uncertainties placed the Ghanaian home at the centre of debates about national stability and the country's future. The 1967 Ideal Home Exhibition was part of this larger NLC refashioning project and represents a point at which gender intersected with the political dimensions of this process. The NLC sponsored events like Ghana's First International Trade Fair as ways to celebrate the country's transition to a free-market, capitalist economy. Aimed mostly towards international audiences, the trade fair strategically portrayed post-coup Ghana's economic potential and to secure foreign aid and private investment. Although visitors to the trade fair and the exhibition took away different messages, publicised images of consumer goods in abundance may have increased NLC support. The implication touted in both shows was the idea that if people supported the ruling regime and turned their backs on Nkrumah's ideologies, they could improve their standards of living and enjoy open access to a wider variety of goods. In a speech broadcast just a few weeks after the coup, Lieutenant-General Ankrah announced that the military government would eliminate shortages in essential commodities and that everything would be done to ensure that adequate supplies were always available in the stores at very reasonable prices.[89]

These ideas were also espoused through gendered messages at the Ideal Home Exhibition. Through advertisements and displays, exhibitors presented a 'domestic ideal' based on a woman's importance as wife, housekeeper and caregiver and a man's authority as head of household. Ideas about stable homes and rigid understandings of gender roles speak to larger ongoing debates in Ghanaian society about the effects of Nkrumah's regime on 'traditional' systems of authority and moral decline. The Ideal Home Exhibition presented a disciplined form of domesticity as vital for the country's economic and political reconstruction.

The Ideal Home Exhibition represents the intersection of gender and politics within a commercial space and further shows how ideas about gender and domesticity are mobilised by political regimes in attempts to restructure and reshape society. The fact that the number of Ghanaian men and women who lived as conjugal partners or in any kind of 'middle-class' domestic household during the 1960s was very small, emphasises this point. The show was largely disconnected from the everyday experiences of Ghanaian men and women, and the items displayed were most likely way beyond average incomes. The logic of a consumer-based household economy did not reflect the demands of most Ghanaians. Responsibilities to extended family, conjugal living patterns, housing shortages, as well as unstable wages and high costs of living did not make room for the consumer society that post-Nkrumah governments, or private investors and advertisers, envisioned.

Notes

Many thanks to Charles Ambler, Andrew Apter, Eileen Boris, Lisa Jacobson, Stephan Miescher, Erika Rappaport, Leila Rupp, Dmitri van den Bersselaar and the two anonymous reviewers for insightful comments on earlier drafts. I am also grateful for the useful comments and suggestions on earlier versions from participants and panellists at the 2005 African Studies Association Conference, the 2006 Mellon workshop of British Historians at the University of California Berkeley and the 2008 International Colloquium on Homes and Homecomings at the University of Nottingham.

1. 'Beentos' is slang for Ghanaians educated overseas, who sometimes placed a certain social value on their foreign experiences. See Emmanuel Akyeampong, 'Africans in the Diaspora: The Diaspora and Africa', *African Affairs* 99 (2000), pp. 1–18, here p. 8.

2. 'It Provides Enough Thrill', *Daily Graphic*, 28 November 1967, p. 7.

3. By 1960, Ghana had a population of around 7 million; 340,000 lived in Accra. Government of Ghana, *1900 Population Census of Ghana, vol. II: Demographic Characteristics* (Accra: Government Printer, 1964).

4. 'It Provides Enough Thrill'.

5. 'A Pat for the Organisers', *Daily Graphic*, 2 December 1967, p. 9.

6. Public Records and Archives Administration Department, Accra (PRAADA), ADM 5/3/141, E. N. Omaboe, 'Ghana's Economy and Aid Requirements in 1967', 20 May 1967; Dennis Austin and Robin Luckman (eds), *Politicians and Soldiers in Ghana, 1966–1972* (London: Frank Cass, 1975); Naomi Chazan, *An Anatomy of Ghanaian Politics: Managing Political Recession 1969–1982* (Boulder, CO: Westview Press, 1983).

7. Konadu also wrote under the pen name K. A. Bediako. His popular novels include *Don't Leave Me Mercy* (1966), *A Husband for Esi Ellua* (1967) and *Night Watchers of Korlebu* (1967).

8. Beyond his literary contributions, published biographical information on Konadu is limited. See Richard K. Priebe, 'Popular Writing in Ghana: A Sociology and Rhetoric', *Research in African Literatures* 9 (1978), pp. 395–432, Ime Ikiddeh, 'The Character of Popular Fiction in Ghana', in Richard K. Priebe (ed.), *Ghanaian Literatures* (Westport: Greenwood Press, 1988), pp. 73–83.

9. John D. Esseks, 'Government and Indigenous Private Enterprise in Ghana', *Journal of Modern African Studies* 9 (1971), pp. 11–29; John D. Esseks, 'Economic Policies', in Dennis Austin and Robin Luckham (eds), *Politicians and Soldiers in Ghana, 1966–1972* (London: Frank Cass, 1975), pp. 37–61, here p. 49; Maxwell Owusu, *Uses and Abuses of Political Power: A Case Study of Continuity and Change in the Politics of Ghana* (Chicago: University of Chicago Press, 1970).

10. Here I refer to the *Daily Graphic*, which followed and published special reports on the Ideal Home Exhibition and was geared mainly towards urban audiences. After independence, the *Graphic* was owned and managed by the Graphic Corporation, a commercial organisation controlled by the Nkrumah Government. Following the coup, the NLC appointed a group of officials to act as a caretaker board and appointed their own Minister of Information Chairman. By 1966, daily sales were about 170,000, yet actual readership was probably much more. The National Archives of the United Kingdom (NA), DO 153/56, Letter to D. K. Middleton, C. R. O. West Africa Political Department 'Ghana Press dismissal of editors by NLC-Confidential Correspondence', 1966.

11. Diana Gladys Azu, *The Ga Family and Social Change* (Leiden: Africa-Studiecentrum, 1974); Christine Oppong, *Middle Class African Marriage: A Family Study of Ghanaian Senior Servants* (London: George Allen & Unwin, 1981); Roger Sanjek, 'Female and Male Domestic Cycles in Urban Africa: The Adabraka Case', in Christine Oppong (ed.), *Female and Male in West Africa* (London: George Allen & Unwin, 1983). For studies, on non-elite women, see Gracia Clark, *'Onions Are My Husband': Survival and Accumulation by West African Market Women* (Chicago and London: University of Chicago Press, 1994); Claire Robertson, *Sharing the Same Bowl: A Socioeconomic History of Women and Class in Accra* (Bloomington: Indiana University Press, 1984).

12. Colonel A. A. Afrifra, *The Ghana Coup: 24th February 1966* (London: Frank Cass, 1967); Richard Rathbone, *Nkrumah and the Chiefs: The Politics of Chieftaincy in Ghana* (Athens: Ohio University Press, 2000); A. K. Ocran, *Politics of the Sword: A Personal Memoir on Military Involvement in Ghana and of Problems with Military Government* (London: Rex Collings, 1977).

13. For important exceptions, see Timothy Burke, *Lifebuoy Men, Lux Women: Commodification, Consumption and Cleanliness in Modern Zimbabwe* (Durham and London: Duke University Press, 1996); Clark, *Onions Are My Husband*; Barbara M. Cooper, *Marriage in Maradi: Gender and Culture in a Hausa Society in Niger, 1900–1989* (Portsmouth: Heinemann, 1997); Robertson, *Sharing the Same Bowl*; Lynn Thomas, *Politics of the Womb: Women, Reproduction, and the State in Kenya* (Berkeley: University of California Press, 2003).

14. For examples on Ghana, see Jean Allman and Victoria Tashjian, *'I Will not Eat Stone': A Women's History of Colonial Asante* (Portsmouth: Heinemann, 2000); Clark, *Onions Are My Husband*; Robertson, *Sharing the Same Bowl*.

15. Amina Mama, 'Khaki in the Family: Gender Discourses and Militarism in Nigeria', *African Studies Review* 41/2 (1998), pp. 1–17; Claire Robertson, 'The Death of Makola and Other Tragedies', *Canadian Journal of African Studies* 17 (1989), pp. 469–94. For comparative histories on similar topics, see Erica Carter, *How German Is She? Postwar West German Reconstruction and the Consuming Women* (Ann Arbor: University of Michigan Press, 1997); Wendy Goldman, *Women, the State and Revolution: Soviet Family Policy and Social Life, 1917–1936* (Cambridge: Cambridge University Press, 1993); Elaine Tyler May, *Homeward Bound: American Families in the Cold War Era* (1988; rev ed. New York: Basic, 1999); Mary Louise Roberts, *Civilization without Sexes: Reconstructing Gender in Postwar France, 1917–1927* (Chicago: University of Chicago Press, 1994).

16. Kwame Nkrumah, 'Christmas Broadcast', 22 December 1961, in Samuel Obeng (ed.), *Selected Speeches of Kwame Nkrumah*, vol. 2 (Accra: Afram Publications Ghana, 1979), pp. 161–70, here 161.

17. Walter Birmingham, I. Neustadt and E. N. Omaboe (eds), *A Study of Contemporary Ghana*, vol. 1: *The Economy of Ghana* (London: George Allen & Unwin, 1967).

18. PRAADA, RG 8/2/1011, Executive Instrument (EI) 344 Price Control, 1962; EI 35 Price Control (Amendment), 1963; EI 93 Price Control (Amendment) Order, 1963.

19. Willie E. Abraham, Chair, *Report of the Commission of Enquiry into Trade Malpractices in Ghana* (Accra and Tema: State Publishing Corporation, 1965). While mostly urban upper and middle classes consumed imported products, these items were not exclusive to them. As early as 1943, the colonial government considered imported goods, such as kerosene, candles, matches, sugar, flour, cotton piece goods and unmanufactured tobacco, as African 'household essentials'. By the 1950s, government surveys added tinned milk, sardines, cigarettes and soap to the most frequently purchased items, especially in the cities. See PRAADA, ADM 5/3/44, W. Ewan Conway, *Report of the Commission of Enquiry into the Distribution and Prices of Essential Imported Goods* (Accra: Government Printing Department, 1943), p. 9; PRAADA, ADM 7/18/3, Gold Coast Office of the Government Statistician, *Accra Survey of Household Budgets*, Statistical and Economic Papers 2 (Accra: Government Printing Department, 1953).

20. Kwame Nkrumah established GNTC between October 1961 and April 1962 when his government bought out two commercial houses – Commonwealth Trust Company and A. G. Leventis – and combined their wholesale and retail functions into one state-owned corporation. 'Ghana National Trading Corporation', *Ghana Business Guide 1969*, p. 246. By 1965, GNTC held a near monopoly over the importation of essential goods. See Abraham, *Report of the Commission of Enquiry*, pp. 6–7.

21. While severe economic crises in Ghana are typically associated with the 1970s, economic problems in the second half of the 1960s created commodity shortages and restricted consumer access to goods. For a more detailed description of the 1964–65 shortages, see Esseks, 'Economic Policies', p. 38.

22. Yet strong opposition to Nkrumah and the CPP existed prior to this. See Jean Allman, *The Quills of the Porcupine: Asante Nationalism in an Emergent Ghana* (Madison: University of Wisconsin Press, 1993).

23. In 1966, the Ghana Army consisted of about 600 officers and 14,000 other ranks. It was then the largest in West Africa and the cost of maintaining it the fifth highest in the continent. The police force, which at independence had numbered about 6,000 men, had grown to 14,000 at the time of the coup. Robert Dowse, 'Military and Police Rule', in Dennis Austin and Robin Luckham (eds), *Politicians and Soldiers in Ghana, 1966–1972* (London: Frank Cass, 1975), pp. 16–36, here p. 16.

24. PRAADA, ADM 5/4/411, 'Interview with the NLC Commissioner for Industries, Major K. B. Agbo, by Managing Director, P. & A. Ltd, Tony Nomah', *Industry in the Service of Ghana*, 1968.

25. ADM 5/4/411, 'Interview with Agbo', p. 9. The NLC offered small-scale state-run enterprises (bamboo and rattan factories) for sale. For larger enterprises, the NLC formed partnerships with Ghanaian, but mostly foreign investors. Esseks, 'Economic Policies', p. 46.

26. Paul Nugent, *Big Men, Small Boys and Politics in Ghana* (Accra: Asempa, 1995).

27. Robertson, 'The Death of Makola', p. 485.

28. Deborah S. Ryan, *The Ideal Home through the 20th Century* (London: Hazar, 1997); Deborah S. Ryan, 'All the World and her Husband: The Daily Mail Ideal Home Exhibition, 1908–1939', in Maggie Andrews and Mary M. Talbot (eds), *All the World and her Husband: Women in Twentieth-Century Consumer Culture* (London and New York: Cassell, 2000), pp. 10–22; Victoria de Grazia, *Irresistible Empire: America's Advance through Twentieth-Century Europe* (Cambridge, MA: The Belknap Press of Harvard University, 2005).

29. Carola Lentz, 'Local Culture in the National Arena: The Politics of Cultural Festivals in Ghana', *African Studies Review* 44/3 (2001), pp. 47–72.

30. Jean Allman, 'Making Mothers: Missionaries, Medical Officers and Women's Work in Colonial Asante, 1924–1945', *History Workshop Journal* 38 (1994), pp. 23–48. 'Home life' and domestic campaigns were quite common throughout colonial Africa. For an excellent collection on similar issues, see Karen Tranberg Hansen (ed.), *African Encounters with Domesticity* (New Brunswick: Rutgers University Press, 1992).

31. Burke, *Lifebuoy Men, Lux Women*, pp. 137–44.

32. The FGGW actively concentrated on ending discrimination against women in employment, marriage and inheritance practices. Although they petitioned on behalf of all women, the organisation's urban bourgeois character did not account for the needs of those living in rural areas or the poor, thus it failed to gain national support. Takyiwaa Manuh, 'Women and their Organisations During the Convention Peoples' Party Period', in Kwame Arhin (ed.), *The Life and Work of Kwame Nkrumah* (Trenton: Africa World Press, 1993), pp. 101–27.

33. Moses Danquah, 'How to Raise Our Living Standards', *Daily Graphic*, 15 August 1956, pp. 7–9; Edith Wuver, 'The Exhibition is Now On: Let's Exploit It!', *Daily Graphic*, 16 August 1956, p. 8.

34. Audrey Gadzekpo, 'Gender Discourse and Representational Practices in Gold Coast Newspapers', *Jenda* (2001), pp. 1–18, here p. 8.

35. 'Happy Home Institute', *Sunday Mirror*, 8 November 1953; Elvis D. Aryeh, 'Organise Young Girls-Teacher', *Daily Graphic*, 11 April 1972. The Ideal Home Makers Club was established in 1971. Aryeh, 'Organise Young Girls'.

36. Danquah, 'How to Raise Our Living Standards', p. 7.

37. 'A Pat for the Organisers'.

38. Lizabeth Cohen, *A Consumer's Republic: The Politics of Mass Consumption in Postwar America* (New York: Vintage, 2004).

39. May, *Homeward Bound*.

40. The NLC held the Ghana International Trade Fair from 1–19 February 1967 in Accra.

41. 'Ghana Plans for a Trade Fair', *Daily Graphic*, 14 December 1966, p. 5.

42. 'Giant Fair Opens Wednesday', *Business Weekly*, 30 January 1967, p. 1.

43. NA, FCO38/56 Ghana: Internal: Fairs and Exhibitions, Summary report on the Ghana International Trade Fair from Harold Medley, British High Commissioner, 25 April 1967, p. 2. Nine African governments including Dahomey (i.e. Benin), Ivory Coast, Liberia, Morocco, Niger, Nigeria, Senegal, Togo and Upper Volta (i.e. Burkina Faso) set up exhibitions and participated in the fair.

44. NA, FCO38/56 Ghana: Internal: Fairs and Exhibitions, The First Ghana International Trade Fair, report from Trade Fair Advisor R. H. C. Hammond to UK Ministry of Overseas Development, 22 February 1967.

45. For instance, the British pavilion measured 36,750 square feet equalling a total of £367,500 in import licences. 'Developing Africa: Ghana's First International Trade Fair', *Business Weekly*, 30 January 1962, p. 2.

46. NA, FCO38/56 Ghana: Internal: Fairs and Exhibitions, Letter from S. J. Gross, Deputy High Commissioner to the Board of Trade Journals Editor, 21 February 1967. For Nkrumah's use of the press, see P. A. V. Anza, 'Kwame Nkrumah and the Mass Media', in Kwame Arhin (ed.), *The Life and Work of Kwame Nkrumah* (Trenton: Africa World Press, 1993), pp. 83–100; Janet Hess, 'Exhibiting Ghana: Display, Documentary and "National" Art in the Nkrumah Era', *African Studies Review* 44 (2001), pp. 59–77.

47. 'Fair – A Scene of Gaiety', *Daily Graphic*, 2 February 1967, p. 1; 'Giant Fair Opens on Wednesday', *Business Weekly*, 30 January 1967, p. 1; 'Thousands Attend the Fair', *Daily Graphic*, 3 February 1967.

48. E.g., photograph of Lt General Ankrah surrounded by foreign dignitaries cutting tape to declare trade fair open, 'Fair – A Scene of Gaiety', *Daily Graphic*, 2 February 1967, p. 1; 'Asantehene Rides to the Fair Site, Other Chiefs Were Present', *Daily Graphic*, 2 February 1967, p. 15; Photograph of 'Tumu Koro, president of the Upper Region House of Chiefs and Lt General J. A. Ankrah, Embracing Each Other', *Daily Graphic*, 2 February 1967, p. 15; Photograph of Lt General J. A. Ankrah with Nigerian federal government representative, *Daily Graphic*, 2 February 1967, p. 15.

49. Through native court reforms Nkrumah dismantled chiefly jurisdiction and replaced chiefs with 'non-traditional' figures. Rathbone, *Nkrumah and the Chiefs*, pp. 1–7, 52–8.

50. NA, FCO38/56 Ghana: Internal: Fairs and Exhibitions, Confidential report from Harold Smedley, British High Commissioner to Herbert Bowden, Secretary of State for Commonwealth Affairs, 25 April 1967, p. 9.

51. Mike Adjei, 'Trade Fair Opens Today', *Daily Graphic*, 1 February 1967, p. 12; 'Ideal Home Exhibition at Trade Fair', *Daily Graphic*, 12 February 1967.

52. For comparisons on the intersection between state interests and public fairs and festivals, see Andrew Apter, *The Pan-African Nation: Oil and the Spectacle of Culture in Nigeria* (Chicago: University of Chicago

Press, 2005); Becky E. Conekin, *The Autobiography of a Nation: The 1951 Festival of Britain* (Manchester and New York: Manchester University Press, 2003); Robert W. Rydell, *All the World's a Fair: Visions of Empire at American International Expositions, 1876–1916* (Chicago: University of Chicago Press, 1984).

53. Photograph of female pavilion guides, *Daily Graphic*, 4 February 1967.

54. For debates on how consumer goods have historically shaped gendered relationships in Africa, see Timothy Burke, '"Fork up and Smile": Marketing, Colonial Knowledge and the Female Subject in Zimbabwe', *Gender & History* 8 (1996), pp. 440–56; Cooper, *Marriage in Maradi*; Jean and John L. Comaroff, 'Home-Made Hegemony: Modernity, Domesticity, and Colonialism in South Africa', in Tranberg Hansen (ed.), *African Encounters with Domesticity*, pp. 37–74; Nancy Rose Hunt, 'Colonial Fairy Tales and the Knife and Fork Doctrine in the Heart of Africa', in Tranberg Hansen (ed.), *African Encounters with Domesticity*, pp. 143–71. For other places, see de Grazia, *Irresistible Empire*; Victoria de Grazia and Ellen Furlough (eds), *The Sex of Things: Gender and Consumption in Historical Perspective* (Berkeley: University of California Press, 1996); Erika Rappaport, *Shopping for Pleasure: Women in the Making of London's West End* (Princeton: Princeton University Press, 2000).

55. Here I rely on Jeremy Prestholdt's theories of similitude, defined as 'a strategic appeal in the space of global interrelation that, through a claim to sameness, seeks to affect the perceptions and policies of more powerful agents'. See Jeremy Prestholdt, *Domesticating the World: African Consumerism and the Genealogies of Globalization* (Berkeley: University of California Press, 2008), p. 18.

56. P. G. Schwegler, a Swiss investor, founded Ghana Pioneer Aluminum in 1959. The company imported aluminum from Russia, but manufactured its final products under the brand name "Red Torch" at its Tema factory. Hans Rudolf Roth, *Because of Kwadua: Autobiography of Hans Rodolf Roth* (Accra: Afram, 2008), pp. 272–3; Also see 'Aluminum Utensils Help Ideal Homes', *Daily Graphic*, 2 December 1967, p. 15.

57. Advertisement for Atico, *Daily Graphic*, 2 December 1967, p. 12.

58. 'Atico Solves Beauticians' Problems', *Daily Graphic*, 2 December 1967, p. 16.

59. 'Ideal Home–Plastic Wares are Useful', *Daily Graphic*, 23 November 1967, p. 17. Prior to 1967, Pioneer Plastic's vinyl floor products would have been popularly known as lino. The use of 'vinyl' reflects a disconnection with Ghanaian consumers.

60. 'A Pat for the Organisers'.

61. 'It Provides Enough Thrill', p. 7.

62. 'Ideal Home–Plastic', p. 17.

63. Oppong, *Middle Class African Marriage*.

64. The majority of Sanjek's interviewees were literate Christian Southern Ghanaians with most being from the Kwawu, Ga and Ewe ethnic groups.

65. Azu, *The Ga Family and Social Change*, pp. 77–82; Roger Sanjek, 'Female and Male Domestic Cycles in Urban Africa: The Adabraka Case'; Oppong (ed.), *Female and Male in West Africa*, pp. 87–9.

66. Sanjek, 'Female and Male Domestic Cycles', p. 88.

67. PRAADA, ADM 7/18/1, I. Neustadt and E. N. Omaboe, *Social and Economic Survey of Tema* (Accra: Office of the Government Statistician in conjunction with the Tema Development Corporation, 1959), pp. 27–9.

68. Audrey Gadzekpo argues that even before the turn of the nineteenth century, elite African women wrote about idealised versions of nuclear family living and companionate marriage. Gold Coast newspapers, which reflected mainly the concerns of the educated elite and later the 'new' elite and emerging middle classes, were full of debates on issues including, domesticity, femininity and women's sphere, marriage, polygamy and inheritance practices. Gadzekpo, 'Gender Discourse and Representational Practices', pp. 2–3. See also Stephanie Newell and Audrey Gadzekpo (eds), *Mabel Dove: Selected Writings of a Pioneer West African Feminist* (Nottingham: Trent Editions, 2004); Christine Oppong (ed.), *Domestic Rights and Duties in Southern Ghana*, Legon Family Research Papers, vols 1–2 (Legon: Institute of African Studies, University of Ghana, 1974); Carmel Dinan, 'Sugar Daddies and Gold-Diggers: The White Collar Single Women in Accra', in Oppong (ed.), *Female and Male in West Africa*, pp. 344–66.

69. The marriage question became a key issue after the passage of the Marriage Ordinance of 1884 (1909), which stated that upon death one-third of a man's estate would go to his lineage and two-thirds to his widow and children. Although very few couples married under the Ordinance, the idea that property should be kept within the nuclear family, and not the deceased's relatives, provoked serious debates throughout the twentieth century. Dorothy Dee Vellenga, 'Who is Wife? Legal Expressions of Heterosexual Conflicts in Ghana', in Oppong (ed.), *Female and Male in West Africa*, pp. 144–55.

70. Dennis Austin, 'Introduction', in Dennis Austin and Robin Luckham (eds), *Politicians and Soldiers in Ghana, 1966–1972* (London: Frank Cass, 1975), p. 2.

71. For a criticism of white-collar working women and urban youth, see Togbi Yao, 'Social Reforms and Economic Planning: They Must Begin and End with the Kitchen', *Sunday Mirror*, 26 August 1967, p. 3.

72. These issues were not specific to Ghana; for Nigeria, Amina Mama argues that military reforms often focused on re-establishing or re-emphasising conservative gender roles. Mama, 'Khaki in the Family', p. 14.

73. Colonel A. A. Afrifa, *The Ghana Coup: 24th February 1966* (London: Frank Cass, 1967), p. 77.

74. Gadzekpo, 'Gender Discourse and Representational Practices', pp. 16–17.

75. Manuh, 'Women and Their Organisations'.

76. 'Maintaining Authority in the Home', *Evening News*, 13 May 1968, p. 6.

77. Ofori-Atta strongly opposed Nkrumah's economic policies and was active during the NLC–Busia period. He was also Deputy Minister of Economic Affairs under Busia. Dr Jones Ofori-Atta, 'To Achieve Social Solidarity Which is Essential for Stable Society Base Values Must be Eschewed', third address at Nkonya Secondary School, *Evening News*, 12 June 1968, p. 3.

78. 'Youth Need Sound Moral Education – Chief', 13 June 1968, p. 5.

79. 'Jiagge – Let's Have Women's Organisation in the Country', *Evening News*, 24 May 1968, p. 5.

80. Dennis Austin, *Politics in Ghana, 1946–1960* (Oxford: Oxford University Press: 1964), pp. 405–7.

81. See e.g., the series of articles by *Evening News* reporter Mike Anane: 'I Maintained 3 Houses in 1962 Boateng', *Evening News*, 15 May 1968, p. 2; 'I Never Gave Pocket Money to My Wife – Atta Mensah', *Evening News*, 4 June 1968, p. 3.

82. T. C. McCaskie, 'Accumulation, Wealth and Belief in Asante History II: The Twentieth Century', *Africa* 56 (1986), pp. 1–23, here p. 18.

83. NA, PREM 11/3369, Prime Minister's Office: Correspondence and Papers, Confidential Letter from the United Kingdom High Commission in Ghana to the Secretary of State for Commonwealth Relations, 17 May 1961.

84. Emmanuel Akyeampong, *Drink, Power, and Cultural Change: A Social History of Alcohol in Ghana, c.1800 to Recent Times* (Portsmouth: Heinemann, 1996), p. 145.

85. Manuh, 'Women and Their Organisations', p. 113.

86. Kojo Bentsil, 'Girls, Give Up Those Luxuries', *Daily Graphic*, 7 February 1966, p. 5.

87. Mabel Dove, 'The Coup Was a Healing Tonic: Examine Your Conscience', *Ghanaian Times*, 15 April 1966, in Newell and Gadzekpo (eds), *Mabel Dove*, p. 118.

88. Tani E. Barlow et al., 'The Modern Girl Around the World: A Research Agenda and Preliminary Findings', *Gender & History* 17 (2005), pp. 245–94. For ongoing debates on the domestic incompetence of educated elite girls, see Gadzekpo, 'Gender Discourse and Representational Practices', pp. 3–7.

89. Major-General Joseph Arthur Ankrah, Chairman of the National Liberation Council, 'Broadcasted Speech on NLC Economic Policies', 2 March 1966.

6 'The Dining Room Should Be the Man's Paradise, as the Drawing Room Is the Woman's': Gender and Middle-Class Domestic Space in England, 1850–1910

Jane Hamlett

In a decorative advice manual, *Our Homes and How to Beautify Them*, published in 1902, H. J. Jennings contended 'that the Dining Room should be the man's Paradise, as the Drawing Room is the woman's . . . The drawing or withdrawing room, is essentially and pre-eminently the ladies' room; as sacred to their influence and rule as the smoking room is to the regnancy of men'.[1] For Jennings and many other domestic advice writers, the ideal middle-class home contained distinctive gendered material cultures. The ideal drawing room was light in colouring and furnished with delicate objects and draperies, while dining rooms were decorated in dark and sombre colours with furniture of oak (see Figures 1 and 2). For larger homes, the morning room and the boudoir were also associated with women, whereas the study, smoking room, billiard room and library were seen as male terrains. Historians have noted the growing importance of gendered spaces for the nineteenth-century middle classes, and the increasing segregation of the middle-class home.[2] But we know little about the extent to which these gendered distinctions were realised in everyday home life, or the social consequences of gendered segregation. On the basis of a new survey of advice literature, inventories and sale catalogues and autobiographies, this chapter examines the relationship between the gendered hierarchy of the home and the way it was organised, decorated and arranged.

There is a growing cross-disciplinary awareness of the function of domestic space and material things in creating meaning within the home. North American studies have examined the mutually constitutive relationship between gender and material culture, noting that 'gendering is the process by which identities are pieced together by active subjects from the materials – objects, ideals, people – at hand'.[3] Theorists have claimed that there is a direct relationship between the extent to which segregation occurs in domestic space and women's wider social power.[4] The sharpening of the divide between male and female space in the middle-class home has been seen as instrumental in women's exclusion from public knowledge and power in nineteenth-century society.[5] This has been widely associated with a broader division of Victorian culture and society into separate spheres.[6] While this has been questioned from a variety

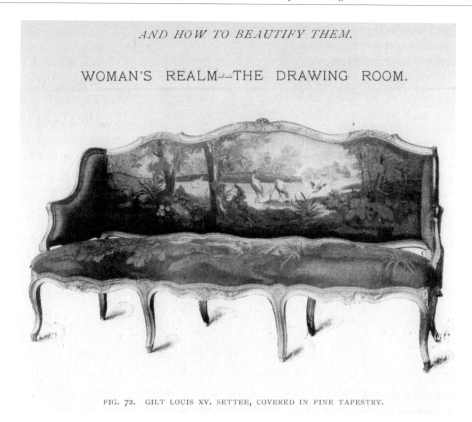

FIG. 72. GILT LOUIS XV. SETTEE, COVERED IN FINE TAPESTRY.

Figure 1: The ideal drawing room, according to H. J. Jennings, *Our Homes, and How to Beautify Them* (London: Harrison and Sons, 1902), p. 173.

of perspectives,[7] Victorian woman's relationship with the drawing room is still often depicted in a negative light. Thad Logan suggests that the densely draped Victorian parlour was produced by the frustrations of confined Victorian females.[8] Juliet Kinchin argues that the association of women with the drawing room symbolised both women's supposed 'innate intellectual inferiority' and their 'objectification within the interior'.[9] This chapter will not only question the extent to which gendered segregation was realised in the home, but also the contention that it should be automatically viewed as negative, exploring how it was viewed by contemporary advice writers, practised in actual homes, and how children reacted to it when they were growing up.

The rise of masculine spaces in the middle-class home has also been seen as evidence of a shift in gender relations. John Tosh argues that during the late nineteenth century, men became increasingly antagonised by the female-controlled customs and practices of the home. In particular, men sought refuge from the five-o'clock tea in an internal flight to the den, study and smoking room.[10] Tosh's analysis incorporates a wide range of data, and offers a number of different models of masculine behaviour: fathers are shown as loving and intimate as well as distant.[11] However, overall his emphasis is on the development of a large scale rejection of domesticity among a new generation of late nineteenth-century men, that was manifested not only in the home, but in the creation of a set of values at odds with domesticity in the public schools,

FIG. 71.   DINING ROOM IN OAK.

Figure 2: The ideal furnishing for the dining room: H. J. Jennings, *Our Homes, and How to Beautify Them* (London: Harrison and Sons, 1902), p. 170.

and above all the exodus of middle-class bachelors to the empire.[12] More recent work has highlighted the existence of exclusively male domesticities outside the home. This emerges in Quintin Colville's study of shipboard material culture in the British navy, in this collection, and Amy Milne-Smith's examination of male domesticity in the club.[13] Smith's analysis is, however, confined to the upper classes. Deborah Cohen's recent study has confirmed that nineteenth-century middle-class men were often active purchasers of goods for the home.[14] However, we know relatively little about the extent to which male spaces were created in these homes, and their impact on the gendered hierarchy of the home.

This chapter, then, reveals the crucial role material objects could play in creating meaning in the home, in reflecting and creating the gendered hierarchies of the middle-class household. Late nineteenth-century advice writers, both male and female, were obsessed with dividing spaces between men and women, and marking out masculine and feminine spaces. Yet rather than reinforcing patriarchal power, female advice writers cautioned against giving priority to masculine space, arguing that the mistress of the house should hold sway in the third sitting room. Spatial division was not necessarily linked to female subjugation. Female domestic advice writers often emphasised the need for a morning room for the lady of the house, linking sexual separation with empowerment. There were, of course, some limits to the expression of gendered identities through everyday material objects. In everyday practice, most middle-class families were unlikely to have the resources to carry out elaborate gendered segregation in their homes. Late nineteenth-century men may have yearned for studies and dens, but they were unlikely to find them in ordinary middle-class homes, where the third reception room was often a multi-purpose breakfast room, a space apparently geared to family sociability as much as sexual separation. Gendered spaces were most frequently found in upper-middle-class or gentry homes where space was plentiful, and those with a husband who worked at home. Here, masculine spaces could be used to reinforce fatherly authority, but the permeability of male spaces could also be used to underline the limits of patriarchal power. Gendered material culture exerted a powerful influence on the children of these homes. Yet as I will also argue below, it did not necessarily reinforce the status quo, in some cases provoking a rejection of the gendered ideals of the Victorian era.

Any study of the nineteenth-century middle classes must confront a problem of definition. During the 1970s and early 1980s, historians refined their view of the social composition of the middle class, noting differences of stratification and occupation.[15] Increasingly, the study of class has shifted from the social to the cultural.[16] Class relations and social institutions are no longer seen as separate from cultural production.[17] Historians of class have also become aware of the importance of other categories: 'social identity is now understood to be a construct in which class is one of a constellation of meanings'.[18] Rather than constructing a single narrative for middle-class domestic practice, this chapter seeks to show differences within this diverse social group. Wealth, the size of the home and the availability of space made a crucial difference to the implementation of gendered divides in the home. The use of gendered suites of rooms in gentry houses is well documented.[19] Occupation was also an important factor: homes that contained a husband who worked from home, such as clerical homes, tended to be organised very differently from those where men were absent for most of the day. Moreover, the homes of those on the fringes of the middle classes such as farmers, shopkeepers and, at the opposite end of the scale, the gentry, have been assessed to reveal the boundaries of social and cultural practice. While several authors have used inventories to reveal a distinctive lifestyle and domestic material culture among the British middle classes,[20] this chapter takes a different approach by systematically considering the evidence of inventories and sale catalogues alongside the cultural representation of gendered spaces in domestic and decorative advice manuals and autobiographies.

From the 1870s onwards, more domestic instruction manuals and guides to home decoration were published.[21] This chapter draws on thirty-two decorative and domestic advice manuals, published between 1864 and 1910, to show how the relationship between gender and domestic space was imagined and represented in cultural discourses. The chapter then turns to inventories and sale catalogues for evidence of room names and contents, to explore the gendering of domestic space in everyday practice. It is true that inventories may not tell us the precise location of objects in the home.[22] This may be particularly the case for the early modern period. As far as the nineteenth century is concerned, inventories and sale catalogues provide more detailed information about use than any other contemporary source. I explore 200 such lists, held in record offices and local archives in the south-east, north-east and north-west of England.

Finally, autobiographies are used to demonstrate the influence of gendered material culture on children in the home. Although autobiographies were for some time considered less than trustworthy, they are now seen as an important source,[23] even though they cannot be viewed as a simple representation of past experience.[24] As Mary Chamberlain puts it, 'memories are complex historical sources, in which what is recalled and recounted may be less revealing than why, how or when recollection takes place'.[25] Accounts of childhood are particularly challenging, as they are driven by a desire to explain the present self.[26] Thus, autobiographies allow us to consider both the experience of gendered material cultures in childhood, and the reflexive consideration and construction of these experiences in relation to the adult self. Four autobiographies that feature an extended commentary of gendered space in the home have been chosen for discussion here.[27] All four accounts are drawn from the late nineteenth century, the time at which the gendered segregation of the home was at its zenith. The accounts also offer the views of male and female children from a range of middle-class homes, revealing the relationship between learning ideas of gender through their home environments and the often complex identities these writers developed in later life.

***

While rooms and goods had been associated with masculinity and femininity in the late eighteenth and early nineteenth centuries, writers of domestic advice placed increasing emphasis on these distinctions in the second half of the nineteenth century.[28] In his treatise on planning, *The Gentleman's House*, first published in 1864, Robert Kerr noted that the drawing room should be 'entirely ladylike'.[29] In *Hints on Household Taste*, first published as a book in 1868, the design reformer Charles Eastlake attacked the femininity of the drawing room and 'the silly knick knacks that frequently crowd the drawing room table'.[30] In contrast, advice writers viewed the dining room as a masculine space, to be decorated in dark colours and sombre oak. These spaces were also increasingly linked to national identity.[31] The oak dining room (often imitation Tudor) was linked to masculine Englishness, the ornate drawing room (often Louis Quinze) associated with French femininity.[32] This system of gendered segregation was, in part, expected to provide a haven for men, both as a welcome respite from the world outside and a serious professional space for those who worked from home. As Kinchin has noted, the study or library was presented as a masculine space that had to be kept quiet and undisturbed, and to suggest serious study with its sober oak furniture.[33] Large homes offered more scope for the gendering of space. Advice manuals such as Kerr's, aimed at the upper middle classes, suggested the gendering of suites of rooms: with boudoirs, drawing rooms and morning rooms as feminine spaces and studies, libraries, smoking rooms and billiard rooms assigned to men. However, while the material culture of these rooms denoted masculinity, advice writers acknowledged that these spaces were subject to varied and complex uses. For example, the dining room in smaller homes could be expected to act also as sitting room, parlour and gentleman's waiting room.[34]

While there was a broad consensus on the gendering of the home, domestic and decorative advice writers disagreed over how much space should be granted for masculine respite. The debate crystallised over the practice of smoking in the home. In *The Gentleman's House*, Kerr gave the male side of the argument, noting, 'The pitiable resources to which some gentlemen are driven, even in their own houses, in order to be able to enjoy the pestiferous luxury of a cigar, have given rise to the

PLATE XXXVI. A SMOKING ROOM CHIMNEY CORNER.   *Photographed at Warings.*

Figure 3: The ideal smoking room: H. J. Jennings, *Our Homes, and How to Beautify Them* (London: Harrison and Sons, 1902), p. 271.

occasional introduction of an apartment specially dedicated to the use of Tobacco'.[35] After cheap cigarettes came on the market in 1883, smoking became more widespread, which may in part explain the increasing vociferousness of the debate. For Jennings, the smoking room was a man's retreat from the working world: 'its keynote should be a rich, shadowy comfort, the room should at once convey a feeling of retirement from the throb and tumult' (see Figure 3).[36] Jane Ellen Panton, however (writing before Jennings), argued that smoking should not be allowed in the home at all, except, perhaps, in the conservatory: 'There is nothing more trying than an atmosphere of stale smoke, and I look forward to a time when men of the rising generation will be a little less selfish than they are at present in their indulgence of a habit'.[37] While fewer men frowned on smoking, the sex of the writer did not necessarily determine their position in the debate. Mrs Haweis, who wrote for the Art at Home series in the 1870s, offered a compromise, suggesting that, while the smoking room was a retreat for tired men, it was ultimately a shared space: 'a very quaint, pleasant, and pretty *sanctum* for both husband and wife and their intimate friends'.[38] These representations of the smoking room offered nineteenth-century homemakers competing and shifting spatial models.

A space for male seclusion in the home was not always given priority. For small middle-class houses with three reception rooms, tastemakers argued over whether husband or wife should hold sway in the 'third sitting room'. Panton argued that the drawing room and dining room were essentials, but in small houses where a third reception room was available, a space for female retreat should be chosen over a study or smoking room. 'Even in a small house I very strongly advise the third room to be set aside emphatically for the mistress's own room – sacred to her own pursuits, and far too sacred to be smoked in on any occasion whatever.'[39] The morning room features in Panton's first book, *From Kitchen to Garret*, which lays out the essentials for a newly wed couple on a budget. The study only appears in her later *Nooks and Corners*, which is aimed at an older, richer couple with more space at their disposal. For Kerr it was simply a retreat. He pictures the morning room as an escape and stresses the need for a door between it and the drawing room: 'it provides for the ladies what is called *escape* in the manner most legitimate of all'.[40] Panton reflected more deeply on the significance of the morning room, suggesting that in addition to seclusion it also offered an expression of female interiority: 'this room can hardly be made too pretty in my eyes, for undoubtedly here will be struck the keynote of the house, for the chamber set aside for the mistress of the house is unconsciously a great revealer of secrets'.[41] Lillie Hamilton French's *The House Dignified*, an American discussion of interior decoration published in 1908, had a similar emphasis: 'you cannot enter this room, even when empty, without recognising that the inner temple of its owner's soul must somehow be a lovely place in which you yourself would like to dwell and find your re-creation'.[42]

Such representations reveal how the morning room was imagined to reinforce femininity, while simultaneously allowing for the expression of feminine interiorities and the construction of a positive female identity. But advice writers also emphasised the room's practical purpose in contributing to feminine freedom. Both Panton and fellow advice writer Mrs Peel stress that the morning room must be seen as an important site for female work.[43] Rather than presenting an opposition between functional male rooms and frivolous female chambers, these writers believed that a room could be both feminine and purposeful. It is often assumed by historians that before Virginia Woolf's famous call for 'a room of one's own', Victorian women had virtually no private space in the home. But these representations suggest that such spaces did exist, if only in the pages of the advice manual. A writer herself, Mrs Panton pushed for an equality of desks: 'if she [Angelina] can copy Edwin's writing table, she will find it a great comfort to her, for the deep drawers will hold paper, envelopes, and the thousand and one things she should never be without'.[44] Peel echoes Panton's suggestion that the morning room should be used as a female workspace: 'Of writing tables there is an endless variety, but as a rule those which are commodious and comfortable are only suitable in style to a mercantile establishment, while others, beautifully designed for boudoirs and drawing-rooms, scarcely commend themselves to the business woman'.[45] While late nineteenth-century men may have become increasingly anxious to carve out a space for themselves in the home, these texts suggest that they did not always succeed. Rather the gendering of space was constantly contested and negotiated as writers argued over which sex should hold sway in the third sitting room. Spatial segregation did not simply enforce the gendered status quo: rather, space was gendered in a variety of ways that could ensure the empowerment or subjection of women.

***

How did such prescriptions compare with the constrictions of practical living? Inventories and sale catalogues from the period reveal room names and contents, showing the extent to which the middle classes chose or were able to follow these recommendations. Approximately 70 per cent of the inventories and sale catalogues examined that included room names contained both a dining room and drawing room. Smaller homes, on the fringes of the lower middle classes, belonging to farmers and shopkeepers, were less likely to label their two main reception rooms in this way, and tended to feature sitting rooms or parlours.[46] However, the survey suggests that middle-class homes had a drawing room and a dining room, and thus had the spatial potential to enact Jennings's divide between masculine and feminine space. Drawing rooms and dining rooms were usually furnished in specially designed suites of furniture, which were the standard commercial product available at this time.[47] Drawing room suites were made from the materials that advice writers associated with femininity, such as oak or rosewood, whereas dining room furnishings were mahogany, or oak in the later period. Thus the design of the main pieces of furniture in these rooms reflected the 'gendered' conventions of advice manuals. The widespread commercial manufacture and marketing of such goods limits the extent to which we can view the choice of such goods as deliberate adherence to advice, though. The clusters of objects in these rooms also hint that the pressures of everyday use may have transcended a strict gendered division of space. For example, although dining rooms apparently adhered to masculine decorative conventions, they were often filled with goods that suggest a variety of uses by different members of the family during the day, rather than male use only. A couple of dining rooms contained writing tables, and one a sewing machine, suggesting female work.[48] It was also common for dining rooms to contain quite substantial collections of books.[49] Of course, inventories cannot tell us who used these objects, but their presence in dining rooms suggests that these rooms were put to a multiplicity of uses.

The ability to create masculine and feminine spaces was clearly linked to levels of wealth and material circumstances. Despite the cultural weight attached to gendered rooms, such as the study, smoking room and morning room, inventories and sale catalogues suggest that these tended to be found in upper-middle-class homes. The size of many houses meant that the third sitting room was rarer than advice manuals suggest. Overall, approximately 30 per cent of the inventories and sale catalogues included a room, that is a study, library, smoking room or billiard room, which could be associated specifically with men. Occupation also made a crucial difference. Men who worked in the home were more likely to need to mark out separate space. Almost invariably, studies were present in the homes of professional men such as clergymen who worked at home. Smoking rooms did become more prevalent in the late nineteenth century but were found almost exclusively in upper-middle-class homes and were too few in number to be viewed as evidence of a wholesale internal 'flight from domesticity'. Aside from the drawing room, feminine spaces were scarcer still. A few upper-middle-class women realised the morning room as imagined by Panton and Peel. For example, Mrs Greenwell, of Clonavon in Barrow, had such a room that included books, a writing table and writing equipment.[50] But in the sample as a whole, only 15 per cent contained a morning room. Again, these rooms were almost always to be found in the homes of the gentry or upper middle classes, suggesting that the majority of middle-class homemakers did not have enough space to divide the home along gendered lines.

It is striking that gendered segregation simply does not seem to have been a priority in many homes. In many middle-class households, the third sitting room was not associated with either sex. Many chose to make the third reception room a 'breakfast room'. These ambiguously named spaces were often multi-purpose, doubling as both male study and female workspace.[51] These rooms clearly had many uses besides breakfast. Some were clearly intended for female work, containing work tables and writing tables. The Blackett household in Leeds contained a 'breakfast room' that included a sewing machine and workbox, and several breakfast rooms in north-west

England also contained sewing machines.[52] But feminine objects often lay side by side with more masculine things. Smoking paraphernalia, for both pipes and cigars, was present in several breakfast rooms in the north-west.[53] But these gender-combined activities in the breakfast room were not only determined by a lack of space in the rest of the house. The sale catalogue of Greenscoe House in Askam in Furness, for example, listed an impressive twenty-six rooms. The catalogue suggests that the library was sparsely furnished and used to store tennis equipment. In contrast, the breakfast room was elaborately kitted out and contained 'a tapestry pile table cover, superior four foot six inch knee hole walnut writing table, inlaid with dark blue leather, a revolving office chair, a rocking chair, two tobacco jars, a hand sewing machine by Singer & Co., and a lady's work basket'.[54] This cluster of goods suggests male and female work and relaxation, implying that the family preferred sociability in the breakfast room to bookish solitude in the library.

Even within the almost exclusively upper-middle-class homes that contained masculine spaces, we can see that the decorative styles which advice writers associated with masculinity were not adopted uniformly. Rather, the contents of libraries, smoking and billiard rooms suggests instead a spectrum of gendered decorative choices linked to, and perhaps compromised by, other needs of the household. Libraries often contained large numbers of chairs and pianos, suggesting family and possibly public sociability as much as male seclusion.[55] The 'smoke room' at Broughton Lodge included a pistol, a 'gents chair' and a cash box with the deeds of the house, suggesting that this room was indeed the heart of masculine power in the home.[56] In contrast, the 'smoke room' at Abbey Road, Barrow, lacked conspicuously masculine objects, instead being shabbily furnished and used to store bicycle equipment; broken and damaged goods were also stored here.[57] A similar spectrum of masculine decoration could be found in the billiard room. Some rooms displayed the typology of masculine décor outlined by Mackenzie. The billiard room at Aldingham Hall was furnished in oak with skin rugs, a crocodile skin, guns, mounted ibex horns, stuffed lizards and Egyptian souvenirs.[58] Stock Park's billiard room was similarly furnished, boasting a pair of buffalo horns and a stuffed platypus.[59] Some billiard rooms were purely used to house a billiard table and other sporting equipment.[60] Others were clearly social spaces, and often included goods that suggested female presence. The enormous billiard room at Bankfield, Urswick included settees, a phonograph and a grand piano.[61] But while sale catalogues and inventories show us the presence of masculine things, they cannot tell us how their owners thought and felt about them. The final section of this chapter explores contemporary interpretations of the meaning of gendered material cultures through autobiographical accounts.

***

Autobiographies can show reactions to gendered spaces and material culture, both in the formation of identities in childhood and in the construction of the adult self. They demonstrate just how provocative the material culture of gender could be, but also some of its limits. Rather than reinforcing adult authority and an acceptance of hierarchy, gendered material culture often provoked resistance in the child that could later solidify into an adult questioning of the system of power relations of the period. This emerges in the childhood autobiography of the novelist and children's writer Noel Streatfeild,

A Vicarage Family: A Biography of Myself, published in 1963. Streatfeild describes the study in the vicarage in her father's parish, St Peter's, St Leonard's-on-Sea, in detail. It is here that authority was meted out: 'the children seldom went into the study for either their father was working or there was someone there to see him, so at all times to be called to the study was an occasion'.[62] The masculinity of the space was reinforced by a sombre decorative style that echoed the prescriptions of advice literature: 'the room seemed dark for there were heavy curtains and two walls were solid with books in dull bindings'.[63] The father's professional role was underlined by the presence of 'a huge roll-topped desk and a swivel feather-seated chair'.[64] This was an intimidating room, and as a child, Streatfeild felt a sense of trepidation on entering it.

However, the young Streatfeild did not simply accept the imposition of adult, masculine authority through this space. The subsequent narrative describes the child Victoria's reactions to her father's remonstrations: 'Victoria felt anxious; surely Daddy was not going to cry ... Worse, was he going to pray with her?'[65] For the adult Streatfeild, the decoration of the room also came to stand for the unequal gendered hierarchy of the age. Thus, the adult Streatfeild wryly notes that the room is decorated with photographs, but only with images of men who have assisted the vicar, whereas 'women church workers were only photographed when they were in their graves'.[66] Masculine spaces and decorative styles were intimidating and reinforced the power of the father, yet their very presence provoked resistance and, in Streatfeild's case, ultimately a questioning of the gendered system of power relations in which she was brought up, and a strengthening of the feminism of her adult self.

The gendered division of space could also be evoked as a symbol of the limits of patriarchal dominance. This is shown in the autobiography of the actor and writer Horace Collins, *My Best Riches: Story of a Stone Rolling Round the World and the Stage*, published in 1941. Collins recounts his theatrical career, providing entertainment in the Anglo-Boer and First World wars, and his involvement with the development of the wireless in the 1920s. Collins characterises the era of his childhood in north-west London as stereotypically Victorian, noting of his architect father that, 'I can recollect him only as a typical Victorian figure. He was a well-set-up man of medium height, with a kindly face, from each side of which grew black bushy whiskers'.[67] The library in the Collins family home was supposedly the father's sacred territory, but Collins reveals: 'The comfortable airy library, surrounded by well-filled bookcases and shelves, on the first floor, was supposed to be my father's sanctum, but it was invaded by the whole household and was the room most frequented'.[68] Collins uses the contemporary expectation that this room would be devoted to adult men to emphasise the impression that this father was not quite in control of his lively brood: 'poor father, overcome by the persistent gabble, would hastily retreat to his bedroom and there remain with a book in comparative peace'.[69] The gendered significance of the space was not ignored, rather its restricted nature lent the invasion a particular cachet. Collins's depiction of the vivacity of his siblings was motivated by his desire to play up their theatrical qualities in the light of their subsequent stage careers. Nonetheless this account clearly demonstrates a humorous subversion of the figure of the Victorian patriarch, through the invasion of the library, his archetypal lair.

Although gendered spaces and material cultures were associated with adult authority, it is important not to lose sight of the fact that decoration could also exert power through pleasure, and for some could provide a formative aesthetic experience.

The smoking room in particular could become the focus of an alternative aesthetic masculinity that transported the viewer beyond the confines of everyday domesticity. This becomes apparent in *A Mingled Chime*, the autobiography of the conductor Sir Thomas Beecham, first published in 1944. Beecham grew up in Lancashire, in the 1880s. His grandfather had made a fortune as a manufacturing chemist, allowing the family to pursue an upper-middle-class lifestyle. Female authority seems to have held sway in the Beecham home, with smoking confined to remote corners of the house: 'in our establishment it was sternly disallowed in most rooms and barely tolerated in any'.[70] Although most of the autobiography deals with Beecham's early career and musical experiences, the smoking room in the Beechams' home, and in particular his father's attire, is discussed in detail. Beecham recalls his father smoking in a 'remote den' on the top floor of his home:

> There he would put on a cap of Turkish design crowned with a long flowing tassel, and a richly coloured jacket decorated with gold-braided stripes and silver buttons. On the rare occasions when I was admitted to this holy of holies I would gaze upon this gorgeous spectacle with rapture while my sire puffed away in placid and silent content, absorbed in reflections which I felt were of world-shaking import.[71]

Beecham's account conveys a sense of the fascination and exoticism that masculine material cultures and practices could arouse in children within the home. Yet it is also worth noting the context in which this description of the smoking room emerges. At this point, Beecham also describes his profound interest, in early childhood, with clothes, of both his father and grandfather. The autobiography itself is driven by a self-conscious desire to explain Beecham's artistic and aesthetic development. Thus within Beecham's present conception of the self as aesthete, the child's past experience of domestic material culture becomes a crucial part of this trajectory. In the elaborate and exotic material culture of the smoking room, the adult Beecham finds a bridge between the cultural limitations of his late Victorian Lancashire home and the aesthetic and highly cultured musical world that he would later inhabit. For both the child and adult Beecham, then, the smoking room offered an alternative aestheticism, a model of masculinity that took him out of the confines of ordinary everyday domesticity and into an alternative aesthetic world.

The glamour and exoticism of adult material culture could repel as well as attract. The significance of gendered material culture in one female child's rejection of femininity is evident in Beryl Lee Booker's autobiography *Yesterday's Child*. From 1896, Booker (formerly Cumming) and her family lived on a wealthy square in central London. Booker was the daughter of a retired military gentleman, and the grandchild of the admiral and Derbyshire country squire, Sir Arthur Cumming. The social position of this family influenced their living practices, and their upper-middle-class home was clearly segregated by gender. Booker remarks: 'He [her father] adored mother, but both went their own gay way and lived the life that suited them best'.[72] Booker's father inhabited his bedroom and dressing room, while her mother held sway in her highly feminised bedroom: 'Mummy's bedroom had walls panelled with a paper covered with bunches of violets or lilac ... It had an off-white pile carpet, and chair covers, and an old dark walnut Norman armoire. The dressing-tables then were of course kidney shaped and draped, with three-fold gilt mirrors'.[73] However, Booker was repelled, rather than entranced, by this room. Her reaction occurred in the context of an uneasy

My Brother and Myself in 1899

Figure 4: Beryl and Charles Lee Booker, 1899, in Beryl Lee Booker, *Yesterday's Child, 1890–1909* (London: Long, 1937), p. 74. © The British Library Board, 10825.i.35.

web of family relationships: her father's favourite, Booker disliked her mother, whom she felt privileged her younger sister.

Rejected by a distant mother, Booker's representation of the exquisite femininity of the space is also cold, and suggests an amoral interest in the worldly and material:

> Mother rustled and glittered round her beautiful bedroom. Often she would be ill, and then perhaps we could be allowed to creep down at teatime to see her lying in beautiful embroidered sheets, threaded with broad white satin ribbons, at the back of her head several down pillows with fine transparent lawn covers, monograms and initials everywhere . . . But we mustn't touch her, or jog the bed, or fidget.[74]

Booker's response to her mother's bedroom shaped her own identity. Much of her later description of herself indicates a rebellion against the feminine excesses of her mother. She describes herself as a tomboy, and when she was allowed a bedroom of her own she clearly used it to express a more ambiguous gendered identity: 'I laid out my treasures, the collection of rubbish from Egypt; and on a table by themselves my dumbbells, embrocation and a book from Mr Sandow telling how to get muscles like his!'[75] Booker and her brother frequently played at being men: Figure 4 shows the pair in military dress.

Booker's autobiography shows how gendered material culture could shape self-fashioning in childhood and early adolescence. Yet this process was complex: Booker's reaction to her mother's bedroom drew on the well-established cultural association between gendered identity and domestic objects, yet her family life pushed her to reject those norms. Booker's later life, her two marriages and four children, were conventional enough, yet the pursuit of her own passions continued to be somewhat in opposition to her conventional femininity. Booker later became a dog trainer, authoring a book on Great Danes that remains in print.[76]

Conclusion

An increasingly conservative Panton, writing in 1910, bemoaned the demise of masculine and feminine spaces in the home, arguing that this was linked to a general decline in marital harmony and the rise of divorce.[77] During the previous era, these spaces had played an important role in the construction of gendered relationships in the home. However, their impact was complex. At the end of the nineteenth century, domestic and decorative advice writers emphasised the importance of devoting individual spaces to husbands and wives, yet disagreed on how this should take place, arguing over who should hold sway in the third sitting room. Previous interpretations have suggested that spatial segregation was synonymous with female subjection, but the female advice writers who championed the morning room took a different view, arguing that women writers could achieve autonomy through the possession of a separate space.

These fantasies of female space may have been confined to the pages of the advice manual. There was relatively little scope for gendered segregation in smaller middle-class homes. Wives who sought a morning room of their own, or late nineteenth-century men who longed for a den to effect an internal flight from domesticity, were likely to be disappointed. Extensive suites of gendered rooms – morning rooms and boudoirs, studies, smoking rooms and billiard rooms – were only to be found in the wealthy homes of the upper middle classes, or spacious gentry mansions. Yet evidence from larger homes also suggests that where men had the option of laying out a masculine domain they did not always do so. More often families chose to use the third sitting room as a shared space, such as a breakfast room, and these rooms were filled with clusters of objects that suggest sociability rather than division and segregation.

In middle-class England, home was the place where men and women first learned to be gendered. In order to understand what 'home' meant, it is essential that we consider the cultural and social meanings of the domestic material world. It was in upper-middle-class homes, and those with a father who worked at home that gendered spaces and material cultures were most strongly felt. Autobiographies demonstrate just how important the gendered material culture of home could be to some Victorian children. Masculine spaces such as the study could be intimidating, yet rather than reinforcing an acceptance of the contemporary hierarchy, gendered spaces could encourage children to question it. Moreover, masculine spaces could also be invoked to highlight the limits of patriarchal power. Finally, these spaces demonstrate that although notions of gender pervaded late nineteenth-century society, they were frequently mutable: within the material culture of gender there was room for manoeuvre.

Notes

1. H. J. Jennings, *Our Homes, and How to Beautify Them* (London: Harrison and Sons, 1902), p. 173.
2. Stefan Muthesius, *The English Terraced House* (New Haven and London: Yale University Press, 1982), p. 39; John Tosh, *A Man's Place: Masculinity and the Middle-Class Home in Victorian England* (London: Yale University Press, 1999), p. 21.
3. Michael S. Kimmel, 'Introduction: The Power of Gender and the Gender of Power', in Katharine Martinez and Kenneth L. Ames (eds), *The Material Culture of Gender: The Gender of Material Culture* (Winterthur: Henry Francis du Pont Winterthur Museum, 1997), pp. 1–7, here p. 2. The Winterthur school of material culture studies has fostered a wide range of work on North American gender and material

culture. See Richard L. Bushman, *The Refinement of America: Persons, Cities, Houses* (New York: Knopf, 1992); Katherine C. Grier, *Culture and Comfort: Parlor Making and Middle-Class Identity, 1850–1930* (Rochester: Strong Museum and University of Massachussetts Press, 1988). The most extensive studies of the relationship between domestic objects and gender in a historical context focus on eighteenth-century Britain. See Amanda Vickery, 'Women and the World of Goods: A Lancashire Consumer and her Possessions, 1751–81', in John Brewer and Roy Porter (eds), *Consumption and the World of Goods* (London: Routledge, 1993), pp. 274–301; Elizabeth Kowaleski-Wallace, *Consuming Subjects: Women, Shopping and Business in the Eighteenth Century* (New York: Columbia University Press, 1997); Margot Finn, 'Men's Things: Masculine Possession in the Consumer Revolution', *Social History* 25 (2000), pp. 133–55; John Styles and Amanda Vickery, 'Introduction', in John Styles and Amanda Vickery (eds), *Gender, Taste and Material Culture in Britain and North America, 1700–1830* (New Haven and London: Yale University Press, 2006), pp. 1–36.

4. Daphne Spain, *Gendered Spaces* (Chapel Hill: University of North Carolina Press, 1992), p. 126.

5. Spain, *Gendered Spaces*, p. 126.

6. Leonore Davidoff and Catherine Hall, *Family Fortunes: Men and Women of the English Middle Class, 1780–1850* (London: Hutchison, 1987), p. 114; Catherine Hall, 'Gender Divisions and Class Formation in the Birmingham Middle Class, 1780–1850', in Raphael Samuel (ed.), *People's History and Socialist Theory* (London: Routledge and Kegan Paul, 1981), pp. 164–75, here p. 166; Tosh, *A Man's Place*, p. 4.

7. Amanda Vickery, 'Golden Age to Separate Spheres? A Review of the Categories and Chronology of English Women's History', *Historical Journal* 36 (1993), pp. 383–414, here p. 401. Also M. Jeanne Peterson, *Family, Love and Work in the Lives of Victorian Gentlewomen* (Bloomington: Indiana University Press, 1989), p. 188; Eleanor Gordon and Gwyneth Nair, *Public Lives: Women, Family and Society in Victorian Britain* (New Haven and London: Yale University Press, 2003), pp. 2–3.

8. Thad Logan, *The Victorian Parlour* (Cambridge: Cambridge University Press, 2001), p. 25.

9. Juliet Kinchin, 'Interiors: Nineteenth-Century Essays on the "Masculine" and the "Feminine" Room', in Pat Kirkham, *The Gendered Object* (Manchester: Manchester University Press, 1996), pp. 18–20.

10. Tosh, *A Man's Place*, pp. 7, 179, 182; also John M. Mackenzie, 'The Imperial Pioneer and Hunter and the British Masculine Stereotype in Late Victorian and Edwardian Times', in J. A. Mangan and James Walvin (eds), *Manliness and Morality: Middle-Class Masculinity in Britain and America 1800–1940* (Manchester: Manchester University Press, 1987), pp. 180–81. Juliette Kinchin, however, argues that gendered identities were slightly less pronounced in the aesthetic interiors of the later nineteenth century. Kinchin, 'Interiors', p. 25.

11. Tosh, *A Man's Place*, pp. 89, 98.

12. Tosh, *A Man's Place*, pp. 175–7.

13. Amy Milne-Smith, 'A Flight to Domesticity? Making a Home in the Gentleman's Clubs of London, 1880–1914', *Journal of British Studies* 45 (2006), pp. 796–818; Amy Milne-Smith, 'Club Talk: Gossip, Masculinity and Oral Communities in Late Nineteenth-Century London', *Gender & History* 21 (2009), pp. 86–106.

14. Deborah Cohen, *Household Gods: The British and their Possessions* (New Haven and London: Yale University Press, 2006), p. 90.

15. See Geoffrey Crossick, 'The Labour Aristocracy and its Values: A Study of Mid-Victorian London Kentish Town', *Victorian Studies* 19 (1976), pp. 301–28. On the lower middle class as a social group, see e.g., A. James Hammerton, 'Pooterism or Partnership? Marriage and Masculine Identity in the Lower Middle Class, 1870–1920', *Journal of British Studies* 38 (1999), pp. 291–321; Peter Bailey, 'White Collars, Gray Lives? The Lower Middle Class Revisited', *Journal of British Studies* 38 (1999), pp. 273–90.

16. See Alan Kidd and David Nicholls, 'Introduction: History, Culture and the Middle Classes', in Alan Kidd and David Nicholls (eds), *Gender, Civic Culture and Consumerism: Middle-Class Identity in Britain, 1800–1940* (Manchester: Manchester University Press, 1999), pp. 5–6. For a contrary view, see F. M. L. Thompson, *Gentrification and the Enterprise Culture: Britain 1780–1980* (Oxford: Oxford University Press, 2001), p. 160.

17. Janet Wolff and John Seed, 'Introduction', in Janet Wolff and John Seed (eds), *The Culture of Capital: Art, Power and The Nineteenth-Century Middle Class* (Manchester: Manchester University Press, 1988), p. 8.

18. Kidd and Nicholls, 'Introduction', p. 6.

19. Mark Girouard, *Life in the English Country House: A Social and Architectural History* (New Haven and London: Yale University Press, 1978), p. 292.

20. See Margaret Ponsonby, *Stories from Home: English Domestic Interiors 1750–1850* (Aldershot: Ashgate, 2007); also Gordon and Nair, *Public Lives*, ch. 4, pp. 107–32, for the second half of the nineteenth century.

21. Michael Snodin, 'Victorian Britain, 1837–1901: Who Led Taste?', in John Styles and Michael Snodin (eds), *Design and the Decorative Arts: Britain 1500–1900* (London: Victoria and Albert Museum, 2001), pp. 369–97, here p. 388.

22. Giorgio Riello, '"Things Seen and Unseen": Inventories and the Representation of the Domestic Interior in Early Modern Europe', unpublished paper, May 2009. Referenced with the author's permission.

23. On the merits of autobiography as a source, see J. P. Roos, 'The True Life Revisited: Autobiography and Referentiality after the "Posts"', *Auto/Biography* 3 (1994), pp. 1–16; Richard N. Coe, *When the Grass Was Taller: Autobiography and the Experience of Childhood* (New Haven and London: Yale University Press, 1984). On autobiography in practice, see Kate Flint, *The Woman Reader, 1837–1914* (Oxford: Oxford University Press, 1993), pp. 187–249.

24. Coe, *When the Grass Was Taller*, p. 1; John Burnett, *Destiny Obscure: Autobiographies of Childhood, Education and Family from the 1820s to the 1920s* (Harmondsworth: Penguin, 1982), p. 11; Mark Philip Freeman, *Rewriting the Self: History, Memory, Narrative* (London: Routledge, 1993), pp. 51–2.

25. Mary Chamberlain, 'Small Worlds: Childhood and Empire', *Journal of Family History* 27 (2002), pp. 186–200, here p. 187.

26. Coe, *When the Grass Was Taller*, p. 41.

27. They are drawn from a wider survey of 200 middle-class autobiographies conducted for my doctoral thesis. Jane Hamlett, 'Materialising Gender: Identity and Middle-Class Domestic Interiors in England, 1850–1910', University of London, 2005.

28. Kinchin, 'Interiors', pp. 12–14; Styles and Vickery, 'Introduction', p. 11.

29. Robert Kerr, *The Gentleman's House* (London, 1864), p. 107.

30. Charles L. Eastlake, *Hints on Household Taste in Furniture, Upholstery and Other Details* (1868; repr. London: Longmans, Green, 1878), p. 126.

31. Jennings, *Our Homes*, p. 73. See also Judith A. Neiswander, *The Cosmopolitan Interior: Liberalism and the British Home, 1870–1914* (New Haven and London: Yale University Press, 2008), ch. 6, pp. 147–78.

32. Robert W. Edis, *Decoration and Furniture of Town Houses* (London: Kegan Paul, 1881), p. 170; Jennings, *Our Homes*, pp. 73, 157.

33. Jennings, *Our Homes*, p. 207; Eastlake, *Hints on Household Taste*, p. 126.

34. Mrs M[artha] J[ane] Loftie, *The Dining-Room* (London, 1878); Edis, *Decoration and Furniture*, p. 170.

35. Kerr, *The Gentleman's House*, p. 124.

36. Jennings, *Our Homes*, p. 221.

37. Jane Ellen Panton, *From Kitchen to Garret: Hints to Young Householders* (London: Ward and Downey, 1887), p. 80.

38. Mrs [Mary Eliza] Haweis, *The Art of Housekeeping: A Bridal Garland* (London: Sampson, Low, Marston, Sarle and Rivington, 1889), p. 34.

39. Panton, *From Kitchen to Garret*, p. 69.

40. Kerr, *The Gentleman's House*, p. 105.

41. Panton, *From Kitchen to Garret*, p. 69.

42. Lillie Hamilton French, *The House Dignified: Its Design, Its Arrangement and Its Decoration* (London and New York: G. P. Putnam's Sons, 1908), p. 68.

43. Panton, *From Kitchen to Garret*, p. 70; Dorothy Constance Peel, *The New Home: Treating of the Arrangement, Decoration and Furnishing of a House of Medium Size to be Maintained by a Moderate Income* (London: A. Constable & Co., 1898), p. 121.

44. Panton, *From Kitchen to Garret*, p. 70.

45. Peel, *The New Home*, p. 121.

46. Examples include valuation of household furniture and dairy utensils belonging to the estate of the late Mr George Robinson of Town End Farm, Biggar, Walney, Barrow in Furness, June 1915, Cumbria Record Office, Barrow in Furness (CROB), BDB/17/1/9; Marriage settlement between William Simpson Ramsay Barrow in Furness in the county of Lancashire electrician and Mary Hannah Atkinson of Barrow in Furness, 26 January 1901, CROB, BDB/17/T2/9/18; Sale catalogue for Tufton Warren Farm, property of Mr J. Earwaker, Whitchurch, 1882, Hampshire Record Office (HRO), 46M84/F91/1; List of household furniture and effects, spring cart and harness, the property of Mr Dumper of Hyde Street, Winchester, to be sold by auction 1862, HRO, 1M90/12; Catalogue of sale of wheelwright's and carpenter's equipment at Mottisford, Romsey, sold by Mr James Jenvey, on behalf of late Mr Alfred Jewel, 1904, HRO, 4M92/N/186/12.

47. For example, the London furniture shop, Heals, sold sets of furniture suitable for the dining room and library furniture in mahogany. *Heal and Sons Catalogue of Dining Room, Library and Drawing Room Furniture* (November 1885), pp. 27–34.

48. West Yorkshire Archive Service, Leeds (WYASL), WYL 295 17 1 4; West Yorkshire Archive Service, Calderdale, Halifax (WYASH), FW 30/30; Valuation of furniture at 7 Framlington Place, *c.* 1870s, Durham Record Office (DRO), D/X 776/243.

49. CROB: BD/TB 8/5/1; BDB/17/SP3/12; BDB/17/SP3/8; BDB/17/SP3/23; BDB/17/3/5.

50. CROB, BDB 17/3/5.

51. Breakfast rooms were mentioned in: Inventory and valuation of the furniture and effects at Cambrian Lodge, Shirley, the property of the late Mrs Flower, 1886, HRO, 4M92/F5/6; Inventory of the heirlooms the property of the late Colonel Warden Sergison of Cuckfield Place, 1849, West Sussex Record Office, SERGISON/1/529; Inventory from Down House, Rottingdean, property of Charles Beard, 1844, East Sussex Record Office, BRD 8/14/1; Catalogue of household furniture sold by auction by Mr Todd, 1875, at Cliff Villa, Headingley, late the property of L. F. Blackett, Esq., dec., WYASL, ACC 2363; List of silver and furniture belonging to Mrs Edith Binnington, 1861, East Riding of Yorkshire Archives, DDX 353 51; Inventory and valuation of household furniture and effects in the dwelling house lately occupied by Mrs Hebden deceased, undated, WYASH, FW31/56; Bill of sale of furniture, chattels and effects in and about Littlebank, Settle, Yorkshire, May 1883, CROB, BD/HJ/12/2/1; Sale catalogue for The Guards, Kirkby, Ireleth, November 1895, CROB, BDB/17/SP3/20; Inventory for Oaklands, Grange over Sands, May 1906, CROB, BDB/17/SP3/18; Inventory of the household furniture at Risedale, Newbarns, Barrow in Furness, 1892, CROB, BDB/17/3/1; Sale catalogue for Greenscoe House, Askam in Furness, March 1891, CROB, BDB/17/SP3/2; Inventory of the household furniture and effects on the premises of Crake House, Sparke Bridge, Colton, November 1902, CROB, BD/HJ/256 2/13.

52. CROB: BD/HJ 12/2/1; BDB/17/SP3/2.

53. CROB: BDB/17/SP3/20; BDB/17/SP3/2. While smoking was not unknown among late nineteenth-century women, cigars and pipe smoking in particular were still associated with bourgeois gentlemanly masculinity. See Matthew Hilton, *Smoking in British Popular Culture, 1800–2000* (Manchester: Manchester University Press, 2000), p. 2.

54. CROB, BDB/17/SP3/2.

55. Sale catalogue of household furniture and other effects at Bird Hill House, Whickham, 1866, DRO, D/St/E5/9/33; Bundle of documents relating to the estate of Mary Ann Bowker who died 1 Feb 1885, including will, HRO, 11M70/D18; Catalogue of the sale of household furniture from 'The Rectory', Upper Clatford, Andover, on behalf of the executors of the Rev. T. Child, 1881, HRO, 46M84/F94/1; Inventory of Clarence House, Dalton in Furness, July 1891, CROB, BDB/17/SP3/13; Sale catalogue for Broughton Lodge, Grange over Sands, April 1902, CROB, BDB/17/SP3/16; Sale catalogue of Croslands, Furness Abbey, January 1910, CROB: BDB/17/SP3/5; BDB/17/SP3/8; BDB/17/SP3/16.

56. CROB, BDB/17/SP3/16.

57. Inventory of 149 Abbey Road, Barrow in Furness, belonging to Mr John Fisher, March 1901, CROB, BDB 17/1/3.

58. Inventory of the household furniture at Aldingham Hall, October 1905, CROB, BDB 17/3/2.

59. Sale catalogue for Stock Park, Lakeside, Windermere, February 1911, CROB, BDB/17/SP3/26.

60. CROB: BDB/17/SP3/5; BDB/17/SP3/16.

61. Inventory of household furniture at Bankfield, Urswick, November 1908, CROB, BDB/17/1/5.

62. Noel Streatfeild, *A Vicarage Family: A Biography of Myself* (London: Collins, 1963), p. 10.

63. Streatfeild, *A Vicarage Family*, p. 10.

64. Streatfeild, *A Vicarage Family*, p. 10.

65. Streatfeild, *A Vicarage Family*, p. 15.

66. Streatfeild, *A Vicarage Family*, p. 11.

67. Horace Collins, *My Best Riches: Story of a Stone Rolling Round the World and the Stage* (London: Eyre and Spottiswood, 1941), p. 11.

68. Collins, *My Best Riches*, p. 33.

69. Collins, *My Best Riches*, p. 33.

70. Thomas Beecham, *A Mingled Chime: Leaves from an Autobiography* (London: Hutchison, 1944), p. 12.

71. Beecham, *A Mingled Chime*, p. 9.

72. Beryl Lee Booker, *Yesterday's Child, 1890–1909* (London: Long, 1937), p. 64.

73. Booker, *Yesterday's Child*, p. 29.

74. Booker, *Yesterday's Child*, pp. 71–2.

75. Booker, *Yesterday's Child*, p. 99.

76. Beryl Lee Booker, *Great Danes of To-day* (Bradford and London: Watmoughs, 1938).

77. Jane Ellen Panton, *Leaves From a Housekeeper's Book* (London: Eveleigh Nash, 1914), p. 49.

7 'There Is Graite Odds between A Mans being At Home And A Broad': Deborah Read Franklin and the Eighteenth-Century Home

Vivian Bruce Conger

Over the forty-four-year marriage between Benjamin and Deborah Franklin, his work frequently took him away from home, but many of those separations were episodic and brief. More important were the long separations during his official trips to England. The first, lasting from 1757 to 1763, separated the couple for five years. Then on 8 November 1764, Benjamin Franklin, the 'ever loving Husband' of Deborah departed from Philadelphia for England for a second time. Upon arriving on the Isle of Wight, he wrote, 'You know whom I love and honour. Say all the proper Things for me to every body'.[1] Thus began their longest and final separation, a separation in which she increasingly assumed the public persona (that is, the male persona) of the Franklin household. His homecoming in 1775 was very different from the first: Deborah died nearly six months before his return to the colonies – it was, in fact, her death that prompted that return.[2] Luckily for historians, they carried on a steady, often complex, correspondence throughout the years before he returned to the city.

Deborah Franklin wrote neither a diary nor an autobiography; her voice comes to us mainly through her letters to her husband. Although their correspondence spanned ten years, for the purpose of this chapter, I concentrate on two years: 1765 and 1766, the years during which she completed work on their new house. Several biographies of Benjamin Franklin briefly touch upon the letters between the two, noting that he 'inundated' his wife with questions, bombarded her with 'no end of advice' and 'deluged' her with detailed instructions and material goods. Deborah dutifully answered his questions, willingly took his advice, skillfully followed his instructions, and placed the goods as best she could given she was alone, overwhelmed and insecure.[3] This interpretation places Deborah in a passive relationship to her husband, and the almost mythological presence of his loud and powerful voice overshadows her presence. More significantly, most biographers gloss over the symbolic significance of the structure and ignore the role gender played in the process of house and household building. While these letters form the structural foundation for examining the ambiguously gendered nature of eighteenth-century houses and households, I erect the framework with material culture analysis, architectural history and theory, and gender studies.

As Bernard Herman reminds us, family taste 'was often companionate and corporate. In the quest for gendered identities expressed in the material culture of the home . . . we tend to forget the conjugal practice of everyday life'. It is through these exchanges that we glimpse a normal give and take between husband and wife, even a typical tension in the hierarchical relationship of the eighteenth-century family. In the seemingly quotidian details we hear Deborah's voice. Yet moving from the mundane to a more nuanced reading of the Franklins' 'material conversations'[4] reveals several literal and figurative constructions embodied in their home: its place in eighteenth-century consumer culture as the couple discussed finishing and furnishing their new house in Philadelphia, and, more significantly, its ambiguously gendered meaning – both ideologically and physically.

Despite the ideal image of an elite eighteenth-century family as a 'unit . . . where husband, wife, and children . . . formed the basic unit of social and economic action', the reality was that not only did Deborah oversee the completion of the house inside and out, she lived the rest of her life in 'his' house without him.[5] Even though Franklin gave his wife power of attorney during his absence, it was an ambiguous legal position at best. She could act as – that is behave like, or even pretend to be – *feme sole* to the extent that she had the right 'to ask, demand, sue for, levy, recover and receive, all such Sum and Sums of Money, Debts, Rents, Goods, Wares, Dues, Accounts' in her husband's name.[6] But as *feme covert* her performative powers were limited; she was legally 'homeless' (that is, she could not own the home she never shared with her husband) and conceptually 'homeless' (in the ideal structure of the home).

Her household variously consisted of her mother, her adopted son, her daughter, relatives, guests, boarders and servants – she permanently assumed the role of head of this complicated household. *His* household consisted of his landlady, Widow Margaret Stevenson, and her daughter Polly as well as friends, relatives and guests who visited him on Craven Street in London. Although labelled 'the patriarch of Craven Street',[7] he was not the male head of household; he was a renter, a lodger. Moreover, as Deborah wrote to her husband about turning the house into an armed fortress during the Stamp Act crisis, he wrote to her about the household goods; as she talked about politics, he discussed domesticity.[8] 'Inhabited space' (what we call architecture) is the site 'of hierarchical . . . arrangements . . . underlying all the arbitrary provisions of a culture';[9] through their sometimes unique living arrangements, husband and wife moved along a continuum of gender identities and cultural assumptions. Although both sometimes appeared to be uncomfortable with this movement, their masculine and feminine roles symbolised the gendered complexity of the eighteenth-century house, a complexity suggested by Deborah's unwittingly tongue-in-cheek comment to her husband about the difference between living overseas and living in Philadelphia.

The Franklin house: 'The Material Culture of Gender, the Gender of Material Culture'

The title of this section is also the title of a book edited by Katharine Martinez and Kenneth L. Ames. They argue, 'Gendering is the process by which identities are pieced together by active subjects from the materials . . . at hand'.[10] That gendering process can be seen through the Franklin house. In theory, early American white middling and elite households consisted of a male head, a wife, their children and servants or slaves.

In exchange for legal, economic and military protection, the household's 'dependents' submitted to male authority. According to eighteenth-century prescriptive literature, the 'patriarchal household' was hierarchical and deferential.[11] The husband, the supreme authority, ruled the household, controlled the family's finances and supervised domestic affairs. He also represented the household in the community. Such fatherly exemplars commanded authority, not only within their own families where 'everyone mov[ed] in a known sphere', but also in the community, where 'good order' was maintained. Men, educated and thus rational and clear-headed, were 'well form'd for government' within the house and within the community.[12]

A married woman had no independent existence or identity; as *feme covert* she was legally subsumed into her husband and she had no rights, no separate identity. Wives submitted to their husbands' mundane and monumental decisions. However, because men felt neither comfortable with, nor confident about, the day-to-day activities of domestic affairs, they left those responsibilities to their wives. Women supervised the 'lived' activities of the household. A woman became 'notable' by running her 'empire' skilfully and smoothly. Her role was to be economical (even though most women had no knowledge of family finances and their husband's business), to work hard and to promote the welfare of the family. Her pride and her recognition came in fulfilling those responsibilities.

As a young man, Benjamin Franklin expressed similar beliefs about married women's roles in three different venues. In 1727, he wrote to his sister that, 'I have been thinking what would be a suitable present for me to make, and for you to receive, as I hear you are grown a celebrated beauty. I had almost determined on a tea table, but when I considered that the character of a good housewife was far preferable to that of being only a pretty gentlewoman, I concluded to send you a spinning wheel'.[13] Three years later and a month after he and Deborah embarked on a common-law marriage, he published *Rules and Maxims for Promoting Matrimonial Happiness Address'd to all Widows, Wives, and Spinsters*.[14] He advised wives to 'Never endeavour to deceive or impose on [their husbands'] Understanding: nor give him *Uneasiness*', to 'Dispute not with him, be the Occasion what it will; but much rather deny yourself the trivial Satisfaction of having your own Will', and to 'have a due Regard to his Income and Circumstances in all your Expences and Desires'. On 10 July 1732, he published his satirical 'Anthony Afterwit'. Afterwit, a tradesman with a spendthrift wife, complained that she 'being entertain'd with Tea by the Good Women she visited, we could do no less than the like when they visited us; and so we got a Tea Table with all its Appurtenances of China and Silver. Then my Spouse unfortunately overwork'd herself in washing the House, so that we could do no longer without a Maid'. To get the family out of this bind, Afterwit sold his wife's entire equipage when she was off on a social visit.[15]

In these selections, Franklin wavered between praising the frugality and criticising the extravagance of all women. But 'in neither capacity could [women] comfortably fit into a theory extolling the achievements of autonomous males'.[16] This may have been a personal predilection, but it also reflected the burgeoning influence of the market economy. Decades later, Franklin aspired to become a gentleman. Not only did he embrace the tea table and all it symbolised, but he strove to prove (and enforce) his rank by the house he lived in and the consumer goods on display in that house; he expected Deborah to aid that goal happily, judiciously, and precisely – but he never entirely abandoned his dislike of the autonomous profligate wife.

Fulfilling their domestic responsibilities may have given women a large measure of pride, but they could also fill women with anxiety, as they did Deborah thirty years later as she strove to rise to Benjamin's newly found status-conscious expectations. For example, responding to several pointed questions Benjamin posed her, Deborah described the glazed doors on the buffet in his room, she counted the number of panes in those doors (there were eight in each), and told him although the 'railes' had not been put up, it was 'promised soon to be dun'. She began to feel overwhelmed by the tasks and perhaps by her desire to please him, for she anguished that, 'every bodey is a fraid they shall doe wrong so every thing is left undun'.[17] She, of course, did not have the luxury of being paralysed by fear, of leaving tasks undone until his return. In that struggle to accomplish all those tasks, Deborah probably gained confidence in her own abilities.

In reality, many households did not adhere to the ideal structure; wives were not completely powerless, and the seemingly normative male authority appears too rigid and too simplistic, especially as the unstable era of the American Revolution made clear. Women could advise their husbands, they could even assume male roles when status allowed it and times demanded it; men were expected to be neither tyrannical nor abusive in wielding their power, and they willingly ceded masculine responsibilities and authority to their wives as necessary. It is within these 'contrasting images of autonomy and subordination', within these ambiguous or flexible gender roles, that the Franklins complicated the household structure.[18]

We can only imagine that Deborah and Benjamin lived contentedly as husband and wife for most of their years together, but there is no evidence one way or the other to prove it. We only enter into their relationship when Benjamin was away. Admittedly, urban Philadelphian households took a 'wide range' of complex forms, and female-headed households were 'a normal occurrence'.[19] However, the Franklins conducted the concluding years of their marriage across continents and through a written exchange between Philadelphia and London – which made it a decidedly untraditional marriage as well as a difficult relationship to pursue. From the start, those letters revealed the way they constructed their relationship, at least on the surface. Every letter Benjamin wrote to Deborah began with 'my dear child'. This phrase seemed to signal the paternalistic, hierarchical relationship between husband and wife. Yet, Deborah began every letter to Benjamin with the exact phrase – suggesting two different interpretations: first, that the companionate marriage of the early republic had an earlier beginning and that this marriage, even long distance, was an affectionate one; and second, that Deborah refused to let her husband infantilise her and in an act of defiance appropriated the phrase and turned it on him. Most likely, both Franklins had found a balance between love and authority that the ambiguously gendered eighteenth-century marriage allowed.[20]

After renting and living in numerous locations over the course of three decades, the Franklins began building their own house in the spring of 1763. Unfortunately all the architectural plans for it have disappeared, but we know that Benjamin hired Robert Smith, 'one of the foremost carpenter-architects in the colonies', and his old friend Samuel Rhoads to oversee the project.[21] By the time Benjamin left for England in late 1764, the framework (the foundation, roof, exterior brick walls, floors and plastered interior walls) had been erected and, not mentioning the role Deborah would play in its completion, he left £550 with the builders to finish the house. According to Susan Stabile, reflecting wider cultural assumptions, eighteenth-century architectural theory gendered domestic structures; 'men and women represented the two spheres of architecture: exterior and interior, public and private',[22] strength and weakness, mind and body, masculine and feminine. The exterior 'reinforced local distinctions . . . the interior engaged social relationships that transcended place and were defined in the competitive culture of Atlantic cosmopolitanism'.[23] That Benjamin confidently walked away once the basic structure of the house was built reflects this bias; the give and take between the Franklins over furnishing the house challenged those cultural assumptions. According to Dell Upton, 'it is never possible to speak of "the" experience of' a house for 'some members have more control over the house than others, some do more work there than others, and all experience it differently according to their places in the domestic community'.[24] As the Franklins demonstrate, often the legal ownership of the house mattered less than the lived experience therein; the actual control of the house acknowledged, represented and challenged seemingly prescribed unequal relationships.

When the house – located on the south side of High Street (now Market Street) between Third and Fourth Streets – was completed in the summer of 1766, insurance records described this typical American Georgian ten-room house as:

> 3 Storys high . . . [with] 3 Rooms on a floor[.] . . . East Room [the dining room] below wainscuted, with frett Cornish all Round, four pedements with frett Bedmolds A Rich Chimney piece, fluted Cullums and half pilasters with intabliture – the other Rooms and passage below wainscuted pedestal high, with frett and dintal Cornish throughout[;] one of sd. Rooms has a Chimney peice with tabernacle fr[a]m[e] pediment &c. All the Second Story wainscoted pedestal high, frett dintal and plain duble Cornish through the whole, a Chimney peice in one of the Rooms with tabernacle frame pediment &c. Chimney Brests Surbass [surbase] Scerting and Single Cornish throughout the third Story – Garet plasterd, a way out on Roof – two Storys of Stairs Rampd. Brackited and Wainscuted[.] . . . [P]ainted inside and out – Modilion Eaves – a Large painhouse [penthouse] . . . [and an] all New – kitchen in Celler.[25]

The land on which the house stood was in part Deborah's inheritance from her mother, and it remained her responsibility to oversee its completion – and until she could, she would remain impatiently in the rented house. 'Yisterday I Spook to Nabor Headock but he ses there is no such Thing as painting till next March . . . so I muste indever to make my self as esey as I can but I did raly think I shold a bin allmoste ready to a mouefed [moved] as soon as this wather has brook up'.[26] Four years earlier (during Benjamin's first trip to England) she made it clear that she was not a patient woman; Deborah, perhaps tired of living in houses picked out by Benjamin, conceivably demonstrating her own desires for upward mobility, and definitely showing signs of a nascent independence, moved 'her household' to a new house she rented from Adam Eckert. These same motivations most likely spurred her frustration in 1765.[27]

Throughout February 1765, the two exchanged letters about the house. A useful way to understand the building at the centre of their transatlantic conversation is as a reflection of the choices they made, which in turn communicated 'a sense of self and their environment'. She wrote about where she was going to put fireplaces, the curious mantel he sent (which she critically nicknamed 'the beste'), laying hearths, the plasterer finishing lathing the staircase and laying the kitchen floor, and getting the rooms ready for the painter (she was going to use the fireplaces to warm up the rooms). She regretted that the work was progressing so slowly even though 'I have not one ower my one att this time'. She appeared to be claiming that the delays were not the fault of a hard-working 'notable' housewife such as herself. She did not want Benjamin to believe she was not up to the task. He wrote about the consumer goods he sent: blankets, bed ticks, new china and mohair cloth for curtains in the blue room, explaining that 'the fashion is to make one Curtain only for each Window. Hooks are sent to fix the Rails by at Top, so that they may be taken down on Occasion'. Then he added, 'I almost Wish I had left Directions not to paint the House till my Return. But I suppose tis done before this time'. She directed the heavy work and oversaw the workers; he made suggestions about interior decorating and stewed in frustration over his lack of control.[28]

Apparently the weather warmed enough, because in April Deborah informed her husband – after noting that he had been absent for five months – that she had been able to get some things into the house and 'yisterday sume of the Sashes was hung and if I wold alow my self I Cold find falte but I donte'.[29] This cryptic phrase suggests that she wanted to more forcefully exert masculine control over the basic construction of the house but dared not – either because women should not criticise men or because Franklin did not always appreciate her temper. Again regretting that he was not there to oversee the move while simultaneously free to flex his authoritarian masculine muscles and patronisingly demonstrate his superior education, Benjamin wrote,

> *I could have wished* to have been present at the Finishing of the Kitchen, as it is a mere Machine, and being new to you, I think you will scarce know how to work it. The several Contrivances to carry off Steam and Smell and Smoke not being fully explain'd to you. The Oven I suppose was put up by the written Directions in my former Letter. . . . *I cannot but complain in my Mind* of Mr. Smith that the House is so long unfit for you to get into, the Fences not put up, nor the other necessary Articles got ready. The Well I expected would have been dug in the Winter, or early in the Spring; but I hear nothing of it. You should have garden'd long before the Date of your last, but it seems the Rubbish was not removed.[30]

Interestingly, when she responded in part to his frustration that he could only challenge Mr Smith through his imagination and in part to ease his mind, she reverted to ideologically prescribed gender roles by acting the demure female and commenting on what Susan Stabile termed the masculine aspects of his house, the exterior: 'I am very glad that you doe approve of my purchous and when it shall pleas God to restore you to your one house I think you will be verey much plesd at the look of it as it dos make a fine Squair and an equil spaise on each sid your house and at this time your man Gorge is a leveling of it and it look much better then when I firste Come into it'.[31] In a bold move, Deborah had purchased a town lot adjacent to the house without Benjamin's sanction. She understood the visual importance of the symmetrical placement of the house on its lot. She also understood she might have transgressed in her independence.

In August, Benjamin sent Deborah a long and varied set of instructions, many of them disguised as questions, about the house. In the specificity of them, there is a sense that he was trying to exert control over a process of house and household building from which he was being excluded. It is also evident that he recognised that she was making decisions on her own and he resented it. After asking for the measurements of the windows, 'for which you would have me bring Curtains', he pointedly added 'unless you chuse to have the Curtains made there'. To reassert his presence in the house, he asked, 'Have you mov'd every thing, and put all Papers and Books in *my*

Room, and do you keep it lock't?' Besides wanting her to draw a picture of the lot she bought (so he could know its size), he also inquired who 'it joins upon'. He understood that placement of the house in the neighbourhood was crucial. He most especially demanded to know who the tenant was – he lived in a small house at the Market Street end of the lot Deborah recently acquired – and what rent he paid. He advised her that she could wait to oil the floors until he returned; he admonished her to 'take great Care of your Fires'; and he challenged her to make sure 'the Vaults' are made because she does 'not have Cellar Room enough'. In closing, he wistfully added, 'I wish you would give me a particular Account of every Room, who and what is in it, 'twould make me seem a little at home'.[32]

Maybe he was worried as well about the expenses she incurred. Under normal circumstances, husbands and wives collaborated on purchases for the household. Billy G. Smith argues that labouring men's wills reveal the great confidence they had in their wives' ability to manage the household alone. This should not come as a surprise because even while both were alive, these wives bore primary responsibility for economic affairs – household as well as helping run the family business – as Deborah Franklin did when she was merely the wife of a printer and postmaster.[33] But wealth and elite status complicated matters. The 'easy access' to consumer goods – especially in the 'empire of goods' of the burgeoning eighteenth-century market economy – gave women increasing chances to challenge the authority of the male head of household and to threaten what were perceived as 'appropriate power relations in the community'.[34] An absent male would radically alter those relationships even further, and the Franklin household was hardly 'normal'. Deborah spoke the common language of goods as skilfully as he.

In a letter written over the space of a week, Deborah responded at length to her husband. While she described everything in detail, there is evidence of her pique at his questions – which she seemed to take as challenges to her ability to see that everything was done properly, evidence of her exerting control over the household and evidence of an unusual (even unfeminine) irreverent attitude toward the interior decorations.

The third floor contained their daughter Sally's room (it had a bed, a bureau, a table, a glass case, books and pictures), the unfinished Blue (Music) Room (it had a harmonica, a harpsichord, gilt sconces, a card table, a china tea set she bought since he 'went from home', a 'very hansom' mahogany table for the tea pot, ornamental china, 'worked Chairs' and wallpaper that had 'loste much of the blume by paisteing of it up'), and Ann Hardy's room (she was a visitor from England), which Deborah could not describe because 'it is keep locked'.

On the second floor was Deborah's bedroom, in which she slept with her maid (she had a bed without curtains, a chest of drawers, a table, a bookcase, 'old' walnut chairs and some family pictures), the 'front room', a small guest bedroom with a bed (that he had sent from England) and a mahogany table and stand, and Benajmin's bedroom. After informing him that she let their son have 'more of your Books then what you laid ought', she then told him that she put all his papers 'into boxes barrels and bages' in the room 'I cale yours'. Again, Deborah is creating her identity as an independent householder – this time in charge of meting out Benjamin's material possessions. There is also a sense here that she did not treat his papers as sacredly as he would have liked, and she chose which room would be his. In this room she also put a desk, a large chest, his harmonica and music, all the materials for his electrical experiments, his clothes and pictures, which she claimed she did not hang for fear that it 'would not be write'.

Most important, however, were the rooms on the first floor. In the 'Northroome', which was not yet complete, she put a table and chairs, a bookcase, some pictures and a small carpet on the floor. The dining room was well appointed with a 'verey hansum' sideboard with two new matching tables and a dozen chairs. Exerting again her independence and reflecting her sense of 'gentle' rank, she sold the old tables because 'they did not sute the room by aney meens'. 'The little Suthroom' (the parlour) contained a 'pritey' card table and chairs, chairs she brought from the parlour of the old house, ornamental china and a new carpet she 'bought cheep'. It also had a worn 'Scotch Carpet' and Benjamin's 'time pees' standing in one Corner. Apparently, people told her the room was 'all wrong'. Wrong because she displayed chairs from the old house, wrong because the carpet was cheap looking, wrong because she placed the furniture carelessly? Deborah cared not about their criticism, and simply replied that 'we shall have all things as thay shold be when you cume home'. Until then she seemed quite satisfied with the room as 'all these things air be cume quite indifrent to me att this time'.

As to his other questions, she wrote that she had used all the chimneys and they worked fine, 'the same man lives in house that did when I bought it but I donte know his name', and the penthouse is not yet completed. Then she appeared to challenge him by saying,

> I fair you have not reseved all my letters[. I told you] mr. Rhodes thought it beste not to dig a volte . . [and] I did write to you in the Spring and since for your orders[.] I hope the Smith will put railes on the house to morro[.] I due take all the Caire of the fiers in my power . . the men keep fier in two rooms while they worked and I did little else but tend them least any acksidente shold happen[.][35]

Perhaps it was not that he did not receive the letters (which was possible), but that he had not read them closely enough or that she perceived he was questioning her decisions or her silence on some issues he thought important but she did not.

When Deborah wrote, 'our Gardin that is to be is a fenesing of[f] but I have two Cartes a bringing durte to rais it as the desente muste Come from the wall to go to the street. I paid to Mr. Smith laste week £39 as I did to Mr. Ervin the Carter. I am to pay this day 6 pounds . . . for the seder postes and fenes', she continued her tactic of willingly (but vicariously) including her husband in the on-going saga of the building process and assuming masculine responsibilities over the house. She continued to assert herself by informing him she had planned 'to write for sume more of the Read Stuef for two Cushins', but instead she found the material in Philadelphia and bought it for '£7 10s. 0d', which was apparently as 'cheep as I Cold get it in Ingland', suggesting, of course, that his buying sprees might be no longer necessary. Although she appeared to include her husband in deciding what to do with the cushions she would make when she wrote, 'if we please [they are] for bouth rooms upstairs', she immediately cut off that possibility by asserting, 'I shall put them down staires'.[36] For Deborah, as for generally all genteel women, shopping was not a frivolous pursuit of a leisured class but 'a form of [gendered] employment'. As Amanda Vickery writes, it 'was most effectively performed by women' whose 'routine decision making' helped create the leisured class.[37] While 'the act of purchase is a performative moment that can reveal the unstable relations of merchant, customer, and consumer good',[38] it can also reveal the unstable relations of husband and wife.

Over the two years during which Deborah oversaw the construction of the Franklin house, she constructed a new identity for herself. In assuming traditional male roles and responsibilities, she became a strong head of household comfortable with making and enforcing decisions, not just about the material goods of the interior – which 'naturally' would have been a woman's sphere – but also about the external structure and the surrounding grounds. She chided, challenged and overrode her husband's wishes. While eighteenth-century gender roles were permeable, Deborah moved too far along the continuum into a role typically associated with the other sex. By so powerfully asserting her voice, she created some discomfort within the Franklin household – and it was only the beginning.

The Franklin household: gendered spaces[39]

Along with the gendered construction of the house, came the gendered construction of the household. According to Robert Blair St George,

> ... women effectively vied with men for control over the household itself. The image of the 'house-body' and its accompanying language play a central role in demonstrating that patriarchal mandate was never absolute. ... The house-body was a gendered body. The productive acreage that surrounded the house consisted of male spatial domains [fields, barns]. Yet within the house women ruled ... [and] the question of how to naturalize the house as a hierarchic body that contained women as subordinate members had no easy answer.[40]

Deborah initially created a unique household, and one wonders how much Benjamin struggled to ensure that she was 'contained' as his subordinate. As she wrote, 'Mr. [John] Foxcrofte Came to town this day[.] ... I had got sume of our things in the new house and beads in the upper roomes [so] he lodges in the room fasing the market street and has his writeing thair all so'. Several months later she explained that when she first began moving into the new house, 'which was in may ..., I stayd in Mr. Foxcroftes house till he Come that is we dressed vitels and slept thair and muefed by degrees to our one house'.[41] Did 'our one house' refer to hers and Benjamin's or hers and Mr. Foxcroft's? It is likely she meant the former and that, in fact, Foxcroft temporarily became a boarder in her house (although it is not clear he paid rent for the room upstairs). This put her in the same ambiguous position as Benjamin's landlady in London. Historian Naomi Tadmor argues that a landlady could have 'a partly servile position in relation to her paying guests, all the more so as they ... [were] clearly her social superiors'. This was not true in the case of Margaret Stevenson; she was 'a landlady [who] retain[ed] the position or moral authority, typical of the mistress and householder'. As such, it was 'her duty to maintain the good order and reputation of *her* establishment'. Clearly, the eighteenth-century household was 'flexible and permeable'; relationships were frequently instrumental rather than sentimental.[42]

Before the Franklins built their new Georgian-style house, gender boundaries appeared more flexible. Deborah ran a shop out of their houses, Benjamin had his post office in the house, and Deborah assisted Benjamin in running his print shop. All these economic activities brought her into the political sphere where she developed networking skills. Thus, the Franklin home 'stood at a crossroads of eighteenth-century gendered interpretations of space'.[43] But there is no evidence of that economic activity in the new house. As Bernard Herman argues, the eighteenth-century urban town house, organised 'around avenues of movement', became the site 'where symbolic action and presentation of self were essential elements of everyday life'. Middle- and upper-class families like the Franklins had the luxury of dedicating certain rooms to private and public activities; each member of the household had their own space within the house and various rooms served dedicated purposes.[44]

As historians have argued, by doing so, eighteenth-century houses created multiple gendered spaces within homes. Areas such as drawing rooms, libraries and dining rooms served as alternatives to public spaces of taverns, coffeehouses and clubs and allowed men to interact politically and intellectually with male peers in their own houses. The dining table was the site of social, cultural and economic exchange, and dinners were primarily masculine affairs. If women were included, they left the table before men did, and often the hostess was the only woman present. At the same time, spaces for women edged them from the house's political, economic and intellectual centre; women congregated in the homosocial realm of the bedroom. There were some mixed sex spaces, such as the parlour for teas, that accommodated a smaller, more intimate public – but it was a public that devalued women.[45] According to Jessica Kross, 'Women without men used far less of the great house than women with men or men alone. There is no record of all-female gatherings for meals in dining rooms or for large discussions in a parlor'.[46]

Here too the Franklins complicated this pattern. Deborah was not a widow but she essentially lived as one. As all widows did, she occupied an ambiguously gendered space and had an ambiguously gendered relationship to the material and social culture of the household. Widows were expected to play the part of male and female, father and mother, masculine and feminine. In reality, Deborah was not a widow; as a married woman living alone, those spaces and relationships were even more ambiguous and complicated as she (sometimes inadvertently and sometimes openly) challenged the gendered construction of the household.

The most radical regendering of the house came on the night of 16 September 1765, when her house took on an overtly political – and military – significance. Angry responses to the Stamp Act occurred throughout the colonies, but many in Philadelphia blamed Benjamin for supporting the Act, and mobs threatened to retaliate. From Deborah's description of the situation, one can feel the tension and perhaps even fear she felt, but also more palpably the strength, control and bravery she exerted.[47] For nine days people kept warning her of the danger she and her family faced. Fearing for her daughter Sally's safety, she sent her to relatives in Burlington, New Jersey. Then 'on munday laste' tensions reached the boiling point when the mob threatened to pull down the newly built house. But she did not face them alone. 'Cusin [Josiah] Davenporte Come and told me . . . it was his Duty to be with me. I sed I was plesed to reseve Civility from aney bodey so he staid with me sum time[.]' She seemed to have control of the situation, however, for she ordered Davenport to 'fech a gun or two as we had none. I maid one room into a Magazin. I ordered sum sorts of defense up Stairs such as I Cold manaig my self'. It is not clear which one of the elegantly furnished, wainscoted and decorated rooms became an armed fortress, but clearly all of the second storey (and maybe third storey) private bedrooms became more than domestic spaces. Later that evening, more than twenty relatives and neighbours helped to guard the house. Despite their offers to stay the night with her, she sent them away.

As her supporters left, they urged her to leave with them, but she refused, adamantly asserting, 'I had not given aney ofense to aney person att all nor would I be maid unesey by aney bodey nor wold I stir or show the leste uneseynis but if aney one Came to disturbe me I wold show a proper resenetement and I shold be very much afrunted'. As she recalled the events, she felt compelled to reiterate to her husband that she would 'not stir as I rely donte think it wold be right in me to stir or show the leste uneseyness at all'. Refusing to be intimidated and putting on a brave face to the outside world, she proved she could protect *her* household. She assumed the male protector role. When Benjamin's reply came several months later, it was notably brief; he wrote simply, 'I honour much the Spirit and Courage you show'd, and the prudent Preparations you made in that [Time] of Danger'. Then he added this intriguing comment: 'The [Woman?] deserves a good [House] that [is?] determined to defend it'. Feminist scholars of architecture suggest that the house constructed the dichotomy between private and public far less than we have previously understood, but in Benjamin's mind had Deborah finally demonstrated enough courage, enough masculine qualities, to begin defining the house as hers?[48]

The image of armed women protecting themselves was not new, but the 'female soldier' lived at the margins – either on the frontier or in captivity; she was not a genteel lady living in the heart of a city in a newly constructed house designed to prove her family's status to others.[49] Historians have argued that because men's houses symbolised their authority and their manhood, those structures 'became target[s] of popular anger' when leaders attemped 'to enforce what the people considered to be illegitimate laws'. Moreover, men who 'had proven themselves to be unmanly' or selfish 'effeminate fops' by acquiring luxury goods occupied these houses. 'Defacing the most visible symbol of their [political] manhood', the mob demonstrated their disrespect for revolutionary leaders.[50] However, the crowd was also attacking a visible representation of an emerging consumer culture that shut them out. The 'lower sort' vented their anger on a house clearly designed to exhibit the Franklins' wealth and power. When defending the house, Deborah was not just protecting her household – her private domain – she also was defending her and her husband's status and visibly securing their role as well-established members of the bourgeois public sphere.

That Deborah simultaneously inhabited a female world was evident when Benjamin thanked 'the good Ladies you mention for their friendly Wishes'. His 'best Respects' went to more than thirteen women who had been visiting with Deborah.[51] That was to be expected. Yet, beyond the unusual circumstances of the Stamp Act brouhaha, Deborah regularly assumed the masculine role of entertaining in the public spaces. For example, she wrote Benjamin that 'Billey and his wife . . . Spente yisterday at our house as did Mr. Williams Brothers. We was att diner. I sed I had not aney thing but vitels for I Cold not get anything for a deserte but who knows but I may treet you with sum thing from Ingland'. Luckily at that point, the mail came, and with whatever arrived from England, she 'had the pleshuer of treeting quite grand-indead, and our little Companey as cheerful and hapey as aney in the world'.[52] Several months later, Benjamin wrote, apparently in response to Deborah informing him that she and a group of his old friends had drunk to his health, 'I am much oblig'd to my good old Friends that did me the Honour to remember me in the unfinish'd Kitchin. I hope soon to drink with them in the Parlour'.[53] He appeared to miss the male camaraderie of the parlour and maybe even resented Deborah's usurpation of male sociability. Like it or not, in their homes and through their letters, women helped the private space of the family emerge into a realm of broader public sociability, and in the process played a crucial role in the creation of a new identity and cultural development.[54]

Still, from the outside looking in – and seemingly a little peeved at Deborah's independence – he wrote, 'it gives me Pleasure that so many of my Friends honour'd our new Dining Room with their Company. You tell me only of a Fault they found with the House, that it was too little; and not a Word of any thing they lik'd in it. Nor how the Kitchin Chimneys perform; so I suppose you spare me some Mortification, which is kind'.[55] The Franklins formed a part of a new bourgeois public sphere, a sphere that was 'the creation of an imagined public space, a powerful, critical voice known as public opinion'.[56] Disagreeing with her expenditure of their social capital, he cringed under that gaze. Perhaps that explains why he ended the letter with, 'I wonder you put up the Oven without Mr. Roberts's Advice, as I think you told me he had my old Letter of Directions'. Did she invite criticism because she did not follow his order? Was he blameless here?

As Daphne Spain argues, houses reflect ideals and realities about relationships between women and men within the family and in society. 'The space outside the home becomes the arena in which social relations (i.e., status) are produced, while the space inside the home becomes that in which social relations are reproduced'. Domestic architecture mediates social relations, specifically those between women and men. Houses are the spatial context within which the social order is reproduced.[57] If that is so, Deborah Franklin turned that order upside down.

But she also partook of what has been described as a more traditionally female ritual. On 3 November 1765, she wrote to her husband that she received the tea he sent, and with it she 'had the pleshuer to treet your old friend John Robertes[,] his Son the Doctor from mereyland[,] thair wifes and Dafter[, and] your verey good friend Mrs. Howel and Dafter to the Number of 13'. A smaller social gathering coalesced when 'good Mr. Rhodes and his son Thomas Franklin and wife dranke tee with us and we had the beste Buckwhate Kakes that ever I maid. They sed I had ought dun my one ought doings. Our good Mr. Mockridg has sente sume of the beste of the flower that I ever saw and we had them hot thay desired thair love to you'. Several months later she wrote that she received 'the butyfull Candel stickes', the set of 'Chaney quite whole[,] and the fine tee Pot . . . for which I give you maney thankes and if I live tell your Birthday I think to fill it with punch and treet sum of your friends'.[58]

As did Benjamin Franklin, men throughout the British Empire recognised the tea table as 'the critical institution in the assertion of women's presence in the emerging public sphere'. David Shields argues that 'women's embrace of tea must be understood as a reaction to the masculine infatuation with coffee and all that it implied', especially the masculine world of the coffeehouse. Those who felt anxiety about the consolidation of women's power dismissed the ritual of tea drinking – and its female devotees – as frivolous, even wasteful. Nevertheless, Benjamin clearly changed his mind once *he* aspired to become a gentleman, for not only did he applaud Deborah's efforts at entertaining his friends and family, he aided those social gatherings by sending her the latest and expensive *accoutrements* from London. While we see the development of a female public sphere, we also recognise a male concern that his friends do not again find fault with his household. A woman's ability to entertain in style reflected her status within the household; her ability to entertain in style reflected his status within the community.[59]

In Deborah Franklin's case, her ability to entertain in style – not only in serving tea in the parlour but also in 'treeting quite grand' in the dining room reflected the gendered nature of the household and her competing masculine and feminine roles as ornament and as head of household.

Conclusion

Not many women built their own houses – or even participated in that process to the extent Deborah Franklin did; the one notable exception, Susanna Wright, interestingly enough was Deborah's good friend. If only correspondence between those women existed! Even if women did not build their own houses, 'they understood architectural form' and the construction of gender around those forms.[60] The Franklins constructed their house and their permeable gendered identities several decades before the ideology of 'republican motherhood' valorised women's roles in the family and the household and women moved from the margins to centre stage in the early nineteenth-century home. Deborah Franklin's letters, replicating the disorder of the building process itself, sheds light on her relationship to the public and personal spaces of the house and the household. As she told her stories, she constructed, deconstructed, and reconstructed those relationships. She left her indelible mark on each room whose lathing, plastering, painting and wainscoting she oversaw; on each room she decorated; on each room she used; and on each room she described in depth. Those marks reveal that Deborah learned to navigate the sometimes calm, sometimes stormy waters of gender in the eighteenth century. She learned – in fact, was forced to learn – new skills generally undertaken by men. She was, by turns, both an active participant and a passive recipient of shifting gender norms. She both resisted and embraced newly created identities around the literal and figurative construction of the Franklin house.

Notes

1. Benjamin Franklin to Deborah Franklin, 9 December 1764, in Leonard W. Labaree, et al. (eds), *The Papers of Benjamin Franklin*, hereafter *PBF* (New Haven: Yale University Press, 1959–), vol. 11, p. 517.

2. In 1763 Benjamin 'came back to the warmest welcome', and in letters to England he boasted of the 'flow of well-wishers coming to his house 'from morning to night'. Claude-Anne Lopez and Eugenia W. Herbert, *The Private Franklin: The Man and his Family* (New York: W. W. Norton, 1975), pp. 96, 174.

3. The cited words or phrases come respectively from Sheila Skemp, 'Family Partnerships: The Working Wife, Honoring Deborah Franklin', in Larry Tise (ed.), *Benjamin Franklin and Women* (University Park: Pennsylvania State University Press, 2000), pp. 19–36, here pp. 31–2; Lopez and Herbert, *The Private Franklin*, pp. 124–30, here p. 124; David Freeman Hawke, *Franklin* (New York: Harper & Row, 1976), pp. 198–9. See also Gordon S. Wood, *The Americanization of Benjamin Franklin* (New York: Penguin, 2004), p. 98; H. W. Brands, *The First American: The Life and Times of Benjamin Franklin* (New York: Anchor Books, 2000), p. 341; Claude-Anne Lopez, *Benjamin Franklin's 'Good House': The Story of Franklin Court* (Washington, DC: US Department of the Interior, 1981), pp. 25–9; Jennifer Reed Fry, '"Extraordinary Freedom and Great Humility": A Reinterpretation of Deborah Franklin', *Pennsylvania Magazine of History and Biography* 127 (2003), pp. 167–96, here p. 185. The most recent discussion of the letters is Edward Cahill's 'Benjamin Franklin's Interiors', *Early American Studies* 6 (2008), pp. 27–58, esp. pp. 47–53. It is an excellent analysis, but it is an analysis that focuses on Benjamin's struggle to maintain *his* image as a virtuous republican citizen while displaying all the trappings of wealth and luxury, an ideological tension of the revolutionary and early national periods. Cahill even admits that Franklin formally appropriated Deborah's voice in his autobiography, p. 43.

4. Bernard L. Herman, 'Tabletop Conversations: Material Culture and Everyday Life in the Eighteenth-Century Atlantic World', in John Styles and Amanda Vickery (eds), *Gender, Taste, and Material Culture in Britain and North America, 1700–1830* (New Haven: Yale University Press, 2006), pp. 37–59, esp. pp. 48, 50–52.

5. Bernard L. Herman, *Town House: Architecture and Material Life in the Early American City, 1780–1830* (Chapel Hill: University of North Carolina Press, 2005), p. 38. Deborah often referred to the house as her husband's: see, e.g., DF to BF, 7 April 1765 and ? August 1765, *PBF*, vol. 12, pp. 101, 224. Perhaps she well understood her legal position for she never called it her house, although she did call it 'our' house on occasion. The Franklins were not alone in their transatlantic construction of their house; Philadelphians Henry and Ann Hill engaged in a similar project with his sister who lived in London – but the key difference was that the married couple were together on one side of the ocean; see Amy Henderson, 'A Family Affair: The Design and Decoration of 32 South Fourth Street, Philadelphia', in Styles and Vickery (eds), *Gender, Taste, and Material Culture*, pp. 267–91.

6. See Linda Sturtz, *Within her Power: Propertied Women in Colonial Virginia* (New York: Routledge, 2002), esp. ch. 3, '"As Though I My Self was Pr[e]sent": Women with Power of Attorney', pp. 71–88.

7. Lopez and Herbert, *The Private Franklin*, p. 149; Lopez, *Benjamin Franklin's 'Good House'*, p. 34. For a description of Franklin's suite of rooms in Stevenson's house and discussion of the 'intimacy between the two households', see Herman, *Town House*, pp. 237–8. In much the way Deborah described the house in Philadelphia as 'his', Margaret Stevenson's house at 36 Craven Street is now a museum and it is called 'The Benjamin Franklin House', http://www.benjaminfranklinhouse.org/site/sections/default.htm

8. DF to BF, 22 September 1765, *PBF*, vol. 12, p. 271; and BF to DF, 9 November 1765, *PBF*, vol. 12, p. 360. See also Fry, 'A Reinterpretation of Deborah Franklin', p. 190.

9. Helen Hills, 'Theorizing the Relationships between Architecture and Gender in Early Modern Europe', in Helen Hills (ed.), *Architecture and the Politics of Gender in Early Modern Europe* (Aldershot: Ashgate, 2003), pp. 3–22, here p. 8.

10. Katharine Martinez and Kenneth L. Ames (eds), *The Material Culture of Gender, The Gender of Material Culture* (Winterthur: Henry Francis du Pont Wintherthur Museum, 1997), p. 2.

11. The secondary literature discussing the eighteenth-century household is vast. For this and the following paragraph, I have drawn on Naomi Tadmor, *Family and Friends in Eighteenth-Century England: Household, Kinship, and Patronage* (Cambridge: Cambridge University Press, 2001), pp. 20–25; Mary Beth Norton, *Liberty's Daughters: The Revolutionary Experience of American Women, 1750–1800* (New York: Little, Brown, 1980), pp. 3–9, 34–9, 61–5; Karin Wulf, *Not all Wives: Women of Colonial Philadelphia* (Ithaca: Cornell University Press, 2000), pp. 25–38, 85–97, 115–17; and Mary Beth Sievens, *Stray Wives: Marital Conflict in Early National New England* (New York: New York University Press, 2005), pp. 17–18.

12. Women did become heads of households when their husbands died, and this greatly complicated the ideal structure of the family. Carole Shammas, *A History of Household Government in America* (Charlottesville: University of Virginia Press, 2002), p. 32, argues that English women were more likely to head households than were colonial American women. For an in-depth discussion of this subject and the sources for the direct quotes, see Vivian Bruce Conger, *The Widows' Might: Widowhood and Gender in Early British America* (New York: New York University Press, 2009).

13. BF to Jane Franklin, 6 January 1727, *PBF*, vol. 1, pp. 100–01.

14. *Pennsylvania Gazette*, 8 October 1730.

15. *Pennsylvania Gazette*, 10 July 1732. David S. Shields, *Civil Tongues & Polite Letters in British America* (Chapel Hill: University of North Carolina Press, 1997), pp. 114–15, calls this one of Franklin's 'finer early satires'. He also noted, 'Franklin was astute enough in his satire not to attempt to turn ladies of quality away from their favorite pastime. The target of his ridicule was women of the middling sort, the would-be gentlewomen who violated the codes of prudence and frugality that regulated middle-class morality'.

16. Ruth H. Bloch, *Gender and Morality in Anglo-American Culture, 1650–1800* (Berkeley: University of California Press, 2003), p. 114. Bloch explored the connections between 'intellectual history and the social history of women by examining [Franklin's] . . . biographical connections to members of the opposite sex', p. 102. She is not alone, for almost every historian who mentions Deborah Franklin does so in and through the context of Benjamin Franklin's writings. Although they reach very different conclusions about Deborah Franklin; the two exceptions are Skemp, 'Family Partnerships: The Working Wife, Honoring Deborah Franklin', and Fry, 'A Reinterpretation of Deborah Franklin'. I similarly turn the tables and examine the social and cultural history of women by looking at Deborah Franklin's biographical connections to the household.

17. DF to BF, 6–13? October 1765, *PBF*, vol. 12, p. 229.

18. Norton, *Liberty's Daughters*, p. 5. For a discussion of permeable gender roles see e.g., Laurel Thatcher Ulrich, *Good Wives: Image and Reality in the Lives of Women in Northern New England, 1650–1750* (New York: Alfred A. Knopf, 1982); Conger, *The Widows' Might*; Mary Beth Norton, *Founding Mothers and Fathers: Gendered Power and the Forming of American Society* (New York: Vintage, 1997); Linda Kerber, *Women of the Republic: Intellect and Ideology in Revolutionary America* (Chapel Hill: University of North Carolina Press, 1980); Rosemarie Zagarri, *A Woman's Dilemma: Mercy Otis Warren and the American Revolution* (New York: Harlan Davidson, 1995); Bloch, *Gender and Morality*.

19. Wulf, *Not all Wives*, pp. 85–90.

20. Sievens, *Stray Wives*, pp. 13–19; Walter Isaacson, *Benjamin Franklin: An American Life* (New York: Simon & Schuster, 2003), p. 81, describes Deborah Franklin as having a 'fierce temper', a temper Franklin possibly tolerated because assertive women were active in the family business, were good housewives, and looked after their husbands' interests.

21. Lopez, *Benjamin Franklin's 'Good House'*, p. 24.

22. Susan M. Stabile, *Memory's Daughters: The Material Culture of Remembrance in Eighteenth-Century America* (Ithaca: Cornell University Press, 2004), pp. 26–32.

23. Hills, 'Theorizing the Relationships', p. 4; see also Herman, *Town House*, p. 39.

24. Dell Upton, *Architecture in the United States* (Oxford: Oxford University Press, 1998), pp. 24–5. He locates the concrete gendering of the home – the distinction between male and female spaces in and control of the house and household – in the nineteenth century, pp. 41–3.

25. The Gunning Bedford Insurance Survey of Franklin House, 5 August 1766, *PBF*, vol 13, p. 379. For a discussion of eighteenth-century American homes, see Victoria Kloss Ball, *Architecture and Interior Design: Europe and America from the Colonial Era to Today* (New York: John Wiley & Sons, 1980), pp. 178–241.

26. DF to BF, 8 January 1765, *PBF*, vol. 12, p. 14.

27. Lopez and Herbert, *The Private Franklin*, pp. 116–17; Lopez, *Benjamin Franklin's 'Good House'*, pp. 24–5; Hannah Benner Roach, 'Benjamin Franklin Slept Here', *Pennsylvania Magazine of History and Biography* 84 (1960); pp. 127–74, see esp. pp. 166–8.

28. Herman, *Town House*, p. 21; DF to BF, 10 February 1765, and 17 February 1765, *PBF*, vol. 12, pp. 44–6; BF to DF, 14 February 1765, *PBF*, vol. 12, p. 62.

29. DF to BF, 7 April 1765, *PBF*, vol. 12, pp. 101–2.

30. BF to DF, 4 June 1765, *PBF*, vol. 12, p. 167. My emphasis.

31. DF to BF, ? August 1765, *PBF*, vol. 12, p. 224.

32. BF to DF, August 1765, *PBF*, vol. 12, pp. 250–51. My emphasis. A vault is an enclosed space used as a cellar or storeroom for provisions.

33. Billy G. Smith, *The 'Lower Sort': Philadelphia's Laboring People, 1750–1800* (Ithaca: Cornell University Press, 1990), p. 185.

34. Mary Beth Sievens, 'Female Consumerism and Household Authority in Early National New England', *Early American Studies* 4 (2006), pp. 354–5, 362, 370. The phrase 'empire of goods' is T. H. Breen's, 'An Empire of Goods: The Anglicization of Colonial America, 1690–1776', *Journal of British Studies* 25 (1986), pp. 467–99.

35. DF to BF, 6–13 October 1765, *PBF*, vol. 12, pp. 293–9.

36. DF to BF, 20–25 April 1767, *PBF*, vol. 14, p. 138. Deborah was indeed being frugal, but she was not alone. According to Richard L. Bushman, 'Shopping and Advertising in Colonial America', in Cary Carson, Ronald Hoffman and Peter Alberts (eds), *Of Consuming Interests: The Style of Life in the Eighteenth Century* (Charlottesville: University of Virginia Press, 1944), pp. 223–51, esp. pp. 248–9, deferential and savvy shopkeepers advertised that they had the cheapest prices because 'genteel customers were considered to be sharp buyers, aware of the best values and demanding the lowest price'. See also Elizabeth Kowaleski-Wallace, *Consuming Subjects: Women, Shopping, and Business in the Eighteenth Century* (New York: Columbia University Press, 1997).

37. Amanda Vickery, *The Gentleman's Daughter: Women's Lives in Georgian England* (New Haven: Yale Nota Bene, 2003), pp. 162–8; Vickery argues that men had control over extraordinary expenses and that their shopping was 'occasional and impulsive, or expensive and dynastic'. Maxine Berg, *Luxury and Pleasure in Eighteenth-Century Britain* (Oxford: Oxford University Press, 2005), pp. 243–5, contends that Vickery portrayed male shoppers incorrectly – that, in fact, men were actively involved in shopping, not just for special purchases, but for the mundane and that they, in fact, took pride in purchasing domestic goods. Ellen Hartigan-O'Connor, 'Collaborative Consumption and the Politics of Choice in Early American Port Cities', in Styles and Vickery (eds), *Gender, Taste, and Material Culture*, pp. 125–49, esp. pp. 141–2, falls in between Vickery and Berg in suggesting that the gendered nature of shopping varied according

to place and time in the colonies. Benjamin Franklin certainly took pride in domestic shopping, but often he purchased luxury goods with which to display his status in the community of which he was an absent member.

38. Ann Smart Martin, 'Ribbons of Desire: Gendered Stories in the World of Goods', in Styles and Vickery (eds), *Gender, Taste, and Material Culture*, pp. 179–200, here p. 181.

39. See Daphne Spain, *Gendered Spaces* (Chapel Hill: University of North Carolina Press, 1992).

40. Robert Blair St George, *Conversing by Signs in Colonial New England Culture* (Chapel Hill: University of North Carolina Press, 1998), pp. 173–80.

41. DF to BF, 7 April 1765, *PBF*, vol. 12, p. 101; DF to BF, ? August 1764, *PBF*, vol. 12, p. 224.

42. Tadmor, *Family and Friends in Eighteenth-Century England*, p. 50; Naomi Tadmor, 'The Concept of the Household-Family in Eighteenth-Century England', *Past & Present* 151 (1996), pp. 111–40, esp. pp. 120–25.

43. Fry, 'A Reinterpretation of Deborah Franklin', pp. 139, 176; Hills, 'Theorizing the Relationships', p. 7.

44. Joan R. Gunderson, *To Be Useful to the World: Women in Revolutionary America, 1740–1790* (New York: Twayne, 1996), p. 135; Herman, *Town House*, pp. 41–2.

45. Jessica Kross, 'Mansions, Men, Women and the Creation of Multiple Publics in Eighteenth-Century British North America', *Journal of Social History* 33 (1999), pp. 385–408, esp. pp. 385–7, 390, 395–8; Herman, *Town House*, pp. 71–2; Barbara G. Carson, *Ambitious Appetites: Dining, Behavior, and Patterns of Consumption in Federal Washington* (Washington, DC: American Institute of Architects Press, 1990), pp. 118–19.

46. Kross, 'Mansions, Men, Women and the Creation of Multiple Publics', p. 399.

47. This and the following paragraph draw on DF to BF, 22 September 1765, *PBF*, vol. 12, pp. 270–74; and BF to DF, 9 November 1765, *PBF*, vol. 12, p. 360. The story is a familiar one, but one that has not been analysed in terms of the gendered construction of the household; see e.g., Wood, *The Americanization of Benjamin Franklin*, pp. 111–13; Lopez and Herbert, *The Private Franklin*, pp. 127–8; Skemp, 'Family Partnerships', pp. 30–31; Gunderson, *To Be Useful to the World*, pp. 150–51.

48. Hilde Heynen, 'Modernity and Domesticity: Tensions and Contradictions', in Hilde Heynen and Gülsüm Baydar (eds), *Negotiating Domesticity: Spatial Productions of Gender in Modern Architecture* (Abingdon: Routledge, 2005), pp. 1–29, here p. 2.

49. Laurel Thatcher Ulrich, ''Daughters of Liberty': Religious Women in Revolutionary New England', in Ronald Hoffman and Peter J. Albert (eds), *Women in the Age of the American Revolution* (Charlottesville: Published for the United States Capitol Historical Society by the University Press of Virginia, 1989), pp. 211–243, esp. pp. 228–36.

50. Anne S. Lombard, *Making Manhood: Growing up Male in Colonial New England* (Cambridge: Harvard University Press, 2003), p. 162. See St George, *Conversing by Signs*, ch. 3, 'Attacking Houses', pp. 206–95.

51. BF to DF, 4 June 1765, *PBF*, vol. 12, p. 166.

52. DF to BF, 12 April 1765, *PBF*, vol. 12, p. 102.

53. BF to DF, 4 June 1765, *PBF*, vol. 12, p. 166.

54. Carolyn Steedman, 'A Woman Writing a Letter', in Rebecca Earle (ed.), *Epistolary Selves: Letters and Letter-Writers 1600–1945* (Aldershot: Ashgate, 1999), pp. 111–33, esp. pp. 115–16, 121.

55. BF to DF, 13 July 1765, *PBF*, vol. 12, pp. 210–11.

56. T. H. Breen, 'The Meaning of Things: Interpreting the Consumer Economy in the Eighteenth Century', in John Brewer and Roy Porter (eds), *Consumption and the Worlds of Goods* (London: Routledge, 1993), pp. 249–60, here p. 257.

57. Spain, *Gendered Spaces*, p. 7.

58. DF to BF, 3 November 1765, *PBF*, vol. 12, pp. 350–51; DF to BF, 12 January 1766, *PBF*, vol. 13, pp. 30–31, 35.

59. Shields, *Civil Tongues & Polite Letters*, pp. 104–6, 113–14; Herman, *Town House*, p. 73.

60. Stabile, *Memory's Daughters*, p. 31.

8 Sexual Politics and Socialist Housing: Building Homes in Revolutionary Cuba

Carrie Hamilton

Feminists have long been concerned with the question of home. Historians of gender and the family have investigated gendered divisions of labour in the household and 'public' sphere,[1] while theorists of migration and globalisation have turned their attention to discourses of home among those displaced by conflict, genocide and/or the search for economic security.[2] Feminist geographers have studied the gendered construction of urban and rural spaces, including the domestic.[3] More recently, concerns with women and gender have expanded to include sexuality, as historians, geographers and queer theorists analyse the construction of sexual terrains.[4]

But notwithstanding the expansive feminist and queer literature on homes and space, this work as a whole pays relatively little attention to housing issues.[5] While contemporary studies of gender, sexuality, home and space sometimes address inequalities in access to housing, most have little to say about the sexual politics of housing policy and provision, their relationship to gendered and sexualised discourses and power regimes, and the vastly different material contexts in which homes are built – literally and figuratively – across time and space.[6] Generally, moreover, this literature displays a bias towards Western, capitalist societies and a lack of attention to developing, socialist or transitional economies.

This chapter addresses some of these imbalances by examining the interconnectedness of home and housing in revolutionary Cuba. It begins by reviewing the secondary literature on Cuban housing and the family, respectively, before analysing a series of interviews from the 'Memories of the Cuban Revolution' oral history project.[7] The related problems of finding a house and being 'at home' run through most of the interviews. While popular and official rhetoric in Cuba, as in most nation-states, often celebrates the family as the centre of national identity, the interviews complicate this narrative, highlighting sites of family conflict as well as support. Family disputes and disunity are exacerbated by gender inequalities, homophobia, racism and an ongoing, acute housing shortage. Historians of race in Cuba have made the link between weaknesses in revolutionary housing policy and persistent racial inequalities.[8] This chapter supplements that work, arguing that the history of housing and homes since 1959 is tied as well to the regime's gender and sexual politics. However, historians and other scholars of the Cuban Revolution usually treat housing and home as separate issues. The aim of this chapter is to begin to historicise the relationship between the politics of housing and home in revolutionary Cuba, drawing on feminist critiques of socialist housing policy as well as feminist and queer theorisations of sexuality and space. It concludes by making the case for comparative histories of sexuality and housing.

Socialism and housing[9]

Even before the 'triumph' of the revolution in January 1959, Cuban revolutionary leaders declared themselves committed to providing adequate and affordable housing for all Cubans. As early as his 1953 'History Will Absolve Me' speech, Fidel Castro recognised what he called the 'tragedy of housing': excessive rents, frequent evictions, high utility rates and crowded and precarious dwellings that plagued poor tenants in both urban and rural areas.[10] As in most large Latin American cities at mid-twentieth century, the Cuban capital Havana was surrounded by extensive squatter settlements and shanty towns.[11] In the countryside, peasants typically lived in *bohíos*, wooden huts with thatched roofs, mud or cement floors, without toilets or bathing facilities.[12] Estimates put the overall housing deficit in 1959 at between 250,000 and 700,000.[13] As Sergio Roca notes, 'the task of the revolution in the housing sector was nothing short of formidable'.[14]

During the early years of the revolution, a series of new housing laws was passed to introduce affordable rents and end property speculation, and there was an initial flurry of new construction.[15] The Self-Help and Mutual Aid programme allowed for the destruction of shanty towns and the relocation of their occupants in newly built units.[16] Additional housing was freed up by the departure of some 200,000 mostly middle-class residents during the first years of the revolution, especially from the wealthy neighbourhoods of Havana.[17] But early promises of adequate housing for all proved difficult to fulfil. Roca calculates that, by the mid-1960s, two-thirds of the population (almost five million people) was still living in substandard or overcrowded housing.[18] Scholars cite a number of explanations for the persistent housing shortage. Kosta Mathéy argues that revolutionary leaders never dedicated the same attention to housing as they did to improving health and education services, or to programmes of agricultural and economic reform.[19] Furthermore, adequate planning and construction were hindered by the departure of many of the country's architects,[20] as well as by the lack of building materials due to the United States embargo, imposed in 1961.[21] The Revolutionary Offensive of 1968, under which all remaining non-agricultural small businesses were nationalised, allowed the government to convert some commercial buildings into dwellings, although the premises often made inappropriate accommodation.[22] That same year, Fidel Castro estimated that, during the first decade of the revolution, only 10 per cent of required housing had been built.[23]

Yet housing provision, especially in Havana, continued to fall behind other priorities and Castro himself declared that housing was the most urgent social problem facing the revolution.[24] During his annual 26 July speech in 1970, the Cuban leader announced a plan for the formation of *microbrigadas* (microbrigades). A certain number of workers would be relieved of their normal duties to build houses for themselves and their colleagues.[25] The microbrigades came at a crucial time for the revolution, as the failure of the ten-million-tonne sugar harvest planned for 1970 forced the government to reconsider its overall strategy, moving closer to the Soviet model of economic and social planning while prompting measures to improve efficiency. The microbrigades were envisaged as a specifically socialist approach to housing provision. The principle of freeing workers from their regular duties to build social housing contrasted with much of the rest of Latin America, where those without shelter were typically left to build their own homes after regular work hours,[26] although this sort of informal practice did continue in socialist Cuba, especially in rural areas.[27] During the 1970s, microbrigades built tens of thousands of dwellings, particularly in new neighbourhoods around Havana. But the success rate of the microbrigades, which were disbanded by the end of the decade and re-formed in the 1980s, was not enough to remedy the housing crisis. Carmelo Mesa-Lago claims that housing was the least successful area of reform during the revolution's first two decades.[28] By the 1980s, the coming of age of the 'baby boom' generation born in the 1960s added further pressure on housing.[29] In response to the housing shortage, Cubans increasingly constructed their own homes and additions.[30] The 1984 Housing Law legalised self-help construction and introduced some forms of renting as well as the *permuta* system, whereby tenants could move by exchanging houses.[31] Moreover, various scholars have argued that the inadequacies of housing provision in the 1970s and 1980s perpetuated pre-revolutionary inequalities, reinforcing what Alejandro de la Fuente calls a 'traditional geography of race and poverty'.[32]

The collapse of the Soviet Union and the socialist Eastern European bloc after 1989 brought the housing crisis, along with all other economic problems in Cuba, to a head. In 1990, Castro announced that Cuba was entering a 'Special Period' of austerity and emergency measures. Since then, Cubans have increasingly had to find creative ways to ease the housing crisis, dividing houses or constructing additions.[33] As many interviewees indicate, others rent or buy properties illegally. In objective terms, the Cuban housing shortage (like most economic and social problems in Cuba) is not as drastic as in much of Latin America, or indeed the rest of the world.[34] But as with other areas of service and consumption in Cuba, the high expectations and promises of the early revolutionary period have widened the gap between aspiration and reality. In the first decade of the twenty-first century, a substantial number of Cubans still live in cramped conditions with extended families. For the younger generation especially, the chance of living alone or with a partner and/or children is negligible. This is the same generation that grew up during the 'Special Period' and has been most exposed to the lifestyle possibilities available to young middle-class people living abroad, through contact with tourists, news from friends and family in North America or Europe and, increasingly, access to new media. Fifty years after the revolutionary victory of 1959, a substantial number of young Cubans envisage their futures abroad, frequently naming the housing crisis as a major motivation for emigration.[35]

Revolutionary homes

Scholars cite a number of explanations for the ongoing housing problems in Cuba: the shortage of professionals and skilled labourers; a lack of materials owing to the US embargo and, more recently, the collapse of the Soviet Union and socialist bloc in Eastern Europe; and the ideological priority accorded educational and health programmes, as well as agricultural reform, industrial development and international solidarity. But although families were most affected by the shortage of dwellings, few scholars have considered the history of socialist housing in relation to family policy.[36]

As in other socialist regimes, many economic measures were 'aimed at abolishing the family as an economic unit of production, as production and distribution came progressively under state control'.[37] The reforms of the early 1960s, followed by the Revolutionary Offensive of 1968, removed most enterprise and land from family hands.[38] Furthermore, many social services historically provided by families, neighbourhood networks or the Church (including health, education and childcare) would subsequently be run by the state. The revolutionary government was concerned to exercise as much influence as possible on the socialisation of new generations.[39] Fidel Castro, Ernesto 'Che' Guevara and other revolutionary leaders celebrated the country's youth as the ideal socialist 'new men' and 'new women', uncontaminated by the bourgeois values of their older relatives. Measures to promote new revolutionary values included universal state schooling that took children away from the influence of parents and multi-generational families and the incorporation of Cubans of all ages into mass organisations. As Lois Smith and Alfredo Padula note, by the early 1960s 'the state was becoming a member of the family'.[40]

But revolutionary family policy was contradictory, reflecting conflicting messages about women's roles in the revolution. While the revolution has made significant advance in promoting women's participation and equality in the workplace and the 'public sphere' generally, it has been much less successful in tackling gender divisions in the home. At the root of this imbalance is the revolutionary emphasis, drawn from classic Marx and Engels, on eliminating gender inequality through the eradication of capitalist class relations, defined in relation to production. Thus the Federation of Cuban Women (FMC), founded in 1960, focused on the construction of the new socialist woman through her incorporation into the workforce and revolutionary organisations and structures.[41] But as Nicola Murray stresses, the 'model of the socialist woman' often clashed with 'the emphasis in Cuban state policy on the role of the family'.[42] At the same time that it shifted the economic and social power of families to the state and promoted women's participation in the workforce, the revolutionary government reinforced the ideal of the nuclear family through, for example, campaigns to encourage heterosexual couples to marry legally.[43]

Moreover, government policy to ease the burden of housework on women through programmes for socialising domestic labour was limited both by economic constraints and the persisting belief that women were more suited than men to domestic work.[44] This view was reflected in the make-up of housing microbrigades, of which women comprised only 22 per cent in 1988.[45] The construction of family homes also reflected, as in other socialist countries, an assumption that cooking and other domestic tasks would be carried out largely in the individual family home.[46] State childcare provision, while impressive, could not meet the requirements of all working mothers, and the tradition of women in extended family networks caring for each other's children may have lessened the pressure on the state to provide universal facilities.[47]

By the mid-1970s, the Cuban government recognised officially that gender equality had not been achieved. On International Women's Day in 1975, a new 'Family Code' came into effect.[48] Article 26 of the code called for women and men to take equal responsibility for domestic labour and childcare.[49] Moreover, the code implicitly acknowledged the family's ongoing importance in the socialisation of youth.[50] It tried to minimise the impact of the older generations by emphasising the role of parents, thus reinforcing the heterosexual couple as the centre of the family unit.[51] Other pieces of legislation during this period likewise reinforced traditional gender roles.[52] According to the 1976 Constitution, 'The state protects the family, motherhood and matrimony'.[53]

How can we explain this substantial gap between pro-family rhetoric and policy, on one hand, and the failure to provide adequate housing for individual families, on the other? Economic shortage alone cannot account for the lack of priority accorded to housing by the revolutionary regime. Comparative studies of gender and socialist housing policy provide some insight here. In their study of women, work and housing in the Soviet Union, Cedric Pugh and Susan Lewin make a direct link between the undervaluation of women's domestic labour and the lack of priority accorded to housing. Because in classic Marxist economics housing is considered to be 'unproductive', it is viewed as less important to socialist planning than the 'productive' sector. Unequal housing provision, while acknowledged in socialist theory as a feature of social inequality, is not perceived as a *cause* of such inequality. This is conceived instead in terms of class relations, which can only be eradicated through the transformation of productive relations. In this model, housing belongs to the 'domestic economy', which in turn is associated with women's unpaid (and therefore non-productive) labour.[54] Of course, as socialist feminists have argued for decades, production is fundamentally dependent on women's unpaid labour in the domestic sphere. But, as Pugh and Lewin write, 'notwithstanding their significance, the domestic labour, the child rearing, and the family roles of women are, like housing, subordinated in socialist theory. Although they have implications for productive work in firms and enterprises, they are essentially seen as unproductive'.[55] Pugh and Lewin's argument makes explicit what is only implicit in references to family, gender and housing in revolutionary Cuba: the low priority accorded to housing under socialist regimes is linked to the hierarchy of production over consumption, which in turn reflects the valuation of 'masculine', 'productive' labour in the public sector above 'feminine', 'unproductive' labour in the home.[56]

This analysis illuminates some of the contradictions in Cuban family policy, but comparisons between Cuba and other socialist states must also take into account economic, social and cultural specificities. The history of housing, gender and sexuality in socialist Cuba must therefore consider the ideological framework of Marxism and the particular historical patterns of family, gender and sexual relations in Cuba, as well as the inconsistent and contradictory impact of revolutionary policy on both of these areas. For example, the official status accorded to the nuclear family by the revolutionary government did not reflect the proliferation of extended and multi-generational families throughout Cuba.[57] According to Helen Safa, matrifocal or mother-centred households, historically strong in Cuba and most of the Caribbean, actually increased after the revolution of 1959, as did consensual unions.[58] If Safa is correct that such patterns reflect 'the levelling of class and racial hierarchies produced by the revolution, combined with greater economic autonomy for women',[59] the regime's attempt to impose a family model historically associated with the white middle classes clashed with its commitments to class, racial and gender equality.

Carollee Bengelsdorf argues that Cuban scholars have yet to investigate adequately the legacy of slavery and racial inequality in relation to family history.[60] Noting the imbalance between revolutionary policy and Cuban social reality, she claims that the privileging of the nuclear family underscores a commitment to the idea of 'modernity' as developed in Marxist theory since the nineteenth century.[61] But it also reflects the race and class privilege of the revolutionary leadership since, as Safa notes, 'legal marriage in Cuba had been a sign of respectability and whitening since colonial times'.[62] Thus in Cuba, as elsewhere, the promotion of the nuclear family model and the denigration of female-headed households reflect a patriarchal and Eurocentric bias.[63] While in agreement with Safa, I caution against her tendency to interpret matrifocal families as a sign of greater levels of social equality as well as of female autonomy and choice. The impact of the revolution on family forms went beyond increased social equality to the radical transformation of most areas of life, including the household economy, often with contradictory effects.[64] Safa's analysis does not consider adequately the material constraints that determine to a great extent where Cubans live and with whom. Nor does it take into account changing values vis-à-vis family relations and the different needs and desires of homosexuals, lesbians and bisexuals.

If women in heterosexual relationships faced the brunt of contradictions in revolutionary policy on women, the family and housing, the needs of homosexual men and lesbians were ignored. Indeed, during the 1960s and 1970s especially, social and political policy aimed to eradicate homosexuality, which was seen as antithetical to revolutionary commitment. Explanations for revolutionary homophobia in Cuba differ, and must take into account various historical, cultural and social traditions.[65] But following the argument above that the lack of priority accorded to housing reflected the gender politics of a Marxist framework that privileged production over consumption and the domestic economy, it is worth considering the construction of homosexuality in revolutionary economic and political theory. Upon adopting Marxism-Leninism as the framework of the revolution, Cuban leaders inherited a set of associations around gender, sexuality, production and class that contributed to the ostracising and eventual persecution of homosexuals as 'counter-revolutionary' or at least 'anti-social' elements. One crucial axis around which such associations clustered was that of labour. As Brad Epps argues, in this tradition homosexuals are viewed as unproductive, both in the biological and economic sense.[66] Engaging in sexual activities that did not lead to the creation of new generations of workers, homosexual men in particular were also stereotyped as non-productive workers engaged in individualistic artistic and intellectual pursuits.[67] The association of homosexual men with unproductive, decadent and parasitic activity was reflected in the frequent conflation in the early revolutionary years between homosexuals and anti-revolutionary emigrants, labelled *gusanos* (worms).[68]

As these arguments show, a history of housing in Cuba must consider the complex relationship between historical factors such as family structure and gender, race and class relations, on the one hand, and the material and ideological conditions that shaped housing policy and practice, on the other. More detailed histories of families and housing in Cuba would be needed to understand the links between tradition, housing needs, family relationships and the aspirations of Cubans of different groups. In the remainder of this chapter, I outline some of the ways in which interviews with Cubans in Havana highlight these patterns and complexities in relation to sexuality.

Memories of home

Housing is a recurring theme in most of the interviews conducted as part of the Memories of the Cuban Revolution oral history project. Several narrators describe their childhood homes in language similar to that used by Castro in his 1953 'History Will Absolve Me' speech. Wooden huts with thatched roofs are remembered as a common feature of an impoverished pre-revolutionary childhood and a miserable dwelling is an important signifier of humble origins, often prefiguring a narrative of revolutionary commitment. Many recount stories of how they acquired houses after 1959: occupying the abandoned mansions of emigrants in wealthy Havana neighbourhoods, building their own houses, participating in microbrigades during the 1970s and 1980s, or acquiring a house illegally on the informal market during or after the Special Period. Some are grateful to the revolution for 'giving' them a home. For most, however, stories of housing revolve around the ongoing dilemma of finding or keeping a home.

The interview with Taty, a black woman born in rural Cuba in 1938, incorporates many of these elements. Taty's life in many ways reads as a success story of the revolution. A poor childhood and insecure family situation forced her to leave school early and work as a domestic servant in her teenage years, which coincided with the dictatorship of Fulgencio Batista in the 1950s. After the revolution, Taty returned to school to study languages while making cakes and other baked goods at home. She sold these in order to help support her mother and sister, with whom she lived even after her marriage in 1971. For the first twenty years of her marriage, Taty continued to work from home, but since 1991 she had been working in a small state factory. She described getting a job outside the home as the best decision of her life, reflecting again the opportunities offered to women by the revolutionary emphasis on women's equality in the labour market.

The sense of improvements in Taty's life is heightened by the contrast with her poor childhood. One of her two younger siblings died because the family could not afford medical treatment. Taty's interview opens with a series of memories of that period, which bring her to tears:

> We lived in a hut with a thatched roof. I remember as a child that the doors were made of zinc. We lived close to an abattoir and the cows escaped and came in one door, flattened the zinc, and went out the other. My father was drunk. He lived and died drunk. He was a barber. He didn't take care of us and he didn't even give us his surname. An aunt of mine, a sister of my mother, the poor thing, struggled selling lottery tickets to give us something to eat.[69]

Following the 1944 hurricane that devastated parts of rural Cuba, Taty moved with her mother and sisters to Havana, where they lived in a *solar*, or humble flat. When her mother remarried, the family moved to a poor neighbourhood on the outskirts of the city. Although the area housed black, white and mixed-raced families and Taty recalls friendships with young people of different groups, the racial division of social and economic space is indicated by her memories of segregated social clubs and job discrimination during the 1950s. In this neighbourhood, where the nearby river frequently overflowed and flooded the house, sending sewage into the streets, Taty's stepfather built a wooden house, made from materials bought at a flea market. Following the revolution, there were plans to abolish the houses and relocate the tenants, but this was never carried through fully and many families were still living in the same deteriorating houses at the turn of the twenty-first century. In 2005, Taty's son was living in the same house her mother had lived in since the 1940s, even though Taty described it as 'ready to be pulled down'. She remembers that in the 1990s she called inspectors from the Housing Ministry to look at the house, but their reply was to offer to put the family on a waiting list for emergency shelter.

Taty married relatively late, aged thirty-four, and lived with her husband and son for about ten years in the attic of her mother's house. In the mid-1980s, the three of them moved to a suburb of Havana, where Taty's husband, deemed an exemplary worker, had been given a flat after his participation in a microbrigade. A decade later, in the 1990s, with her mother increasingly ill, Taty moved back to her old neighbourhood through the *permuta* system. In 2005, she described her current house as a place where she 'lived well', in spite of her difficult thirty-two-year marriage. Her thirty-one-year-old son, on the other hand, was living alone in the leaky wooden house, raising pigs on top of his regular job at a fishery in order to make improvements on the house and to accommodate his new partner and her small son. Taty's reflection on her son's situation reveals an awareness of the differing impact of the revolution on their lives. While she and her husband benefited from many of the social and economic improvements after 1959, including access to housing and work, their son, born in the heyday of the revolution, struggles to meet ends meet in the early twenty-first century.

Taty's interview also incorporates several wider trends in the history of Cuban housing: the miserable conditions in rural Cuba and working-class Havana during 1940s and 1950s; the mixed record of the revolutionary government in re-housing tenants in the 1960s and the particular impact this had on poor black families; the successes of the microbrigade projects and the rewards given to exemplary workers in the 1970s and 1980s in the form of houses; and the function of the *permuta* system and the self-help approach to housing since the 1990s, with people working on the informal market in order to make improvements to their living spaces. Moreover, the interview highlights how family, gender and sexual relations shape, and in turn are shaped by, housing issues. Most interesting is the evidence of a cross-generational pattern of women relying for housing on marriage and their husband's financial status or standing, a pattern that continued after the revolution. Taty's mother gained a house for herself and her children by marrying in the 1940s; Taty was likewise able, eventually, to have a family home thanks to her husband's employment and political connections. For the younger generation, however, opportunities are scarcer and Taty's son finds himself repairing an old house for his new family.

Sex, gender and housing

Taty's interview is not the only in which themes of family, gender, race and sexual relations merge through tales of housing. A notable feature of the interviews as a whole is that they complicate the popular myth of the exceptionally close Cuban family. In narrators' memories and descriptions of their current situations, family is as often a source of conflict and pain as one of support and comfort, and tensions with relatives are invariably aggravated by claustrophobic living conditions.

Lily is a black woman from the same neighbourhood as Taty, but some twenty-eight years younger. Born in eastern Cuba in 1965, as a child Lily moved to Havana, where her parents were given a house. She became pregnant while at boarding school, aged fifteen, which brought an end to her formal education. Subsequently, she worked in a series of temporary jobs, including cleaning, cooking and factory work. At the time of the interview in 2005, Lily, then aged forty, was living with her three children in the upstairs of her mother's house, with her siblings residing downstairs. Lily's life story is characterised by instability in many areas: work, housing and relationships. She describes herself as someone who did not think carefully about finding attentive and responsible fathers for her children and talks about problems of physical abuse and alcoholism in her relationships. In particular, Lily recalls the difficulty of having to share a house with her ex-husband (whom she describes as 'a bit of a womaniser') and his demanding mother. In describing this situation, Lily addresses the two Cuban interviewers directly, 'You know what the housing situation is like'.[70] At another point in the interview, she expresses faith that 'El Comandante' (Fidel Castro) would help her solve her housing problems.[71] As with many of the interviewees, Lily identifies the revolution with 'Fidel' and bestows him with a god-like power to solve the country's problems as well as her own.

The case of Lily underscores the problems faced by many Cuban single mothers with limited economic resources. Whereas Taty and her mother found homes through heterosexual relationships, for Lily marriage meant being trapped in cramped living quarters with an unfaithful husband and his difficult mother. Nena, a white woman from a working-class family, was born in the mid-1950s in a neighbourhood close to that where Taty and Lily live. Her situation demonstrates that although black Cubans have been disproportionately affected both by weaknesses in revolutionary policy to decrease inequality and the economic crisis since 1990, patterns of social exclusion are also shaped by class and gender. In racially mixed poor areas, white women may face similar challenges to their black neighbours. Nena's life story revolves around tales of domestic violence, prison, difficult relationships, abandonment and struggles to find adequate work and housing. As a child, Nena lived through her father's attempted murder of her mother and his subsequent imprisonment. She was raised by her grandparents and finished secondary school before doing a sewing course. After finishing her studies, Nena worked for a brief time in a factory and then describes her work life as earning a living as she could, 'a little here, and a little there', implying that she was working largely selling bits and pieces on the informal market. When the interviewers ask her why she doesn't get an official job, she scoffs at the idea of working legally for negligible pay that would not even cover her rent.

In fact, at the time of the interview in 2005, Nena was not paying rent, or at least, not in cash. After a number of marriages (by which she probably means consensual unions rather than, or as well as, official ones), Nena was living in a house belonging to a man in prison. She had had a relationship with this man several years earlier and he had subsequently been imprisoned after killing his wife. Nena visits the prison regularly to bring him provisions, talk and have sexual relations. In exchange, she lives in his house, a practice known as *hacer pabellón*. She describes this as an amicable arrangement, one she engages in contentedly, but without much affection. But at the time of the interview, the deal was under threat because one of the prisoner's daughters wanted to come and live at the house. When asked towards the end of the interview to talk about any fears or uncertainties she had, Nena cites the threat of losing her home.[72]

The stories of Taty, Lily and Nena incorporate some of the ways in which housing and heterosexual relationships converge in socialist Cuba, producing both conflict and creative solutions. The cases of Taty and Lily, living with problem husbands and extended families, are representative of a wider social trend. During the 1960s and 1970s, housing conditions were often cited as a reason for divorce.[73] Even after formal separation, many couples were forced to continue living together, dividing areas of their small houses however they could.[74] Historically, as these stories indicate, racial and economic inequalities have been major factors in limiting access to adequate housing. Although more privileged Cubans are not immune from housing problems, they often have more options for dealing with them, as the following example shows. Katia is a white woman born in 1943 to a lower-middle-class provincial family. She has a university degree and has worked in various government jobs. Katia has been active in revolutionary politics all of her adult life, though has never been a member of the Communist Party. At the time of the interview in 2007, she was sharing a large house with her aged mother and aunt in a historically wealthy neighbourhood of Havana.

Katia describes at length her mother's attempt to control her friendships, relationships and movements during Katia's childhood and adolescence. For Katia, then, marriage in 1968 to a man she had dated for three years was experienced as a form of liberation. But the young couple was not able to find a house of their own and had to live with Katia's parents. In desperation, Katia placed an advertisement in the classified section of a newspaper to buy or rent a room in a house where she and her husband could have some privacy. The following day, however, the newspaper rang to inform her that the classified section of the paper had been closed.[75] According to Katia, the only way of acquiring a house at that time was for someone in the family to die or to move to the United States. In this way, people from historically middle-class families were in an advantageous position, as their relatives were most likely to leave the country. Indeed, several members of Katia's extended family had emigrated in the early 1960s. But by the time of her marriage in 1968, official restrictions on emigration had slowed the flow of travel to Miami. Consequently, Katia and her husband lived with their sons in houses belonging to other family members until their separation in the early 1990s. She describes the strain this put on her marriage:

> I should also mention the fact of living collectively, which didn't help. Because my mother was the one who cooked. So at mealtime she was the one who served him, she put his food down on the table. My mother didn't understand that a woman wouldn't wait on her husband, as we say here. Waiting on was to take off his shoes, serve his meals. And I was never like that. I think that I could make a dessert and present it to him, I could make a drink and toast him. But not that systematic thing. Because I didn't have the time, with the children. Because that was something else to keep in mind. There are many Cuban women who think that having a child, giving a man a child will unite the couple. And that's not true. It's the opposite. I say it divides. It's logical. That being who's born and you have to dedicate time to him or her. And when you work outside the home time is short and so your relationship as a couple isn't the same. I mean, maybe you want to make love but the child is crying and so the thing is different. Or you live with other people. Maybe if you lived alone, and you want to make love at two in the afternoon. Understand? Or be intimate, not just, any kind of intimacy. So it makes it uncomfortable. So I think living together in marriage is disastrous with another person. It's too much. And when there's a child, I say it again, it doesn't unite. It separates. And the man tries to get on with his life.[76]

Katia's memory of living with an older mother who imposed on her daughter pre-revolutionary views about a woman 'serving' her husband, indicates that the revolutionary leaders' fears that multi-generational families could reinforce the power of tradition over new revolutionary values were not without foundation. Moreover, in Katia's experience, collective living took a toll on the sexual and emotional relationship of the younger couple and she, as the wife, bore the brunt of the conflict between domestic and outside duties. Katia's story thus highlights some of the tensions and contradictions that the Family Code of 1975 attempted to redress, albeit with limited success. Her claim that collective living made sexual intimacy difficult is similarly indicative of a wider social pattern. The challenge of finding private spaces for sexual relations predates the revolution. A historical solution has been the creation of *posadas*, private rooms rented for intimate encounters. During the early revolutionary period, as part of a wider campaign to promote sexual respectability (which included brothel closures, the 'rehabilitation' of prostitutes and widespread persecution of homosexuals), the revolutionary government attempted, unsuccessfully, to shut down the *posadas*.[77] In an oft-cited 1965 interview with Fidel Castro, the journalist Lee Lockwood asked the Cuban leader if the *posadas* were still permitted because of the housing shortage in Havana.[78] In response – and avoiding further discussion of the housing shortage – Castro defended the decision to maintain the *posadas*, saying they satisfied a 'social need'.[79] As Luis Salas noted in the late 1970s, however, the *posadas* were reserved for heterosexual couples. This policy was another mechanism through which revolutionary government and popular prejudice combined to hinder homosexual encounters.[80] Lourdes Arguelles and B. Ruby Rich claim that *posadas* were used by lesbians and homosexuals in the 1980s, but that access to them probably depended on connections with the manager as well as the latter's interpretation of official policy.[81] Pachy, a white homosexual man who migrated to Havana from a rural village in the 1980s to study at university, recalls that in those years he was dating a woman but still found ways to meet other men in *posadas*:

> Well, with her I had a normal sex life. I also continued the homosexual life. I went out with her, I met up with a guy and he said, 'I'm at such and such hotel with my girlfriend, if you two want to come by'. But it was a lie. He was telling me the number of the hotel room and that so I could go and be with him, understand?[82]

Queer homes

As the example of the *posadas* suggests, the themes of sex and housing converge in particular ways for Cubans who identify as homosexual or lesbian,[83] a result of the combined impact of official policy, popular prejudice, wider social and economic patterns and material constraints. Homosexuals and lesbians in Cuba, as in other countries, often migrate from provincial cities and rural areas in search of sexual relationships and friendship, as well as economic opportunity. In the context of an acute housing shortage and the lack of an open rental market, many of these migrants have to fend for themselves.[84] Pachy, the young man who sneaked into *posadas* in the 1980s, recalls that after moving to Havana he had relationships with men he picked up at the bus station or in parks in order to find a place to sleep for a few nights or weeks. Ricardo, a younger homosexual man, was evicted from his home by his stepfather who objected to the friends he brought home. Ricardo, who was taken in by an older male friend, stressed that he did not have to have to sleep in the streets or have sex with anyone in order to find a place to live, suggesting that he knows cases of people in a similar situation who have.[85]

For Havana residents who live with their families in the capital, a homophobic atmosphere at home may prevent them from bringing lovers home, or even receiving friends in their small quarters.[86] Having to meet outside their homes requires access to, among other things, means of travel. For this reason, the challenges of finding private spaces for sexual relations and social contact was worsened for homosexuals and lesbians during the Special Period, when public transport virtually disappeared due to petrol shortages.[87] Even if they do visit their lovers' homes, homosexual and lesbian couples may find it more difficult to live together. This has been the case of Katia who, after a twenty-five year marriage to a man, became involved in another long-term relationship, this time with a woman. Although she had lived at home with her husband, her mother's disapproval of her new relationship, and the general silence with which it was treated in the family, meant that the lesbian couple lived separately throughout their seventeen-year union. Even lesbian couples who manage to find housing together may be subject to surveillance by neighbours, as indicated in the interview with a woman asked to 'watch over' two lesbians in her block as part of her work for the local FMC.[88]

* * *

The double bind of housing for homosexuals is exemplified in a pair of interviews with Eusebio, a white man born in 1971 in the same neighbourhood where Taty, Lily and Nena live. At the time of the interviews, he was working as an accountant in a state firm. Previously, he had worked in his chosen profession as a nurse, but had left his job after the mother of one of his patients falsely accused him of trying to seduce her son. Eusebio's case demonstrates again that gender and race privilege can ameliorate, but not necessarily eliminate, housing problems. It also underscores the fact that for homosexuals and lesbians access to housing is about more than acquiring a physical place of residence.

The youngest of three siblings with a deceased father, at the time of the interview in 2005, Eusebio was living alone with his mother in what he describes as 'a big house, but not remotely pleasant. I have a room of my own, but little good it does me'.[89] Eusebio's mother disapproves of his sexuality and his friendships and does not permit him to receive guests or even to take phone calls. Consequently, Eusebio spends most of his time 'in the street', at the houses of acquaintances or meeting with friends in public places, returning to his home on the outskirts of Havana only to sleep. This is in spite of the fact that he finds the street violent and has more than once narrowly escaped attack in his own neighbourhood. Furthermore, Eusebio does not identify with what he perceives as the unsavoury behaviour of homosexual men who frequent public places.[90] He has proposed to his mother that they divide their house in two (a common solution to housing problems), but she refuses. Living on her pension and his small state salary, they cannot afford to rent another dwelling.

Eusebio opens his first interview with direct reference to the housing crisis: 'The situation we have here, that a certain group of people don't have their own home, we have to live with our parents, we cannot live with whom we want. This is something fundamental here'.[91] Unlike most of the interviews, this one was conducted away from his home and Eusebio begins by explaining why. He returns time and again to the topic of housing in both interviews, along with related stories of family conflict, ongoing problems at work and fear of aggression in the street. Although many of these problems go beyond the realm of sexuality, Eusebio's stories of discrimination in the workplace, violence and family rejection merge to form a narrative fundamentally shaped by experiences of homophobia. Asked about his plans for the future, Eusebio makes it clear that he wants to follow many of his generation (including his ex-boyfriend) by emigrating. He cites the housing crisis and homophobia as his main motivations for wanting to leave Cuba.

Laura is a friend of Eusebio and the aunt of his former partner. Ten years older than Eusebio and living in another area of Havana, Laura does not share his dream of leaving the country. But she does suffer from similar housing problems. Laura was, in her words, 'born with the revolution'.[92] Six months old in January 1959, she was the youngest child in a middle-class black family from the provinces that moved to Havana during the 1960s. Laura completed secondary school and went to work in a state firm. She was a member first of the Young Communists and later the Communist Party. In spite of her insider position, she continues to live in a relatively poor neighbourhood in a house she shares with her mother and an older brother with whom she is not on speaking terms.

Laura was first interviewed in the living room of this house in 2005. When, over a year later in 2006, I proposed to do a second interview with Laura, she asked to be interviewed somewhere else, so that she would be able to talk more freely. In this second exchange, she spoke at some length about the impossibility of resolving her housing situation, since according to the state she was registered as housed. Similarly to Eusebio, Laura had attempted unsuccessfully to convince her mother and brother to divide their house. When asked about intimate relationships, Laura spoke of a male partner with whom she could not live because neither of them had their own home. At the time, Laura was in her late forties and the partner over fifty.

At Laura's own request, I contacted her at the end of 2007 for a third interview. At this point, she told me that the partner she had spoken of in the previous interview was a woman. When we discussed the fact that she had changed her partner's gender in her second interview, Laura spoke more openly about the homophobia in different areas of Cuban society, including her workplace and in the Party. This time we conducted the interview in the house of a friend, a middle-aged, mixed-race, single heterosexual woman whose home acts as a place of social gathering and refuge for a small community of homosexuals and lesbians. At the time of this third interview, Laura was sleeping on the couch in this house, returning daily to her mother's house to clean and prepare her meals.

Laura's situation not only highlights the particular problems faced by queer Cubans, especially those with limited financial resources. It also points to one of the ironies of contemporary Cuban history for the generation 'born with the revolution'. In Laura's first interview, she speaks at length about the importance of the *beca*: the scholarships given to many Cuban children to study in boarding schools, away from their families. Laura experienced the *beca* as a form of liberation from what she described as a stifling and strict upbringing. Several decades later, still politically active and working for a modest salary, Laura finds herself living with and caring for her aged mother, who continues to exercise control over her social and personal life.

Scholars of race in Cuba have pointed to the ways in which the failures of revolutionary housing policy reinforced pre-revolutionary inequalities in both time and space. Poor housing continued to be concentrated in regions or neighbourhoods inhabited predominantly by black Cubans at the same time that the lack of new housing contributed to the dominance of multi-generational households in which traditional views about race and racism were transmitted in private, countering the regime's attempts to educate young people in the ideals of racially equality.[93] As the interviews analysed here suggest, this argument can be extended to incorporate gender and sexuality. An analysis of housing therefore provides an excellent opportunity to examine critically the intersections of class, race, gender and sexuality in revolutionary Cuba.

At the same time, an investigation of housing and related social issues prompts us to consider the complex role of families in relation to the state. Although an early aim of revolutionary leaders was to curb the influence of the family and to promote the role of state institutions and mass organisations, families continued to be not only a key location of socialisation but also an important source of economic survival. This was true particularly during the Special Period, when family networks were crucial in providing access to food and other scarce resources. Families often continued to provide for their members when the state was unable to do so. In some cases, families could also counter-balance the effect of official and popular homophobia, as with the case reported by Lawrence La Fountain-Stokes, of a mother who traded her large residence for two smaller ones through the *permuta* system so that her son and his lover could live alone together.[94] In other instances, however, such as those of young people evicted from their homes by their parents,[95] lack of family support exacerbates wider patterns of exclusion.

The issue of housing therefore points to the importance, but also the limitations, of families in helping Cubans to confront material shortages. Moreover, by focusing on how Cubans seek to build homes in the face of poverty and adversity, we find sites of resistance and creativity as well as oppression and exclusion. Nena's arrangement with the prisoner whose house she rents in return for sex is one example. Another is the small apartment where Laura often sleeps and where Eusebio and others come together for meals and visits. This queer home, created out of necessity but also friendship and solidarity, in which Habaneros of different racial, gender, sexual and generational groups share their lives, represents its own kind of revolutionary space.

Cubans, like people in all societies where material resources are limited, rely variously on solidarity, social and familial networks, insider connections, luck, wits, illegal activity, or a combination of these, to find solutions to their problems, including around housing. Since the 1990s, they have also relied increasingly on access to foreign currency. Although buying and renting a house is technically illegal in Cuba, with enough convertible pesos arrangements can be made.[96] Saray and Nancy, two young lesbians in Santiago de Cuba, both with university training and professional experience but no official jobs, 'rent' a flat using money sent to them by Nancy's girlfriend living overseas.[97] Marielis, a mixed-race woman who studied French at university in the 1980s and now lives in a good-sized flat in Havana with her teenage daughter, began collecting dollars when they were first legalised in 1993 while working in the tourist industry. She was eventually able to arrange to 'buy' a flat, which she later exchanged for her current home. Marielis acknowledges that her unusual housing situation goes some way in protecting her from the everyday impact of homophobia.[98] Other lesbians and homosexuals take advantage of their housing situations to increase their incomes. Ricardo, whose stepfather kicked him out of the family home for being gay, speaks of his pride in getting a house through his own 'struggle', via a series of formal and informal jobs, and now rents his spare room to male friends and their female companions, typically tourists.[99] As these examples suggest, housing is an important commodity on the thriving informal market and finding and renting living space is one aspect of the new Cuban entrepreneurialism. Whereas during the 1960s and 1970s many Cubans thanked the revolution for giving them a home, since the Special Period resourceful young Cubans like Ricardo take pride in their individual 'struggles' to acquire and even make money out of their homes.

Towards a history of sexuality and housing

As this preliminary study makes clear, much work remains to be done on the inter-connectedness of housing and relations of power in revolutionary Cuba, including sexuality. A history of housing and sexuality would involve rethinking housing policy in relation to the intersection of class, race, gender and sexuality. For example, the history of the microbrigades could consider how pushes to construct family homes literally helped to construct the heterosexual nuclear family as the revolutionary ideal. The inter-generational pattern of women attaining housing through formal or informal heterosexual relationships tends to confirm the overall conclusions of studies of gender in Cuba, that the revolution has been much more successful at challenging inequality in the 'public' sphere than in private. However, more detailed studies of such patterns, and their relationship to housing policy and provision, would be needed to substantiate this thesis.

With regard to histories of homosexuality, the issue of housing likewise points to new areas of research. To date, research on queer Cuba has been characterised by a focus on male homosexuality, especially in relation to cultural production, representation and use of public spaces. These studies frequently cite the 'invisibility' of lesbians and their relative protection from official homophobia that targeted gay men.[100] But the stories of Eusebio and Laura, cited above, indicate that official and popular homophobia affects men and women in similar ways in relation to housing. An analysis of housing could therefore contribute to a more inclusive history of homosexuality in Cuba.

The case of Cuba points both to the possibilities and the challenges of a comparative or transnational history of queer housing. Existing studies of queer homes conducted in western capitalist contexts attest to similar issues of marginalisation, family conflict and the desire for private space as a refuge from day-to-day forms of homophobia, whether in public or at home, cautioning us against the temptation to see Cuban homophobia as exceptional.[101] But even though these studies challenge the idea that homes are always a refuge for queers, especially when forced to live with their families of origin, they tend to assume that privacy – whether in the form of separate rooms or moving house – is accessible and available to most queers, even if this access is unequal and mediated by class, race, religion and geographical location. In other words, the existence of adequate housing is largely taken for granted, as is the existence of communal public gathering spaces, such as bars, saunas, parks, streets and so on. The widespread availability of both private and public queer spaces in western, capitalist urban areas contrasts radically not only with Cuba, but with much of the rest of the world.[102] Not only do Cuban queers contend with an acute shortage of housing; they also struggle to find meeting places in public, since there are no private bars and public meeting places are subject to frequent police and public harassment. As Abel Sierra Madero argues, to speak of a 'gay community' in Cuba is to import terminology inappropriate to the contemporary Cuban context.[103]

While Madero and others correctly warn against writing a Cuban history of sexuality in the model of the West, there may be more valuable parallels with other countries. Comparative studies of housing and sexuality outside the capitalist West indicate that, even when governments name housing as a top priority, this often clashes with other political and economic priorities. In the case of socialist Cuba, housing, defined as an item of consumption, was subordinated to the 'productive' sphere. In his study of the legacy of apartheid in South Africa, Glen Elder argues that housing policy, like much else, has been refracted through a 'heterosexualized fog' and that housing provision has privileged nuclear families and men at the expense of working mothers and women generally.[104] Moreover, early promises of housing provision were soon sacrificed to a macroeconomic plan, constructed in consultation with the World Bank, which marginalises women as both producers and consumers.[105] The case of South Africa, with its radical differences from Cuba, nonetheless serves as a salient warning. As outsiders celebrate reforms under the new leadership of Raúl Castro, including proposed changes to the housing law, there is good reason to believe that such reforms may exacerbate, rather than ameliorate, existing inequalities in housing provision. Historians and other theorists of gender and sexuality have shown how the spaces in which people live, work, struggle, form communities and find pleasure are fundamentally shaped by social power relations as well as wider political and economic contexts. As historians and other scholars of sexuality call for increased attention to transnational perspectives and a reconsideration of questions of class and materialism, research into housing policy and provision can make an important contribution to developments in the history of sexuality.

Notes

1. For an example from Cuban history, see K. Lynn Stoner, *From the House to the Streets: The Cuban Women's Movement for Legal Reform, 1898–1940* (Durham and London: Duke University Press, 1991).
2. See Sara Ahmed, Claudia Castañeda, Anne-Marie Fortier and Mimi Sheller (eds), *Uprootings/Regroundings: Questions of Home and Migration* (Oxford: Berg, 2003).
3. Doreen B. Massey, *Space, Place and Gender* (Cambridge: Polity, 1994).
4. Beatriz Colomina (ed.), *Sexuality and Space* (New York: Princeton Architectural Press, 1992); David Bell and Gill Valentine (eds), *Mapping Desire: Geographies of Sexualities* (London: Routledge, 1995).
5. But see Rose Gilroy and Roberta Woods (eds), *Housing Women* (London: Routledge 1994); Linda McDowell, 'City and Home: Urban Housing and Sexual Division of Space', in Mary Evans and Clare Ungerson (eds), *Sexual Divisions: Patterns and Processes* (New York: Tavistock, 1983), pp. 142–63; Leslie K. Weisman, *Discrimination by Design: A Feminist Critique of the Man-Made Environment* (Urbana: University of Illinois Press, 1994).
6. A notable exception is Glen S. Elder, *Hostels, Sexuality and the Apartheid Legacy: Malevolent Geographies* (Athens: Ohio University Press, 2003).
7. The project is funded by the Ford Foundation and Swedish development agency SIDA and is directed by Professor Elizabeth Dore at the University of Southampton, co-hosted by the Cuban National Centre for Sexual Education (CENESEX) in Havana. From 2004 to 2007, a team of UK and Cuban researchers interviewed some 100 Cubans – of different generations, socio-economic status, gender, racial identity, religious practice and sexual orientation – in and around Havana and Santiago de Cuba. All names of interviewees have been changed to protect their anonymity.
8. Alejandro de la Fuente, *A Nation for All: Race, Inequality and Politics in Twentieth-Century Cuba* (Chapel Hill and London: University of North Carolina Press, 2001), p. 313.
9. For the purpose of this chapter, I focus on housing provision rather than design and planning. These areas are largely interdependent but the limited space here does not allow for a detailed exploration. On socialist urban planning, see Roberto Segre, Mario Coyola and Joseph L. Scarpaci, *Havana: Two Faces of the Antillean Metropolis* (Chichester: John Wiley & Sons, 1997).
10. <http://www.granma.cubaweb.cu/marti-moncada/jm01.html>. See also Segre et al., *Havana*, p. 186.

11. Sergio Roca, 'Housing in Socialist Cuba', in Oktay Ural (ed.), *Housing, Planning, Financing, Construction*, vol. 1 (New York: Pergamon Press, 1979), pp. 62–74, here p. 63; Lois M. Smith and Alfredo Padula, *Sex and Revolution: Women in Socialist Cuba* (New York and Oxford: Oxford University Press, 1996), p. 149. For a description of one of Havana's largest pre-1959 shanty towns, Las Yaguas, see Douglas Butterworth, *The People of Buena Ventura: Relocation of Slum Dwellers in Postrevolutionary Cuba* (Urbana, Chicago and London: University of Illinois Press, 1980), pp. 3–17.

12. Roca, 'Housing', p. 63.

13. Roca, 'Housing', p. 63.

14. Roca, 'Housing', p. 63.

15. Segre et al., *Havana*, pp. 186–9.

16. Segre et al., *Havana*, p. 131.

17. Kosta Mathéy, 'Recent Trends in Cuban Housing Policies and the Revival of the Microbrigade Movement', *Bulletin of Latin American Research* 8 (1989), pp. 67–81, here p. 67; Segre et al., *Havana*, p. 187.

18. Roca, 'Housing', p. 64.

19. Mathéy, 'Recent Trends', p. 67.

20. Antoni Kapcia, *Havana: The Making of Cuban Culture* (Oxford: Berg, 2005), p. 127, citing N. Torrents, *La Habana* (Barcelona: Ediciones Destino, 1989), p. 129.

21. Segre et al., *Havana*, p. 188.

22. Kapcia, *Havana*, p. 127. One interviewee recalls moving with her family around 1970 to a cafeteria in central Havana that was being converted into a dwelling: 'There were holes and from out of the holes crawled rats. It was awful, with those iron doors'. Interview with Irina, Havana, November 2005.

23. Roca, 'Housing', p. 66.

24. Roca, 'Housing', p. 68.

25. Mathéy, 'Recent Trends', p. 69.

26. Segre et al., *Havana*, p. 203.

27. Roca, 'Housing', p. 70.

28. Carmelo Mesa-Lago, *The Economy of Socialist Cuba: A Two-Decade Appraisal* (Albuquerque: University of New Mexico Press, 1981), p. 172.

29. Mathéy, 'Recent Trends', p. 70.

30. Segre et al., *Havana*, pp. 208–9. According to Smith and Padula, *Sex and Revolution*, p. 150, while the Cuban media hailed the successes of the microbrigades, it virtually ignored the widespread evidence of self-built homes during the first three decades of the revolution.

31. Kapcia, *Havana*, pp. 149–50.

32. de la Fuente, *A Nation for All*, p. 313. See also Mesa-Lago, *Economy*, p. 174. Nadine T. Fernández notes that a 1992 study of housing in Havana indicated that areas with high levels of black residents tended to have a higher proportion of housing in poor condition than predominantly white neighbourhoods. Nadine Fernández, 'The Color of Love: Young Interracial Couples in Cuba', *Latin American Perspectives* 23 (1996) pp. 99–117, here p. 107.

33. Segre et al., *Havana*, p. 214; Smith and Padula, *Sex and Revolution*, p. 150.

34. Mathéy, 'Recent Trends', p. 67. This is still true in the early twenty-first century, the economic crisis notwithstanding.

35. Various interviews conducted as part of the Memories of the Cuban Revolution oral history project. See note 7.

36. Smith and Padula, *Sex and Revolution*, is an exception.

37. Maxine Molyneux, 'Socialist Societies Old and New: Progress Towards Women's Emancipation?', *Feminist Review* 8 (1981), pp. 1–34, here p. 17.

38. Smith and Padula, *Sex and Revolution*, p. 146.

39. Smith and Padula, *Sex and Revolution*, p. 146.

40. Smith and Padula, *Sex and Revolution*, p. 147.

41. Nicola Murray, 'Socialism and Feminism: Women and the Cuban Revolution: Part 1', *Feminist Review* 2 (1979), pp. 57–73, here p. 64.

42. Murray, 'Socialism and Feminism: Part 1', p. 64.

43. Murray, 'Socialism and Feminism: Part 1', p. 64.

44. Murray, 'Socialism and Feminism: Part 1', p. 66.

45. Mathéy, 'Recent Trends', p. 73. The 1996 film *Mariposas en el andamio* (*Butterflies on the Scaffold*), directed by Margaret Gilpin and Luis Bernaza, is shot in the Havana neighbourhood of La Güinera, a former squatters' community with a predominantly poor, black Cuban population, where the majority of microbrigaders are women. The head of the microbrigade is an older black woman, Fifi, who tells the

story of how the people of La Guïnera welcomed a group of transvestites into the community through their incorporation into the cabaret performed at the cafeteria used by microbrigade workers. Notwithstanding the film's title, and although the film makes some interesting interventions in relation to understandings of work, workers, sexuality, gender and the revolutionary 'new man', there is little attempt to analyse the relationship between the drag performances and the construction of new homes in the neighbourhood. Thus we do not learn much about where the transvestites themselves live, whether any of them have been housed in the new buildings built by the microbrigades or whether homosexual or lesbian identified people form part of the brigades. Nor does critical commentary on the film interrogate the housing connection.

46. Smith and Padula, *Sex and Revolution*, p. 145; Molyneux, 'Socialist Societies', p. 17. Douglas Butterworth's study of the relocation of Las Yaguas residents reaffirms this pattern during the 1960s. See Butterworth, *The People of Buena Ventura*.
47. Murray, 'Socialism and Feminism: Part 1', p. 65; Molyneux, 'Socialist Societies', p. 3.
48. For a review of different interpretations of the Family Code, see Carollee Bengelsdorf, '(Re)considering Cuban Women in a Time of Troubles', in Consuelo López Springfield (ed.), *Daughters of Caliban: Caribbean Women in the Twentieth Century* (Bloomington and Indianapolis: Indiana University Press, 1997), pp. 229–55, here pp. 248–9 *n*. 5.
49. Molyneux, 'Socialist Societies', p. 16.
50. Bengelsdorf, '(Re)considering Cuban Women', pp. 248–9 *n*. 5.
51. Bengelsdorf, '(Re)considering Cuban Women', p. 233.
52. Nicola Murray, 'Socialism and Feminism: Women and the Cuban Revolution, Part 2', *Feminist Review* 3 (1979), pp. 99–108, here p. 102.
53. Cited in Marifeli Pérez-Stable, 'Cuban Women and the Struggle for "Conciencia"', *Cuban Studies* 17 (1987), pp. 51–72, here pp. 64–5.
54. Cedric Pugh and Susan Lewin, 'Women, Work and Housing in the Soviet Union in Pre-Perestroika Times: Marxist Theory and Socialist Practice', *Journal of Housing and Environmental Research* 5 (1990) pp. 339–57.
55. Pugh and Lewin, 'Women, Work and Housing', p. 339.
56. Of course, gendered hierarchies in relation to work and production also exist in capitalist societies, but the different ideologies and roles of the state must be taken into account in comparisons between socialist and capitalist gender politics.
57. Bengelsdorf, '(Re)considering Cuban Women', p. 230.
58. Helen Safa, 'The Matrifocal Family and Patriarchal Ideology in Cuba and the Caribbean', *Journal of Latin American Anthropology* 10 (2005), pp. 314–38, here pp. 315–16.
59. Safa, 'The Matrifocal Family', p. 315.
60. Bengelsdorf, '(Re)considering Cuban Women', p. 234.
61. Bengelsdorf, '(Re)considering Cuban Women', p. 232.
62. Safa, 'The Matrifocal Family', p. 315.
63. Safa, 'The Matrifocal Family', p. 316.
64. For example, the extension of families to include members outside the neighbourhood was sometimes motivated by material incentives: a new member of the household meant an addition to the food ration book. Butterworth, *The People of Buena Ventura*, pp. 51–2.
65. I discuss these in greater detail in my manuscript-in-progress, *Sexual Revolutions: Passion and Politics in Socialist Cuba*.
66. Brad Epps, 'Proper Conduct: Reinaldo Arenas, Fidel Castro, and the Politics of Homosexuality', *Journal of the History of Sexuality* 6 (1995), pp. 231–83, here p. 241.
67. See Jose Yglesias, *In the Fist of the Revolution: Life in Castro's Cuba* (Harmondsworth: Pelican, 1970), p. 271.
68. José Quiroga, 'Homosexualities in the Tropic of Revolution', in Daniel Balderston and Donna Guy (eds), *Sex and Sexuality in Latin America* (New York: New York University Press, 1997), pp. 133–51, here p. 136.
69. Interview with Taty, Havana, February 2005.
70. Interview with Lily, Havana, December 2005.
71. The interviews cited here were conducted before Fidel Castro announced his retirement in early 2008.
72. Interview with Nena, Havana, April 2005.
73. Butterworth, *The People of Buena Ventura*, p. 59; Smith and Padula, *Sex and Revolution*, p. 150.
74. Smith and Padula, *Sex and Revolution*, p. 150.
75. This was around the time of the Revolutionary Offensive of 1968 and the classifieds may have been closed as part of the general attack on private businesses.

76. Interview with Katia, Havana, December 2007.
77. Hugh Thomas, *Cuba: The Pursuit of Freedom* (New York: Harper & Row, 1971), p. 1,434 *n*. 38.
78. Lee Lockwood, *Castro's Cuba, Cuba's Fidel* (1967; Boulder, CO and Oxford: Westview Press, 1990), p. 105.
79. Lockwood, *Castro's Cuba*, p. 106. In the 1980s, married couples living together sometimes queued to get into *posadas*. See Smith and Padula, *Sex and Revolution*, p. 150.
80. Luis Salas, *Social Control and Deviance in Cuba* (New York: Praeger, 1979), p. 171.
81. Lourdes Arguelles and B. Ruby Rich, 'Homosexuality, Homophobia, and Revolution: Notes toward an Understanding of the Cuban Lesbian and Gay Male Experience, Part 1', *Signs: Journal of Women in Culture and Society* 9 (1984), pp. 683–99, here p. 697. Arguelles and Rich blame the housing crisis on a combination of 'the limited resources of an underdeveloped nation and the punitive effect of the US blockade' (p. 696). While these are both important factors, weaknesses in revolutionary policy must also be taken into account, as argued above.
82. Interview with Pachy, Havana, April 2005.
83. I use the term 'queer' here to incorporate a variety of non-heterosexual identities or relationships. With reference to individual narrators, I employ translations of the terms the narrators use to define themselves. Cuban men who have same-sex relations usually use the Spanish word *homosexual*.
84. Since the Special Period, the government put restrictions on internal migration to Havana in order to curb the overcrowding in the capital.
85. Interview with Ricardo, Havana, October 2006.
86. For an example of the centrality of housing issues in Cuban lesbian life stories, see the oral history interview with 'Carmen', who constructed an illegal extension to her mother's house in Havana during the 1970s in order to have some privacy. '¡No, no, yo me voy!', in Juanita Ramos (ed.), *Compañeras: Latina Lesbians* (London and New York: Routledge), pp. 54–60.
87. Ian Lumsden, *Machos, Maricones, and Gays: Cuba and Homosexuality*, (Philadelphia: Temple University Press, 1996), pp. 93–4.
88. Interview with Elisa, Havana, December 2005.
89. Interview with Eusebio, Havana, September 2005.
90. Eusebio's presentation of himself as 'normal' in opposition to homosexuals in the street – characterised as too showy, promiscuous and effeminate – is repeated in other interviews with self-identified homosexual men. This 'othering' of certain homosexual men, and especially transvestites, is probably a reaction to both official homophobic attacks on feminine men and popular associations of homosexuality with men who 'show off' in public.
91. Interview with Eusebio, Havana, September 2005.
92. Interview with Laura, Havana, September 2005.
93. de la Fuente, *A Nation for All*, pp. 313, 337; Fernández, 'The Color of Love', pp. 106–7.
94. Lawrence La Fountain-Stokes, 'De un pájaro las dos alas: Travel Notes of a Queer Puerto Rican in Havana', *GLQ* 8 (2002), pp. 7–33, here pp. 23, 33 *n*. 40.
95. Various interviews conducted as part of the Memories of the Cuban Revolution oral history project. See note 7.
96. The convertible peso or CUC replaced the US dollar in 2005.
97. Interviews with Saray and Nancy, Santiago de Cuba, December 2007.
98. Interview with Marielis, Havana, December 2007.
99. Interview with Ricardo, Havana, October 2006. Although Ricardo does not elaborate, he is presumably speaking of Cuban men who have sexual relations with foreign women in exchange for money.
100. Brad Epps, 'Proper Conduct: Reinaldo Arenas, Fidel Castro, and the Politics of Homosexuality', *Journal of the History of Sexuality* 6 (1995), pp. 231–83, here p. 232 *n*. 2; Allen Young, *Gays under the Cuban Revolution* (San Francisco: Gay Fox Press, 1981), p. 3.
101. Jayne Egerton, 'Out but not Down: Lesbians' Experience of Housing', *Feminist Review* 36 (1990), pp. 75–88; Sarah Elwood, 'Lesbian Living Spaces: Multiple Meanings of Home', in Gill Valentine (ed.), *From Nowhere to Everywhere: Lesbian Geographies* (New York: Haworth, 2000), pp. 11–28; Andrew Gorman-Murray, 'Homeboys: Uses of Home by Gay Australian Men', *Social and Cultural Geography* 7 (2006), pp. 53–69; Lynda Johnston and Gill Valentine, 'Wherever I Lay My Girlfriend, That's My Home: The Performance and Surveillance of Lesbian Identities in Domestic Environments', in Bell and Valentine (eds), *Mapping Desire*, pp. 99–113; Linda Peake, '"Race" and Sexuality: Challenging the Patriarchal Structuring of Urban Social Space', *Environment and Planning D: Society and Space* 11 (1993), pp. 415–32.

102. For the argument that understandings of lesbian identity in India and South Africa, for example, must take into account lesbians' daily struggles for survival, including violence, poverty and housing problems, see Amanda Lock Swarr and Richa Nagar, 'Dismantling Assumptions: Interrogating "Lesbian" Struggles for Identity and Survival in India and South Africa', *Signs: Journal of Women in Culture and Society* 29 (2003), pp. 491–516, here p. 506.
103. Abel Sierra Madero, *El otro lado del espejo: La sexualitdad en la construcción de la nación cubana* (Havana: Casa de las Américas, 2006), p. 225.
104. Elder, *Hostels*, pp. 12, 138.
105. Elder, *Hostels*, pp. 137–9.

9 'The White Wife Problem': Sex, Race and the Contested Politics of Repatriation to Interwar British West Africa

Carina E. Ray

> Return is as much about the world to which you no longer belong as it is about the one in which you have yet to make a home.[1]
>
> Saidiya Hartman

As the First World War came to a close, 'black' men from Britain's overseas colonies and their white wives and lovers came to embody the fears and anxieties that gripped Britain's economically depressed port cities.[2] Black men were accused of taking jobs from white British men and stealing 'their' women. White women who partnered with black men were cast as depraved and immoral traitors, who selfishly prioritised their own sexual and material desires above the good of the nation. Working-class inter-racial couples became targets of abuse on the increasingly tense streets of Britain's port cities and, when a series of violent race riots swept through the ports in the summer of 1919, they were largely blamed for their outbreak. White mobs, ranging in size from a few hundred to several thousand, indiscriminately attacked black men, harassed and assaulted their white partners, and destroyed the multiracial settlements they called home.[3] In the wake of the riots, some of these couples attempted to leave their hostile environs for the British colonies, especially in West Africa and the West Indies, where many of the men in question came from. Their desire to take up residency overseas, however, led to the immediate implementation of a policy which I call the 'policy of prevention', designed to keep European women married to working-class black men out of the colonies. This was especially the case for British West Africa and marked an important shift from the prewar period, when colonial social conventions and their attendant racial taboos were the primary mechanisms that, at the very least, kept European women and black men from openly liaising with one another.[4] During the interwar period, state power was also used to ensure that the West African colonies were kept free of such couples.

While the origins of the policy of prevention are to be found in the immediate aftermath of the 1919 race riots, it continued to guide colonial authorities' decision-making processes throughout the interwar years. By and large, it was West African men who were domiciled in Britain and married to white British women that sought joint repatriation as their economic positions worsened during this time period. Given that British women did not lose their natal citizenship upon marriage to British colonial subjects, they were simply denied entry to the colonies and expected to remain in Britain with or without their husbands. Faced with this difficult choice, some couples separated upon the man's return to West Africa, while others remained together in Britain. By the late 1920s, however, the Colonial Office was confronted with a few cases involving West African men married to German women, who were either seeking to be repatriated or were facing deportation from Germany. These cases were far more complicated because, upon marriage to foreigners, the women in question inherited their husbands' citizenship status. British authorities were therefore left with a choice: allow the couples to settle in Britain or in the colonies. While comparatively less common, these complex cases became the battleground upon which British metropolitan and colonial authorities most vigorously fleshed out their anxieties about where inter-racial couples should be permitted to make home. The second half of this chapter focuses on one of these cases in order to illuminate how concerns about race, sex, gender, class, nationality, religion and space informed the contested politics of repatriation to British West Africa during the interwar years.

The case studies under consideration also offer a glimpse into the social world of the West African diaspora in Britain and mainland Europe during the interwar years and provide valuable insight into the challenges faced by many inter-racial couples in carving out an existence for themselves in a world that was distinctly unreceptive to their unions. Indeed, the struggles of these families represent the longing for homecoming. For these couples, however, homecoming was inextricably linked to what might appropriately be called 'home-leaving'. While many West African men had lived in Europe for decades and came to regard it as home, and for their wives Europe had always been home, during the interwar years metropolitan racism, gendered citizenship laws that penalised European women for marrying foreign men and racialised economic discrimination compelled these working-class families to search for home across the Atlantic in the colonies. As we will see, however, they searched in vain. Ultimately, domestic anxieties over the way in which Britain's empire was remaking the metropole were trumped by colonial concerns about the threat European women living in 'native fashion' with their working-class African husbands posed to race-based colonial authority. From the anxious voices of British empire builders emerges a sense of their own awareness of the fragility of colonial rule. While competing tensions between the domestic and overseas organs of the British state dominate the relevant archival records, we must bear in mind that it was the most mundane of longings on the part of inter-racial couples that provoked such intense debates about who could make home where. In highlighting their actions and voices, when and where they emerge in the archival record, these couples speak for themselves in ways that underscore the extent to which they challenged and defied, to the best of their abilities, the colonial state's determination to 'quarantine' them in Britain and continental Europe.

Not all mixed race couples were barred from taking up residency in British West Africa. A handful of wealthy West African men who were able to demonstrate to colonial authorities that they could maintain their white wives at a standard deemed suitable to European womanhood were allowed to make the colonies home. This caveat underscores the importance of class status and gender, rather than race alone, in the decision-making processes of colonial authorities. It also demonstrates that in contrast to settler colonial regimes, in places like Southern Rhodesia and South Africa, the administered colonies of British West Africa stopped short of implementing the most draconian forms of sexual segregation through the use of anti-miscegenation laws and barbaric extralegal measures such as lynching. Rather, to keep the colonies free of all but a handful of wealthy inter-racial couples, colonial authorities used a combination of strategies, including denying passports to the white wives of working-class African men, refusing to pay the cost of their passage to West Africa, and classifying them as 'undesirable immigrants' under the provisions of the colonies' Immigration Restriction Ordinance. While not the focus of this chapter, these strategies were complemented by earlier but comparatively less vigilant efforts on the part of colonial administrators to bring an end to the far more frequent occurrence of sexual relationships between European colonial officers and African women through the use of official anti-concubinage circulars during the early twentieth century.[5] This in turn helps to underscore the importance of paying attention to the spectrum of colonial anxieties that accompanied the gendered, racial and spatial configurations of mixed race couples, as well as the forms (illicit, casual, marital) their relationships took. Indeed, if we are to use panic and bureaucratic strong-arming as yardsticks, preventing European officers from cohabiting with African women was a far less pressing issue than keeping lawfully married working-class black men and white women out of the colonies.

Reflecting on the deep-seated anxieties surrounding the existence of inter-racial unions between black men and white women during the interwar years in Britain, Lucy Bland usefully suggests that, if we are to fully understand the complexity of inter-racial relationships during this period, we must undertake the difficult work of documenting the voices of the 'women and men who negotiated their personal and sexual relationships in the face of a barrage of both official and cultural hostility', while paying particularly close attention to 'their experiences, the impact of prejudice upon them, and their strategies of survival and support'.[6] Foregrounding their experiences in our analysis of the colonial archive provides a more complete view of the various worlds these couples were attempting to negotiate. Laura Tabili has done just this by charting the thwarted struggles of a handful of British and mixed-race British–Somali women to make the British Protectorate of Somaliland their home in the face of the exclusionary practices of colonial authorities who believed that the presence of these women living intimately among 'native' populations posed a 'threat to colonial racial and gendered hierarchies, and British credibility'.[7] In what follows, I also take up Bland's mandate and in so doing provide a broader historical context, indeed the precedent for understanding Tabili's work on British Somaliland, by looking at the history of mixed-race couples who sought to make home in British West Africa during the interwar years.

Riots, repatriation and the policy of prevention

Although black communities and mixed marriages in Britain long predate the First World War, during the war itself increasing numbers of black seamen came to its ports from different parts of the world to fill the labour vacuum in the shipping industry that resulted from the drafting of white British men into the military. The majority of these seamen originated from Britain's colonies in the West Indies and West Africa, as well as from India, the British Somaliland Protectorate and Aden. While seamen from India, known as *lascars*, had always made up a significant number of the colonised labour hired on British vessels, the contracts they were hired under greatly restricted their ability to reside in Britain; as a result, settlement rates were highest among seamen from the West Indies, West Africa, Somaliland and Aden. Ethnic settlement patterns differed from port to port; for instance, Liverpool was inhabited mostly by West Indians and West Africans, while Cardiff had a higher percentage of men from Aden and Somaliland. At the close of the war, most of these men, along with considerable numbers of demobilised soldiers from the colonies, remained in the country's seafaring districts. Together, they competed with white British men for an increasingly limited number of maritime jobs.

Economic hardship in the ports, created by the post-war depression and racialised job competition within the shipping industry, offers a compelling explanation of the underlying cause of the riots. In Jacqueline Jenkinson's study of the 1919 riots, she examines a series of smaller riots between January 1919 and the outbreak of major rioting in June and finds that in each of the cases racial violence was a direct result of competition over jobs.[8] Moreover, the initial incidence of racial violence that led to the outbreak of rioting in Liverpool in June was attributed to tensions between black seamen and white foreign labour, in this case Scandinavians, who were in direct competition with each other for jobs not already taken by white British seamen.[9] Yet, it was the notion that black men were consorting with white women that garnered the most attention from the press, local and national authorities, as well as everyday observers. The 'sex problem', as one newspaper dubbed it, became a primary explanatory framework for understanding, and in many cases rationalising, the impetus behind the riots.[10] The attention given to the 'sex problem' by contemporary observers, including policy makers, suggests that, in addition to job competition, anxieties over race and sex played an important role in the move towards proposing repatriation as an appropriate solution to the social and economic problems deemed responsible for the riots.

Indeed, within days of the major outbreak of violence in June, local and national authorities began drawing up plans to repatriate black men to the colonies in an attempt to restore calm and order (and more specifically, racial order) to the port cities. The Colonial Office, however, feared that if the repatriations were handled inappropriately, they would cause instability by returning disgruntled men to the colonies. Disturbances had already broken out in Sierra Leone as early as July 1919 over the ill-treatment of black men in the British ports.[11] How much more unrest could be expected if the victims of the riots, many of whom had participated in the war effort, were forcibly returned to the colonies?

Anxious about the stability of the West African colonies, the Colonial Office not only insisted that the repatriation scheme be voluntary, it was also equally adamant that the white wives of 'natives' should be prevented at all costs from going to West Africa with their husbands. In fact, rioting had barely come to a stop in June 1919, and the Colonial Office had already decided to refuse repatriation facilities to black men who insisted on returning with their white wives.[12] Given that the men in question had no funds to repatriate themselves, let alone their wives, by refusing to pay passage fees, British authorities effectively made it impossible for black men who desired joint repatriation to return to the colonies with their white wives. On 30 July 1919, this policy was solidified during a meeting at the Ministry of Labour, which had

Table 1: Employment and Marital Status of West African Seamen Living in Liverpool

Marital and Employment Status	Sierra Leone	Gold Coast	Nigeria	**Totals**
Single Unemployed	78	18	21	**117**
Single Employed	33	10	7	**50**
Married Unemployed	5	1	5	**11**
Married Employed	6	4	0	**10**
Totals	**122**	**33**	**33**	**188**

Source: Report on the Repatriation of Negroes, National Archives, Home Office Papers 45/11017–377969/44

assumed responsibility for the repatriation scheme. At the special insistence of the Colonial Office, the Ministry of Labour instructed the local committees responsible for facilitating the scheme in the seven main ports (Salford, Liverpool, Cardiff, Glasgow, Hull, South Shields and London), not to repatriate black men with their white wives.[13] As one Colonial Office adviser later put it, the 'white wife problem' was, as the phrase suggests, particular to white women.[14] This is underscored by the fact that the government agreed to pay the cost of repatriating the few black men, like Joseph Queashie from the Gold Coast, who were married to black women.[15]

It is difficult to ascertain the exact number of West Africans and their white wives who were adversely affected by this policy, but the statistical information available suggests that their numbers were by no means negligible. In a survey conducted by the Liverpool Police shortly after the riots, a total of 188 men from British West Africa were identified as residing in Liverpool. The police, however, suspected that the actual number was much higher and suggested that the lower number reported was the result of 'an exodus of negroes from the city to inland towns since the question of repatriation arose' and added that 'those who have not left are probably in hiding'.[16] As Table 1 indicates, of the 188 West African men identified, twenty-one were married, eighteen of these to white women resident in Liverpool and three to African women who resided in West Africa. Of the eighteen men married to white women, eleven were willing to be repatriated back to West Africa with their white wives.

The willingness of 50 per cent of married West Africans to accept repatriation compared to 47 per cent of single West Africans indicates that the authorities were wrong in believing that marriage to white women created ties to the metropole that could not be broken as easily as those of single men. Rather, it was the authorities' policy of prevention that kept these men in Britain because it barred them from returning to the colonies with their wives. Thus, if we are to understand fully the range of different imperatives that shaped the unwillingness of West Africans to be repatriated and ultimately led to the schemes' widely recognised failure, we must acknowledge that, in addition to unsatisfactory remuneration packages and the desire, indeed the right to remain in Britain, for some West Africans the policy of prevention was also a major factor.[17] A representative from the Local Government Board said as much when he expressed his belief that 'the white wife constituted a big difficulty'.[18]

The Colonial Office's refusal to repatriate West Africans with their white wives contrasts sharply with its concession to allow black men from other parts of the British Empire, namely West Indians, to return home with their white wives at the government's expense.[19] According to Jenkinson, by September 1919 the government had reverted to its pre-riot scheme in which 'repatriation for white wives and families was to be considered and granted on receipt of proof that a marriage had taken place, and that the sailor was in fact, from the colony to which he wished to return'. Although Jenkinson refers to the reintroduction of this non-restrictive scheme broadly as a 'concession by the government [to allow] the white wives and families of black men to be repatriated with them', her evidence is limited to West Indians and, in one instance, to a black Canadian.[20] Colonial Office records indicate that this concession was never contemplated for West Africans. Thus, while it is unclear whether the pre-riot scheme Jenkinson refers to was ever applied to the West African colonies, there is no doubt that, immediately following the 1919 riots, a clear policy of prevention emerged, which remained unique to the West African colonies for several years, before expanding to incorporate other parts of British Africa.

While not completely enthusiastic about its concession, implicit in the Colonial Office's decision to repatriate West Indians with their white wives was *its* belief that a different set of racial politics was at work in the West Indies, where it imagined that the region's long history of intermixture between Europeans, Africans and indigenous peoples had created more racially egalitarian societies. This myth and its repercussions on colonial policy were not new. A decade earlier, the West Indian colonies were intentionally excluded by the Colonial Office from a widely distributed anti-concubinage circular on the grounds that enforcing such a directive 'where black and white live together, often intermarry, and where you have every shade of colour living side by side in social union, would be a great blunder'.[21] Similarly, the Colonial Office felt that race relations in the West Indies could withstand the presence of working-class black men married to white women. It is critical to note, however, that local colonial authorities vehemently disagreed and tried to convince the Colonial Office not to repatriate inter-racial couples to the West Indies.[22] Here we have a classic example of the different perspectives and agendas that characterised the colonial project as it was carried out in the metropole and in the colonies, and the kind of discord that could arise between those who wielded their power from imperial centres and the 'men on the spot'.[23]

Thus, the Colonial Office pursued very different strategies in its management of inter-racial sexual relations throughout its diverse empire. In fact, it explicitly acknowledged that 'the case of West Africans with white wives was on a somewhat different footing from white wives of natives of the West Indies'. In support of this assertion, Colonial Office civil servant, Alexander Fiddian, cited the system of residential racial segregation in some parts of the West African colonies as a major obstacle. Using Nigeria as a case in point, he noted that 'in various Nigerian townships a white woman would be supposed not to live in the native reservation and a native not to live in the European reservation unless he did so as his wife's servant!'[24] The irony here is that residential segregation ordinances were, in part, designed to curb the far more common occurrence of sexual relations between European men and African women in the colonies, yet they were now being used as an excuse to exclude legally married African men and European women from making the colonies home.[25] While Fiddian made recourse to legalities in order to justify his claim of West African exceptionalism, the volumes of correspondence produced by these repatriation requests reveal that colonial officials refused to repatriate Africans and their white wives because they steadfastly believed that a European woman living with a working-class African posed a major threat to the stability of colonial race relations by calling into question the whole notion of European racial prestige. The Colonial Office was simply not willing 'to face the consequences of letting an Englishwoman . . . go to West Africa as the wife of a black man'.[26] In short, the decision to allow working-class West Indians but not working-class West Africans to be repatriated with their white wives must be read against the particular dynamics of race, sex and class relations in each of these colonial spheres, and more specifically against the way in which the Colonial Office, situated in the metropole, read (or misread) such relations in its overseas colonies.

Citizenship and repatriation policy

While the Colonial Office's policy of prevention kept the West African colonies free of working-class mixed race couples in the immediate aftermath of the 1919 race riots, it did not stop West Africans and their white wives from petitioning for repatriation. Before turning to their cases, it may be helpful to return to Laura Tabili's work on the Somaliland Protectorate in order to make some important observations about the policy of prevention's geographic and temporal expansion, as well as its formalisation in the early 1920s. In January 1923, the Protectorate enacted legislation to prohibit the entry of the white wives of Somali men on the grounds that they were 'undesirable non-natives'. As Tabili points out, this legislation was not limited to the Protectorate, but rather 'effectively exclud[ed] European wives from all of British East Africa'.[27] Tabili makes the argument that 'it was a colonial government with an immediate stake in local social and political relations, not metropolitan empire-builders, who initiated debate regarding "the desirability of allowing European women married to natives to proceed to Tropical Africa"'.[28] The evidence discussed earlier, however, indicates that 'metropolitan empire-builders' in London's Colonial Office were the first to initiate this debate during the summer of 1919. What was precedent-setting about events in the Somaliland Protectorate, however, was that they marked the first time *formal* colonial legislation was used to exclude the white wives of African men from the colonies. The original incarnation of the policy of prevention, conversely, depended on non-legislative measures, namely refusing to pay the passage fees of inter-racial couples to the colonies. Its success immediately after the riots was made possible by the fact that these couples were typically working-class, if not impoverished, and could not fund their own travel. As a measure designed in response to the riots and the repatriation schemes that followed in their wake, the policy of prevention clearly did not anticipate the possibility that inter-racial couples could, or would, make it to the colonies on their own.

In the case of the Somaliland Protectorate, the government's hand was forced when Somali native Ismail Noor and Edith, his British wife, financed their own travel from Cardiff to Aden before being detained by British authorities in January 1923. In less than a week, the Protectorate's governor enacted shotgun legislation to prevent Edith from entering Somaliland. This marked the geographic expansion of the intention behind the policy of prevention from West Africa to East Africa, its temporal expansion beyond the immediate post-riot period, and the policy's formalisation into legislation.[29] It also foreshadowed what would take place in West Africa during the late 1920s and 1930s with regard to the deployment of legislative measures to meet the challenges of increasingly complex repatriation cases, and the more active role local colonial governments would begin to play in these matters.

Like the immediate post-riot period, most interwar cases involved British colonial subjects married to British women, whose citizenship status remained unchanged upon marriage. Given that these women were entitled to remain in Britain, as were their husbands, requests for joint repatriation from such couples were quickly rejected and generally left little documentation. Yet, it is still possible to glean a sense of the difficulties they faced when denied the ability to make home in the colonies. By way of example, Ena Parker's desperation to be jointly repatriated to the Gold Coast with her husband John 'Akok' Parker, in October1933, stemmed from the fact that John was suffering from severe tuberculosis and had been warned by his doctor that he would not live through another English winter. This fact was compounded by the constant threat of homelessness they lived under, as underscored in the following excerpt from one of Ena Parker's repatriation requests:

> In addition to his illness, we have been knocked about and hounded from one house to another. As soon as we get the tenancy of a house and they find out my husband is a coloured man we have to move. We have just received the tenancy of a corporation house, they knew my husband was a coloured man, and all full particulars as soon as we moved in the people on the row signed a petition against us the result is we are on notice to quit. There is nothing against my husband's character only that he is a coloured man. As this is our only means of living (letting apartments) we shall become chargeable to the Guardians and rather that I beg you to try and see your way clear to send both myself and my husband back to his home in the West Coast of Africa, all this is very upsetting and is making my husband's condition worse.

In a final desperate appeal for assistance, Mrs Parker closed her letter by drawing attention to her husband's service in the First World War, which included being torpedoed on the Foylemore in 1917: 'He fought for his country in the war [and] now his country offers no shelter . . . We have only till November 6th before we are thrown on the streets. So I beg you please try and use your influence to get us to Africa'.[30] Her request fell on unreceptive ears. Alex Fiddian, of the Colonial Office, informed her that repatriation would be considered for her husband only.[31] Upon further pressure from Mrs Parker, the Colonial Office sent her request to the Governor of the Gold Coast, Sir Shenton Thomas, for his consideration. As expected, Thomas agreed to fund John Parker's repatriation provided Ena did not accompany him.[32] She categorically refused, however, to be separated from her husband. We do not know whether John Parker lived through the winter of 1933–34.

Aside from the government's well-known views on the subject in general, it was specifically noted that 'the conditions under which [Ena Parker] would have to live would be most unsuitable'. Here 'unsuitable' referred to the fact that John Parker's home town was a small fishing village where it was doubted 'whether there is a single iron roofed home in the place'.[33] In short, colonial authorities regarded Mrs Parker's potential living conditions and, most especially, the physical home she would inhabit in her husband's village, as completely inappropriate for a white woman. Such concerns were at the root of the unwillingness of colonial authorities to repatriate not only the Parkers, but also other inter-racial couples who made similar requests for repatriation to British West Africa.[34] While not further elaborated on in the Parker case, the kinds of anxieties provoked by the spectre of a European woman living in 'native fashion', as one colonial bureaucrat put it, emerge in greater detail in the case of the Annan family. 'Native fashion' not only implied at best a working-class lifestyle; it also referenced the cultural milieu of the colonies' African populations. To live in 'native fashion' was to 'go native' – no other transgression frightened colonial elites more, especially when it involved European women.

The case of Gold Coaster Alfred Annan and his wife Frieda was distinguished by the fact that she was a German citizen and the couple was resident in Germany.[35] Upon marriage, Mrs Annan inherited the citizenship status of her husband and was therefore no longer technically entitled to the right to remain in Germany, nor were her husband and children.[36] Their story vividly underscores the risks involved for women who married across national, as well as race lines.[37] Unwanted in the colonies and in Britain itself, the fate of the Annans became the subject of much diplomatic and legal wrangling, which in turn produced voluminous archival records that chart their struggles for home. Emerging from this case is a clear sense of the way colonial authorities were increasingly called upon to clarify and formalise the grounds on which the white wives of all but a few wealthy West Africans could be legally refused entry into the colonies.

Our first glimpse of the Annans occurs in September 1927 when Mr Annan, having been denied assistance by the British Consulate in Berlin because he had no papers that could prove his status as a British subject, wrote to the Colonial Office requesting that his family be repatriated to the Gold Coast. Born in 1888 in Accra, Annan had apparently come to Germany in 1901 as the personal servant of a 'coloured man' named Larsen, who eventually died. Annan subsequently became a seaman working in the German merchant marines. While his whereabouts during the First World War are unclear, after the war Annan lived in Germany, where he occasionally found employment as a singer and step-dancer.[38] After a courtship of at least two years he married twenty-three-year-old Frieda Meyer in early 1927. By August of that year they had two children, a girl and a boy. As his family grew and became increasingly impoverished, Annan decided that it would be best to resettle them in the Gold Coast. Once the Colonial Office had ascertained that Annan was a native of the Gold Coast and that his wife was white, it instructed the Foreign Office to have the consulate in Berlin inform Annan that 'it is not possible to give any assistance towards his repatriation if his wife and family accompany him to West Africa, but . . . if he is willing to return to the Gold Coast without them, the Secretary of State will be prepared to refer his case to the Government of the Gold Coast for consideration'.[39]

Nothing more was heard from the Annans until the early autumn of 1930 when they came into the hands of the German authorities who were seeking to deport them. The radical change in the position of the Annan family can be explained in relation to two major interrelated events. First, the Great Depression, which started in 1929, wreaked havoc on the German economy and led to several calls for the expulsion of foreigners. Equally important was the increasing popularity of the Nazi Party, which became the second largest political party in Germany at the September 1930 elections, the very month the Annans were targeted for deportation, alongside the hardening conservatism of the Weimar government. While the different *Länder* (administrative divisions) each devised their own policies to deal with 'unwanted' foreigners, it is fair to say that across Germany as a whole, a couple like the Annans would have felt increased hostility. Inter-racial marriage was scorned by Hitler in *Mein Kampf*, by 1930 a bestseller, and the fact that Frieda Annan was Jewish, while probably playing little role in her deportation from Germany in 1932, along with her husband and children, was of greater consequence in later years when the British sought to remove the Annans back to Germany, as we will see.

When Alfred Annan returned to the British Consulate in Berlin to renew his application for a passport, he informed the consulate that the German government had agreed to repatriate his entire family to the Gold Coast. Accordingly, the consulate contacted the Foreign Office to approve the issue of a passport to Annan. Despite having been turned down by colonial authorities three years earlier, the Foreign Office forwarded the request to the Colonial Office, which then took the issue up with the Gold Coast government. Lord Passfield, the Secretary of State for the Colonies, reiterated in his dispatch to Governor Slater of the Gold Coast the undesirability of sending Annan's wife and children to the Gold Coast and indicated his desire to adhere to the standard policy of refusing to repatriate such families.

The German government's intervention in the case, however, posed a new challenge to the colonial authorities. As Lord Passfield remarked, 'if the German Government is prepared to provide the necessary funds for the repatriation of the whole family, it will hardly be possible to prevent their embarkation'.[40] Up until this point, the method through which the colonial authorities had prevented white women from accompanying their working-class African husbands to the West African colonies was to refuse to pay their passage fees. The policy succeeded in achieving its goal because these couples did not have the financial means to repatriate themselves. The exception to this *de facto* rule occurred in 1922 when Mr Samuels, a Gold Coaster employed by the government as a prison instructor, returned from Europe with his Irish wife at their own expense. The couple, having made their own way to the Gold Coast, was accepted into the colony. However, within a year of their arrival Mr Samuels died, leaving his wife destitute and forcing the government to pay the cost of her repatriation back to Britain. The outcome of the Samuels's case heightened colonial authorities' concerns about the class status of mixed-race couples seeking residency in the colonies. After all, if a case involving a fairly well-paid Gold Coaster employed in the government service ended in the destitution of his European wife, what would become of a woman like Frieda Annan, the wife of a working-class African?

Given the German government's intention to deport the family and the Colonial Office's uncertainty about how to prevent their embarkation, the Gold Coast government launched its own investigation into what it could do to stop the Annans from being sent to the colony. The colony's attorney general, Mr Abrahams, was consulted on the matter and, while admitting that there was no way Annan himself could be refused permission to enter the Gold Coast, he contended that Annan's wife and children could be refused under several sections of the Immigration Restriction Ordinance. In particular, section 5(6) of the Ordinance allowed immigrants to be excluded on the grounds of their entry being 'undesirable'. While Abrahams argued that it was 'obviously undesirable in the interests of the wife and children themselves that they should come here particularly at a time of economic stress', he was concerned with the social stability of the colony rather than with the family's prospects.[41] In a rebuke to his colleagues for apparently failing to see things the same way, Abrahams warned:

> ...undue emphasis is laid upon the interests of the Annan family, and the possibility of their becoming a financial burden on the colony, and insufficient emphasis upon what in my opinion is the only factor for consideration, namely whether the residence in the Colony of a European

woman under conditions to which this woman would probably be forced to live is undesirable in the interests of the Colony.[42]

In short, while the Annan family's entry into the colony posed a number of different potential hazards, Abrahams contended that these threats formed a hierarchy of danger, at the top of which was the intensely subversive nature of Mrs Annan's presence in the colony as the white wife of a destitute African man. Like Edith Noor, the case of Frieda Annan

> . . . illustrates the apparent threat a woman out of place could pose, symbolically and materially, to the stability of imperial rule, a power system to which racial but also gendered and class, spatial and sexual boundaries remained integral . . . These women violated imperial sexual categories and spatial boundaries, not only by marrying implicitly 'downwards' across the colour line, but also by seeking to move geographically and culturally 'backwards' from metropole to colony.[43]

Following the attorney general's advice, the government opted to prohibit the entry of Mrs Annan and her children as 'undesirables' until Mr Annan could prove that he had 'means sufficient to maintain her in a manner not altogether unbefitting a European woman and to make reasonable provision for her and her children in case of his death'. As articulated by one of Governor Slater's advisers, the caveat allowing the family entry into the colony if Annan could meet certain financial requirements was a ploy designed to force the family onto the Home Authorities in light of their impending deportation:

> The German government has a perfect right to deport Mr Annan and his family. If we refuse the wife and children permission to land here presumably they will have to remain in the United Kingdom. In that event I feel certain that the Home Authorities will not be long in forcing us to accept them. However, we can bluff by replying . . . that it is not possible to admit Mrs Annan and her children to this colony unless Mr Annan can show on arrival here that he could earn at least £20 per month.[44]

There was some debate, however, over how high to set the sum Annan was asked to meet. Attorney General Abrahams not only felt that the sum originally proposed might be interpreted as being purposely prohibitive, he also thought it unnecessarily high for 'the type of European woman who would marry an "illiterate African sailor"', since such a woman 'would hardly expect a refined standard of life and probably has never enjoyed a substantial measure of comfort'.[45] He then added, 'German women of the lower order are notably frugally-minded'. His comments are suggestive of the role that nationality and class played, in addition to race and gender, in the decision-making processes of colonial authorities in these kinds of cases. As a white woman who had chosen to marry an 'illiterate African sailor', Mrs Annan was automatically looked down upon by the authorities; her nationality, class status and gender combined to transform her into an impoverished penny-pincher who could justifiably be provided with a more modest standard of living befitting a European woman of her particular station. By no means constituting a formal policy, references to nationality in this and other cases suggest a slightly more relaxed attitude towards the question of repatriating non-British white women to West Africa on the part of some colonial officials. That no repatriations of this description occurred, however, indicates that such officials were in the minority.

Regardless of whether the sum in the Annan case was scaled back as a result of Mrs Annan's nationality and class status, the stipulated amount of £20 per month along with the £300 death insurance policy that Annan was required to provide was indeed prohibitively high. Nonetheless, it cleverly allowed the Gold Coast government not to appear completely unreasonable and overly preoccupied with the question of race. With the legal solution of the Immigration Restriction Ordinance now in place, Governor Slater's response to the Colonial Office was crafted to highlight why Mrs Annan and her children could not be admitted to the colony. Having used the Samuels case as an example of the fate that had befallen the white wife of a regularly employed African civil servant, Governor Slater went on to paint a frightening picture of the even greater consequences of a European woman married to an 'illiterate sailor' living in 'one room of a house crowded by Africans of the labouring class' in the 'native quarter' of Accra:

> It is not difficult to conceive of the tragic conclusion to such a ménage, very possibly with repercussions on public peace and good order. Nor can I view without disquiet the effect upon the less cultured majority of Africans of a European woman living the life of an African labourer; I regard it as thoroughly undesirable in the interests of the colony that a European woman should be perceived to be living in a state of social degradation.[46]

Whereas the repatriation of Mrs Samuels back to England after her husband's death had rid the colony of the sight of a European woman living in destitution, Governor Slater further argued that, if a similar situation were to occur, the government would be unable to deport Mrs Annan back to Germany, as she had lost her German citizenship upon marrying Annan. As a result, Governor Slater predicted that 'her residence in the Gold Coast would be continued in the same depressed and degraded condition'.[47] She would in effect become the permanent liability of the Gold Coast government. Slater's description illustrates the way in which the presumed subversiveness of Frieda Annan's presence in the colony was constituted not only through race and gender, but also class and space. After all, white women were already resident in the colonies at this time, but the vast majority of these women were, as Tabili aptly points out, 'wives of British colonial functionaries who inhabited a hermetic all-European society as the dependents of colonising men, affirming gendered and racial as well as colonial hierarchies between men and women, colonisers and colonised'.[48] Annan's imagined home, in sharp contrast, was located in a bustling 'native quarter' thereby allowing working-class Africans to both participate in and be exposed to her 'social degradation'. In violating the colony's racial geography, the purported location of Mrs Annan's home would physically transgress the divide between colonised and coloniser that was so essential to colonial rule. Here one sees that while colonial ideologies were overtly fixated on 'keeping the natives in their place', their success was arguably more dependent upon keeping Europeans in *theirs*. Finally, it should be noted that in alleging that Mrs Annan's presence would have a deleterious effect on working-class Africans, Governor Slater conjured up the spectre of Black Peril. Resorting to such alarmist measures is but one indication of the acute anxieties that the 'white wife problem' produced in colonial authorities.

The Gold Coast government was well aware that its determination to keep the Annan family out of the colony would put it at odds with British national authorities, who were also loathe to accept the family. The colony's attorney general summed this up as follows:

> This is an ugly situation. It looks as if German patience has been exhausted and that these wretched people will be landed in England and there taken in according to international understanding. But

I think we must stick to our guns and refuse to accept them as long as we can. It may be hard on England but in a way it would be worse for the Gold Coast and we can ... justify exclusion by our law. It may be that the Home Office will press the Colonial Office to force our doors open, but until then we should refuse to open.[49]

His prediction turned out to be true. After nearly two years of diplomatic wrangling, the Germans deported the Annans in March 1932 to the British port city of Hull. Adamant about refusing the family entry to the Gold Coast, the Colonial Office prepared itself for 'a squabble with the Home Office'. In the words of one Colonial Office civil servant, the Home Office was 'certainly not in a position to compel us to raise a finger, certainly not to send a white woman to West Africa with a black man, even if he is her husband'.[50]

The extent to which the Home Office and local authorities continued to pressure the Colonial Office to repatriate the family to the Gold Coast is unclear; however, from the numerous letters that Mr Annan sent to the colonial authorities it seems very clear that local authorities attempted to make life as miserable as possible for them. Shortly after the family's arrival in the city, Alfred Annan lamented to the Secretary of State for the Colonies that his wife and children had been placed in a separate state institution from him, a fact that was making Frieda ill. He went on to say, 'I am left here in a strange town, with a wife and five children. I don't want to hang about here, I want to get back home, to Accra, Gold Coast, so if you could assist me in any way I should be extremely obliged to you'.[51] In a September 1932 letter to Governor Hodson of the Gold Coast, Annan recounted his family's increasing destitution and the indignities they were subjected to at the hands of British domestic authorities: 'On account of unemployment I was imprisoned for 6 months by this English Government and my poor ... children were kicked about and beaten. During these 6 months the government has sold all my furniture and cloth, so now I stand naked with my poor children'.[52] In another letter, sent eight years later to the Colonial Office, Annan again requests to be repatriated with his family in order to escape the harassment of local authorities at the onset of the Second World War:

... send me and my family home. I think I could live more better at home than in England ... Why I am not satisfied is because my children are being neglected ... Now my name in Britain is called Foreign as people assault me by calling us German spies also the Hull government. I am under a British colony therefore I am neither, my wife is a Russian Jew and the people put down she is a spy ... I can see this great day every body should not consult people to assault people, but the Hull Government follow such *low down* people themselves detectives keep coming and upsetting my home about us being spies for any reason at all. They also brought soldier with a gun and threatened them [his children] about mum and dad being a spy and did they know anything.[53]

In closing his letter, Annan sought to assure the Colonial Office that his wife would be able to adjust to life in the Gold Coast: 'My wife understands African food although she is a jew. Never mind African people walk barefooted but not in England'. That Frieda Annan was Jewish redirects our attention to the additional factor of the racialisation of religion, in addition to race, class, gender and nationality, as a source of marginalisation and persecution for the Annans, particularly as the linked phenomena of antisemitism and Germanophobia intensified in the context of wartime Europe. Throughout the letter, Annan drew attention to the relentlessness with which local authorities in Hull disturbed, indeed invaded his home, rendering it a site from which he needed to flee. In stark contrast, Annan's imagined home in the Gold Coast was where he could protect, feed and clothe his wife and children. Home was where he and Frieda would cease to be 'foreigners' and 'spies'. Annan knew, however, that he could not claim his rightful identity as a British subject in 'England': to do that he would have to make home in the Gold Coast. As late as 1941, the Annans were still petitioning colonial authorities to repatriate them to the Gold Coast. Their efforts proved futile, as did those of other similarly situated couples.[54]

The class caveat

There is one important caveat to the colonial authority's 'policy of prevention': it allowed the white wives of wealthy African men who could demonstrate that they could maintain their wives in a standard suitable to European womanhood to proceed to the colonies at their own expense. While the economic requirements African men were forced to meet in order to be granted permission to reside in the colonies with their white wives severely limited the numbers of these couples in West Africa, those who could meet these requirements appear not to have been discouraged from entering the colonies. There are six such documented cases for the Gold Coast, Nigeria and Sierra Leone, and in each case the husband was extremely well off. These couples included the Akereles of Lagos, Nigeria, and the Asafu-Adjayes of the Gold Coast. Mr Akerele was a wealthy barrister and the government of Nigeria raised no objections when he brought his white wife with him to Nigeria.[55] Similarly, the Gold Coast raised no objection to Dr I. B. Asafu-Adjaye who brought his white wife and nine-year-old child with him to Kumasi where he established a medical practice.[56] Yet, where any doubt lingered about the probable class status of an inter-racial couple, the colonial authorities erred on the side of extreme caution. By way of example, in 1935 a young doctor, Mr M. O. Phillips, who had recently finished his medical studies in Britain, was not allowed to return home to Nigeria with his white wife and their child. Instead, the Colonial Office advised him to return alone and if 'he was successful in finding work and in a position to support [his family], the question might then be considered whether [they] might join him'.[57]

Notwithstanding the stringent criteria employed by the Colonial Office, this caveat further amplifies the importance of class considerations in the decision-making processes of colonial authorities as they determined the eligibility of mixed-race couples to establish homes in West Africa. Race and class were mutually constitutive and, as far as the colonial authorities were concerned, the European community's racial prestige would be all but obliterated by the presence of a European woman living in 'native fashion' with her African husband. On the other hand, the white wives of wealthy African men were afforded the kinds of lifestyles deemed racially appropriate for European women. Arguably the European wives of extremely wealthy Africans may have enjoyed a more comfortable lifestyle than the wives of European government officers who often lived on modest budgets. We might also consider whether the presence of one or two wealthy African men living with their white wives in each West African colony may have worked in favour of colonial officials who wished to portray themselves as not entirely unreasonable where matters of race were concerned. Indeed, it was not uncommon for civil servants to refer to the few inter-racial couples that had been allowed to make the colonies home when justifying why they barred others from doing the same.[58]

More practically, colonial authorities had no legal grounds on which they could prevent these couples from entering the colonies provided they could fund their own passage and could show that they had adequate resources at their disposal to prevent them from being deemed 'undesirable immigrants'. With the exception, however, of a handful of wealthy couples, the colonial administration's policy of prevention was successful in stopping the vast majority of mixed race couples from taking up residence in British West Africa precisely because they lacked the financial resources necessary to fund their own repatriation and to meet the requirements of the Immigration Restriction Ordinance. This policy, therefore, provides a key to understanding why it was not until the era of independence that larger numbers of African men resided in West Africa with their white wives.

Hitherto, the paucity of such relations has been explained primarily through colonial social conventions that militated against European women having sexual relations with African men. Within British West Africa's expatriate societies, as Barbara Bush notes, 'powerful sexual taboos policed white female sexuality, which could only be broken covertly'.[59] Indeed, if and when such relations occurred they were shrouded in secrecy and therefore rarely made their way into the archival record. We know now, however, that these social conventions were not the only mechanism through which the colonies were kept free of the 'white wife problem'. The colonial state exercised its power through the use of both legislative and non-legislative measures to accomplish this goal as well. Perhaps most succinctly put by J. A. Rogers in his three-volume series on sex and race, 'Africa was no place for the white wife of a black man' and colonial authorities did all in their power to ensure that such women could not, and did not, reside in the colonies.[60]

As the Annans' family history poignantly demonstrates, such couples did not passively resign themselves to this fate, rather with vigour and passion they fought to keep their families united and to realise their dreams. Their struggles are one indication of how powerful the desire, indeed the longing for home can be. Equally, the imperial anxieties that their struggles generated suggest that the seemingly ordinary desire for home can become extraordinarily threatening when it fails to conform to gendered, classed, raced and spatial norms. If we now know something of their struggles, and have been able to add their voices and experiences to the historical record, doing so only highlights how much more there is to know.

The quotation by Saidiya Hartman that opened this article captures the in-betweenness inherent in the process of 'return'. It is in equal measure informed by the 'world to which you no longer belong' and 'the one in which you have yet to make home'. This meditation on return is helpful in addressing one of the central questions posed by this volume on 'Homes and Homecomings': how might we historicise the idea of 'being at home'? The very nature of seeking to 'return' home, an impulse that runs through this historical narrative, is dependent upon *not* 'being at home'. Thus, we can only historicise the idea of 'being at home' if we are able to fully appreciate what it means to be without a home or to be in a constant state of searching for one. In identifying the socio-historical conditions that produced the gendered, raced and classed discourses that regulated what kinds of people were allowed to make homes together and where their homes could be located, we are one step closer to under-standing why, for couples like the Annans, home remained a longing rather than a reality.

Epilogue

As this chapter was going to press, I located and interviewed Alfred and Frieda Annan's four surviving children. The Annans had a total of seven children, two of whom were born in Hull. In 1941, they moved to Cardiff after a fellow Gold Coaster persuaded Alfred that he could obtain better employment there, and Frieda's connections secured the family a sizeable home. Shortly after, Alfred joined the war effort as a fireman aboard a munitions ship, the SS *Cape Corso*. On 2 May 1942, Alfred Annan and forty-three other crew members died when the *Cape Corso* was torpedoed by the Germans. Although distraught by her husband's death, Frieda – known in Cardiff for her strength of character – supported her family by taking in boarders and cleaning homes until her death in 1974. For readers interested in learning more about the Annans, I will discuss them in my forthcoming book on the politics of race in colonial Ghana.

Notes

I would like to thank the anonymous reviewers along with the members of the Homes and Homecomings colloquium for providing indispensable suggestions on how to structure this chapter more effectively.

1. Saidiya V. Hartman, *Lose Your Mother: A Journey along the Atlantic Slave Route* (New York: Farrar, Straus and Giroux, 2007), p. 100.
2. I use the term 'black' rather than 'coloured', even though the latter term was more widely used in Britain to refer to a broad range of people during the time period under consideration here. Indeed, West Indians, West Africans, Portuguese, Indians, Sinhalese, Malays, Egyptians, Somalis and Arabs (generally from Aden) were all referred to as coloured. It was also not uncommon for persons to describe themselves as coloured, when not identifying themselves in more specific ways. As a term that originated out of the colonial experience and formed part of the lexicon of British racism and imperialism, it is no longer used and has been replaced by black in both popular and academic usage.
3. See Jacqueline Jenkinson, 'The 1919 Riots', in Panikos Panayi (ed.), *Racial Violence in Britain in the Nineteenth and Twentieth Centuries* (London and New York: Leicester University Press, 1996), pp. 92–111; Neil Evans, 'Across the Universe: Racial Violence and the Post-War Crisis in Imperial Britain, 1919–1925', in Diane Frost (ed.), *Ethnic Labour and British Imperial Trade: A History of Ethnic Seafarers in the UK* (London: Cass, 1995), pp. 59–88; Robin Cohen and Roy May, 'The Interaction between Race and Colonialism: A Case Study of the Liverpool Riots of 1919', *Race and Class* 16 (1974), pp. 111–26.
4. This is not to deny the existence of relationships between European women and African men in the colonies; however, they were extremely rare in comparison to relationships between European men and African women. See e.g., Charles Van Onselen, *Studies in the Social and Economic History of the Witwatersrand, 1886–1914* (Johannesburg: Ravan Press, 1982), pp. 45–6, 49–54; Jock McCulloch, *Black Peril, White Virtue: Sexual Crime in Southern Rhodesia, 1902–1935* (Bloomington: Indiana University Press, 2000); John Pape, 'Black and White: The "Perils of Sex" in Colonial Zimbabwe', *Journal of Southern African Studies* 16 (1990), pp. 699–720.
5. For the Gold Coast, see Carina Ray, 'Policing Sexual Boundaries: The Politics of Race in Colonial Ghana' (unpublished doctoral thesis, Cornell University, 2007), pp. 59–184. See also Ronald Hyam, 'Concubinage and the Colonial Service', *Journal of Imperial and Commonwealth History* 14 (1986), pp. 170–86; Ann Laura Stoler, 'Sexual Affronts and Racial Frontiers: European Identities and the Cultural Politics of Exclusion in Colonial Southeast Asia', in Frederick Cooper and Ann Laura Stoler (eds), *Tensions of Empire: Colonial Cultures in a Bourgeois World* (Berkeley: University of California Press, 1997), pp. 198–237; Ann Laura Stoler, *Carnal Knowledge and Imperial Power: Race and the Intimate in Colonial Rule* (Berkeley: University of California Press, 2002); Ann Laura Stoler, *Race and the Education of Desire: Foucault's History of Sexuality and the Colonial Order of Things* (Durham: Duke University Press, 1995); Anne McClintock, *Imperial Leather: Race, Gender, and Sexuality in the Colonial Conquest* (New York: Routledge, 1995); Durba Ghosh, *Sex and the Family in Colonial India: The Making of Empire* (Cambridge: Cambridge University Press, 2006).
6. Lucy Bland, 'White Women and Men of Colour: Miscegenation Fears in Britain after the Great War', *Gender & History* 17 (2005), pp. 29–61, here p. 52.

7.   Laura Tabili, 'Empire Is the Enemy of Love: Edith Noor's Progress and Other Stories', *Gender & History* 17 (2005), pp. 5–28, here p. 10.

8.   Jenkinson, 'The 1919 Race Riots', pp. 93–6. See also Cohen and May, 'The Interaction between Race and Colonialism', pp. 118–19; Evans, 'Across the Universe', pp. 68–70.

9.   Head Constable, Liverpool, to Watch Committee, 17 June 1919, National Archives (NA), Home Office (HO) 45/11017/377969/28. Also see Cohen and May, 'The Interaction between Race and Colonialism', p. 114.

10. *Western Mail*, 13 June 1919.

11. Cohen and May, 'The Interaction between Race and Colonialism', p. 123; Evans, 'Across the Universe', p. 79.

12. 'Repatriation of Coloured Men: Note on Conference at Colonial Office', 19 June 1919, NA, HO 45/11017/377969/21.

13. Ministry of Labour to Chief Constables of Salford, Liverpool, Cardiff, Glasgow, Hull, South Shields, London, in 'Minutes of Meeting at Ministry of Labour', 30 July 1919, NA, HO 45/11017/377969/98.

14. Minute by Mr Maclennan, 'Passports: Mr Oladele Adebayo Ajose and his White Wife Beatrice', 23 March 1936, NA, Colonial Office (CO) 554/103/3.

15. Minute by Mr Maclennan, 'Passports: Mr Oladele Adebayo Ajose and his White Wife Beatrice', 23 March 1936, NA, CO 554/103/3. In order to be jointly repatriated with their black wives, this group of men had to wait until ships with special accommodation for women became available. The fact that there were far fewer repatriation requests from West African men married to black women was a reflection of the fact that they primarily partnered with white women in the ports. This was largely due to the demographic makeup of early twentieth-century British port cities, which were home to smaller numbers of black women than men. On Queashie's repatriation, see Colonial Office (draft letter) to the Secretary of the Repatriated British Civilians Help Committee, 11 November 1919, 'Natives Awaiting Repatriation', NA, CO 554/44.

16. 'Report on the Repatriation of Negroes', NA, HO 45/11017/377969/44.

17. On the failure of the repatriation, see Cohen and May, 'The Interaction between Race and Colonialism', pp. 12–21; Jenkinson, 'The 1919 Race Riots', pp. 103–5; Evans, 'Across the Universe', p. 81.

18. Mr Francis, Local Government Board, as recorded by an unnamed author in an untitled report on the Colonial Office conference on the repatriation schemes, 19 June 1919, in 'Position of Coloured Men Stranded in the UK', NA, CO 323/814/28.

19. See 'Case of Jamaican Seaman, T. Savis', 12 August 1919, NA, CO 137/735, no. 46926.

20. Jenkinson, 'The 1919 Race Riots', p. 106.

21. See T. C. Macnaghten to R. L. Antrobus, 6 January 1909, in 'Memo by Col. Seely, Case of Mr. Silberrad and Mr. Haywood', NA, CO 533/52, no. 45005.

22. See e.g., 'Repatriation of D. Russell and Family', 18 June 1919, NA, CO 137/735, no. 37977.

23. Frederick Cooper and Ann Stoler have usefully characterised these kinds of differences and discontinuities as 'tensions of empire'. See 'Between Metropole and Colony: Rethinking a Research Agenda', in Cooper and Stoler (eds), *Tensions of Empire*, pp. 1–56.

24. Minute by Alexander Fiddian, 'Repatriation of Natives with White Wives: Minutes as to policy to be adopted in regard to', 7 August 1919, NA, CO 137/735, no. 48782.

25. In her study of race relations in British West Africa, Barbara Bush notes that the policy of residential segregation was not only instituted to limit the spread of diseases from Africans to Europeans, it was also 'justified on the basis of the undesirability of too much "social intercourse" or familiarization between European and African'. Specifically, she cites the Nigerian Townships Ordinance as exemplifying this trend. The Ordinance 'stipulated that no natives, except bona fide domestic servants, were to reside in the European reservation (at least fifty yards to the rear of white residences) and no European was allowed to live in non-European areas'. Similar residential segregation ordinances were also institutionalised in the Gold Coast. On Nigeria, see Barbara Bush, *Imperialism, Race, and Resistance: Africa and Britain, 1919–1945* (London: Routledge, 1999), pp. 77–8.

26. 'Repatriation of Natives with White Wives: Minutes as to policy to be adopted in regard to', 8 August 1919, NA, CO 137/735, no. 48782.

27. Tabili, 'Empire Is the Enemy of Love', p. 8.

28. Tabili, 'Empire Is the Enemy of Love', p. 8.

29. One possible explanation for why the policy of prevention does not appear to have originally been applied to East Africa in the wake of the riots is that there were comparatively few East Africans who married white women in the British ports. Rather, it was West Indians and West Africans who were identified as having the highest rates of intermarriage with white women. Anecdotal evidence of the tendency of Somalis, in particular, not to marry white women is provided by J. A. Rogers who notes in his survey of inter-racial

sex that 'At Cardiff, Wales, one could always make the Arab and the Somali boys angry by saying that they were going to marry white women'. Rogers suggests that this was not only the result of a colour difference, but also of religion. J. A. Rogers, *Sex and Race: Negro-Caucasian Mixing in All Ages and All Lands*, 3 vols (New York: J. A. Rogers Publications, 1940), vol. 1, p. 148.

30. The Register General of Shipping and Seamen forwarded her letter to the Colonial Office. Ena Parker to Register General of Shipping and Seamen, 23 October 1933, 'Mr and Mrs John Parker – Repatriation of, from England to the Gold Coast', Ghana, Public Records and Archives Administration Department (PRAAD), Accra (ACC), Colonial Secretariat Office (CSO) 21/14/47.

31. 'Mr and Mrs John Parker – Repatriation of', Alex Fiddian to Ena Parker, 1 November 1933. PRAAD, ACC, CSO 21/14/47.

32. 'Mr and Mrs John Parker – Repatriation of', G. S. Northcote, Governor's Deputy, Gold Coast to Secretary of State, Colonial Office, 18 January 1934. PRAAD, ACC, CSO 21/14/47.

33. 'Mr and Mrs John Parker – Repatriation of', File Minute, 19 December 1933. PRAAD, ACC, CSO 21/14/47.

34. These couples included the Canns and the Roberts. On the Canns, see 'Repatriation of Natives to West Africa/Destitute Natives', 10 March 1927, NA, CO 554/74/8. For the Roberts, see 'White Wives of Natives', NA, CO 554/105/6, 1936.

35. While most British colonial subjects in Europe resided in Britain, others were scattered across the continent. This was especially the case after the war when employment opportunities in Britain became increasingly scarce. On British colonial subjects, especially those that were distressed, across mainland Europe and parts of the British Empire, see Amy Robinson, 'Tinker, Tailor, Vagrant, Sailor: Colonial Mobility and the British Imperial State, 1880–1914' (unpublished doctoral thesis, Stanford University, 2005).

36. German women were not alone in this regard. European women of other nationalities, including but not limited to British, Swiss and French women, along with women from North and South America were all at various times in the nineteenth and twentieth centuries at risk of losing their citizenship upon marriage to a foreign national. See e.g., Brigitte Studer, 'Citizenship as Contingent National Belonging: Married Women and Foreigners in Twentieth Century Switzerland', *Gender & History* 13 (2001), pp. 622–54; Kif Augustine-Adams, '"She Consents Implicitly": Women's Citizenship, Marriage, and Liberal Political Theory in Late-Nineteenth and Early-Twentieth-Century Argentina', *Journal of Women's History* 13 (2002), pp. 8–30.

37. German men, as was the case for men in other parts of the world, did not lose their citizenship upon marriage to foreign women and were often able to confer their citizenship status on to their wives and children. The caveat to this is that after 1935 German men who were Jewish lost their citizenship under numerous conditions. I would like to thank Karen Adler for bringing this to my attention.

38. Foreign Office, Mr G. Lyall, British Consulate, Berlin to the Secretary of State, 22 November 1927, NA, CO 554/74/8.

39. Colonial Office to Foreign Office, 23 December 1927, NA, CO 554/74/8.

40. Secretary of State, Colonial Office to Governor Slater, 'Mr Alfred Annan, alias Alfred Larsen – Repatriation of to the Gold Coast', 6 October 1930, PRAAD, ACC, CSO 21/14/6.

41. Minute, Attorney General Abrahams, 3 January 1931, 'Mr Alfred Annan, alias Alfred Larsen – Repatriation of to the Gold Coast', PRAAD, ACC, CSO 21/14/6.

42. Minute, Attorney General Abrahams, 3 January 1931. PRAAD, ACC, CSO 21/14/6.

43. Tabili, 'Empire Is the Enemy of Love', p. 13.

44. Minute, 25 February 1932, 'Mr Alfred Annan, alias Alfred Larsen – Repatriation of to the Gold Coast', PRAAD, ACC, CSO 21/14/6.

45. Minute, 15 January 1931, 'Mr Alfred Annan, alias Alfred Larsen – Repatriation of to the Gold Coast', PRAAD, ACC, CSO 21/14/6.

46. Governor Slater to Secretary of State Lord Passfield, 'Mr Alfred Annan, alias Alfred Larsen – Repatriation of to the Gold Coast', Colonial Office, 21 January 1931, PRAAD, ACC, CSO 21/14/6.

47. Governor Slater to Secretary of State Lord Passfield, 21 January 1931, PRAAD, ACC, CSO 21/14/6.

48. Tabili, 'Empire Is the Enemy of Love', p. 12.

49. Minute, 25 February 1932, Attorney General Abrahams, 'Mr Alfred Annan, alias Alfred Larsen – Repatriation of to the Gold Coast', PRAAD, ACC, CSO 21/14/6.

50. Minute, 15 March 1932, 'Repatriation of Natives to West Africa/Destitute Natives/A. Annan', NA, CO 554/89/5.

51. Alfred Annan to Colonial Office, 17 March 1932, 'Repatriation of Natives to West Africa/Destitute Natives/A. Annan', NA, CO 554/89/5. Annan, who was illiterate, appears to have used letter writers.

52. Alfred Annan to Governor Hodson, 25 September 1932, 'Mr Alfred Annan, alias Alfred Larsen – Repatriation of to the Gold Coast', PRAAD, ACC, CSO 21/14/6.

53. Alfred Annan to Colonial Office, 18 December 1940, 'Repatriations: Alfred Annan', NA, CO 554/123/17.

54. The cases of Michael Egali from Nigeria and Herbert Helden from the Gold Coast were complicated by the fact that their wives were German and Italian, respectively. Both couples were denied entry to the British West African colonies. On the Egalis, see 'Repatriation of destitute natives to West Africa, M. B. Egali: Passport facilities for Mrs. Egali', NA, CO 554/93/1, no. 1405/1. For the Heldens, see 'Repatriations: Herbert Helden and Wife (An Italian) from Barcelona to the Gold Coast', PRAAD, ACC, CSO 21/14/67.

55. Memorandum by Mr Maclennan on the position of white wives of natives desirous of entering West Africa, 1936, 'White Wives of Natives', NA, CO 554/105/6.

56. Other such couples include the Ajoses and the Boardmans, who entered Nigeria in 1936 and 1939, respectively; and an unnamed Sierra Leonean man who entered Sierra Leone with his white wife in 1936. For the Asafu-Adjaye and Boardman families and the unnamed Sierra Leonean man and his white wife, see Memorandum by Mr Maclennan, 'White Wives', NA, CO 554/105/6. For the Ajoses, see Minute, Mr Maclennan, 3 November 1936, 'Passports – Mr Oladele Adebayo Ajose and his White Wife Beatrice', NA, CO 554/103/3.

57. The Phillips case is referenced in the Ajose file. See 'Passports: Mr Oladele Adebayo Ajose and his White Wife Beatrice', NA, CO 554/103/3.

58. See e.g., Memorandum by Mr Maclennan, 'White Wives' and 'Passports – Mrs S. Oyadiran', NA, CO 554/118/2.

59. Bush, *Imperialism, Race, and Resistance*, p. 86.

60. Rogers, *Sex and Race*, vol. 1, p. 148. See also Bush, *Imperialism, Race, and Resistance*, p. 86.

10 From Husbands and Housewives to Suckers and Whores: Marital-Political Anxieties in the 'House of Egypt', 1919–48

Lisa Pollard

During the 1919 revolution, from which Egypt emerged as a nominally independent nation-state after forty years of British occupation, elite nationalists used images of their homes, marriages and domestic relations to demonstrate that they were ready for self-rule. On the eve of the July Revolution of 1952, in which a handful of military officers swept away the institutions that revolutionaries had fought for in 1919 – a constitutional monarchy, a parliament and a liberal economic structure – middle-class Egyptians used images of households in disarray to decry the failures of those institutions to flourish. This chapter examines cartoons from the urban, middle-class press between the 1919 era and the late 1940s to trace the transformation of the household from its role as a site of promise, in which monogamous husbands and their educated (house)wives presaged the nation's potential, to a place of treachery and deceit, where men were suckers and women lost their virtue. It argues that, while the institution of marriage actually flourished in Egypt's inter-revolutionary period, home life served as a symbol through which middle-class Egyptians critiqued their nation's postcolonial political experience.

A generation of historians working on the turbulent period between Britain's occupation of Egypt in 1882 and the military coup that secured the nation's complete independence seventy years later has used gender as a lens through which to capture how the national experience was made personal and immediate for Egyptians. They have demonstrated the various ways in which Egypt and its inhabitants were imagined and represented as gendered bodies, both by outsiders and by Egyptians themselves.[1] And they have illustrated the impossibility of separating the gendering of Egypt from that of its political struggle: nationalists of both sexes fought to save 'Egypt as a woman' from the aggressions of outsiders, and to nurture 'mother Egypt' once her independence had been secured.[2] While independent Egypt's political institutions were initially male-only spaces, the image of the nation as gendered feminine blurred the boundaries between masculine political acts and the feminine national arena in which those acts would resonate.[3] Furthermore, while women in newly independent

Egypt were excluded from the political realm, and enjoined to shape the nation from their homes, men were also required to display an attachment to domestic life (along with a certain predilection for nurturing activities) in order to signal their commitment to the (masculine) realm of politics and the (feminine) image of the nation.[4]

Within this gendered history, the home, its practices and its inhabitants have emerged as central to our understanding of the struggle for Egypt's sovereignty.[5] If we take the Egyptian revolutions of 1919 and 1952 as historical bookends, we see a strong father figure appear to put the 'house of Egypt' in order, to end British interference in Egyptian affairs and to instate new political and economic institutions. The iconography attendant to both revolutions suggests that Egypt's father would both guarantee the success of the nation-state, and model proper marital and domestic behaviour. Mothers were also central to revolutionary imagery: in the decades surrounding the 1919 revolution, elite revolutionaries used the presence in the home of a reformed, educated housewife to herald Egypt's readiness for self-rule. The exemplars of Egyptian modernity were the home of the revolution's leader, Sa'ad Zaghlul, and his wife, Safiyya. Their dwelling was referred to, then as now, as *beit al-ummah*, or house of the nation.[6] By contrast, in the years following the July Revolution of 1952, Gamal abdel Nasser's regime linked women's high level of visibility outside the home and in the workforce to a kind of triumph of the domestic realm: thanks to his economic and political platforms, women would succeed at making home life so secure that they could then contribute to the formal workforce – all the while taking care of their homes and families.[7] In each case, successful home life and stable domestic relationships marked the end of one era and presaged a new order of things.

In each revolutionary period, the press and other venues circulated images of the home. Those images presented modern women as the embodiments of Egypt's national aspirations. While men featured less often in the cartoons and caricatures that depicted the domestic realm, their masculinity – understood as their very ability to lead and defend Egypt, to build a strong economy and to shape national identity – was constructed through proximity to, and marriage to, 'lady Egypt' and the ideals that she embodied. 'Family men', in gendered representations from both revolutionary eras, claimed 'manliness' for themselves both through their successes outside the home and through close relationships to their homes, wives and families.[8]

In the inter-revolutionary years, however, the popular press also crafted an increasingly cautionary tale about the manly stature of married men and about homes and home life. While the home presaged the triumph of the body politic, it also portended calamity. Historian Hanan Kholoussy has shown that, by the end of the 1920s, a discourse of crisis fully surrounded marital life, reflecting not only the anxieties that Egyptians experienced about marriage – its cost and durability, among other aspects – but also concern about the condition of the political realm.[9] In other words, two dominant discourses about marriage circulated in the years after 1919: one suggested that home life presaged great personal and political success; the other that it would ruin the men who participated in it. While Kholoussy claims that the discourse of 'marital crisis' abated in 1936, as Egypt gained fuller independence from the British and greater confidence in its political future, this chapter will argue that as the nation appeared to flounder in the late 1940s, the home once again became a stand-in for political commentary and critique. On the eve of the July Revolution, images of marital and domestic life '1919 style' appeared to threaten and emasculate husbands, rather than guarantee them the political and economic enfranchisement that had been the promises of the revolution.

The link between the body politic and marital and domestic practices has its roots in what we think of as the building of 'modern Egypt'. To be precise, four specific historical events coupled domestic and marital behaviour to the form and function of the modern nation-state, shaping the 'family politics' of the modern era by politicising the domicile, attaching it to the establishment and function of the modern political arena.[10] The first was the state building activities of Mohammed 'Ali Pasha (*r.*1805–48), father of what many historians consider the modern, centralised Egyptian nation-state. The rise of new elites and, with them, new sensibilities about marital and domestic life, coupled with various projects undertaken by Mohammed 'Ali, served to make monogamy, single-family dwelling, and new domestic practices synonymous with state reform.[11] New projects and practices also served to define Egypt and an Arabic-speaking caste of civil servants, as distinct from the greater Ottoman Empire – politically, culturally and territorially.

The second event was the British occupation of Egypt in 1882. While Egyptian elites had begun to link monogamy with modernity, and to think of single-family living arrangements as 'Egyptian', Europeans were emphasising Egypt's polygamy, extended families, unchanged domestic practices and supposedly bizarre sexual habits as indicative of its degraded 'national' culture. And it was frequently those familial stereotypes that British colonial officials exploited when they occupied Egypt in 1882 and began setting up the framework for an occupation that would last – in various guises – until 1956. The British did not claim that they were occupying Egypt because of the sexual practices of the ruling classes. They did imply, however, that they had to stay in Egypt because of the moral turpitude of elite male Egyptians – a condition that the British linked to home life.

Given the role that homes and home life (both real and imaginary) played in both state building and in shaping a colonial occupation, it should come as no surprise that the language of secular bourgeois nationalism and its calls for an end to the occupation were first made in a similar register. Evidence of an emerging relationship, constructed between Egyptian nationalism and family practices, can readily be found in the press, party literature and school textbooks that extend back to the years of the British occupation of 1882. From the 1890s onwards, for example, *effendi*[12] (secular, bourgeois) nationalism was most frequently articulated in discussions about marriage, domestic habits and children that took place in weekly and monthly periodicals.[13] Egyptians who worked within the colonial administration translated early nationalist discussions about home life and its role in nationalism into concrete lessons for school children, thereby creating a curriculum that linked proper domestic manners to independence. These lessons also mapped, overtly, onto political discourse once the British allowed Egyptians to form parties beginning in 1907. The People's Party (hizb al-ummah), for example, linked the eventual establishment of constitutionalism in Egypt to an educational system that would reinforce familial relationships.[14]

But it was in 1919, as Egyptians staged a revolution against British colonial rule, that the linking of a modern, independent, constitutional Egypt with the home and its practices reached a crescendo. The domestic-nationalist imagery that was rooted in the 1890s was put to use by the *effendi* nationalists who supported Sa'ad Zaghlul (1859–1927) and the Wafd[15] in their quest to secure, first, a place for themselves in the post-war negotiations in Versailles and, ultimately, independence from the British. *Effendi* propaganda during the 1919 revolution drew on discussions about the domicile that had been in circulation since the 1890s to create a definable revolutionary iconography of family life.

The iconography of 1919 had two important functions. The first was to show the British that the elite class and domestic relations that had defined British understandings of Egypt at the time of the occupation no longer applied. In other words, middle-class nationalists demonstrated (both to each other, and to the British) that polygamy, the harem, extended family households and the failed political realm that accompanied them (at least in the British imagination) were no longer regnant in Egypt – necessitating the end of the occupation. The second was to cement the relationship between the elite political leadership that emerged from the First World War (the Wafd, and, at its head Sa'ad Zaghlul) to the Egyptian masses. During the revolution, Zaghlul emerged as the symbolic father of the revolution and of the nationalist movement that had made the revolution possible – a relationship that was forged, at least symbolically, by connecting him to the masses through a nationalist lineage. Wafd members and their supporters were thus portrayed as family men, and as good nationalists who fed the nation's children.[16] Wafd members wrote poetry glorifying men willing to nurture the nation's youth.[17] Revolutionaries chanted slogans in which they claimed lineage from Zaghlul himself.[18] Each verse, chant and image attributed the parentage of independent Egypt to Zaghlul and the Wafd, infusing the revolutionary movement with the images and the vocabulary of earlier state-building projects. By the time the British agreed to grant the Egyptians limited independence, self-government and a constitution in 1922, the re-formed family had been linked to the movement that produced semi-independent Egypt.

The 1919 revolution was indeed rich in familial, domestic symbolism. Cartoons and political caricatures were common to the press in the revolutionary era, allowing even the illiterate access to revolutionary iconography as it appeared in print. If the most common portrayal of the 'Egypt' that nationalists struggled to liberate was female, her most typical depiction was as a mother figure. Cartoon depictions of Egypt as a woman typically embodied the ideals of early twentieth-century nationalism: Pharaonic garb linked modern Egypt to its ancient past. The veil evoked debates that raged in early twentieth-century Egypt over the 'new Egyptian woman'.[19] Most typically she was 'modern', wearing the latest fashions (either local or European, and with or without a veil), and chic footwear. Regardless of her attire, lady Egypt was modest, virtuous and attractive – the object of nationalists' desires. She was respectful of men, and deferential to them, and she conveyed the idea that both tradition and new forms of modernity could be combined.[20]

Cartoon images of a mother Egypt suggested the parallel reforms of home and nation, and it was through such images that ideal housewives and mothers were linked to the emerging body politic. One such cartoon had lady Egypt breast-feeding Bank Misr (the Bank of Egypt), nurturing the nascent financial institution and reminding the viewer that home-grown domestic reform linked the nation's aspirations to the homes of its citizens (Figure 1). The 1919-era press was full of quotes from young revolutionaries who claimed to wish that they had a mother like lady Egypt, one who was educated in the domestic sciences and the *belles lettres*, a woman who raised good sons for the nation. In this discourse, the housewife was virtuous, modest and devoted to her home (both her own home and the national one) and to the care of her young.

Figure 1: The newborn Bank Misr and the foreign banks in Egypt.
Source: *al-Lata'if al-Musawwara* (*Illustrated Niceties*), 2 August 1920.

This picture represents the newborn Bank Misr and the foreign banks in Egypt. Bank Misr is represented as a newborn baby being breast-fed the milk of his mother. And who is his mother? None other than the Egyptian Nation, the beloved, splendid Egyptian Nation sitting on its oldest and most famous manifestation – the Sphinx. While mother Egypt attends to breast-feeding her newborn – about whom she is overjoyed – the child's older brothers sidle up to take a look. Their eyes are full of jealousy and rage, but they cheer each other on by saying: 'Will the baby live? Will the baby live?' We say: 'Yes the baby will live if he continues to nurse from the breast of his mother'.

But young male revolutionaries also suggested that their aspirations included marriage to a woman who embodied the virtues of lady Egypt. Accompanying the rush to illustrate lady Egypt's qualities in the years around 1919 was a discourse that idealised such marriage. In poetry, fiction and articles from the political press it was not uncommon for men to compare their beloved to lady Egypt, and to long for relationships with women who embodied her virtues. While men frequently desired to be the son or the brother of a 'woman like her', they were just as likely to articulate their desires to marry her.[21] As Kholoussy indicates, bourgeois masculinity in the 1919 era was defined by marriage, by men's ability to choose suitable companions and to set up modern households with them. Men who chose bachelorhood over matrimony threatened to erode the very nation that their supposedly more masculine counterparts were fighting to liberate.[22] Furthermore, at precisely the same time as familial imagery emerged as central to a nationalist agenda, Egyptian lawmakers endeavoured to make marriage and the family more permanent by limiting men's access to divorce.[23] Thus, making (and maintaining) a family with the reformed, educated 'new Egyptian woman' – both the literal woman and her symbolic counterpart, the nation – modelled independence and political success for the nation and the new Egyptian man.[24]

Indeed, to complete the image of Sa'ad as the father of the revolutionaries, Egyptians adopted his wife Safiyya (1876–1946) as the 'mother of the Egyptians' (*umm al-masriyyin*). Photographs of the couple were central to revolutionary-era iconography, in which the Zaghluls emerged as a loving, companionate couple.[25] The pair captured revolutionaries' imagination as a family; in turn, the Zaghluls called Egyptians their children. Indeed, by 1921 Safiyya referred to nationalists as her 'devoted sons', carving out a political role for herself as their symbolic mother.[26] The couple's home, meanwhile, played an iconic role in the revolution as 'the house of the Nation', or *beit al-ummah*, serving as a meeting place for the Wafd and as a starting place for demonstrations.[27] National attention was continuously focused on *beit al-ummah*, in which Safiyya was both an ideal companionate wife, a model homemaker and a proper lady (she met with male politicians from behind a screen, for example), linking the revolution to the decades of domestic debates that had preceded it.[28] To keep house like the Zaghluls became a revolutionary as well as a personal standard.

Revolutionary-era iconography and Egyptians' ideation of the Zaghlul couple suggested that political successes such as the Wafd's victory in securing a place for Egypt at the post-war negotiations was intertwined with marriage and correct domestic habits. For women, right political behaviour – political 'femininity' – meant to be a housewife, Safiyya Zaghlul style. Political 'masculinity' was derived, in part, from the desire to marry lady Egypt.[29] And the masculine political ideal derived from the amount of time Egyptian husbands cared to spend in 'lady Egypt's' presence, raising children and enjoying the delights of home. Marrying and setting up a house had both a personal and public dimension: Egypt's independence and its future as a constitutional regime appeared to rely on it.

But the political promises evoked by the domestic symbolism of 1919 were tarnished by political failure. The first blow to the Egyptian family was Sa'ad's failure to reach the kind of agreement he wanted with the British. By February 1922, Zaghlul had secured for Egypt a limited form of independence. At the same time, however, Egypt's first constitution – penned while Zaghlul was in exile – quashed many of the ideals of the revolutionary period even as it formed the basis of an arrangement with the British that would last until 1936. The constitution displaced Zaghlul as the titular 'father of the Egyptian nation' in favour of a heavy-handed, unpopular king, Fu'ad (r.1917–36), the brother of the puppet ruler the British had placed on the throne early in the First World War. In order to gain Egypt's nominal independence, the Wafd had to agree to a body politic in which the king had unchecked power. Many nationalists broke ranks with the Wafd as the result of the constitution, blaming its weaknesses on Zaghlul and forming new political parties to compete with it. Furthermore, Zaghlul was marginalised from politics after the British linked him to the 1924 assassination of a colonial official. The result of the revolution was thus an Egypt with a somewhat powerless representative government, an unpopular king, a disgraced symbolic father and a factionalised nationalist fraternity. Turf wars became the order of the day, as rival parties vied for seats in a parliament that struggled to function. (During Fu'ad's reign, not a single elected parliament sat for a complete session.) In King Fu'ad, the father of the revolution thus had a powerful rival, one who was less than keen on the idea of a constitution, or on representative government, the ranks of which would be filled with 'Sa'ad's sons'.[30] Fu'ad in fact played a behind-the-scenes role in suppressing Article 23 of the Constitution, which claimed that 'all powers emanate from the nation', dealing a powerful blow to the symbolic Egyptian family.[31] And the fraternal bonds the Wafd had managed to create, however weak, were challenged as Sa'ad's 'sons' split ranks in favour of rival politicians. The father of the nation was no longer master of his household, and *beit al-ummah* lost its political, as well as its symbolic pride of place.[32]

The fraternal ranks of the generation of 1919 would continue to be fragmented throughout the 1930s and 1940s. Economic challenges brought by the Great Depression and the Second World War shook the remaining confidence that Egyptians had in the Wafd (as well as its rivals) and in Fu'ad and his son and successor Faruq (*r.*1936–52), resulting in the further proliferation of political parties. The ranks of the Muslim Brotherhood, founded in 1928, swelled in the 1930s and 1940s. That organisation's popularity resulted from its exceptional infrastructure (the organisation provided services that a floundering state often could not). Its popularity also stemmed from the increased disenchantment of Egypt's growing middle and lower middle classes with the secular politics and the party rivalries of the 1919-era elite.[33] Communist groups proliferated in the 1930s and the 1940s, as did paramilitary parties like Young Egypt, bringing with them not only the further fragmentation of the 1919 ideal but challenges to Egypt's national identity. The secular, 'Pharaonic' ideals that were proclaimed by the generation of 1919 were now challenged by competing identities: for some, Egypt was an Arab entity, for others an Islamic one, for others still a communist one.[34] Such challenges to Egypt's identity came to a head in 1948, as the government's failure to respond adequately to the conflict between Arabic Palestinians and incoming Jews in British Mandate Palestine was seen by the Egyptian populace as a failure to help 'fellow' Arabs and 'fellow' Muslims who were, beginning in the 1930s, seen by many Egyptians as constituting part of the Egyptian national family.

Sa'ad's sons were also split by changes within the ranks of the *effendiyya* itself. The *effendi* class grew steadily throughout the 1920s and 1930s, as an increased number of lower-middle-class males received the secondary and university diplomas that allowed them access to government jobs and to the prestige associated with civil servant positions. But these latecomers shared neither the tastes nor the economic good fortunes of their predecessors. The Great Depression made fashioning themselves after the elite founders of the Wafd difficult, if not impossible. While the numbers of their ranks grew, their opportunities in business and in government shrank as the state and the market contracted in size and in strength. Consequently, alternative political platforms, like those of the Muslim Brotherhood, became more appealing than the Wafd, and *effendi* males began to choose alternative role models for self-fashioning.[35] In such a climate, Sa'ad Zaghlul's image as father and husband lost much of its personal and political patina.

In the 1930s, Egypt experienced two crises, both of which served as a national reminder of the failures of 1919. The first, in 1930, was the former Wafdist Prime Minister Isma'il Sidqui's (1875–1950) abrogation of the 1923 constitution in favour of a yet more conservative version. By 1935, the result was rioting and demonstrations led by Egypt's university students, at the helm of whom stood the Wafdist Youth Vanguard, determined to regain the 1923 version of the constitution, despite its limitations. As a result of the rioting, the British feared for the country's stability. By 1936, both the Wafd – once again in control of parliament – and the British found common cause in their alliance against fascism. An Anglo-Egyptian treaty, secured by the Wafd in August 1936, seemed to guarantee Egypt's eventual independence and a lessened British presence. The signing of the treaty was regarded by most Egyptians and foreigners as a final step towards Egypt's full independence and as a new victory for the Wafd. British reluctance to make good on the treaty after the Second World War evoked the failures of 1919 and did little to restore the legitimacy, or the legacy, of the Wafd. The signing of the treaty came to be viewed as a crisis, rather than a victory. *Effendi* Egyptians' nostalgia for an earlier era in which the promises of 1919 had yet to be broken is reflected in this cartoon from 1935 (Figure 2). In it, 'Al-Misry Effendi' (The Egyptian

Figure 2: 'Does history repeat itself? After years of patience and forbearance … it seems like the only thing to do is to look for 1919 and go back to it'. Source: *Ruz al-Yusuf*, 20 May 1935, p. 7.

Effendi) who, by the early 1930s had emerged in the popular press as a kind of Egyptian middle-class 'everyman', longs for the ideals of 1919. The title reads: 'Does history repeat itself?' Al-Misry Effendi says to himself, as he digs through a stack of calendars, 'after years of patience and forbearance . . . it seems like the only thing to do is to look for March 1919 and go back to it'. In March 1919, the hopes of the revolution had not yet been dashed by the realities of the 1923 Constitution or continued struggles for full independence.

If the failure of the revolution's father to secure a fully independent Egypt delivered the first blow to 1919-era ideals, the second blow came from the elite Egyptian women who refused to play house – who did not conform to their role as 'mother Egypt'. For many women, 'lady Egypt' was but a symbol, embodying their commitment to the nation but not defining their actual domestic arrangements. At the same time, 'mother Egypt' did not embody their aspirations for actual political agency. As soon as the constitution had been promulgated, many activist women split from the Wafd. The wives and daughters of many Wafd members (and their later detractors) had formed the Wafd Women's Auxiliary in 1919. The Auxiliary was instrumental to the success of the revolution, and Wafd women hoped to parley their revolutionary experiences into suffrage. Once the Egyptian Constitution was made public in 1923, and women learnt that they had not been enfranchised, the many members of the Auxiliary dissociated themselves from the Wafd and formed the Egyptian Feminist Union, or the EFU. The EFU championed Article 3 of the new constitution: 'They [Egyptians] equally enjoy civil and political rights and are equally subjected to duties and public obligations to race, language or religion'.[36] As women became more insistent on a role for themselves in the political realm, men seemed to have concluded that the right place for them was in the home, in the schoolroom and at the helm of beneficent organisations – but not in parliament. And as the EFU continued to struggle for greater access to post-secondary education, divorce and suffrage – a struggle that continued until 1954 – women with extra-domestic aspirations were labelled as threatening. Those women were chastised not only for putting pressure on men and on the struggling nation-state, but also for threatening to destroy the family that was its cornerstone.[37]

As Sa'ad's paternal image was tarnished and women challenged Mother Egypt, the domestic images that were so central to 1919 began to lose their pride of place in the press. Cartoon images in the political press seemed quickly to become focused on the activities of independent Egyptian men as they built the political, educational and economic institutions that they had recently achieved through revolution. As the revolution died down, cartoonists and caricaturists were less occupied with a mother Egypt who had proven to be unreliable than they were with a new image: men who left the gendered–feminine, nationalist–domestic activities of 1919 behind in order to build the state. This marginalising of domestic images corresponds with the heightened *effendi* male preoccupation, aptly described by historian Wilson Jacob, with physical strength in response to the allegedly effeminising effects of colonialism (and, quite likely, as a more visibly potent alternative to the domestic ideals of 1919).[38] In this new phase of caricaturing, men laid bricks for the foundations of a new legal system and of the new parliament building. They swung anvils to hammer out the foundations of a new legal system. They constructed government buildings.[39] Cartoons showed men taking each other on in the boxing ring, symbolic of the struggle for prominence in the arena of party politics.[40] At the same time, cartoonists depicted governing

Figure 3: 'The road to Parliament'. Source: *Al-Kashkul*, 13 November 1927.

institutions – obtained as the result of a revolution infused with gendered–feminine virtues – as female-free space. 'The Road to Parliament', for example, had no women on it (Figure 3).

In the stead of the gendered–female depictions of Egypt from the 1919 era, ugly, misogynistic depictions of the real women who made demands on the public realm were growing in number. The highly celebrated writer and educator Nabawiyya

Musa (1886–1951) appeared as almost ape-like in a cartoon depicting her negotiating with a state body (the Ministry of Education) over what kind of headwear Egyptian students would don on campuses.[41] Likewise, Hoda Sha'rawi (1879–1947), who founded the EFU and who is still considered to be the mother of Egyptian feminism, was frequently depicted as ugly and clownish in her interactions with male politicians.[42] Safiyya Zaghlul was lampooned by the anti-Wafdist periodical *al-Kashkul* (*The Notebook*) as an ugly crone, yanking the ear of Prime Minister Mustafa Nahhas (1879–1965) in approbation as he visits *beit al-Ummah*.[43] Here, the attractive qualities of women, 1919 style, are nowhere to be seen; even *beit al-ummah* has been taken over by a hag.

Accompanying the challenges to the ideals of 1919 was the rise of the 'marriage crisis' discourse, which, Hanan Kholoussy reminds us, emerged most prominently in the Egyptian press in the late 1920s. The discourse was concerned with the habits of the *effendiyya*, and appeared in the middle-class press as a heightened intellectual preoccupation with the question of whether or not young men were marrying, and whether or not they were choosing proper wives.[44] Letters to the editor, columns and editorials all seemed to capture the rising concern of middle-class readers with bachelors and bachelorhood. Concern over and complaints about marriage had certainly emerged before; beginning in 1898 and continuing until 1919, men protested against the costs of marriage and carped about the low government salaries that kept them from paying dowries and purchasing apartments.[45] But, beginning in the late 1920s, marriage appeared in the press as an institution under fire. Despite what appeared to be stable marriage rates and the marriage laws of 1920 and 1929, which reduced men's access to divorce, pundits claimed that bachelorhood was on the rise, and that young men were refusing to marry.[46] Similarly, they claimed that legalised prostitution had led to the popularity of bachelorhood.[47] When men did give in to marriage, analysts claimed that they often divorced. A frequent joke in the press equated the length of the average marriage with the typical Egyptian parliament or cabinet. While divorce rates were actually down in the 1930s as the result of the changes in personal status laws that will be discussed below, the public perception was one of a high divorce rate and of 'crisis'.[48]

And yet, despite their beleaguered reputation in the press, and their retreat from symbolic space, the home and the family continued to be the mainstays of nationalism and state-building in the inter-revolutionary decades, and the idea that the home and family formed the basis of the nation continued to circulate. The Ministry of Education, for example, persisted in peddling the home as central to shaping Egyptian nationalism – however contested that nationalism remained. In the decades between 1919 and the July Revolution, state-produced school books still enjoined males to marry a living equivalent of 'lady Egypt', and to shape their marital and domestic habits so as to support her.[49] In other words, the lessons offered to schoolchildren on the eve of a second revolution were not so different from 1919: the very bricks that supported clean, well-ventilated, well-organised domiciles were still labelled the foundation of the nation. State officials continued to ask Egyptian schoolchildren to keep their houses in order and their domestic relationships intact, despite the failures of their symbolic mothers and fathers outside the home.

The inter-revolutionary Egyptian government also committed itself to the family's role in the nation by promulgating a number of marriage laws. Laws prohibiting the marriage of minors, the personal status laws of 1920 and 1929 and various legislative manoeuvres against polygamy were each designed to encourage monogamy and companionate marriage. Such laws were not designed to grant agency to Egyptian men or women, *per se*, but were, rather, geared towards cementing monogamous marriage as the building block of the nation.[50]

By the late 1930s, however, the tensions between two seemingly contradictory discourses surrounding marital and domestic life remained unresolved. In 1939, the Egyptian government created a new institution, the Ministry of Social Affairs, in part to fortify the Egyptian household. The ministry succeeded the short-lived High Commission for Social Reform, founded in 1936, which was established in order to tend to 'fixing' the social order and the family.[51] Accordingly, the family emerged as one of the main targets of the Ministry of Social Affairs.[52] In its early days, the new ministry apparently flirted with the idea of opening a 'school of marriage' to teach men and women to stay married and to focus appropriate attention on their households.[53]

Civil organisations echoed the government's call to improve the condition of the home and the family: the efforts of many of the *gama'iyyaat igtima'iyya* (social associations) that proliferated in the 1930s and 1940s (and many of which were funded by the Ministry of Social Affairs after 1939) fixed their attention on marriage and the domicile. Some offered 'model homes' to teach domestic and marital ideals to the urban poor and working classes, like the Society for Social Service, established in the suburb of Heliopolis, adjacent to Cairo, in the early 1940s. The society also offered legal domestic intervention for families in need of their assistance.[54] Certain social associations provided lecture series for their membership, in which marriage and home life and their attendant benefits were on the bill. The subject of 'new' women and their educational and political demands was certainly included among the lecture topics. It was quite often the subject of getting men to want to stay home – 1919 style – that audiences were treated to in lectures, however.[55] Some of the societies made explicit reference to their space – sporting fields, libraries and restaurants – as ideally suited for men. Indeed, *gama'iyya* space was described as thus because there men would be surrounded by ideas and practices that they could, in turn, take home and teach their wives and families, making the club an extension of the home.[56]

The periodical of the Ministry of Social Affairs, *Magallat al-Shu'un al-Igtima'iyya* (*Magazine of Social Affairs*), also made specific reference to the 'public space' of the *gama'iyyaat* as preferable to the coffee-house if men had to spend time away from home. Ideally, at least according to the ministry, men would learn to play games and musical instruments and take up hobbies and spend their leisure time fully ensconced in domestic bliss.[57] Shoring up marriage and home life seemed not fully focused on stemming the feminist tide (although the inter-revolutionary press did blame the feminist movement for spoiling home life). Rather, the goal of government and civic organisations seemed also to be teaching (or re-teaching) men a set of habits and ideals that would make them want to stay at home, and creating institutions that would help men infuse their families with civic ideals.

The message that the house should be a place where men spent leisure time and in which they cultivated relationships and not simply a place to sleep – 'a hotel' – was one frequently delivered by *Magallat al-Shu'un al-Igtima'iyya*:

> There are those among us who see their house as a hotel or restaurant. They leave early to go to work. They come for lunch in a hurry; they're silent as they eat. Then they dive into bed for a nap.

Then they go to a café ... So their house is a hotel for sleeping and a restaurant for eating ... Children ... might confuse their fathers' roles with their mothers. They come to think that their fathers' only place is in the café or the club, not the house.[58]

The magazine offered a remedy. While it did not refer to the ideals of 1919 specifically, it laid them out rather precisely: remind women that when they did their jobs well, home life was attractive to men (and teach those who did not know the arts of modern homemaking). Remind men that support of the national project required choosing home life over the café or club. Remind both husbands and housewives that their performance of the proper domestic and familial roles would shape the next generation.[59]

By the end of the 1940s, the home had recaptured its earlier pride of place as a common trope for discussing the body politic. Columns expressing apprehension about marriage and divorce, gender asymmetry in the schoolroom and its effects on marriage, and the dangers of bachelorhood were a frequent press staple.[60] To be sure, depictions of strained domestic relations must be read as powerful critiques of the feminist movement, and of women's continued demands for greater inclusion in public life. The feminist movement had indeed grown, both in membership and in political orientation. So too had the number of women who sought higher education and employment outside the home. But it can hardly be claimed that the 1940s witnessed elite and middle-class women's wholesale abandonment of the home in favour of politics and the public realm.[61] (Indeed, feminists themselves continued to argue for maintaining domestic and household management training in schools for girls.)[62] Thus the reappearance of caricatured domestic scenes as political commentary in the popular press must also be seen as the re-emergence of an earlier pattern within nationalist discourse. In the late 1940s, the tropes were subtler than they had been in 1919: female cartoon figures were not labelled 'Egypt', nor were their male counterparts referred to as 'nationalists'. And the message delivered about home life was decisively bleaker than that delivered during the revolution: what had once promised independence now pointed to failure, treason and deceit.

The Second World War years had been hard on Egypt; at their end, the British appeared no closer to a full withdrawal than they had been in 1936, upon the signing of the Anglo-Egyptian Treaty. Student demonstrations were frequent in the mid-1940s. And, while the number of students had increased, the issues carried over from 1936: the economy lagged, the political realm was fragmented, the king was ineffective and the British were still in Egypt. In a second round of rioting, the failures of the 1923 Constitution united a second generation of nationalists whose aspirations were also not met by Egypt's original struggle for independence. Indeed, the slogan of political demonstrations in the second half of the 1940s was 'total independence' (*istiqlal tam*) – the same slogan that had given shape to 1919. In addition, when, in 1947, the British turned their Palestine Mandate over to the United Nations, and when the UN voted to partition Palestine, Egyptians felt that the Arab people had been betrayed – first by the British, and now by an international body. King Faruq hesitated to send Egyptian troops to the aid of Palestinians, and when he did it was discovered that the troops had been sent forth with substandard equipment. Thus the corruption of his palace and Faruq's wont for interference with parliament emerged as the objects of great ire and outcry. The legacies of British imperialism were again apparent and official, Egyptian political institutions appeared at their most inept.

Figure 4: 'The Discomforts of Home: Drink A Glass of "Awtar" and Leave Your Troubles For Others'. Source: *Al-Ithnayn wa Dunya*, 29 December 1947.

In this tumultuous era, the home appeared as a place from which men had to break at all costs. In stark contrast to the call in the Ministry of Social Affairs's magazine for men to stay home, a 1947 advertisement, for example, encouraged men to 'check out'. In a 1947 advertisment for a drink called Awtar, 'The Discomforts of Home: Drink A Glass of "Awtar" and Leave Your Troubles For Others', an *effendi* husband runs away from his home (Figure 4). This house is indeed a site of discomfort: a harried wife irons clothes while her food catches fire. In her arms, the baby screams while a toddler blasts his toy trumpet. Another child swings from the chandelier. Family pets add to the chaos: canine–feline antics knock over a potted plant. Home life does not nurture this *effendi* Egyptian, nor does he embrace his family. Rather, his glance at his watch tells us that he's got somewhere else to be, or that he has fled, just in the nick of time.[63]

If the apprehensions over men's willingness to marry had seemed to define the political anxieties of an earlier age, the fate of men once they had entered into the marital contract seemed to define this later one. One periodical in particular, *Akhir Sa'a (The Latest)*, seemed to capture this new wave of anxieties about escaping from home life, publishing a stream of cartoons about the pitfalls of both the home and of marriage.[64] Indeed, *Akhir Sa'a*'s cartoons appear to have been the calling card of what has been referred to as an overtly political, if politically unaligned periodical.[65] Stylistically, *Ahkir Sa'a* offered its readers the kind of mixed bag of topics that had been common to the political press in the early twentieth century, although the journal's intended audience would have broadened by the 1940s to include the new middle- and lower-middle-class ranks of the *effendiyya*. In the style reminiscent of the early twentieth century, *Akhir Sa'a*'s editorial staff comfortably juxtaposed photographs of bathing beauties against serious articles about the idiosyncrasies of Egyptian royalty, Egyptians' obsession with party politics (*hizbiyya*), student movements, economic crises, the problem of continued British presence and the failure of Egyptian (and Arab) foreign policy in Palestine. The journal's discontent with the status quo was not disguised, whether it came to politics, marriage or domestic 'crisis'.

It is impossible to know if the 'women' who are represented in *Akhir Sa'a*'s cartoons are real – in other words whether they were meant to represent the Egyptian women whose aspirations challenged the discourse of 1919 or to symbolise the nation itself. What is clear, however, is that in relation to the female figures in these cartoons, men look foolish, incapable and duped. In these images, marriage and domestic life did not embolden men or connect them to the political realm as they had three decades previously: rather, domestic space appeared as ineffective as parliament.

In 1919, men had been the actors in political cartoons. To be sure, Lady Egypt and Mother Egypt took centre stage, but it was men who longed for them, reached for them, interacted with them and, sometimes, clothed them. In one cartoon from 1922, as the constitution was being written, for example, a group of four males surrounds Lady Egypt (one of the men bears a strong resemblance to Sa'ad Zaghlul, the leader of the 1919 revolution). They play the role of tailors, creating a new garb for this Lady Egypt. She commands them: 'My dress is missing something. I want a new one of a different sort'. She has voice in this caricature, but the men possess the means of making her new dress. She is at the centre, but it is the men's actions that will lead Egypt into a new era. Femininity inspires, but it does not dominate.[66]

In the late 1940s, by contrast, men appear subject to the whims of women. Frequently, they are spoken about but do not appear. 'Susu', who frequented the pages of *Akhir Sa'a*, had much to say about men and their outmoded expectations of women: 'Picture this!' she says, for example. 'These days, men's thoughts are backward-looking and outdated. And their thoughts are very "country". They understand loyalty to mean that a girl loves only one man'.[67] So too did these two young women who discuss their future married life: 'Daddy is very conservative. Imagine! He is determined to know the name of the man who wants to marry me!'[68] When men are present in these cartoons, they frequently react to women's follies, but seem to lack the wherewithal to respond. In one, a suitor on a bent knee blanches at his beloved's response to his proposal: 'Tell me quickly how much you love me', she says, 'because there are others waiting'.[69] Here, the trappings of manliness appear similar to 1919: this is a modern man in a western suit and tie. And the object of his affection is clearly a modern woman. She sports a dress and heels. She sits on a couch in what appears to be a well-ordered, modern household. In other words, the props of this image are straight out of 1919. But the 'hero' here is not successful at winning the object of his affection; rather, he is rebuffed and a mockery is made of the very institution he seeks.

Perhaps the most lampooned man in *Akhir Sa'a* was 'Lion Effendi' or 'Mighty Man'.[70] As his title suggests, he was symbolic of Egypt's educated middle classes, whose socio-economic and political aspirations were put on display in 1919, but whose relationship to the political realm had been severely strained by the late 1940s. As his name does not suggest, he is tiny, skinny and dwarfed by his wife. Unlike her name, 'The Skinny Lady', this woman is huge – obese, even. She is so huge, in fact, that she overwhelms everything around her. In one depiction, Mighty Man appears to try to put her in perspective, but she dominates all that surrounds her – including him.[71] Furthermore, she is enormously obtuse: unclear about her size and her condition, she claims that her doctor told her to increase her size and strength. She uses Mighty Man as a dumbbell, accordingly.[72]

A number of readings of 'The Skinny Lady' are possible. She could be a self-critique of the *effendi* class, which, by the 1940s, was frequently called selfish and self-focused,[73] of the *effendiyya*'s growing size, its pretence and its alleged penchant for consumption.[74] Skinny Lady might also be a critique of the tastes of the generation of 1919 for heavy women – in other words, a means of distinguishing one political generation from another – and, thereby, a commentary on the diminished success of the Wafd.[75] And Skinny Lady might represent the growing size of the feminist movement by the late 1940s, as well as its proliferation into several branches.[76] She might well be a stand-in for the nation-state, swelled in size but not in substance, eager to control the aspirations of the *effendiyya*, and determined to squash the men who might resist or challenge her – the girl of 1919 all grown up and overwhelming. She might tell us a thing or two about middle-class males' anxieties about marriage. In any case, marriage to Skinny Lady made Mighty Man irrelevant. 'It drives me crazy', she says in one image. 'Every time I put Mighty Man somewhere, I forget where I put him'.[77] In the chaos of their household, in the dross of their material possessions, Mighty Man has been overlooked (Figure 5).

And as if irrelevance were not enough, marriage to, and cohabitation with Skinny Lady was outright life threatening: she could squash you, apparently without thinking about it. Skinny Lady rolls over in bed and exclaims: 'It drives me crazy! Mighty Man was under the pillow with the keys! Where did he go?'[78]

Skinny Lady was just one of several female figures in late 1940s cartoon space who seemed to contradict the 1919 ideals of demure, adoring women. The women of *Akhir Sa'a* certainly have the agency to talk back to men. But what they had gained in agency since 1919 they had lost in physical appeal, at least in comparison to their 1919-era counterparts. Their features have become coarse; they have large mouths that grimace and pout. The modernity of women in the 1919 era (high heels and western clothes) has given way to the comparatively risqué: their blouses and dresses are low-cut and tight, their breasts are prominent. They smoke, in defiance of norms for that time. While men remain in relationship to female figures in the late 1940s, the male gaze

رفيعه هانم . حاجه تجنن . .! كل ما احطـالسبعافنديـفى حته . . ارجع انسى انا حطينه فين !؟

Figure 5: 'It drives me crazy! Every time I put Mighty Man somewhere, I forget where I put him'.
Source: *Akhir Sa'a*, 18 May 1948.

does not reflect the longing for the gendered-feminine representations of the nation that were so central to 1919. Like the rebuffed suitor, men seem to recoil from these women.

As for the home in late 1940s cartoons, it would appear to have the material trappings of 1919 – its furniture is modern, as is its décor. It possesses the proper technology: telephones and refrigerators, irons and ironing boards. In other words, at first glance, 1919-era notions of order, cleanliness and proper furnishings seem to be present. But upon closer inspection, households are no longer shaped by the ideals of 1919: fathers cease to be consulted about marriage. Men are thought of as accessories (Skinny Lady puts Mighty Man with her keys), rather than companionate partners. Houses are in disarray. Women are lousy housewives. As one man leaves his wife, in apparent repudiation of their partnership, pictures hang crookedly on the wall and furniture is overturned.[79] In one home, gender roles have been fully reversed: a fashionably dressed woman comes in to find her husband and children. He is in his pyjamas and robe. The children are unruly; two of them squall while one pulls mischievously at the belt of her father's robe. A final child sits at his feet and screams. Again, the décor looks modern, but the scene evokes nothing of 1919. She says: 'Your friends must be really jealous of your domestic happiness'.[80] Home life has apparently brought this man little more than chaos, naughty children and an absentee wife (Figure 6).

But wives and fiancées were not the only sources of men's troubles. Indeed, a third figure emerged in *Akhir Sa'a*: 'the Prostitute' (al-Ghaaniya). Debates about prostitution proliferated in the Egyptian press and parliament in the late 1940s, as they had throughout the 1930s. In both decades, the conclusion was similar: alleged increases in prostitution were a sign of men's indifference to marriage, and of social

الزوجة – لازم كل اصحابك يحسدوك على سعادتك المنزلية !

Figure 6: 'Your friends must really be jealous of your domestic happiness'. *Akhir Saʻa*, 7 January 1948.

decay.[81] As far as *Ahkir Saʻa* was concerned, the renunciation of wives brought men as few rewards as marriage. Like wives, 'Al-Ghaaniya' seemed to prey upon men, usually for their money. One says, 'If you've got change, see about giving me a 100-pound note so that I can pay the taxi'.[82] And they were frequently caught in the act of questioning men about their bank accounts: 'Up to now, you have not honoured me with the name of the bank you deposit your money in'.[83] And, like 'honest' women, they duped their suitors and made fun of their values: 'My boyfriend is very conservative. If he knew I was meeting you like this he'd shoot me!'[84] As a 'substitute for marriage', relationships with prostitutes appeared to offer few rewards.

A secondary message from the 'Prostitute' series is that extra-marital relationships (or prostitution instead of marriage) would fail to produce a legitimate new generation. Children were evoked in 1919-era imagery at every turn. And the message delivered by earlier images of the breast-feeding mother Egypt and the adoption of the Zaghluls as adoptive 'parents' was that the revolution, like marriage, would produce a new generation of capable 'sons'. When children in later cartoons are evoked or depicted at all, it is as naughty, unruly brats. And with 'The Prostitute', Egyptian men would – at best – produce a generation of bastards.

That the generation of 1919 had, however, failed to produce capable sons – nationalists who could oust the British or steer parliament clear of rivalries and kings – was made clear in a series in *Akhir Saʻa* called 'The New Generation' (al-gil al-gadeed). The expression, 'the new generation' was what the press called the post-1919 political generation; in its cartoon form, it illustrated youth that refused to follow the example of their parents. Typically, a young boy and a young girl were pictured talking together, although sometimes parents were included in the images. In one, a boy says to his female friend: 'Daddy is really backward-looking! Picture this! He does not want me drinking whisky!'[85] The courtship and marital habits of the 1919 generation were also rejected by 'the new generation'. One girl says: 'Our engagement has gone on a long time. People are starting to talk'.[86] (Long engagements were not at all uncommon in Egypt. They were typical among the generation of 1919.) And 'the new generation' was apparently rejecting monogamy. A woman asks a friend why her son is crying. The answer: 'I found him a fiancée, but he refuses! He wants four!'[87] What, indeed, had happened to Sa'ad's sons?

As reflected in such images, the failures of 1919 to secure a fully independent nation translated into anxieties over marriage and home life in the intra-revolutionary period, and the domestic and familial ideals that were so central to the 1919 revolution thus lost their lustre. The symbolic home and happy marriage as measures – or promises – of political success declined in appeal as the result of the failure of the 'father' of that revolution, Sa'ad Zaghlul, to deliver both full independence from the British as well as a fully functioning constitutional regime. Whereas modern homes and monogamous marriages were substitutes for political success in 1919, they emerged, over the course of three politically and economically turbulent decades, as potential sites of crisis, failure, treason and deceit. In 1936, with the signing of the Anglo-Egyptian Treaty, 'marriage crisis' discourse lost its pride of place in the press as Egyptians sensed that the promise of full independence (as they had fought for it in 1919) was finally at hand. But as the Second World War and an escalating crisis in Palestine kept the British ensconced in Egypt, as palace corruption became more visible, and as parties competed to define and to govern the nation, marriage and domestic relations emerged once again as the metaphor for an unhappy nation. While suitors and husbands were emboldened by their proximity to lady Egypt in 1919, later cartoon images depicted men as duped, overwhelmed, robbed and, sometimes, literally squashed by their home lives. Connubial and domestic bliss could no longer embody national success as the political contract that was symbolically shaped through them continued to flounder. Accordingly, the aspiring revolutionary qua family man from 1919 found little domestic or political bliss by the late 1940s.

Complete independence, the object of the revolutionaries' greatest desire, would not come to Egypt until a second revolution obtained it. During the July Revolution, Gamal abdel Nasser presented himself as the nation's new father and declared that he would put the nation back in order. His regime swept away many of the political institutions of 1919 – the monarchy and the multi-party parliamentary system – and replaced them with a brand of socialism that would define the nation for a generation. Nasser fulfilled many of the unkept promises of 1919, especially the departure of British troops from Egyptian soil. Through land redistribution and the nationalisation of capital, Nasser reduced the fortunes (and the power) of Egypt's most elite classes. By opening up the educational system and creating a new industrial economy, Nasserism dismantled the *effendiyya* and attempted to create a new, classless society. An unchallenged father, with new ranks of sons, could thus begin to put the national household – *beit al-ummah* – back in order.

While marriage would remain central to Egyptian nationalism throughout the Nasser era, the scenes of domestic drama would change. Women would no longer be required to support the nation from the household, and hence, the pressure on men to marry the living equivalent of a 1919-style 'mother Egypt' lessened. In Nasser's Egypt, domestic success was guaranteed by women's visibility in the public sphere; a spate of new, locally produced appliances and gadgets lightened women's household burdens, allowing them to contribute to the paid workforce.[88] While women's departure from the domicile would create a whole host of new anxieties about the collapse of gender roles and the threatened disintegration of gender hierarchies, it did seem to put an end to the kinds of marital anxieties that were so common to the inter-revolutionary era. As husbands, housewives, suckers and whores were replaced by worker citizens – the daughters and sons of the new state, to borrow Laura Bier's phrase – marriage once again offered promise, and augured well for a new generation.[89]

Notes

Earlier versions of this chapter were given at the 2006 annual meeting of the Middle East Studies Association of America, at the University of South Carolina, at the Arab Families Working Group in Cairo in 2007, and at the University of Nottingham in 2008. The questions and comments from each group of listeners shaped and honed my arguments immeasurably. My colleagues Tammy Gordon, Paul Townend and Lynn Mollenauer offered invaluable insights and critiques, as did the anonymous reviewers of this article. I am particularly indebted to Hanan Kholoussy for her careful readings and valuable critiques.

1. Beth Baron, *Egypt as a Woman: Nationalism, Gender and Politics* (Berkeley: University of California Press, 2005); Marilyn Booth, 'Woman in Islam: Men and the "Women's Press" in Turn-of-the 20th-Century Egypt', *International Journal of Middle East Studies* 33 (2001), pp. 171–201; Hoda Elsadda, 'Imagining the "New Man": Gender and Nation in Arab Literary Narratives in the Early Twentieth Century', *Journal of Middle East Women's Studies* 3/2 (2007), pp. 32–55; Wilson Chacko Jacob, 'Working out Egypt: Masculinity and Subject Formation between Nationalism and Colonial Modernity, 1870–1930' (unpublished doctoral thesis, New York University, 2005); Lisa Pollard, *Nurturing the Nation: The Family Politics of Colonizing, Modernizing and Liberating Egypt, 1805–1922* (Berkeley: University of California Press, 2005).
2. Baron, *Egypt as a Woman.*
3. Margot Badran, *Feminists, Islam, and Nation: Gender and the Making of Modern Egypt* (Princeton: Princeton University Press, 1995).
4. Hanan Kholoussy, 'The Making and Marrying of Modern Egyptians: Gender, Law, and Nationalism, 1898–1936' (unpublished doctoral thesis, New York University, 2008); Pollard, *Nurturing the Nation.*
5. Kholoussy, 'The Making and Marrying of Modern Egyptians'; Pollard, *Nurturing the Nation*; Mona Russell, *Creating the New Egyptian Woman: Consumerism, Education and National Identity, 1863–1922* (New York: Palgrave Macmillan, 2004).
6. Baron, *Egypt as a Woman*; Pollard, *Nurturing the Nation.*
7. Laura Elizabeth Bier, 'From Mothers of the Nation to Daughters of the State: Egyptian Women and the Gender Politics of Nasserist Rule' (unpublished doctoral thesis, New York University, 2005).
8. Badran, *Feminists, Islam, and Nation*; Pollard, *Nurturing the Nation.*
9. Kholoussy, 'The Making and Marrying of Modern Egyptians'.
10. The following summary of those four events is taken from Pollard, *Nurturing the Nation*, unless otherwise indicated.
11. Baron, *Egypt as a Woman*; Russell, *Creating the New Egyptian Woman.*
12. *Effendi* is a difficult term to pin down. It was used most frequently to connote a new class of Egyptians: those educated in the nascent, national educational system and who had a vested interest in the nation. The *effendiyya* were not necessarily land-owning elites; rather their elite stature was the result of their education and their proximity to the state apparatus.
13. Pollard, *Nurturing the Nation*; Russell, *Creating the New Egyptian Woman.*
14. From a speech given by secular nationalist Ahmed Loutfi al-Sayyid, head of the People's Party, on 17 May 1908, at the Club of the People's Party in Cairo, cited in *Discours politiques prononcés par Ahmed Lutfi al-Sayyid* (Cairo: Imprimérie al-Jaridah, 1909), pp. 5–6.
15. The Wafd (delegation, in Arabic) was a group of land-owning elites who demanded to represent Egypt in the post-war negotiations.

16. Baron, *Egypt as a Woman*; Pollard, *Nurturing the Nation*; Russell, *Creating the New Egyptian Woman*.
17. See e.g., Hafith Ibrahim's 'Malga'a al-Huriyya' and 'To Children', which are included in 'Abd al-Rahman al-Rafa'i, *Shua'r'a al-wataniyya fi misr* (Cairo: Dar al-Kuttub al-Misriyya, 1966).
18. National Archives (NA), Foreign Office (FO), 848/12. Taken from a circular intercepted by British intelligence in December 1919, 'Ihna awlad Sa'ad', or 'We are Zaghlul's Children'.
19. Badron, *Feminists, Islam, and Nation*; Baron, *Egypt as a Woman*; Pollard, *Nurturing the Nation*; Russell, *Creating the New Egyptian Woman*.
20. This chapter by no means presents a comprehensive survey of the Egyptian press. The periodicals discussed here were printed in Cairo and targeted at an educated, upper-class readership and, later, a middle-class readership. Nor does the chapter provide a receptivity study, a project that, unfortunately, lies outside its scope.
21. Pollard, *Nurturing the Nation*, ch. 6, pp. 164–204.
22. Kholoussy, 'The Making and Marrying of Modern Egyptians'.
23. Hanan Kholoussy, 'The Nationalization of Marriage in Monarchical Egypt', in Arthur Goldschmidt, Amy J. Johnson and Barak A. Salmoni (eds), *Re-Envisioning Egypt 1919–1952* (Cairo: American University of Cairo Press, 2005), pp. 317–50.
24. Elsadda, 'Imagining the "New Man"'.
25. Baron, *Egypt as a Woman*, p. 140.
26. Baron, *Egypt as a Woman*, p. 143.
27. Baron, *Egypt as a Woman*, p. 144.
28. Baron, *Egypt as a Woman*, pp. 141–4.
29. Indeed, as Baron has argued, cartoon depictions of lady Egypt came, more and more frequently, to resemble Safiyya.
30. The British claimed that Fu'ad resisted the constitution, agreeing to it only to maintain the favour he had won by his association with Zaghlul. Allenby claimed that, if left to his own devices, Fu'ad would have restored the kind of rule that characterised Isma'il's reign. NA, FO 141/516/1443, 23 April 1923.
31. NA, FO 141/576/14431, 'Royal Rescript No. 42 of 1923 Establishing a Constitutional Regime in the Egyptian State'.
32. For an excellent discussion of the 1923 Constitution and citizenship see Mervat Hatem, 'The Pitfalls of the Nationalist Discourses on Citizenship in Egypt', in Su'ad Joseph (ed.), *Gender and Citizenship in the Modern Middle East* (Syracuse, NY: Syracuse University Press, 2000), pp. 33–57.
33. By the 1930s, *effendiyya* had come to include university-educated members of the middle and lower-middle classes and therefore the title had lost some of its panache.
34. Israel Gershoni and James P. Jankowski, *Redefining the Egyptian Nation, 1930–1945* (Cambridge: Cambridge University Press, 1995).
35. Jacob, 'Working out Egypt'; Lucie Ryazova, 'Egyptianizing Modernity through the "New Effendiya": Social and Cultural Constructions of the Middle Class in Egypt under the Monarchy', in Goldschmidt et al. (eds), *Re-Envisioning Egypt*, pp. 124–63.
36. The Egyptian Constitution of 1923, cited in Badran, *Feminists, Islam, and Nation*, p. 86.
37. Badran, *Feminists, Islam, and Nation*; Cynthia Nelson, *Doriyya Shafiq, Egyptian Feminist: A Woman Apart* (Gainesville: University Press of Florida, 1999); Bier, 'From Mothers of the Nation'.
38. Jacob, 'Working out Egypt'.
39. See e.g., *al-Kashkul* (*The Notebook*), 17 August 1923; 19 November 1923; 31 July 1925.
40. *Al-Kashkul*, 3 July 1925.
41. *Al-Kashkul*, 15 January 1923. Wilson Jacob, 'Working out Egypt', claims that debates over proper 'Egyptian' headwear were part of the sartorial experimentation that accompanied 'working out' Egyptian masculinity.
42. See e.g., *al-Lata'if al-Musawwara*, 9 June 1924; *al-Kashkul*, 22 May 1931, cited in Baron, *Egypt as a Woman*, pp. 173 and 184 respectively.
43. *Al-Kashkul*, 30 January 1931, cited in Baron, *Egypt as a Woman*, p. 158.
44. Kholoussy, 'The Making and Marrying of Modern Egyptians'.
45. Kholoussy, 'The Making and Marrying of Modern Egyptians', pp. 48–50.
46. Kholoussy, 'The Making and Marrying of Modern Egyptians'.
47. Laura Bier, 'Prostitution and the Marriage Crisis: Bachelors and Competing Masculinities in 1930s Egypt', paper given at the annual meeting of the Middle East Studies Association of America, San Francisco, 2001.
48. I thank Hanan Kholoussy for making this point clear to me. Personal communication, 2 February 2008.

49. Barak Salmoni, 'Pedagogies of Patriotism: Teaching Socio-Political Community in Twentieth-Century Turkish and Egyptian Education' (unpublished doctoral thesis, Harvard University, 2002); Barak Salmoni, 'The Limits of Pedagogical Revolution: Female Schooling and Women's Roles in Educational Discourse, 1922–1952', in Thomas Ewing (ed.), *Revolution and Pedagogy: Interdisciplinary and Transnational Perspectives on Educational Foundations* (New York: Palgrave Macmillan, 2005), pp. 61–86.

50. Kholoussy, 'The Nationalization of Marriage in Monarchical Egypt'.

51. Idarat al-'Ama lil Sh'un al-Igtima'iyya, *Wizarat al-shu'un al-igtima'iyya: nishatha wa tataurha wa khidamaatha* (Cairo: Dar al-Kuttub, 1955).

52. Omnia al-Shakry, *The Great Social Laboratory: Subjects of Knowledge in Colonial and Postcolonial Egypt* (Stanford: Stanford University Press, 2007).

53. Articles about the school appeared in the Egyptian journal *al-Thaqafa* (*Culture*) in 1939. Many of Egypt's cultural luminaries defended the school (Ahmed Amin and Tawfiq al-Hakim, for example) or, by contrast, ridiculed it (Taha Hussein). *Al-Thaqafa*, December 1939.

54. Dar al-Watha'iq al-Qawmiyya (DWQ) (Egyptian National Archives), 'Abdiin Collection, Box 203, 'Social Service Society of Heliopolis'.

55. DWQ, 'Abdiin Collection, Box 203, 'Service Society for the Peoples of the Luxor Province in Cairo'.

56. DWQ, 'Abdiin Collection, 'Societies, Clubs and Sporting Entities'.

57. See e.g., *Magallat al-Shu'un al-Igtima'iyya*, July 1941, pp. 37–50; August 1941, pp. 1–10.

58. 'The House is not a Hotel or a Restaurant', *Magallat al-Shu'un al-Igtima'iyya*, March 1940, pp. 72–4.

59. 'The House is not a Hotel or a Restaurant', p. 73. Reporters and readers alike used the press over the course of the 1930s to counsel men to re-embrace home life. See Kholoussy, 'The Making and Marrying of Modern Egyptians', ch. 1, pp. 47–108.

60. Bier, 'From Mothers of the Nation', introduction, pp. 1–31.

61. Bier, 'From Mothers of the Nation', introduction, pp. 1–31.

62. Badran, *Feminists, Islam, and Nation*, chs 8 and 9, pp. 142–64 and 165–91 respectively.

63. Thanks to Mona Russell for sharing this cartoon with me.

64. This does not by any means represent a survey of the late 1940s press. Rather, I chose to focus this discussion on *Akhir Sa'a* because its cartoons and caricatures seemed most representative of debates about marriage and politics, much like *al-Lata'if al-Musawwara*'s cartoons had in the 1919 era.

65. Ami Ayalon, *The Press in the Arab Middle East* (Oxford: Oxford University Press, 1995). Ayalon calls *Akhir Sa'a* an unaligned political journal. The periodical was established in 1934. Its editor in the late 1940s was Mahammed al-Taba'i. Cartoons and caricatures all but disappeared from the periodical by the early 1950s, and were replaced with photographs.

66. *al-Lata'if Al-Musawwara*, 3 April 1922.

67. *Akhir Sa'a*, 4 February 1948. Many thanks to Dena al-Adeeb and Riham Shebl for their help translating these cartoons. They are not, of course, responsible for my interpretations.

68. *Akhir Sa'a*, 3 March 1948.

69. *Akhir Sa'a*, 18 January 1948.

70. As per my own translation.

71. *Akhir Sa'a*, 11 February 1948.

72. *Akhir Sa'a*, 11 January 1948.

73. Ryzova, 'Egyptian Modernity through the New *Effendiyya*'.

74. My thanks to Alan Mikhail for this insight.

75. Thanks to Lynn Mollenauer for drawing this to my attention. In *Palace Walk*, the first of his Cairo Trilogy, Naguib Mahfouz gives vivid descriptions of the large wives of elite men. Naguib Mahfouz, *Palace Walk*, tr. William Hutchins and Olive E. Kenny (New York and London: Doubleday, 1990).

76. Bier, 'From Mothers of the Nation'; Nelson, *Doriyya Shafiq*.

77. *Akhir Sa'a*, 18 May 1948.

78. *Akhir Sa'a*, 1 February 1950.

79. *Akhir Sa'a*, 7 January 1948.

80. *Akhir Sa'a*, 7 January 1948.

81. Laura Bier, 'Prostitution and the Marriage Crisis'; 'Imad Ahmed Hilal, *al-Baghaya fi Misr, Dirasah Tarikhiyya Ijtima'iyya* (Cairo: al-'Arabi lil Nashr wal-Tawzi', 2001).

82. *Akhir Sa'a*, 21 January 1948. Even in 2008, 100 Egyptian pounds is an impossibly high amount for a taxi ride. Since 100 Egyptian pounds often appeared in the press as the standard but very high sum that middle-class men were required to pay as a dowry, this image must be a reminder of the unavailability of marriage. I thank Hanan Kholoussy for bringing this to my attention.

83. *Akhir Sa'a*, 14 February 1948.

84.   *Akhir Sa'a*, 3 March 1948.
85.   *Akhir Sa'a*, 11 January 1948.
86.   *Akhir Sa'a*, 1 September 1948.
87.   *Akhir Sa'a*, 18 January 1949.
88.   Bier, 'From Mothers of the Nation'.
89.   Bier, 'From Mothers of the Nation'.

11 Double Displacement: Western Women's Return Home from Japanese Internment in the Second World War

Christina Twomey

At the end of the Second World War, Hilda Bates returned home to London. Bates was one of 130,000 Allied civilian nationals (approximately 40,000 of whom were women) captured and interned by the Japanese in the Asia–Pacific region in the Second World War.[1] She was forty-four years old, single and had lived in the British protectorate of North Borneo since the mid-1930s, with occasional visits home on leave. Sister Bates had trained as a nurse in London; in North Borneo her official title was 'Health Visitor'. Hilda Bates loved living in East Asia, fond as she was of swimming and warm weather, but years of internment had soured her appetite for it. The first letter Bates wrote after release was to her sister, Nora. 'In future it's Great Britain for me', she wrote in September 1945. 'How I long for home – I think I preferred air raids at home to Jap rule here'.[2] By November, Bates had completed the long sea journey back to England and was living with her sister at Gray's Inn. 'Poor old London', Bates confided to her diary:

> It's a very different place [from] the Town I knew, everyone looks lined & worn, but the atmosphere is the same. One looks back on the nightmare of the last $3\frac{1}{2}$ years – sometimes [one] even wakes up in the night & wonders if it can be over – & then thinks – what of the future? It certainly doesn't look like a world of peace & plenty – one realizes that at Home here they've had their particular Hell to a lesser extent than ours – but let's hope whatever happens that it will be PEACE.[3]

There is a cautious note of optimism struck here; whatever the difficulties and changes, London was home and peace was its own reward. The capitalisation of 'Home' in Bates's diary emphasises the significance she accords to it. Home is not just her sister's flat, a domestic and familial place; it is also a proper noun, a national space which she inhabits as a British woman.

Like many war diaries, the one written by Bates ends with liberation and home-coming, yet it also includes a brief postscript, written in March 1946:

> I couldn't find peace of mind in England – I felt lost and out of touch – everyone had done their Bit in the war – I'd merely been in internment – it's a strange new world, I don't feel part of

it – I'm going back to Borneo to help restart the medical Health service there . . . there's sun there & warmth & people who have had the same experiences as I've had.[4]

For Hilda Bates, homecoming did not live up to the promise it had held for her through years of internment during the war. The bitterness of Bates's description of 'merely' being interned belied her earlier certainty that the 'Hell' endured in Britain had somehow been 'lesser' than her own experiences in Borneo. It also exposed the ways in which her own war experiences did not fit any of the available categories for doing one's 'bit' in terms of war duties or war service. A sense of home now appears to belong more with the community of people who had suffered in war as Bates had, rather than through any ties of family or nation. It was a feeling Bates had already anticipated before her return to Britain, when she confided to her diary that it was 'noticeable . . . that we are all nervous of getting home and meeting our people. There seems a great bond between barbed wire friends'.[5]

Bates was not the only former internee who returned to her home society to discover an obsession with the European war, at the expense of recognising the suffering experienced by those who had been in the Pacific theatre.[6] The sense of disenchantment Hilda Bates felt upon her return did have some antecedents in the experiences of British families with long-standing colonial connections. Elizabeth Buettner's study of British families in India found that 'home' had dual meanings for them too, as both national and domestic space.[7] To expatriates of any sort, whether by choice or enforced as in the case of internees, these ideas of home lent themselves to nostalgia and idealisation. On return, cultural connections appeared to be strongest with other expatriates rather than Britain itself; the reality of life 'at home' struggled to meet the fantasy nurtured about it.[8] The disappointments of homecoming were, in that sense, familiar and indeed, amplified, given the circumstances of internees' absence. Although there were continuities with other expatriate groups, the confluence of homecoming with a particular experience of the war, and with changing ideas about empire, posed particular challenges for former internees.

This chapter explores the sense of displacement rather than relief felt by women like Hilda Bates who returned from Japanese captivity. Western women's return from internment exposed the dual meaning of home as both the natural realm for women and as a national space; former internees had a problematic relationship with both. Released internees were women who had spent the war in a culturally uncertain space – away from the home, as prisoners of non-white men – and responses to their liberation and homecoming reflected these tensions and ambiguities. For white women who had spent the war as captives of the Japanese, homecoming prompted questions about their femininity and sexual integrity. Yet return home to the nation was also fraught, because women had to find a way to narrate their particular experiences of war within the languages and frameworks available to them, none of which particularly allowed space for women's experience to be central to the tale.

Empire, internment and gendered understandings of war

Hilda Bates was one of the growing number of British women who lived in the colonies in the years following the First World War. Prior to that time, colonial service had been viewed primarily as a male vocation; but the interwar period saw, as Barbara Bush has described it, a 'feminization of imperial discourse and practice'.[9] Women trained in the health and education fields began to enter the colonial service, and missionary women worked the colonial field in greater numbers. Despite the gradual increase in women professionals, most British women in the colonies were present as the wives or daughters of men with positions in bureaucracy, commerce or agriculture. The Colonial Office encouraged the marriage of its male members during this period, in the belief that domestic life and responsibilities would curb the worst excesses of frontier masculinity and prevent sexual liaisons between British men and women of colour. This was a period when empire was being recast as offering improvements to the welfare of its subject citizens, and British women were seen as valuable for the contribution that both their labour and the civilising influence their femininity might bring. The bellicose imperialism of the nineteenth century had been tainted by the advent of the First World War, even though some of the assumptions that underpinned it remained unchanged.

The continuing belief in the superiority of European civilisation, for example, meant that the Japanese invasion of the colonial possessions of the British, Dutch and Americans in south-east Asia, and the defeat of their armies, was as unanticipated as it was shocking. Defeated military personnel spent the rest of the war in prisoner-of-war camps. Allied civilians – men, women and children – were interned. Despite the fact that the Japanese had no policy on civilian internment, hundreds of camps were created throughout the region.[10] The conditions of internment varied depending on the size and location of the camps. Internees faced extremely harsh conditions on Java and Sumatra, and in New Guinea, where men and women were separated, accommodation was inadequate, sanitation poor and food always in scarce supply. In locations where mixed-sex camps were established, such as on Hong Kong and in the Philippines, the dwindling supplies of food by the end of the war and inadequate medication took their toll. Of 130,000 Allied civilians who spent the war in internment camps, 15,000 had died by the time of its conclusion.[11]

The liberation of the camps, and the repatriation services provided by governments to assist with return home, differed markedly between civilians and military personnel, and between nations. The first camps to be liberated were in the Philippines, which the United States reoccupied in February 1945. General MacArthur insisted all civilian US citizens return to their homeland 'unless there was a very good reason' that they should not.[12] Given the extent of destruction to homes and businesses caused by the fighting on the Philippine islands, very few people had any option but to leave. The US government charged its own citizens, newly released from captivity by the Japanese, $275 for the privilege of transporting them home. The Australian government initially acquiesced to the user pays principle for its own nationals but, after bitter protests about the injustice of charging civilians to return home from internment, Australian and British internees received free transport on hospital ships, troopships and aeroplanes.[13] As American, British and Australian forces liberated other camps throughout the region, internees were supplied with the food and essential medicines that they lacked. In all cases, the immediate assistance was generous but short term. Unlike military personnel, released civilian internees were not entitled to ongoing government assistance with the costs of their rehabilitation and re-establishment. The British and Australian governments did not insist that released internees return to their countries immediately, and some people chose to remain behind in the places that had been home to them for many years. They hoped to regain control of their dwellings or re-establish businesses destroyed by the war.

The distinctions drawn between civilian internees and prisoners of war in the repatriation process was indicative of a larger process that ultimately rendered the history of civilian internment less visible than its military counterpart. Civilians become displaced in narratives of war that focus largely on the military in general, and servicemen in particular.[14] The cultural tendency for war stories to be male stories has often been the subject of feminist critique. In response, historians have been active in recovering and analysing histories of war's impact on women – in terms of family life, trauma and loss, wartime employment, shifts in gender relations, and the experiences of women in the services – but symbolic centrality in the commemoration of war remains with soldiers.[15] Furthermore, western civilians captured by the Japanese were an uncomfortable reminder of the failure of Allied forces in a battle against an enemy long constructed as racially inferior. The fact that some of those captives were women rubbed salt into the wound, a reminder that white men had failed those whom they were most meant to protect.

These tensions and ambivalences at the heart of the internment story have also meant that its historiography has been slow to develop, particularly in English-speaking countries. The Dutch, who were the most numerically preponderant group of internees owing to their large colonial presence in the Netherlands East Indies, had an earlier, empirical tradition of scholarship on internment.[16] Extensive academic research into the experiences of British, American and Australian civilian internees is a more recent phenomenon, although there have been occasional studies of particular groups and camps.[17] Despite the recognition that women's wartime internment experiences were long overlooked because they were an uncomfortable reminder of men's 'failure' to fulfill their half of what Penny Summerfield has called the 'wartime gender contract', female internment also posed other contradictions to wartime narratives.[18] The theoretical and conceptual literature on gender and war has largely overlooked the challenges that female imprisonment poses to one of war's traditional, if ultimately chimerical dichotomies: that between the gendered domains of military front and home front.[19] Whatever the actualities and lived experiences of war, for men and women both, there have been powerful cultural associations linking men with the battlefield and women with the hearth. The internment camp, no longer a battlefield but hardly a place of refuge, struggled to fit within this dichotomy, and consequently posed contradictions to gendered understandings of wartime experience. There has been important work identifying military prisoners of war as men who, once defeated and confined, entered a culturally feminised condition of passivity and containment.[20] Yet internment created dilemmas for women, who also found themselves in a culturally ambiguous zone.

These ambiguities had implications for the ways in which women experienced their internment, but they had even greater ramifications once women were released and they returned home. Female internees were returning home from a place that had been constructed as a site of sexual danger for them. Women's internment by the Japanese was broadly perceived by westerners to carry with it the danger of sexual violation. There were many reasons for this, not the least of which was awareness of the potential for rape to be used as a weapon of war, and longstanding racial discourses which had constructed non-white men as sexually deviant and potentially violent.[21] Despite the spurious basis of claims about the innately violent man of colour, they were enmeshed in the power relations of colonialism and had been used to regulate both subject peoples and the movements of white women within the empire.[22] The relatively well-known atrocities committed by the Japanese army during the invasion of China in the late 1930s, most infamously in Nanjing in 1937–38, meant that, in the case of the Japanese military, however, these fears were not without foundation. Furthermore, British and Chinese nurses had been raped and killed during the invasion of Hong Kong in December 1941, further fanning public fears and speculation.[23] More critically, many of the female internees had been isolated from their traditional 'protectors', white men. Hence, women internees were forced to manage and negotiate relations with their male captors in the absence of men from their own cultural groups.

Homecoming, sex and femininity

Release from the camp meant facing up to the concern and, at times, voyeuristic curiosity, of friends, family and media about the sexual dangers of camp life. Interest in the sexual fate of female captives had a long history in western cultures, was immediate upon the release of women interned by the Japanese, and has been a constant in media and creative responses to their plight in the ensuing period.[24] When the 'Angels of Bataan', United States military nurses interned in the Philippines, were released, an editorial in the *New York Times* speculated: 'Only those who were with them in their captivity can know the dread that must have haunted these nurses during three dragging years'.[25] Australian military nurses confronted directly speculation about their sexual fates, by holding a press conference confirming that they had come under intense pressure to perform sexual work for the Japanese but had successfully resisted the attempt to make them into 'prostitutes'.[26] It was not just the media who were interested. Sometimes family members were prepared to ask direction questions. Phyllis Montefiore, a British woman who had spent the war in Santo Tomas internment camp in Manila, described her brother, Ian, greeting her at Southampton Quay after her journey home from the Philippines. Montefiore's brother lived north of London, so the pair had a hotel meal and then returned to the car for the long journey home. Montefiore recalled that, 'When we were comfortably settled and driving along, I shall never forget the first questions Ian asked me: "Were you raped by the Japanese? Are they your own teeth?"'[27]

Montefiore had not been raped, nor was it a particularly common experience for western women interned by the Japanese. Several hundred Dutch women were forcibly recruited from camps in the former Dutch East Indies to work as part of the Japanese military's systematic programme of sexual slavery, but a great deal of research has shown that it was Asian women in Japanese-occupied territories who were the most likely targets of sexual attack.[28] The memoirs of British, American and Australian women mention the fear of sexual violence, particularly early in their captivity, and the ongoing sexual innuendos and leering of their guards, but deny that they were raped or that it was widespread in the camps. The point here is not so much to quantify the extent of sexual violence within the internment camps, but to underscore the fact that women faced intense questioning and speculation about their sexual experiences upon release. It may have been as much a defence and protection of their reputation to deny sexual violence, as it was any statement of fact about its incidence. One Dutch woman, Jan Ruff-O'Herne, who suffered severely as a result of her abduction from the camp by the organisers of a Japanese sexual slavery unit, admits that her reticence to discuss the matter for almost fifty years stemmed from shame about the sullying of her own reputation and good name.[29]

There is a further sense, however, in which homecoming revealed the internment camps as sexually over-determined, rather than solely as a site of sexual danger for women. While speculation about the sexual fates of female captives suggests women were imperilled by their internment, other evidence points to the ways in which some internees were frightened that return home would expose the ways their war experiences had in some way defeminised them. This fear is present in the writings of Miss P. M. Briggs, a nurse at the General Hospital in Alor Star in Malaya when war broke out, who found herself interned on Sumatra after the ship on which she had attempted to flee was captured by the Japanese. By the end of the war, Briggs had been malnourished for many years, weighed thirty-eight kilos and had scabies on her hands. She was conscious that starvation had taken away some of the more obvious bodily markers of femininity. Recovering in hospital after her release, Briggs could not help but stare at the staff because 'they all seemed to have such large busts and behinds'.[30] Ostensibly this is a comment on the bodies of other women, but textually it serves to reinforce the lack of these features in Briggs's own body at the end of the war. Hilda Bates also expressed overt anxiety about the potential for defeminisation in her diary. 'It would be fun – or would it', she pondered, 'to see oneself in a mirror larger than 6 × 6 because looking around we all seem a funny shape – seats have gone and we go IN where we should be OUT'.[31] When Bates heard that peace had been declared, the first thing she ruminated upon was her physical appearance: 'I couldn't sleep, it all seemed so impossible & once or twice I was almost frightened of going out in the world after so long. What would it be like – would we appear strange?'[32] Interned women also knew something not so apparent to the outside world. The effects of long-term starvation meant that many of the women in the internment camps had stopped menstruating.[33]

As these comments reveal, some women feared that they had somehow been de-sexed by their presence in camp. In this version of events, women were placed uncomfortably close to conditions associated with masculinity – daily interaction with the enemy, physical separation from those at home, tough material conditions – and were in danger of losing their femininity as a result of their experiences. This was certainly an aspect of women's internment picked up by the news media in early reports about their release, with journalists and war correspondents deliberately interpolating women's freedom as the chance to return to full, fertile femininity. Reporting on the liberation of Australian army nurses from captivity provides an example of the ways in which journalists focused heavily on the necessity for women to purchase make up, have their hair done and return to conspicuous consumption as a way of confirming to themselves and the nation that they had emerged from the ambiguous zone of the camp with their femininity firmly intact.[34]

The ambiguity of the camp was further underlined by the way in which women sometimes experienced it as an excessively feminine space. These tensions could exist within the same individual. While Hilda Bates, for instance, feared that her confinement in camp had compromised her womanliness, at least in physical terms, in another sense she felt that living in a world without white men meant that she had become too accustomed to predominantly female company. 'One still feels all wrong outside the barbed wire & talking to a man', she commented in the early weeks of freedom, when she and the other women from the camp began visiting their male counterparts who had been housed separately from them.[35] A day later she visited the clinic that housed very ill male prisoners of war and again commented about 'feeling very shy about meeting so many men'.[36] One incident recorded in the diary vividly records Bates's anxiety:

> Life is hectic – rather too much so as our one desire is to be quiet after the excitement however there is no hope of that, forces pour in – we can't even change our clothes, they stay to meals & on our beds & talk! Never were there such talkers. In the middle of it an American pops his head in the window & calls 'Say, Honey, hold everything' & snap goes the camera![37]

A much later memoir, prepared by Bates in the 1980s, omits this wonderfully evocative image of a woman who feels so keenly the presence and observation of men, symbolised here by the American's camera looming through her window. The memoir constructs a much more stoic Hilda, one prepared to admit to disappointment and frustration, but some of the specifically gendered concerns of her homecoming – most notably her fear of having to interact with large numbers of men again – have been effectively erased.

Internment, war and empire

When writing about her captivity, Hilda Bates slipped into a mode in which war again became centrally about soldiers' experiences. In August 1945, she wrote, 'Looking back over the years I realised how fortunate we had been ourselves – it was the soldiers one felt for – the best years of their lives wasted'.[38] Yet two months earlier, lying in hospital with a dysentery-like complaint, one of things Bates reflected upon was that she was about to turn forty-four and her current feeling of 'hating these wasted years when I could have done so much'.[39] Bates, a professional nurse, had 'wasted' the war years as much as any soldier had done in a prisoner-of-war camp, but talk of the 'wasted lives' of imprisoned soldiers was part of the language of war in a way that her own internment was not. Just as the 1980 memoir expunged some of the gendered specificities of Bates's homecoming as a female internee, her earlier diary reinstates the symbolic centrality of the soldier as the representative of the nation at war.

Soldiers returning from war, however displaced, traumatised or equivocal they may feel, do at least have a symbolic place in which their service for the nation during a time of conflict might be recognised. The archetypal returnee is a male soldier, yet women returning from internment were female and civilian, and they struggled to find a presence in prominent narratives about war, suffering and sacrifice. Even military nurse prisoners of war, who at least had the imprimatur of service, felt displaced. A nurse of the Queen Alexandra's Imperial Military Nursing Service (QAIMNS), Mrs D. Ingram, who had nursed wounded soldiers during the battle for Hong Kong before surrender and internment, was resentful about the reception she and her colleagues received when returning home to Britain.[40] Ingram felt particularly bitter that there was no specialist medical care given to nurses returning from captivity. In May 1946 she and her matron from Hong Kong days marched in a victory parade with the Queen Alexandra nursing contingent and 'as we passed the saluting base I could lip read the King saying to the Queen (who held the programme) "Who are these?"'[41] Later in the account, Ingram suggests that the king did not recognise her contingent because they were wearing a new khaki uniform, in contrast to their more familiar grey and scarlet. However, it is possible to read the king's lack of recognition in another way, particularly given Ingram's frustration at the way she had been treated. His question can be interpreted as a comment on the way in which war spent as a female prisoner of war had rendered Ingram's suffering invisible and unspeakable.

If women in uniform felt their internment experiences had been obscured and overlooked, this sense of invisibility was even more profound for civilian internees. A teenager who had spent the war interned with her British parents in Shanghai, Miss E. Gander, described her journey home aboard a ship packed with service personnel. 'They were part of the victorious armed services and very matey with each other', Gander recalled, 'but anyone without a uniform felt an oddity'. 'We felt like the forgotten people', she remembered, 'a motley, ragged group completely out of touch with the rest of the world, to be looked on as freaks'.[42] A similar experience haunted the homecoming of Dr Cicely Williams, a prominent British pediatrician who had spent the war interned in Changi, where she had been one of the leaders of the women's section.[43] On the journey home from Singapore, Dr Williams's ship stopped at Colombo, where she and several other distinguished figures were invited to lunch at Government House. Williams later spoke about her experiences that day, a conversation rendered thus by her biographer:

> 'Tell us about some of your experiences', said a woman brightly, as if asking them to describe a holiday. The gulf between them widened beyond communication. Cicely could only mutter incongruously.
>
> 'We weren't really fit for human company.'
>
> 'Nonsense', said the woman, briskly, but not unkindly, and started to ask naïve questions. Had the Japanese behaved unspeakably? How much had they had to eat? Was it true that some people had escaped? They tried to shield her from the horrors yet still to entertain her. Cicely thought they weren't doing too badly.
>
> But suddenly the woman turned away and started to talk to a friend. Cicely heard her speak in a high distinct voice.
>
> 'Why on earth does the old man insist on having these poor jailbirds here? It's ghastly for us having to listen to their stories.'
>
> Shocked, Cicely stared across the harbour. In a subtle way she felt more deeply and treacherously wounded than at any time during her imprisonment.[44]

Like the teenaged Miss Gander from Shanghai, even a senior figure such as Dr Williams could experience homecoming as an event compromised by the ignorance of her company and the invisibility of internment in publicly accepted narratives of suffering in war.

In the late 1940s, the dominant story about the Second World War was that it had been 'the people's war'. This narrative could encompass the European war; it was less easily applied to the war in the Pacific, which concerned the defence of empire. Civilian internees were part of the imperialist presence in East Asia; the story of them participating in a 'people's war' was difficult to maintain. Yet the 1940s were a 'transitional moment' in the way both war and empire were represented in Britain.[45] Wendy Webster's study of film in the 1940s and 1950s has argued that Britain's retreat from imperial power led to the transposition of heroism and martial masculinity from films about empire to those about the Second World War. As women and civilians became conspicuous by their absence from stories about the Second World War, they re-emerged in films about empire, where white women in particular frequently symbolised weakness and vulnerability.[46]

A Town Like Alice (1956), a film based on Nevil Shute's 1950 novel, contained reference to war, empire and internment and established an influential narrative about them. Jean Paget, a young British secretary, was the central figure of the film, which followed her fate as a captive of the Japanese in wartime Malaya and her relationship with an Australian prisoner of war. The film was essentially a romance, but it also explored questions about the inversion of an imagined racial order and the loss of white prestige through the figure of the white woman captive. In keeping with empire films of the early 1950s, 'partnership' between Britain and colonised peoples was also a key theme, with Jean Paget returning after the war to bestow the gifts of modern technology upon the Malayan women who had assisted her during captivity.[47] *A Town Like Alice* received wide distribution, particularly in Britain and Australia. For British audiences in particular, the war in *A Town Like Alice* was a context for an exploration of themes attendant upon the end of empire.[48] It made viewers aware of the wartime internment of civilians, but did not ultimately ensure their inclusion in a national story about the Second World War; nor did it prompt scholarly research or a better public understanding of that experience. The film reinforced a perception that internment was a female fate, despite the fact that the majority of civilian internees were men.

Internment, return and romance

As *A Town Like Alice* makes clear, romance was one existing narrative trope into which women could readily fit their war experiences. 'Like so many romances', ran the first line of a book which was actually about a traumatic internment in Burma, 'mine began with a telephone call'.[49] There were some internment memoirs published in the early post-war period, although very few had wide international distribution or commercial success.[50] The one exception was American woman Agnes Keith's *Three Came Home* (1947), which was made into a Hollywood film in 1950. Keith, a writer by profession, produced what remains one of the most sophisticated internment memoirs, although the film version is more reminiscent of a captivity narrative. Similar to other lesser-known works in this genre, Keith's memoir begins with the separation of husband and wife during the Japanese occupation and ends with the reunion of the couple. While the anxiety of separation from their husbands was obviously a serious concern for internees, romance at first seems an odd narrative choice for this topic. But it becomes less odd when we consider how the broader culture validated and endorsed romance as one of the key ways women experience war.

Recourse to a trope about romance is common in women's war memories, because this is where their experiences of war have a more natural 'home'. War is a time when, often, gender stereotypes are both undermined – in terms of women's entry into 'non-traditional' spheres – and heightened, owing to the need to contain the implicit threat that such boundary crossing might imply. The emphasis on recruitment into the services and into war industries was always accompanied by implicit reminders of the ongoing womanliness of those who chose to serve. The increased masculinisation of the public sphere in times of war, when men's roles as both protectors of their own women and aggressors against enemy men is emphasised, allowed few entry points for women. Experiencing war as a willing helpmate in the effort was one of them; engaging in romantic interludes with serving men was another.

The operation of the narrative trope of romance, and its link to the validation of women's war experiences, can also be seen in the reflections of Phyllis Montefiore. Montefiore had arrived in the Philippines in August 1940 as the wife of 'Jag', a 'naval architect' who had 'been sent out to supervise the building of motor torpedo boats for the Filipino government'.[51] The marriage between Jag and Phyllis Montefiore was not stable, and did not survive the pressures of internment. 'We had both realised for some considerable time (even before our internment) that our marriage had irretrievably broken down', she later reflected.[52] Montefiore's papers include two accounts of internment. One is a diary written during her time in Santo Tomas. The diaries composed during the end of war and during Montefiore's homecoming period reveal an obsession with the minutiae of social interaction in the camp and her uncertainty about her future as a divorced woman. The descriptions of her release and journey back to England via the United States are punctuated by moments of despair about her prospects and ongoing efforts to readjust to freedom after so many years of captivity. 'I had great difficulty in realizing I was free and there would be no more sudden warning over a loud speaker to line up for roll call', Montefiore wrote in 1945.[53] The diaries read as the words of an anxious and uncertain woman.

The other inclusion in Montefiore's papers is a typescript memoir of internment entitled 'A Bit of Camp 1942–45'. The memoir is not dated, but appears to have been compiled in the 1970s using the original diaries.[54] The play on the word 'camp' stemmed from Montefiore's theatrical ambitions, which she pursued in Santo Tomas by becoming heavily involved in the entertainment programme. Her professional acting in the post-war period included cameo roles in early BBC television dramas in the late 1950s and 1960s.[55] The typescript memoir erases the earlier uncertainty and instead focuses on the pleasure Montefiore derived from delaying her return home and picking up some acting work with a touring troupe, 'The International Revue', that entertained US army troops stationed in the Philippines. The trip back to England via the United States (which she disliked apart from San Francisco, which was described as 'like the continent, without the filth') is constructed as a series of exciting romantic interludes, rather than the very contingent and unsettling process it appears to have been in the diaries.

One example illustrates this process of rewriting and rescripting. The diaries describe a journey east from San Francisco where she made 'new friends' who were very interested in her internment experience and were 'incredible that I appeared normal, comparatively speaking'.[56] When the train reached Chicago, Montefiore decided to disembark. This is how she describes her weekend in the diary:

> I believe in seizing every opportunity and as I thought it unlikely I would visit the States again in the near future if ever I thought I might as well take as much of a look around as I could in the given time. Curiously I bumped into some of my friends from the Camp, so we had a high old time on the Saturday night eating giant sized steaks and dancing to Charlie Spivak. This was Fairyland to me. I was certain I'd wake up any minute with a Japanese leering at me, but oh NO! It was really true.[57]

The main feature of Montefiore's weekend in Chicago, from the impression she has left in her diary, was her reunion with former internees and her ongoing fear that freedom from the Japanese did not mean freedom from the trauma she had felt in her captivity.

The same train journey to Chicago and weekend there is described in the following way in the 1970s typescript memoir:

> I met some delightful people and one particularly charming Naval Officer, who appointed himself CO of my travelling needs and comforts, and I raised no objections when he suggested I get off with him at Chicago, which was his destination before going to a resettlement Centre. We spent two happy days there, but I did not care for the city, after San Francisco. He saw me off on the Monday and we corresponded for several years, but as always, there must be an end. Still, I had collected another pleasant memory.[58]

The 'friends from camp' have gone, to be replaced by a Naval Officer. As Montefiore was interned in a civilian camp, there is no possibility that the Naval Officer was resident with them, although he may well have joined the group for a night out dancing to Charlie Spivak. Montefiore's ongoing discomfort with freedom and adjustment to life outside the camp walls has also been replaced with the bland aside that she had 'collected another pleasant memory', rather than being reminded of some more sinister ones.

Montefiore's rewriting of this episode may well stem from an unwillingness to revisit some of the difficulties that the process of release and homecoming may have inspired. It is well documented that in the post-war years the emphasis on overcoming trauma was directly linked to injunctions to forget about it and get on with life.[59] Transcribing diary notes about unpleasant memories might have appeared unseemly and unnecessarily maudlin and not in accordance with the picture Montefiore attempted to paint of herself in the document prepared for more public perusal. In this reading, a successful war was one in which difficult memories were quickly overcome. Yet Montefiore makes some interesting narrative choices, which tell us something not just about personal remembering and forgetting, but also about the ways in which the broader culture validates women's experience of war.

In rewriting her own history to provide a publicly sanctioned and easily under-stood experience of homecoming – as refeminisation, as opportunity for romance – Montefiore writes out what was specific about her experience of war. The sense of dis-placement from others, the pleasure she takes in spending time with former internees who know her experience better than those who are simply surprised she is not mad, is subsumed in a textual move that makes homecoming a time for romance rather than a longer process of rehabilitation. For Hilda Bates, single long before the war and destined to remain so after its conclusion, the prospect of release and homecoming was also bound up with ideas of romance. Her excitement is as palpable as her fear at the prospect of meeting so many men, from whom she had been separated for so long. Yet, in the end, she made the more realistic choice and decided to return to what had become her true 'home' – life as a much-admired nurse in the relatively remote districts of North Borneo.

It was only in the 1970s and 1980s that alternative narrative choices emerged as ways in which women might recount their experiences of war and internment. One was a construction of the camps as the sites of women's agency. The creators of the successful BBC television series *Tenko* (1981–85), influenced by the women's movement of the 1970s, viewed the internment camps as 'a "laboratory" in which there was a great deal to be learned about women'.[60] And yet, older interpretations died hard. Joan Didion recalled one Californian summer in the early 1980s, when she and her husband would stop writing for the afternoon, have a swim and then watch *Tenko* wrapped in their towels. 'There seemed for some a level at which the husband was held responsible for the ordeal of imprisonment', she later recalled. 'There seemed a sense, however irrational, of having been abandoned.'[61]

The accounts of British women's return from captivity analysed here suggest that in the 1940s and 1950s former internees had experienced a double displacement. For them, the focus was not so much abandonment as it was despair that homecoming, which had been so longed for, could be so fraught. Internees had endured a war spent outside their 'home' country, imprisoned by the enemy; they had also been removed from the supposedly natural feminine realm of the domestic 'home' and been confined in the ambiguous zone of the internment camp. The ambiguity of the camp gave licence to both the media and family members to question released internees about their sexual integrity – a discussion scarcely imaginable for a respectable woman to engage in before the war. Yet this public discussion belied a more complex relation between internment, femininity and homecoming, one in which it was equally possible for a woman to feel defeminised by her experience of captivity. This displacement was matched by the difficulty former internees faced in having their war experiences recognised as part of the story of the nation's experience of war. In one sense this was because of the dominance of the European theatre of the war in memories and public discussion of it; in another, it was because war spent as an internee did not fit any of the available categories for understanding and interpreting war. In some cases this led women to write out their own gender-specific experiences of war and substitute the sufferings of male soldiers as again central to the tale. In others, it meant the substitution of a romantic narrative for a traumatic one. In either case, it meant that return home from an ambiguous zone resulted in a difficult transition, which exposed how contingent the meaning of home was for those so long absent from it. In their absence home had changed, and reminders of an empire that was in the process of being dismantled were a discomfiting presence.

Notes

1. For statistics on the number of people imprisoned and interned by the Japanese, see Van Waterford, *Prisoners of the Japanese in World War II: Statistical History, Personal Narratives and Memorials Concerning POWs in Camps and on Hellships, Civilian Internees, Asian Slave Laborers and Others Captured in the Pacific Theater* (Jefferson, NC: McFarland, 1994).
2. Hilda Bates to Nora, 11 September 1945, Imperial War Museum (IWM), 91/35/1, Papers of Miss H. E. Bates (IWM, Bates Papers).
3. Hilda Bates, Diary, 25 November 1945, IWM, Bates Papers.
4. Bates, Diary, 26 March 1946, IWM, Bates Papers.
5. Bates, Diary, 23 September 1945, IWM, Bates Papers.
6. Gerald Horne, *Race War: White Supremacy and the Japanese Attack on the British Empire* (New York: New York University Press, 2004), pp. 5–7.
7. Elizabeth Buettner, *Empire Families: Britons and Late Imperial India* (London: Oxford University Press, 2004), pp. 188–9.
8. Buettner, *Empire Families*, pp. 190–91.
9. Barbara Bush, 'Gender and Empire: The Twentieth Century', in Philippa Levine (ed.), *Gender and Empire* (Oxford: Oxford University Press, 2007), pp. 77–111, here p. 90.
10. Utsumi Aiko, 'Japanese Army Internment Policies for Enemy Civilians During the Asia–Pacific War', in Donald Denoon, Mark Hudson, Gavan McCormack and Tessa Morris-Suzuki (eds), *Multicultural Japan: Palaeolithic to Postmodern* (Cambridge: Cambridge University Press, 2001), pp. 174–209.
11. Bernice Archer, *The Internment of Western Civilians under the Japanese, 1941–1945: A Patchwork of Internment* (London: Routledge Curzon, 2004), pp. 1–15.

12. Cited in Frances Cogan, *Captured: The Japanese Internment of American Civilians in the Philippines, 1941–1945* (Athens: University of Georgia Press, 2000), p. 309.
13. Christina Twomey, *Australia's Forgotten Prisoners: Civilians Interned by the Japanese in World War Two* (Cambridge: Cambridge University Press, 2007), pp. 146–9.
14. Archer, *The Internment of Western Civilians*, p. 8.
15. Lucy Noakes, *War and the British: Gender, Memory and National Identity* (London: I. B. Tauris, 1998), p. 2.
16. The earliest and most influential Dutch study is Dora van Velden, *De Japanse Interneringskampen voor burgers gedurende de tweede wereldoorlog* (Groningen: J. B. Wolters, 1963). For a Dutch study written in English that is more theorised, see Esther Captain, 'The Gendered Process of Remembering War Experiences: Memories about the Second World War in the Dutch East Indies', *European Journal of Women's Studies* 4 (1997), pp. 389–95.
17. For studies of civilian internment, see A. V. H. Hartendorp, *The Japanese Occupation of the Philippines* (Manila: Bookmark, 1967); Lavinia Warner and John Sandilands, *Women beyond the Wire: A Story of Prisoners of the Japanese, 1942–1945* (London: Michael Joseph, 1982); Joseph Kennedy, *British Civilians and the Japanese War in Malaya and Singapore, 1941–45* (London: Macmillan, 1987); Margaret Brooks, 'Passive in War? Women Internees in the Far East 1942–45', in Sharon Macdonald, Pat Holden and Shirley Ardener (eds), *Images of Women in Peace and War: Cross–Cultural and Historical Perspectives* (London: Macmillan, 1987), pp. 166–78; Lynn Z. Bloom, 'Till Death Do Us Part: Men and Women's Interpretations of Wartime Internment', *Women's Studies International Forum* 10 (1987), pp. 75–83; Shirley Fenton Huie, *The Forgotten Ones: Women and Children under Nippon* (Sydney: Angus & Robertson, 1992); Bernice Archer and Kent Fedorowich, 'The Women of Stanley: Internment in Hong Kong, 1942–45', *Women's History Review* 5 (1996), pp. 373–99; Bernice Archer, '"A Low–Key Affair": Memories of Civilian Internment in the Far East, 1942–1945', in Martin Evans and Ken Lunn (eds), *War and Memory in the Twentieth Century* (Oxford: Berg, 1997), pp. 45–58; Cogan, *Captured*; Theresa Kaminski, *Prisoners in Paradise: American Women in the Wartime South Pacific* (Lawrence: University Press of Kansas, 2000); Twomey, *Australia's Forgotten Prisoners*.
18. Penny Summerfield, 'Gender and War in the Twentieth Century', *International History Review* 19 (1997), pp. 3–15.
19. Nicole Dombrowksi (ed.), *Women and War in the Twentieth Century: Enlisted with or without Consent* (New York: Garland, 1999); Marilyn Lake and Joy Damousi, 'Warfare, History and Gender', in Joy Damousi and Marilyn Lake (eds), *Gender and War: Australians at War in the Twentieth Century* (Cambridge: Cambridge University Press, 1995); Miriam Cooke, 'Wo-Man, Retelling the War Myth', in Miriam Cooke and Angela Woollacott (eds), *Gendering War Talk* (Princeton: Princeton University Press, 1993), pp. 177–204; Margaret Randolph Higgonet, Jane Jenson, Sonya Michel and Margaret Collins Weitz (eds), *Behind the Lines: Gender and the Two World Wars* (New Haven: Yale University Press, 1987).
20. Robin Gerster, *Big-Noting: The Heroic Theme in Australian War Writing* (Melbourne: Melbourne University Press, 1987), pp. 222–36; Joan Beaumont, *Gull Force: Survival and Leadership in Captivity 1941–1945* (Sydney: Allen & Unwin, 1988); Gavan McCormack and Hank Nelson (eds), *The Burma–Thailand Railway: Memory and History* (Sydney: Allen & Unwin, 1993); Stephen Garton, *The Cost of War: Australians Return* (Oxford and Melbourne: Oxford University Press, 1996).
21. Carolyn Nordstrom, *Rape: Politics and Theory in War and Peace* (Canberra: Peace Research Centre, 1994); Claudia Card, 'Rape as a Weapon of War', *Hypatia* 11 (1996), pp. 5–14.
22. See Amirah Inglis, *Not a White Woman Safe: Sexual Anxiety and Politics in Port Moresby, 1920–1934* (Canberra: Australian National University Press, 1994). More recent work that explores the anxieties about intimacy that were central to the colonial project is included in Ann Laura Stoler (ed.), *Haunted by Empire: Geographies of Intimacy in North American History* (Durham, NC: Duke University Press, 2006); Levine (ed.), *Gender and Empire*; Angela Woollacott, *Gender and Empire* (London: Palgrave Macmillan, 2006).
23. Yuki Tanaka, *Hidden Horrors: Japanese War Crimes in World War II* (Boulder, CO: Westview Press, 1996), pp. 79–104.
24. Interest in the fate of white women captives was nothing new – there is a long history of the circulation of captivity narratives in American and British cultures. See Christopher Castiglia, *Bound and Determined: Captivity, Culture Crossing and White Womanhood from Mary Rowlandson to Patty Hearst* (Chicago: University of Chicago Press, 1996). For a broader history of captivity in British culture, see Linda Colley, *Captives: Britain, Empire and the World, 1600–1850* (London: Jonathan Cape, 2002). See also Christina Twomey, 'Retaining Integrity? Sex, Race and Gender in Narratives of Western Women detained by the Japanese in World War II', in Bob Moore and Barbara Hately-Broad (eds), *Prisoners of War, Prisoners of Peace: Captivity, Homecoming and Memory in World War II* (Oxford: Berg, 2005), pp. 175–84.

25. *New York Times*, 28 February 1945, p. 22.
26. See Christina Twomey, 'Australian Nurse POWs: Gender, War and Captivity', *Australian Historical Studies* 36 (2004), pp. 255–74.
27. Diary of Phyllis Montefiore, IWM, 84/42/1, Hearnden, Mrs. P.
28. After the revelations of Korean women in the early 1990s, the Dutch government commissioned Bart van Poelgeest to prepare a report on Dutch women's involvement in what was then called 'forced prostitution'. Van Poelgeest concluded that approximately 200–300 Dutch women were involved in the system of military sexual slavery. See Bart van Poelgeest, 'Oosters stille dwang: Tewerkgesteld in de Japanse bordelen van Nederlands–Indie', *NRC Handelslad*, 8 August 1992; repr. in *ICODO Info* 93/3 (1993), pp. 13–21. Esther Captain suggests this figure is an arbitrary one. Esther Captain, 'Spreken over gedwongen prostitutie en zwijgen over verkrachtingen: Bronnengebruik in een zaak over Japanse legerbordelen in Nederlands Indie', *ICODO Info* 94/1 (1994), pp. 37–48. (Translations from Dutch by Loes Westerbeek.) See also Ustinia Dolgopol, 'Pragmatism, International Law and Women's Bodies', *Australian Feminist Studies* 11 (1996), pp. 227–42.
29. Jan Ruff–O'Herne, *50 Years of Silence* (Sydney: Tom Thompson, 1994).
30. Miss P. M. Briggs, IWM, 82/24/1.
31. Bates, Diary, 26 April 1945, IWM, Bates Papers.
32. Bates, Diary, 17 August 1945, IWM, Bates Papers.
33. This is commented upon in Agnes Keith, *Three Came Home* (1948; London: Corgi, 1973), p. 96. For further discussion see Archer, *The Internment of Western Civilians*.
34. For a fuller explication of this argument, see Twomey, 'Australian Nurse POWs'.
35. Bates, Diary, 6 September 1945, IWM, Bates Papers.
36. Bates, Diary, 10 September 1945, IWM, Bates Papers.
37. Bates, Diary, 13 September 1945, IWM, Bates Papers.
38. Bates, Diary, 17 August 1945, IWM, Bates Papers.
39. Bates, Diary, 12 February 1945, IWM, Bates Papers.
40. See Brenda McBryde, *Quiet Heroines: Nurses of the Second World War* (London: Chatto & Windus, 1985), pp. 74–116, 198–229; Jean Bowden, *Grey Touched with Scarlet: The War Experiences of the Army Nursing Sisters* (London: Robert Hale, 1959), pp. 57–105, 170–85. The current nomenclature is Queen Alexandra's Royal Army Nursing Corps.
41. Mrs D. Ingram, 'Experiences of an Army Nurse in WW2', p. 10. IWM, 93/18/1, Papers of Mrs D. Ingram.
42. Memoirs of Miss E. Gander, p. 102, IWM, 86/44/1.
43. See Anne Pimlott Baker, 'Williams, Cicely Delphine (1893–1992)', *Oxford Dictionary of National Biography* (Oxford: Oxford University Press, 2004); Naomi Baumslag, 'Cicely Delphine Williams: Doctor of the World's Children', *Journal of Human Lactation* 21 (2005), pp. 6–7.
44. Ann Dally, *Cicely: The Story of a Doctor* (London: Gollancz, 1968), p. 236.
45. Wendy Webster, *Englishness and Empire, 1939–1965* (Oxford: Oxford University Press, 2005), p. 55.
46. Webster, *Englishness and Empire*, pp. 55–8, 89.
47. Webster, *Englishness and Empire*, p. 90. Jack Lee (dir.), *A Town Like Alice* (Britain, 1956).
48. Australian audiences were far more concerned with its representation of the male POW and the Japanese. See Christina Twomey, 'Revisiting *A Town Like Alice*', *Australian Feminist Studies* 21 (2006), pp. 85–102.
49. Hilda R. Corpe, *Prisoner Beyond the Chindwin* (London: Arthur Barker, 1955), p. 13.
50. In Australia, Betty Jeffrey's *White Coolies* (Sydney: Angus & Robertson, 1954), an account of the experience of nurse prisoners of war, was a notable exception. Jeffrey was interned alongside civilian women and children, although she was a military prisoner.
51. Phyllis Montefiore, 'A Bit of Camp, 1942–45', p. 1, memoir n.d., in IWM, 84/42/1, Papers of Hearnden, Mrs. P. Although she later become Mrs Hearnden, I have chosen to use the name 'Montefiore' here because this is the name Phyllis was known by in camp and during her later acting career.
52. Montefiore, 'A Bit of Camp', p. 76, IWM, 84/42/1.
53. Diary of Phyllis Montefiore, in IWM, 84/42/1, Hearnden, Mrs. P.
54. Montefiore, 'A Bit of Camp', p. 1 refers to it being twenty–six years since release from internment, which would make the date of the typescript 1971, IWM, 84/42/1.
55. Montefiore appeared in *Private Investigator* (1958), *Maigret* (1960), *Dr Finlay's Casebook* (1962), *The Baron* (1966) and *The Saint* (1966). See <www.tv.com/phyllis–montefiore/person/172510/summary.html> (accessed 11 March 2008). In the memoir, Montefiore comments: 'I spent my convalescence writing innumerable letters and succeeded in landing a job in Repertory. I am happy to say I followed this up with various other engagements and finally achieved my ambition to appear on the West End stage. I was indeed fortunate enough to appear with some of our biggest stars and also on television

and radio. Now unfortunately I am partially disabled by virtue of various operations three on my head, so my theatrical career is sadly curtailed except for the odd broadcast', IWM, 84/42/1. Montefiore does not comment on the nature of the disability, or whether it stemmed from internment.

56. Montefiore, Diary, IWM, 84/42/1.
57. Montefiore, Diary, IWM, 84/42/1.
58. Montefiore, 'A Bit of Camp', p. 1, IWM, 84/42/1.
59. Joy Damousi, *Living with the Aftermath: Trauma, Nostalgia and Grief in Post-War Australia* (Cambridge: Cambridge University Press, 2001).
60. Warner and Sandilands, *Women beyond the Wire*, p. 15.
61. Joan Didion, *The Year of Magical Thinking* (New York: Vintage, 2007), p. 161.

INDEX